READING
FOR RESULTS

As part of Houghton Mifflin's ongoing commitment to the environment, this text has been printed on recycled paper.

READING
FOR RESULTS

FIFTH EDITION

Laraine E. Flemming
South Central Community College

HOUGHTON MIFFLIN COMPANY
Boston   Toronto
Dallas   Geneva, Illinois
Palo Alto   Princeton, New Jersey

Sponsoring Editor: Mary Jo Southern
Managing Development Editor: Melody Davies
Associate Project Editor: Danielle Carbonneau
Production/Design Coordinator: Martha Drury
Manufacturing Coordinator: Sharon Pearson
Marketing Manager: George Kane

Cover art: Copyright John Martin/The Image Bank

Photograph credits: Page 7, Library of Congress; p. 18, © 1992 by Marianne Barcellona; p. 37, UPI/Bettmann Newsphotos; p. 59, © Yosuke Yamahata/Magnum Photos, Inc.; p. 72, © 1992 Capital Cities/ABC, Inc. Ann Limongello; p. 81, The Bettmann Archive; p. 83, Copyright © by John Spragens, Jr. 1979/Photo Researchers, Inc.; p. 87, *Benjamin O. Davis, Jr., American, an Autobiography*, published by Smithsonian Institution Press, copyright 1991 Smithsonian Institution. Photograph courtesy General Davis; p. 111, UPI/Bettmann Archive; p. 122, Brown Brothers; p. 123, Photo courtesy of Colorado Historical Society; p. 126, Photofest; p. 131, Photofest; p. 154, UPI/Bettmann Archive; p. 178, Copyright Mail Newspapers PLC/Solo; p. 184, Brown Brothers; p. 186, Preben Dehlholm, Fotograf Dehlholm, copyright Forhistorisk Museum, Moesgard, Denmark; p. 200, Brown Brothers; p. 228, Artwork courtesy of the artist and Mill Pond Press, Inc. Venice, FL 34292-3505; p. 233, Brown Brothers; p. 238, Tom Smart/The Gamma-Liaison Network; p. 275, © Sargent copyright 1986 Austin American-Statesman. Reprinted with permission of Universal Press Syndicate. All rights reserved; p. 291, Copyright © 1989 Tri-Star Pictures, Inc. All rights reserved; p. 315, © Cornell Capa/Magnum Photos, Inc.; p. 315, © Abbas/Magnum Photos, Inc.; p. 326, UPI/Bettmann Newsphotos; p. 326, UPI/Bettmann Newsphotos; p. 360, UPI/Bettmann Newsphotos; p. 366, Gjon Mili, *Life Magazine* © Time Warner, Inc.

Acknowledgments: Copyrights and Acknowledgments appear on pages 491–492, which constitute a continuation of the copyright page.

Printed in the U.S.A.

ISBN: 0-395-63327-3

123456789-DH-96 95 94 93 92

Contents

To the Instructor

This fifth edition of *Reading for Results* continues to offer the same clear, step-by-step approach to improving reading comprehension that has made the previous editions so successful. First, students learn how to discover the key elements in individual paragraphs. Then they apply what they have learned to longer *multiparagraph selections drawn from textbooks, magazines, and newspapers.* Abundant and varied exercises give students ample opportunity to practice and review what they have learned. In addition, throughout the text, *critical thinking questions and writing assignments* encourage students to evaluate the author's point of view and to develop their own perspective on the issues they encounter in their reading.

As always, the reading selections have been carefully chosen to stimulate students' interest and to enlarge their background knowledge in a variety of areas, such as history, natural science, psychology, current events, and film. From its first edition, an essential goal of this text has been to encourage the notion that reading is a source of both knowledge *and* excitement, thus the inclusion of engaging and thought-provoking readings on such topics as the custody rights of fathers, the long struggle for civil rights, and the lonely battle of Lyle Alzado.

New Features in This Edition

More Extended Vocabulary Instruction Chapter Two still provides instruction and practice in how to use context clues, structural analysis, and the dictionary, but the coverage of vocabulary is now integrated throughout the text. Chapters Three through Eight now include:

1. **New Vocabulary.** New words to look for are listed on the opening page of each chapter.
2. **Working with Words.** A list of prefixes and roots is introduced in each chapter and is followed by exercises.
3. **Stories Behind the Words.** Five words with colorful origins appear at the end of each chapter.
4. **Vocabulary Review.** End-of-chapter reviews test students'

knowledge of the words and word parts introduced in the chapter.

Thus students have an opportunity to see and use new words in a variety of different contexts, making it easier for them to enlarge their vocabuary. In addition, each set of exercises incorporates some of the words already introduced in previous chapters, so that students get a chance to review and refine their understanding of new words.

Reading Longer Selections   Chapters Six and Seven have been completely rewritten to help students more readily adapt what they have learned about individual paragraphs to longer, multiparagraph selections. Both chapters now include more *academic readings* drawn from history, psychology, business, sociology, and science texts.

Writing Summaries   In addition to learning how to use informal outlines and charts to take notes, students now learn *how to write summaries*. Chapter Six offers a four-step sequence for reducing an entire page of text to a paragraph or two without eliminating any essential information. Students learn not just how to create summaries but also how to decide when a summary would be more effective than an outline or a chart.

Making Inferences   Teaching students how to draw the appropriate inference from explicit statements in the text has always been an important goal of this text. However, in this edition, instruction in drawing logical inferences receives even greater attention. Explanation, practice, and review of this essential skill have been included throughout the text.

Using Transitional Signals   Like making inferences, understanding the verbal signals that transitions provide is an essential reading skill. This edition has expanded the coverage of what transitions are and how writers use them.

Critical Reading   Chapter Eight, "Critical Reading," has been completely revised. The section on facts and opinions has been expanded to include more explanation and more exercises. In addition, students learn how to *identify an author's tone* and use that tone to discover the author's *degree of bias*. In the section on analyzing and evaluating arguments, special emphasis is given to the kind of *informal fallacies* that can discredit a seemingly sound argument.

Improving Reading Rate   A brief discussion of how to improve reading rate by strictly defining purpose, eliminating regressions, enlarging vocabuary, and using the author's organization has been added to this edition. Each selection in the appendix concludes with a word count so that students can immediately evaluate their reading rate. Each reading is accompanied by a set of ten questions designed to test students' comprehension after they have been reading at accelerated rates of speed.

Additional Readings   Most of the longer selections in the appendix are new, and they cover a wide variety of topics, from Anna Quindlen's passion for rock-and-roll to the stereotypes that confront people with disabilities. The questions that follow each reading have a dual purpose. They test students' understanding of the material, and they provide a complete and comprehensive review of all skills covered in *Reading for Results*.

Expanded Ancillary Package   *Instructor's Annotated Edition* provides answers to the exercises in the student text.

Instructor's Resource Manual offers materials for individualizing instruction. It includes additional explanation and exercises for every major topic introduced within the text. If a student has difficulty with one of the end-of-chapter review tests, the instructor can readily provide additional explanation and practice. Also included are sample midterm and final exams that instructors can adapt to fit their needs and a sample syllabus based on how I have used this text over the years. Although the book is purposely designed to adapt to student and teacher needs, I have found the organization outlined in this sample syllabus to be particularly effective.

Computerized Exercises, available on disk for teachers who have access to computers, offers additional materials for review.

Also Available   Students pleased by the results of their work with this text will also benefit from using READING FOR THINKING, a new text that reviews the comprehension strategies taught in READING FOR RESULTS and then expands the instruction on critical reading. Students read, analyze, and evaluate four units of longer readings that have been expressly chosen for their stimulating content and expository style. Used in combination, these two texts provide a comprehensive introduction to all the reading strategies essential for understanding, evaluating, and responding to expository texts.

Acknowledgments

I would like to thank the following reviewers for their contributions:

Suzanne Garza Weisar, San Jacinto South, TX
Patricia L. Rottmund, Harrisburg Area Community College, PA
Carolyn W. Carmichael, Kean College, NJ
Barbara L. Cheek, Pierce College, WA
Louise M. Tomlinson, The University of Georgia
Terrence J. Foley, Henry Ford Community College, MI
Michael E. Erickson, Monroe Community College, NY
Dolores Segura, Austin Community College
Jane M. Harmon, Lakewood Community College, MN

Special thanks go to a trio of fine editors: to Melody Davies for all her hard work on the manuscript; to Danielle Carbonneau for shepherding the book through composition; and to Mary Jo Southern for her continued enthusiasm and support of *Reading for Results*.

Laraine Flemming

First Things First: The Importance of Pre-reading a Chapter

When you're reading a novel, you probably let the story unfold without looking ahead to find out how it ends. Part of the pleasure of novel reading is the suspense of wondering what will happen next.

But this strategy, appropriate for novels, is not the most efficient method of reading textbooks. Authors of textbooks are not usually interested in creating suspense. They want to communicate a large body of information as quickly and efficiently as possible.

Aware of the difference, experienced readers shift strategies when they turn from novels to textbooks. They don't wait to see what happens. Instead, they **pre-read** or preview portions of a chapter *before* they actually begin reading. Experienced readers know that advance information about a chapter will give their reading a **goal** or purpose. Knowing what to look for, they find it easier to direct their attention and concentration to key places in the chapter. Thus they can speed up or slow down their reading with confidence.

Pre-reading gives you mental flexibility. Once you know what the author wants you to understand, you can make informed decisions about what is essential information and what is not. You can then decide which portions of the text require close and careful reading and which ones can be read at a normal rate.

Pre-reading can also help you divide the text into manageable units of study. Through pre-reading you can identify the natural divisions in the chapter's structure. Then based on those divisions, you can divide the chapter into manageable portions or sections of text.

Generally to avoid concentration "burn-out" and sagging motivation, you need to limit your study sessions to forty or fifty minutes with breaks between each one. Pre-reading will help you de-

1

cide exactly how much you need to read during each individual session. Having a goal, in this case a particular number of pages to cover, will help you maintain a high level of concentration.

Pre-reading should take only a few minutes—no more than fifteen or twenty, depending on the type of material.

☐ Read the title, introductory paragraphs, and any questions, objectives, or outlines.
☐ Raise questions about the chapter.
☐ Study the visual aids.
☐ Read any concluding sections titled summary, review, questions, or key terms.
☐ Map the chapter's contents.
☐ Consider what you already know about the subject at hand.

Pre-reading does not take much time, but it pays big dividends. It will help you understand and remember what you read.

A Six-Step Strategy for Pre-reading

Step 1: Read the Title, Introductory Paragraphs, and any Questions, Objectives, or Outlines

The title of a chapter like **Theories of Mate Selection** or **People and Motivation** usually identifies the **topic** or subject under discussion.

Titles, however, can also help you *predict what direction the chapter will take.* For example upon seeing the title **People and Motivation** in a business text, you might predict that the author is going to define motivation. Because you probably know how important motivation is to getting things accomplished, you might also predict that the author is going to explain what managers do to encourage a high degree of motivation among employees.

Making predictions based on the title and introduction is important. Your first **tentative** or temporary predictions create an immediate purpose: You are reading to confirm, modify, or even contradict your first guess about the chapter's contents. Giving this kind of determined focus to your reading helps you quickly identify key points in the chapter. They will usually be the points that confirm or contradict your initial predictions.

In addition to introducing the title, authors often use the first page or two to **explicitly** or directly identify key points in the chapter. In effect they tell readers: Here's what to look for and pay attention to while you are reading.

Different authors use different methods to explain what's important and what to look for. Some authors, for example, may begin with a list of **learning objectives.** This list from a business text tells you what the author expects you to know after reading the chapter:

Promotion

LEARNING OBJECTIVES

1. Recognize the role of promotion
2. Know the purposes of the three types of advertising
3. Become aware of the advantages and disadvantages of the major advertising media
4. Identify the major steps in developing an advertising campaign
5. Know the various kinds of salespersons, the personal-selling process, and the major sales management tasks
6. Understand the sales promotion objectives and methods
7. Recognize the types and uses of publicity and the requirements for effective use of publicity
8. Know what factors influence the selection of promotion-mix ingredients

(Pride, Hughes, and Kapoor, *Business*, p. 415.)

Other authors may provide you with a **chapter outline** that announces the topics to be addressed.

Historical Views of Abnormal Behavior

Abnormal Behavior in Ancient Times

Demonology, Gods, and Magic
Early Philosophical and Medical Concepts
Conflicting Views During the Middle Ages
Witchcraft and Mental Illness: Fact or Fiction?

Growth Toward Humanitarian Approaches

Resurgence of Scientific Questioning in Europe
Establishment of Early Asylums and Shrines
Humanitarian Reform

The Foundations of Twentieth-century Views

Changing Attitudes Toward Mental Health
Growth of Scientific Research

Unresolved Issues on Interpreting Historical Events

Summary

(Carson, Butcher, and Coleman, *Abnormal Psychology*, p. 29.)

Still others may offer a list of questions to help direct your attention while you are reading. Find the answers to those questions, and you have found the key points in the chapter.

Psychology and Psychologists

Survey Questions

☐ What is psychology? What are its goals?
☐ How did psychology emerge as a field of knowledge?
☐ What are the major trends and specialties in psychology?
☐ Can psychology be applied to improve study skills and grades?
☐ How does psychology differ from false systems that also claim to explain behavior?

(Coon, *Introduction to Psychology*, p. 3.)

Chapter previews are yet another way of telling readers what's to come.

Inflation and Unemployment

PREVIEW If you were graduating from college today, what would your job prospects be? In 1932, they would have been bleak. A large number of people were out of work, and a large number of firms had laid off workers or gone out of business. At any time, job opportunities depend not only on the individual's ability and experience, but also on the current state of the economy.
Economies operate in cycles, periods of expansion followed

by periods of contraction. These cycles have a major impact on people's income and standard of living. When the economy is growing, the demand for goods and services tends to increase. To produce those goods and services, firms hire more workers. So as the economy expands, the unemployment rate falls. Economic expansion also has an impact on inflation. As the demand for goods and services goes up, the prices of those goods and services also tend to rise. During periods of recession, the unemployment rate goes up and inflation tends to slow. Both unemployment and inflation are affected by business cycles in fairly regular ways. But their effects on individual standards of living, income, and purchasing power are much less predictable. (Boyes and Melvin, *Economics*, p. 181.)

In addition to chapter objectives, outlines, questions, or previews, authors frequently provide their readers with a **statement of purpose.** This is a sentence or a paragraph that identifies what the chapter is supposed to accomplish. Look, for example, how the authors of the above preview identify the goals of their chapter:

> In this chapter we describe the business cycle and examine measures of unemployment and inflation. We talk about the ways in which the business cycle, unemployment, and inflation are related. And we describe their effects on the participants in the economy. (Boyes and Melvin, *Economics*, p. 182.)

Increasingly authors of textbooks use introductions to identify explicitly what each chapter should accomplish. Now that you are aware of this practice, make sure you use that introductory material to guide your reading. By knowing what a chapter is supposed to accomplish, you automatically have a better idea of what you should look for and pay attention to during your reading.

Step 2: Raise Questions About the Chapter

In addition to using the author's questions, outlines, or previews to guide your reading, get into the habit of developing your own questions. Let's say you're reading a chapter titled **Theories of Mate Selection.** Even before you read the author's introduction, use words like *who, what, how, why, when,* and *where* to pose questions such as What are the theories of mate selection? How many are there? What distinguishes one from the other?

As you pre-read, look at the **major** and **minor headings.** They too can help you create your own questions. Major headings identify the topics or issues discussed in the chapter. Minor headings indicate what aspects of those topics the author intends to address.

For an example, look at these major and minor headings.

Learning Disabilities

Causes of Learning Disabilities

Helping Children with Learning Disabilities

Each of these headings can be turned into questions. Again you just need to add words like *who, what, how, why, when,* and *where.* What are the causes of learning disabilities? How do we recognize a learning disability? How can we help children with learning disabilities? Questions like these should be written in the margins. Then you can read to find the answers.

Like headings, material that has been emphasized in some way is a good source for questions. As you flip through the pages of a chapter, look for words, phrases, or sentences that have been emphasized through repetition, **boldface** or *italics.* For example, in the following passage you probably can define the word *anesthetic,* but what about *analgesic*? If you don't know what that word means, you could pose a question in the margins: What is an analgesic?

> Most traditional hospital maternity facilities consist of separate rooms for labor, delivery, and recovery. Physicians, usually obstetricians, serve as the primary birth attendant, with assistance from nurses. Emergency equipment and trained personnel are quickly accessible should the need arise. **Analgesics** and **anesthetics** are options typically available only in this setting. High-risk pregnancies especially benefit from technological advances found in the hospital setting. (Greenberg, Bruess, Mullen, and Sands, *Sexuality,* p. 296.)

Each time you can answer a question posed during pre-reading, you will feel a sense of accomplishment. That sense of accomplishment will motivate you to keep reading even the most difficult and detailed assignments.

Step 3: *Study the Visual Aids*

Authors of textbooks use a variety of visual aids—photographs, boxes, charts—to highlight significant information. During your pre-reading, take advantage of this practice and look over any visual aids included in the chapter. Read the captions as well. Here again your goal is to *get as much advance knowledge about the chapter as you possibly can.* Look, for example, at the way one group of authors uses a cartoon to highlight their discussion of President Franklin D. Roosevelt's court-packing plan.

Roosevelt's Court-Packing Plan

What Roosevelt requested was the authority to add a federal judge whenever an incumbent* who had already served at least ten years failed to retire within six months of reaching age seventy. He wanted the power to name up to fifty additional federal judges, including six to the Supreme Court. Though Roosevelt spoke of understaffed courts and aged and feeble judges, it was obvious that he envisioned using the bill to create a Supreme Court sympathetic to the New Deal. (Norton, et al. *A People and a Nation*, p. 748.)

President Roosevelt's court-packing plan provoked an outcry from Democrats as well as Republicans. Roosevelt's miscalculation resulted in a major defeat for his administration. Library of Congress.

---

* incumbent: person still in office.

Simply by looking at the cartoon and reading the caption, you already understand one of the author's key points: Roosevelt's plan to pack the Supreme Court infuriated Republicans and Democrats alike.

Many authors of textbooks also use **marginal annotation** to highlight key terms or thoughts. They use the margins of a page to repeat a definition or point already introduced within the chapter. Marginal annotations, shown in the following example, are an excellent source of pre-reading information.

The Meaning of Organization Design

We can define **organization design** as the overall configuration of positions and interrelationships among positions within an organization. More specifically, let's think of the design of an organization as being like a jigsaw puzzle, it consists of a number of pieces put together in a certain way. (Van Fleet, *Contemporary Management*, p. 238.)

For the most part, textbook authors don't illustrate or annotate minor points in their explanation. They illustrate only major ones. Therefore the time you spend looking at illustrations and annotations is well worth your while.

Step 4: Read any Concluding Sections Titled Summary, Review, Questions, or Key Terms

Many authors use the final pages of a chapter to summarize key points. It is their way of saying to readers: Here is what you should have learned from reading this chapter.

In addition to summaries, authors frequently provide a list of **review questions.** These questions can help you test your mastery of the chapter. If you can answer most of them, you have understood the chapter. If you can answer only a few, some re-reading is in order.

Then, too, authors often use the last page to list key terms. This is their way of making sure you do not fail to recognize the vocabulary essential to understanding their topic.

Obviously the final pages of a chapter can be a real gold mine for pre-reading. Look, for example, at how much you can learn from the last two pages of a chapter on marketing.

CHAPTER REVIEW

Summary

Marketing is the process of planning and executing the conception, pricing, promotion, and distribution of ideas, goods, and services to create exchanges that satisfy individual and organizational objectives. Marketing adds value in the form of utility, or the power of a product or service to satisfy a need. It creates time utility by making products available when customers want them, place utility by making products available where customers want them, and possession utility by transferring the ownership of products to buyers.

Business people focused on the production of goods from the Industrial Revolution until the early twentieth century, and on the selling of goods from the 1920s to the 1950s. Marketing received little attention up to that point. After 1950, however, business people recognized that their enterprises involved not only production and selling but also the satisfaction of customers' needs. They began to implement the marketing concept, a business philosophy that involves the entire business organization in the dual process of satisfying customer needs and achieving the organization's goals.

Implementation of the marketing concept begins

and ends with marketing information—first to determine what customers need, and later to evaluate how well the firm is meeting those needs.

A market consists of people with needs, the ability to buy, and the desire and authority to purchase. Markets are classified as consumer, industrial, and reseller markets.

A marketing strategy is a plan for the best use of an organization's resources to meet its objectives. Developing a marketing strategy involves selecting and analyzing a target market and creating and maintaining a marketing mix that will satisfy that market. A target market is chosen through the total market approach or the market segmentation approach. A market segment is a group of individuals or organizations within a market that have similar characteristics and needs. Businesses that use a total market approach design a single marketing mix and direct it at the entire market for a particular product. The market segmentation approach directs a marketing mix at a segment or segments of a market.

A firm's marketing mix is the combination of product, price, distribution, and promotion that it uses to reach a target market. To achieve a firm's marketing objectives, marketing-mix strategies must begin with an assessment of the marketing environment, which in turn will influence decisions about marketing-mix ingredients. Market measurement and sales forecasting are used to estimate sales potential and predict product sales in specific market segments. Strategies are then monitored and evaluated through marketing research and the marketing information system, which stores and processes internal and external data in a form that is conducive to marketing decision making.

In the next chapter we discuss two elements of the marketing mix: product and price. Our emphasis will be on the development of product and pricing within a marketing strategy.

Key Terms

You should now be able to define and give an example relevant to each of the following terms:

marketing	place utility
utility	time utility
form utility	possession utility

marketing concept
market
marketing strategy
marketing mix
target market
total market approach
market segment
market segmentation
sales forecast
marketing information system

marketing research
buying behavior
consumer buying behavior
organizational buying behavior
personal income
disposable income
discretionary income

Questions and Exercises

Review Questions

1. How, specifically, does marketing create place, time, and possession utility?
2. How is a marketing-oriented firm different from a production-oriented firm or a sales-oriented firm?
3. What are the major requirements for a group of individuals and organizations to be a market? How does a consumer market differ from an industrial market?
4. What are the major components of a marketing strategy?
5. What is the purpose of market segmentation? What is the relationship between market segmentation and the selection of target markets?
6. What are the four elements of the marketing mix? In what sense are they "controllable"?
7. Describe the forces in the environment that affect an organization's marketing decision.
8. What major issues should be specified prior to conducting a sales forecast?
9. What is the difference between a marketing information system and a marketing research project? How might the two be related?
10. Why should marketers try to understand buying behavior?
11. How are personal income, disposable income, and discretionary income related? Which is the best indicator of consumer purchasing power?
12. List five reasons why consumers make purchases. What need is satisfied in each case?
13. How might a marketing manager make use of information about consumer trends?

(Pride, et al. *Business*, pp. 344–5.)

Armed with the information contained on these final pages, you would know exactly how to distribute your attention and concentration while reading.

Step 5: Map the Chapter's Contents

Maps give visual form to a chapter's content and organization. Making a map and keeping it by you while you read will help you understand how each section of a chapter relates to the larger whole.

Begin your map by writing the chapter title or statement of purpose in the middle of the page. To make it stand out, put a box, circle, or star around it. Then attach a series of spokes to that center statement. On each spoke, write out the major headings in the chapter.

A map based on this chapter would look something like this:

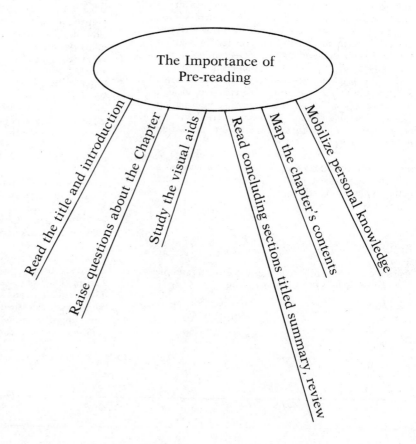

Once you have made a map, you can use it to *monitor your comprehension* as you read. Each time you complete a chapter section, find the heading on your map and see if you can *recite the key points* introduced underneath that heading. Your recitation will help you decide whether you have really understood the author's message. It will also help you remember what you read. Every time you *translate an author's words into your own,* you are that much closer to understanding and remembering new information.

Step 6: Consider What You Know Already About the Subject at Hand

Whenever possible, *consider what you yourself might already know* about the chapter topic. If, for example, you're reading a chapter titled "The Media and Political Campaigns," make every effort to mobilize your own personal knowledge about this issue. Is it true that the media tend to follow the front-runner in a presidential election more closely than other candidates? Do you think that media coverage of primary returns before the polls close affects the outcome? Do you think journalists should or should not probe the private lives of presidential candidates? What you want to do at this point is bring to consciousness any and all prior knowledge you might have about a chapter's contents. This kind of intellectual gearing up will help you understand and remember key points in the chapter. It will help you connect the world you know with the one represented on the printed page.

Whatever you do, don't skip this last step, assuming it's the author's job to tell you what you need to know. Reading is creative. It requires you to make the appropriate connections between sentences and *help create the text you read.* This task becomes easier when you can call upon your own personal knowledge.

D I G G I N G   D E E P E R

What do you think? Should journalists probe a candidate's private life? In your opinion, does the public need to know about a candidate's private life? Why or why not?

Exercise

Directions: Pre-read the accompanying chapter. Then answer the following questions.

1. Based on your pre-reading of the title and first page, which prediction seems the most appropriate?

   a. The author will discuss current questionable business practices.

   ⓑ. The author will discuss questionable business practices in the past but concentrate on how improvements or changes have been made.

   Explain your answer: The chapter preview specifically mentions

   "questionable business practices common before the 1930s" but then

   focuses on consumerism and "models of social responsibility"

   _____

2. List at least three ways the authors identify key points in the chapter.

1) learning objectives	4) chapter summary
2) chapter preview	5) list of key terms
3) annotation in the margins	6) discussion questions

3. Below are five different headings. Identify each one as an M (major) or m (minor) heading. If you need to, refer to the chapter to check your answers.

   Affirmative Action Programs __m__

   Training Programs for the Hard-Core Unemployed __m__

   Employment Practices __M__

   The Four Basic Rights of Consumers __m__

   Consumerism __M__

4. Now use some or all of those headings to create questions that could be used to guide your reading of the chapter.

Sample questions: What are affirmative action programs?

What training programs are offered for the hard-core unemployed?

How does the author define *consumerism*?

What are the four basic rights of consumers?

5. Based on your pre-reading, circle those terms you think are important to define.

waste sites
ad hominem
(caveat emptor)
civil rights
(minority)
(whistle blowing)

6. Why does the chapter have a picture of a young boy eating at McDonald's?

McDonald's is an example of a company that encourages ethical behavior.

_____

7. Based on your pre-reading, do you think the author will

a. assume you already have a good definition of the word *ethics*.
(b). provide a definition of the word *ethics*.

8. Based on your pre-reading, the chapter will

(a). discuss government regulation of business before 1914.
b. not discuss government regulation of business before 1914.

Explain why you chose a or b.

The table on page 21 suggests the author will, to some

degree, discuss regulation of business prior to 1914.

9. Based on your pre-reading, what are the three major areas of social responsibility for business?

consumerism, employment practices, and the environment

10. Make a map of the sample chapter.

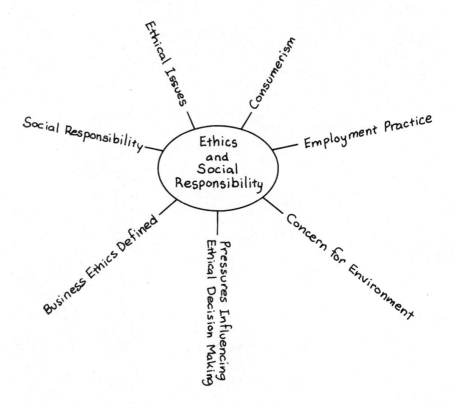

ETHICS AND SOCIAL RESPONSIBILITY

LEARNING OBJECTIVES

1 Understand the types of ethical concerns that arise in the business world

2 Recognize the ethical pressures placed on decision makers

3 Understand how ethical decision making can be encouraged

4 Be aware of how our current views on the social responsibility of business have evolved

5 Understand the factors that led to the consumer movement and list some of its results

6 Recognize how present employment practices are being used to counteract past abuses

7 Be aware of the major types of pollution, their causes, and their cures

8 Become familiar with the steps a business must take to implement a program of social responsibility

CHAPTER PREVIEW

We begin by defining business ethics and examining ethical issues confronting business people. Next, we look at the pressures that influence ethical decision making and how it can be encouraged. Then we initiate our discussion of social responsibility by reviewing questionable business practices common before the 1930s and describe how public pressure brought about changes in the business environment after the Great Depression. We define and contrast two present-day models of social responsibility, the economic model and the socioeconomic model. Next, we present the major tenets of the consumer movement, which include consumers' rights to safety, to information, to choice, and to a full hearing of complaints. We discuss how ideas of social responsibility in business have affected employment practices and environmental concerns. We consider the commitment, planning, and funding that go into a firm's program of social responsibility.

Business Ethics Defined

Ethics is the study of right and wrong and of the morality of choices made by individuals. An ethical decision or action is one that is "right" according to some standard of behavior. **Business ethics** is the application of moral standards to business situations. Business ethics has become a public concern because of recent cases of unethical behavior. The Wall Street insider trading scandals and the questionable pricing tactics of federal defense contractors such as General Dynamics Corp. are just two examples of unethical behavior.

Ethical Issues

Business people face ethical issues daily. These issues stem from a variety of sources. While some issues arise infrequently, others occur regularly. Let's take a closer look at several ethical issues.

Fairness and Honesty

Learning Objective 1
Understand the types of ethical concerns that arise in the business world

Fairness and honesty in business are important ethical concerns. Besides obeying all laws and regulations, business persons are expected to refrain from knowingly deceiving, misrepresenting, or intimidating others. Lying is also a business problem. According to a Roper Public Opinion Research Center poll, 72 percent of Americans surveyed sometimes lie. Also, 54 percent of the respondents believe that people are less honest than they were ten years ago.

Organizational Relationships

It is sometimes tempting to place personal welfare above the welfare of others or the welfare of an organization. Relationships with customers and coworkers often create ethical problems since confidential information is expected to be kept secret and all obligations are expected to be honored. Specific issues that arise include taking credit for others' ideas or work, not meeting one's obligations in a mutual agreement, and pressuring people to behave unethically.

Conflict of Interest

Conflict of interest results when a business person takes advantage of a situation for his or her own personal interest rather than for the interest of his or her employer. Sometimes payments and gifts make their way into business deals. A bribe is anything given to a person that might unfairly influence that person's business decision. All bribes are unethical.

Communications

Business communications, especially advertising, can present ethical questions. False and misleading advertising is unethical and can infuriate customers. Sponsors of advertisements aimed at children must be especially careful to avoid messages that are misleading. Advertisers of health-related products must also take precautions to guard against deception.

Pressures Influencing Ethical Decision Making

Learning Objective 2
Recognize the ethical pressures placed on decision makers

Business ethics involves relationships between a firm and its investors, customers, employees, creditors, and competitors. Each group has specific concerns, and each exerts some type of pressure on management.

Investors want management to make sensible financial decisions that will boost sales, profits, and returns on their investments.

Customers expect that a firm's products will be safe, reliable, and reasonably priced.

Employees want to be treated fairly in hiring, promotion, and compensation.

Creditors require that bills be paid on time and that the accounting information furnished by the firm be accurate.

Competitors expect that the firm's marketing activities will truthfully portray its products.

Although there are exceptions, when business is good and profit is high, it is relatively easy for management to respond to these expectations in an ethical manner. However, concern for ethics can dwindle under the pressure of low or declining profit. In such circumstances, ethical behavior is most likely to be compromised.

Expanding international trade has also led to an ethical dilemma for many American firms. In some countries, bribes and payoffs are an accepted part of business. In 1977, the U.S. government passed the Foreign Corrupt Practices Act, which prohibits these types of payments, but it is hard to enforce this act. By 1978, in response to the government's promise of leniency for firms disclosing information voluntarily, more than 400 U.S. companies admitted to making $800 million in questionable foreign payments. Government agencies have prosecuted several companies for "illegal payoffs," in spite of the fact that there is as yet no international code of business ethics. Some U.S. firms that refuse to make direct payoffs are forced to hire local consultants, public relations firms, or advertising agencies. Without stronger international laws or ethics codes, such cases are difficult to investigate. Much of the evidence and many of the people are overseas and cannot be prosecuted effectively.

Encouraging Ethical Behavior

A quick test to check if a behavior is ethical, if there is not a company policy regarding it, is to see if others approve of it. Ethical decisions will always withstand scrutiny. Openness will often create trust and help build solid business relationships.

What affects a person's inclination to make either ethical or unethical decisions is not entirely clear. Three general sets of factors are believed to influence the ethics of decision making. First, an individual's values, attitudes, experiences, and knowledge influence decision making. Second, the absence of an employer's official code of ethics may indirectly encourage unethical decisions. Third, the behaviors and values of others, such as coworkers, supervisors, and company officials, affect the ethics of a person's decisions.

McDonald's, which produces hundreds of millions of pounds of paper and plastic waste annually, has become a proponent of recycling. The company urges its New England customers to dispose separately of polystyrene packaging and then collects and recycles it. McDonald's has taken other steps as well, including making its napkins from recycled paper.

Learning Objective 3
Understand how ethical decision making can be encouraged

Most authorities agree that there is room for improvement in business ethics. A more problematic issue is whether business can be made more ethical in the real world. The majority of viewpoints on this issue suggest that government, trade associations, and individual firms can establish acceptable levels of behavior.

The government can do so by passing more stringent regulations. But regulations require enforcement, and the unethical business person always seems to "slip something by" without getting caught. Increased regulation may help, but it surely cannot solve the entire ethics problem.

Trade associations can provide (and some have provided) ethical guidelines for their members to follow. These organizations of firms within a particular industry are also in a position to exert pressure on members that stoop to questionable business practices. However, enforcement varies from association to association, and because trade associations exist for the benefit of their members, very strong measures may be self-defeating.

Employees have an easier time determining what is acceptable behavior if a company provides them with a code of ethics. This is perhaps

corporate code of ethics *a guide to acceptable and ethical behavior as defined by an organization*

the most effective way to encourage ethical behavior. A **corporate code of ethics** is simply a guide to acceptable and ethical behavior as defined by an organization. Uniform policies, standards, and punishments for violations encourage employees to behave ethically. Of course, such a code cannot possibly cover every situation, but general guidelines should be sufficient for most employees. Specific details could deal with prohibited practices such as bribery.

Even if employees want to act ethically, it may be difficult to do so. Unethical practices often become ingrained in an organization. Employees with high personal ethics may then take a controversial step called whistle blowing. **Whistle blowing** is informing the press or government officials about unethical practices within one's organization. Whistle blowing could have averted disasters and prevented needless deaths and injuries in the *Challenger* space shuttle disaster and the toxic gas leak at Union Carbide Corp. in Bhopal, India. Engineers in both cases voiced their concerns to upper-level management but were reluctant to present their apprehensions to the press or news media. How can it be that employees know about life-threatening problems and let them pass? In the words of one Union Carbide employee, "Most of the engineers at Union Carbide think of themselves as part of the company. Besides, if you were identified, that would be the end of your career." Naturally, whistle blowing can have serious repercussions for an employee, yet those who take this step feel that the benefit to society outweighs any personal consequences they may suffer.

whistle blowing *informing the press or government officials about unethical practices within one's organization*

Social Responsibility

social responsibility *the recognition that business activities have an impact on society, and the consideration of that impact in business decision making*

Social responsibility is the recognition that business activities have an impact on society, and the consideration of that impact in business decision making. Obviously, social responsibility costs money. It is perhaps not so obvious—except in isolated cases—that social responsibility is good business. Consumers eventually find out which firms are acting responsibly and which are not. And, just as easily as they cast their dollar votes for a product produced by a company that is socially responsible, they can vote against the firm that is polluting the air or waterways, against the food product that contains the insecticide EDB, and against the company that survives mainly through bribery.

Social Responsibility Before the 1930s

Learning Objective 4
Be aware of how our current views on the social responsibility of business have evolved

During the first quarter of the twentieth century, businesses were free to operate pretty much as they chose. Government protection of workers and consumers was minimal. This was indeed a period of laissez-faire business conditions. (Remember, *laissez-faire* is a French term that implies there shall be no government interference in the economy.) As a result, people either accepted what business had to offer or they did without.

Working Conditions Before 1930, working conditions were often deplorable by today's standards. The average workweek was in excess of sixty hours for most industries, and there was no minimum-wage law. Employee benefits such as paid vacations, medical insurance, and paid overtime were almost nonexistent. Work areas were crowded and unsafe, and industrial accidents were the rule rather than the exception.

In an effort to improve working conditions, employees organized and joined labor unions. But during the early 1900s, businesses—with the help of government—were able to use such weapons as court orders, force, and even the few existing antitrust laws to defeat the attempts of unions to improve working conditions.

Consumer Rights Then as now, most people in business were honest people who produced and sold acceptable products. However, some business owners, eager for even greater profits, engaged in misleading advertising and sold shoddy and unsafe merchandise.

During this period, consumers were generally subject to the doctrine of **caveat emptor,** a Latin phrase meaning "let the buyer beware." In other words, "what you see is what you get," and too bad if it's not what you expected. Victims of unscrupulous business practices could take legal action, but going to court was very expensive and consumers rarely won their cases. Moreover, there were no consumer groups or government agencies to publicize their discoveries and hold sellers accountable for their actions.

In such an atmosphere, government intervention to curb abuses by business would seem almost inevitable. But there was as yet no great public outcry for such intervention.

caveat emptor *a Latin phrase meaning "let the buyer beware"*

In the early 1900s it was not unusual for children to work twelve-hour days under highly dangerous conditions. The "breaker boys," some of the most exploited children during this period, worked in mines separating rocks from chunks of coal.

PICKING SLATE

Government Regulation Prior to the 1930s, most people believed that competition and the action of the marketplace would correct abuses in time. Government became involved in day-to-day business activities only when there was an obvious abuse of the free-market system.

Six of the more important federal laws passed between 1887 and 1914 are described in Table 2.1. As you can see, these laws were aimed more at encouraging competition than at correcting business abuses, although two of them did deal with the purity of food and drug products. Such laws did little to curb abuses that occurred on a regular basis.

Social Responsibility After the 1930s

The collapse of the stock market on October 29, 1929, triggered the Great Depression and years of economic problems for the United States. As we noted in Chapter 1, U.S. production fell by almost one-half, and up to 25 percent of the nation's work force was unemployed. At last public pressure mounted for government to "do something" about the economy and about worsening social conditions.

When Franklin Roosevelt was inaugurated president in 1933, he instituted programs to restore the economy and to improve social conditions. Laws were passed to correct what many viewed as the monopolistic abuses of big business, and various social services were provided for individuals. These massive federal programs became the foundation for increased government involvement in the dealings between business and American society.

As government involvement has increased, so has everyone's awareness of the social responsibility of business. Today business owners are concerned about the return on their investment, but at the same time most of them demand ethical behavior from professional business managers. In addition, employees demand better working conditions, and

TABLE 2.1 Early Government Regulations that Affected American Business

Government Regulation	Major Provisions
Interstate Commerce Act (1887)	First federal act to regulate business practices; provided regulation of railroads and shipping rates
Sherman Antitrust Act (1890)	Prevented monopolies or mergers where competition was endangered
Pure Food and Drug Act (1906)	Established limited supervision of interstate sale of food and drugs
Meat Inspection Act (1906)	Provided for limited supervision of interstate sale of meat and meat products
Federal Trade Commission Act (1914)	Created the Federal Trade Commission to investigate illegal trade practices
Clayton Act (1914)	Eliminated many forms of price discrimination that gave large businesses a competitive advantage over smaller firms

consumers want safe, reliable products. Various advocacy groups echo these concerns and also call for careful consideration of our delicate ecological balance. Managers must therefore operate in a complex business environment—one in which they are just as responsible for their managerial actions as for their actions as individual citizens.

consumerism *all those activities intended to protect the rights of consumers in their dealings with business*

Consumerism consists of all those activities that are undertaken to protect the rights of consumers in their dealings with business. Consumerism has been with us to some extent since the early nineteenth century, but the movement came to life only in the 1960s. It was then that President John F. Kennedy declared that the consumer was entitled to a new "bill of rights."

The Four Basic Rights of Consumers

Learning Objective 5
Understand the factors that led to the consumer movement and list some of its results

Kennedy's consumer bill of rights asserted that consumers have a right to safety, to be informed, to choose, and to be heard. These four rights are the basis of much of the consumer-oriented legislation that has been passed during the last twenty-five years. These rights also provide an effective outline of the objectives and accomplishments of the consumer movement.

The Right to Safety   The right to safety means that products purchased by consumers must

▶   Be safe for their intended use

▶   Include thorough and explicit directions for proper use

▶   Have been tested by the manufacturer to ensure product quality and reliability

There are several reasons why American business firms must be concerned about product safety. Federal agencies such as the Food and Drug Administration and the Consumer Product Safety Commission have the power to force businesses that make or sell defective products to take corrective actions. Such actions include offering refunds, recalling defective products, issuing public warnings, and reimbursing consumers—all of which can be expensive. Second, consumers and the government have been winning an increasing number of product-liability lawsuits against sellers of defective products. Moreover, the awards in these suits have been getting bigger and bigger. Producers of all-terrain vehicles, for example, have faced a number of personal injury lawsuits. Another major reason for improving product safety is the consumer's demand for safe products. People will simply stop buying a product that they believe is unsafe or unreliable.

The Right to Be Informed   The right to be informed means that consumers must have access to complete information about a product before they buy it. Detailed information about ingredients must be provided on food containers, information about fabrics and laundering methods must be attached to clothing, and lenders must disclose the true cost of borrowing the money that they make available for customers to purchase merchandise on credit.

In addition, manufacturers must inform customers about the potential dangers of using their products. When they do not, they can be held responsible for personal injuries suffered because of their products. For example, General Electric provides customers with a twenty-page booklet that describes how they should use an automatic clothes washer. Sometimes such warnings seem excessive, but they are necessary if user injuries (and resulting lawsuits) are to be avoided.

The Right to Choose   The right to choose means that consumers have a choice of products, offered by different manufacturers and sellers, to satisfy a particular need. The government has done its part by encouraging competition through antitrust legislation. The more competition there is, the greater the choice available to consumers.

Competition and the resulting freedom of choice provide an additional benefit for consumers: They work to reduce the price of goods and services. Consider the electronic calculators that are so popular today. The Bowmar Brain, one of the first calculators introduced, carried a retail price tag in excess of $150. The product was so profitable that Texas Instruments, Rockwell International Corp., and many other firms began to compete with Bowmar Instrument Corp. As a result, calculators can now be purchased for under $10.

The Right to Be Heard   This fourth right means that someone will listen and take appropriate action when consumers complain. Actually, management began to listen to consumers after World War II, when competition between businesses that manufactured and sold consumer goods increased. One way firms got a competitive edge was to listen to consumers and provide the products they said they wanted and needed. Today, businesses are listening even more attentively, and many larger firms have consumer relations departments that the buying public can easily contact via toll-free phone numbers. Other groups listen too. Most large cities and some states have consumer affairs offices to act on the complaints of citizens.

Employment Practices

Learning Objective 6
Recognize how present employment practices are being used to counteract past abuses

minority   *a racial, religious, political, national, or other group regarded as different from the larger group of which it is a part, often singled out for unfavorable treatment*

We have seen that a combination of managers who subscribe to the socioeconomic view of business's social responsibility and significant government legislation enacted to protect the buying public has considerably broadened the rights of consumers. The last two decades have seen similar progress in affirming the rights of employees to equal treatment in the workplace.

Everyone who works for a living should have the opportunity to land a job for which he or she is qualified and to be rewarded on the basis of ability and performance. This is an important issue for society, and it also makes good business sense. Yet, over the years, this opportunity has been denied to members of various minority groups. A **minority** is a racial, religious, political, national, or other group regarded as different from the larger group of which it is a part, often singled out for unfavorable treatment.

The federal government responded to the outcry of minority groups during the 1960s and 1970s by passing a number of laws forbidding job discrimination. Now, more than twenty-five years since passage of the first of these (the Civil Rights Act of 1964), abuses still exist. An example is the disparity in income levels for whites, blacks, and Hispanics. Lower incomes and higher unemployment rates also affect Native Americans, handicapped persons, and women. Responsible managers have instituted a number of programs to counteract the results of discrimination.

Affirmative Action Programs

An **affirmative action program** is a plan designed to increase the number of minority employees at all levels within an organization. Employers with federal contracts of more than $50,000 per year must have written affirmative action plans. The objective of such programs is to ensure that minorities are represented within the organization in approximately the same proportion as in the surrounding community. If 25 percent of the electricians in a geographic area where a company is located are black, then approximately 25 percent of the electricians it employs should also be black. Affirmative action plans encompass all areas of human resources management: recruiting, hiring, training, promotion, and pay.

Unfortunately, affirmative action programs have been plagued by two problems. The first involves quotas. In the beginning, many firms pledged to recruit and hire a certain number of minority members by a specific date. To achieve this goal, they were forced to consider only minority applicants for job openings; if they hired nonminority workers, they would be defeating their own purpose. But the courts have ruled that such quotas are unconstitutional even though their purpose is commendable. They are, in fact, a form of discrimination called reverse discrimination.

The second problem is that not all business people are in favor of affirmative action programs, although most such programs have been reasonably successful. Managers not committed to these programs can "play the game" and still discriminate against workers. To help solve this problem, Congress created (and later strengthened) the **Equal Employment Opportunity Commission (EEOC),** a government agency with the power to investigate complaints of employment discrimination and the power to sue firms that practice it.

The threat of legal action has persuaded some corporations to amend their hiring and promotional policies, but the discrepancy between men's and women's salaries has not really been affected. For more than thirty years, women have consistently earned only about 60 cents for each dollar earned by men.

Training Programs for the Hard-Core Unemployed

For some firms, social responsibility extends far beyond placing a help-wanted ad in the local newspaper. These firms have assumed the task of helping the **hard-core unemployed:** workers with little education or vocational training and a long history of unemployment. In the past, such workers were often routinely turned down by personnel managers, even for the most menial jobs.

Obviously such workers require training; just as obviously this training can be expensive and time-consuming. To share the costs, business and government have joined together in a number of cooperative programs.

National Alliance of Businessmen (NAB) *a joint business-government program to train the hard-core unemployed*

One particularly successful partnership is the **National Alliance of Businessmen (NAB),** a joint business-government program to train the hard-core unemployed. The NAB is sponsored by participating corporations, whose executives contribute their talents to do the actual training. The government's responsibilities include setting objectives, establishing priorities, offering the right incentives, and providing limited financing.

Concern for the Environment

The social consciousness of responsible managers and the encouragement of a concerned government have also made the public and the business community partners in a major effort to reduce environmental pollution, conserve natural resources, and reverse some of the worst effects of past negligence in this area.

pollution *the contamination of water, air, or land through the actions of people in an industrialized society*

Pollution is the contamination of water, air, or land through the actions of people in an industrialized society. For several decades, environmentalists have been warning us about the dangers of industrial pollution. Unfortunately, business and government leaders either ignored the problem or weren't concerned about it until pollution became a threat to life and health in America. Consider the following list.

Learning Objective 7
Be aware of the major types of pollution, their causes, and their cures

▶ According to the Environmental Protection Agency, sixty-eight areas are known to exceed the national air-quality standards for ozone, with an additional twenty-eight areas expected to be added to the list. Approximately 140 million Americans populate these polluted regions.

▶ Approximately 2.7 billion pounds of toxics, some carcinogens, were released into the air by American industry in 1987.

▶ Only 38 of the 1,175 hazardous waste sites included on the Superfund national cleanup priority list have been cleaned up. The General Accounting Office predicts that more than 425,000 sites may actually need cleanup.

These are not isolated cases. Such situations, occurring throughout the United States, have made pollution a matter of national concern. Today Americans expect business and government leaders to take swift action to clean up our environment—and to keep it clean.

Effects of Environmental Legislation

As in other areas of concern to our society, legislation and regulations play a crucial role in pollution control. Of major importance was creation of the **Environmental Protection Agency (EPA),** the federal agency charged with enforcing laws designed to protect the environment.

Once they are aware of a problem of pollution, most firms respond to it rather than wait to be cited by the EPA. But other owners and managers take the position that environmental standards are too strict. (Loosely translated, this means that compliance with present standards is too expensive.) Consequently, it has often been necessary for the EPA to take legal action to force firms to install antipollution equipment and clean up waste storage areas.

Experience has shown that the combination of environmental legislation, voluntary compliance, and EPA action can succeed in cleaning up the environment and keeping it clean. However, much still remains to be done.

CHAPTER REVIEW

Summary

Ethics is the study of right and wrong and of the morality of choices. Business ethics is the application of moral standards to business situations. Because ethical issues arise in business situations every day, the business person should make an effort to be fair, to consider the welfare of customers and others within a firm, to avoid conflicts of interest, and to communicate honestly.

Investors, customers, employees, creditors, and competitors each exert specific pressures on a firm. Business people should not compromise their ethics to either satisfy or mislead any group. Because no international business code of ethics exists and since payoffs are sometimes part of international business practices, U.S. firms are sometimes directly or indirectly faced with ethical dilemmas when engaged in foreign business operations.

Any ethical action should be able to withstand open scrutiny. A person's individual values, the absence of an employer's code of ethics, and coworkers' attitudes and behaviors all influence a person's ethical decision making. The government, trade associations, and individual firms can help establish a more ethical business environment. An ethical employee working in an unethical environment sometimes resorts to whistle blowing to bring a particular situation to light.

In a socially responsible business, management realizes that its activities have an impact on society, and that impact is considered in the decision-making process. Before the 1930s neither workers, consumers, nor government had much influence on business activities; as a result, business gave little thought to its social responsibility. All this changed with the Great Depression. Government regulation and a new public awareness combined to create a demand that businesses act in a socially responsible manner.

According to the economic model of social responsibility, society benefits most when business is left alone to produce profitable goods and services. According to the socioeconomic model, business has as much responsibility to society as it has to its owners.

Most managers adopt a viewpoint somewhere between these two extremes.

Three major areas of social concern to business and society are consumerism, employment practices and the environment. The consumer movement has generally demanded—and received—attention from business in the areas of product safety, product information, product choices through competition, and the resolution of complaints about products and business practices.

Legislation and public demand have prompted some businesses to correct past abuses in employment practices—mainly with regard to minority groups. Affirmative action and training of the hard-core unemployed are two types of programs that have been used successfully.

Industry has contributed to the pollution of our land and water through the dumping of wastes, and to air pollution through vehicle and smokestack emissions. This contamination can be cleaned up and controlled, but the big question is who will pay for it. Present cleanup efforts are funded partly by government tax revenues, partly by business, and, in the long run, by consumers.

In this chapter and in Chapter 1, we have used the general term *business owners* and the more specific term *stockholders*. In the next chapter, wherein we discuss the various forms of business and business ownership, you will see who these people are.

Key Terms

You should now be able to define and give an example relevant to each of the following terms:

ethics
business ethics
corporate code of ethics
whistle blowing
social responsibility
caveat emptor

economic model of
   social responsibility
socioeconomic model of
   social responsibility
consumerism
minority

affirmative action
  program
Equal Employment
  Opportunity
  Commission (EEOC)
hard-core unemployed
National Alliance of
  Businessmen (NAB)

pollution
Environmental
  Protection Agency
  (EPA)

Questions and Exercises

Review Questions

1. Why might an individual with high ethical stand-ards act less ethically in business than in his or her personal life?
2. How would an organizational code of ethics help ensure ethical business behavior?
3. How and why did the American business environment change after the Great Depression?
4. What are the major differences between the economic model of social responsibility and the socioeconomic model?
5. What are the arguments for and against increased social responsibility for business?
6. Describe and give an example of each of the four basic rights of consumers.
7. There are more women than men in the United States. Why, then, are women considered a minority with regard to employment?
8. What is the goal of affirmative action programs? How is this goal achieved?

9. What is the primary function of the Equal Employment Opportunity Commission?
10. How do businesses contribute to each of the four forms of pollution? How can they avoid polluting the environment?
11. Our environment *can* be cleaned up and kept clean. Why haven't we simply done so?

Discussion Questions

1. Besides the catastrophic effects of the oil spill on the environment, what has been the effect on Exxon?
2. To what extent can and should an oil company prepare for a major oil spill?
3. How can an employee take an ethical stand regarding a business decision when his or her superior has already taken a different position?
4. Overall, would it be more profitable for a business to follow the economic model or the socioeconomic model of social responsibility?
5. Why should business take on the task of training the hard-core unemployed?

Exercises

1. Write out four "guidelines" that can be included as part of the code of ethics that prevails at your school or at a firm where you have worked.
2. Research and report on one case in which the EEOC or the EPA successfully brought suit against one or more firms. Give your own evaluation of the merits of the case.

(Pride, et al. *Business*, pp. 34–63.)

Review Test: Chapter One

1. Why is pre-reading important?

   Pre-reading provides a purpose and that purpose encourages mental

   flexibility. Readers have a basis for distributing attention and concentration.

2. What are two functions of the title during pre-reading?

   (1) Announces the topic

   (2) Provides the basis prediction

3. What are at least three methods authors use to tell you, on the opening page of a chapter, what is important?

   (1) Lists of learning objectives   (4) Chapter previews

   (2) Chapter outlines   (5) Statements of purpose

   (3) Lists of questions

4. How can headings help you during pre-reading?

   Readers can use them to raise questions.

5. What is the difference between major and minor headings?

   Major headings identify the topics discussed; minor headings tell you

   what aspects of those topics will be discussed.

6. What is marginal annotation?

   Writing in the margin that emphasizes key terms or points

7. What can you expect to find on the last page or two of a chapter?

Lists of key terms, summaries, discussion questions
_____

_____

8. How can mapping a chapter help you?

Mapping will help you see relationships among topics.
_____

9. Why is reading creative?

The reader has to make the right connections between sentences.
_____

10. Identify the six steps for pre-reading:

(1) Read the title and any introductory questions, outlines, objectives.
_____

(2) Raise questions about the chapter.
_____

(3) Study visual aids.
_____

(4) Read any concluding sections called *Summary, Review,* or *Questions.*
_____

(5) Map the chapter.
_____

(6) Consider what you know about the subject.
_____

Building Your Vocabulary

Pre-reading is a powerful strategy for improving your comprehension. But to really improve your reading skills, you also have to make a commitment to regular vocabulary work. Pre-reading will not help you much if you don't know what the words mean.

One of the best ways to discover what a word means is to look it up in the dictionary. However, sometimes looking up all the words you don't know in a difficult text can confuse you. By interrupting yourself too often, you lose track of what you're reading.

Still that does not mean you should just skip over unfamiliar words as if they were not there. On the contrary, use **word analysis** and **context clues** to derive a tentative or temporary definition, one that will allow you to continue reading until you are finished and can look up the unfamiliar words.

This chapter will show you how to develop and combine strategies for working with words.

- ☐ Use *prefixes*, *suffixes*, and *roots* to analyze new words.
- ☐ Become familiar with common context clues.
- ☐ Know what to expect from your dictionary.
- ☐ Collect words with interesting histories.
- ☐ Enlarge your vocabulary of *specialized terms*.
- ☐ Use a variety of strategies to learn new words.

Word Analysis

When we use the term **word analysis,** we mean that it is possible to take an unfamiliar word, figure out what a part or parts of the word mean, and come up with a definition. For example, let's say you came across the following sentence: "He thought it might be a good idea to study dermatology." Suppose that you did not have the slightest idea what the word *dermatology* means. It would undoubtedly help if we told you that *derma* means "skin" and *logy* means "study of." Then you would be able to figure out that dermatology is the study of skin.

At this point, you may be asking yourself how word analysis can save time since you have to go to a dictionary to find out what parts of a word mean. The answer is simple: *Learn some of the most commonly used prefixes, suffixes, and roots.* That way you will have these useful clues to word meaning with you at all times. When you see an unfamiliar word, you can check if it contains a familiar prefix, suffix, or root. If it does, you may be able to figure out a definition without turning to the dictionary.

1. **Prefixes** can consist of one letter, two letters, or a group of letters. Prefixes are word parts that appear at the beginning of many different words (*re*turn, *ex*clude, *semi*circle).
2. **Suffixes,** like prefixes, can consist of one letter, two letters, or a group of letters. But unlike prefixes, they do not appear at the beginning of words; instead, they always appear at the end (farm*er*, hypnot*ist*, gentle*ness*).
3. A **root** is that part of a word to which prefixes and suffixes are attached in order to form new words (re*spect*, *spec*ulate, and intro*spect*ion).

Context Clues

Although word analysis is extremely useful, simply combining the meanings of the parts of a word will not always give you the best definition. For example, take the following sentence: "I can't imagine a more credulous person; he actually believed that I was attacked by men from Mars on my way home from the party."

If you don't know what the word *credulous* means, it will help to explain that *cred* means "belief" and *ous* usually means "full of."* You can then take "full of belief" for a first definition of the word *credulous*. But what exactly does that mean? You can imagine a bottle full of milk, but what is a person full of belief?

---

* *ous* can also mean "in possession of," or "having."

If you read the sentence again with the first definition in mind, you will understand what *credulous* means. The person who is described as credulous obviously believes a story that most people would laugh at. A person who is credulous, then, is ready to believe something most people would not. As a matter of fact, he or she is ready to believe almost anything. This second definition, derived from context, explains the first one, which was derived from word analysis. Someone who is full of belief is ready to believe anything.

The **context** of a word is the sentence, paragraph, or selection in which the word appears. Whenever you use the sentence, paragraph, or passage in which a word appears to discover its meaning, you are using context clues. Here are three examples of important context clues.

Example Clue

The context of a word often contains an example of behavior associated with the word; for instance, "His feelings for his cousin were *ambivalent;* sometimes he delighted in her company and sometimes he couldn't stand the sight of her." From this sentence, it is clear that someone with ambivalent feelings tends to have mixed emotions. Certainly, the sentence gives an example of someone who is in conflict: ". . . sometimes he delighted in her company and sometimes he couldn't stand the sight of her." Since that's an example of what it's like to be ambivalent, we can say that *ambivalent* in this sentence means "conflicting."

Contrast Clue

The context may also tell you what the word does *not* mean; for example, "She wanted to give me the impression of being *erudite,* but instead she gave me the impression that she knew absolutely nothing." It is clear from this sentence that if someone is erudite, he or she is the opposite of someone who knows nothing. It wouldn't be very sensible to claim that a person who is erudite knows everything, but we can say that someone who is erudite knows a great deal.

Restatement Clue

The context may actually contain a definition of the word; for example, "His *redundancy* was not one of the things that pleased me about his style. As a matter of fact, the way he repeated himself drove me almost insane." There are two sentences in this example. From the first one we learn that redundancy is irritating; from the second, we learn that redundancy means "repetition."

Example, contrast, and restatement context clues are very important. Nevertheless, keep in mind that most context clues are not so obvious. Often you have to combine ideas in a paragraph or selection with your own knowledge and experience to figure out the meaning of a word. The following sentences illustrate this point.

> For months he had dreamed of being able to *redeem* his medals. He had been unable to think of anything else. Now with the vision of the medals shimmering before him, he hurried to the pawnshop.

In this short selection, none of the context clues previously presented appear. However, it is still possible to figure out that the word *redeem* in this context means "reclaim" or "recover." Most people go to a pawnshop to buy or to sell, and it is doubtful that the man described as hurrying to the pawnshop would be in such a rush to sell something he had dreamed of for months. Clearly, he is going to buy back what he has already sold.

Remember, too, that the use of context clues, like word analysis, has its limitations. Take, for example, the following sentence: "She was an *articulate* student, ready and willing to speak on every subject." Here the word *articulate* means "capable of speaking clearly and expressively." However, given the description of the student's behavior—she was "ready and willing to speak on every subject"—it would be just as easy to assume that *articulate* means "talkative."

Sometimes context clues alone are simply not good enough to lead you to the correct definition of a word. Rely on them only when you have no choice—for example, if you are taking a test and cannot look up a word. Whenever you can, use word analysis and context clues together. Combining these two methods will usually lead you to the correct definition of a word.

However if combining context and word analysis doesn't lead to a definition of the word that makes sense, and you cannot understand the sentence without understanding that particular word, it is time to turn to the dictionary. The purpose of this section is *not* to discourage you from ever using the dictionary while you are reading. Rather, the purpose is to discourage you from using it so often that you lose your train of thought.

Exercise 1

Directions: Read the following list and then look at the sentences that follow. Each sentence contains an italicized word that may not be familiar to you. Use context and word analysis to figure out the meaning of the italicized word in the sentence.

Write the letter *c* after the sentence if you are able to use context clues. Do not mark the sentence at all if there are no context clues.

1.	circum	(Latin prefix)	around
2.	inter	(Latin prefix)	between
3.	loqu, locut	(Latin root)	speak, talk
4.	spec	(Latin root)	see, look
5.	scrib, script	(Latin root)	write
6.	ven	(Latin root)	come
7.	ous, ious	(Latin suffix)	full of, in possession of, having

Example: He had been silent and withdrawn in his youth, but old age had made him *loquacious.* __C__

The word *loquacious* in this sentence means

talkative

Explanation: In this example, you can use word analysis and context clues. You know that *loqu* means "talk" and the suffix *ous* means "full of." Thus someone who is *loquacious* is "full of talk."

The context of the word also contains a clue. It tells you that someone who is loquacious is the opposite of someone who is silent and withdrawn. Someone who is not silent is willing to talk. The person is not only willing but, as you learned from word analysis, he or she is full of talk, or talkative.

Do the rest of the sentences in the same manner.

1. American colonists did not like British *intervention* in their affairs. __C__

The word *intervention* in this sentence means

interference

2. After his accident he was decidedly more *circumspect* when driving in heavy traffic. __C__

The word *circumspect* in this sentence means

careful, watchful, cautious

3. What formula do you use to figure out the *circumference* of a circle? _____

The word *circumference* in this sentence means

measurement around

4. Her actions were rigidly *circumscribed* by the club's rules and regulations; she could not make any decisions for herself. __C__

The word *circumscribed* in this sentence means

controlled, limited, defined

5. The scientists were unable to read the strange *script*. __C__

The word *script* in this sentence means

writing

6. After their families forbade them to meet, the young lovers used the coachman as their *intermediary* to carry their letters back and forth. __C__

The word *intermediary* in this sentence means

go-between, an agent between two parties

7. Because she came dressed as Cher in fishnet and feathers, her mother accused her of making a *spectacle* of herself. __C__

The word *spectacle* in this sentence means

object of interest or curiosity

A powerful speaker, Martin Luther King could hold an audience spellbound with his eloquence.

8. The singer Lena Horne was one of the few performers who managed to *circumvent* the Jim Crow* laws that once ruled Las Vegas. A star attraction, she insisted on having a room normally reserved for white people only, and she got what she wanted. __C__

   The word *circumvent* in this sentence means

   avoid, get around

9. The document was written *circa* A.D. 1500. _____

   The word *circa* in this sentence means

   around

10. Martin Luther King was famous for his *eloquence:* he could hold an audience spellbound by the power of his words. __C__

    The word *eloquence* in this sentence means

    brilliance in speaking, gift for speaking

---

* Jim Crow laws: a practice or policy of keeping the races separate or segregated in public places.

11. When the waiter *interceded* in the fight, he was knocked unconscious. __C__

The word *intercede* in this sentence means

interfere, come between, act as mediator
_____

12. He decided to take *elocution* lessons because he knew his new job required a lot of public speaking. __C__

The word *elocution* in this sentence means

speaking
_____

13. After much *speculation*, she decided to enter the religious order and give up all worldly contact. _____

The word *speculation* in this sentence means

thought
_____

14. There was an *inscription* on the back of the locket, but it was written in a foreign language. __C__

The word *inscription* in this sentence means

writing
_____

15. Because they stopped talking as soon as she arrived, she felt like an *interloper* in their conversation. __C__

The word *interloper* in this sentence means

intruder
_____

Definition and Context

Notice that when we ask you to give a definition, we always ask what a word means within a sentence ("The word *speculation* in this sentence means . . ."). We never ask you to define a word outside of a particular context.

That's because the meaning of a word depends on its context.

In the following sentence, for example, the word *speculation* means "thinking": "After hours of *speculation*, he could still not make up his mind." But *speculation* in this sentence has a different definition: "Her *speculation* in stocks had cost her a great deal of money." Here the word *speculation* refers to business dealings involving a certain amount of risk; the word does not refer to the consideration of an object or idea. Clearly, the meaning of a word can change when its context changes.

Never assume that a word has only one meaning. **Most words have several meanings, and all word definitions are dependent on context.**

If you think you know the definition of a word but find that your definition just doesn't make sense in relation to the rest of the sentence, use context clues and word analysis to work out another meaning. If that's not possible, look up the word and try to find a definition that fits the particular context of the word that is puzzling you.

Exercise 2

Directions: Read the following list and then look at the sentences that follow. Each sentence contains an italicized word that may not be familiar to you. Use context and word analysis to figure out the meaning of the italicized word in the sentence.

Write the letter *c* after the sentence if you are able to use context clues. Do not mark the sentence at all if there are no context clues.

Note that whenever possible we have included prefixes, suffixes, or roots you have already learned.

1.	in, im, il	(Latin prefix)	into, not
2.	super	(Latin prefix)	over, above
3.	vid, vis	(Latin root)	see
4.	brev	(Latin root)	short
5.	clar	(Latin root)	clear
6.	cred	(Latin root)	believe
7.	er, ar, or	(Latin suffix)	one who has something to do with the idea expressed in the root

1.   The *brevity* of his letter convinced her that she could no longer consider him a good friend. _____

The word *brevity* in this sentence means

shortness
_____

2. His story about being attacked on the way home was hardly *credible;* he didn't have a mark on him. __C__

The word *credible* in this sentence means

believable

3. I just can't give any *credence* to what he says; it's impossible to believe him after all the lies he's told. __C__

The word *credence* in this sentence means

belief

4. His *supercilious* attitude offended them; he acted as if they were not good enough to talk to him. __C__

The word *supercilious* in this sentence means

arrogant

5. It was *evident* that she was uncomfortable because she kept picking imaginary threads off her coat and fixing her scarf. __C__

The word *evident* in this sentence means

obvious

6. After hearing the story about the UFOs, he had an *incredulous* look on his face. _____

The word *incredulous* in this sentence means

unbelieving, skeptical

7. You'll have to *abbreviate* that phrase. _____

The word *abbreviate* in this sentence means

shorten

8. Because she had been able to foresee the storm, they believed her to be a *visionary*. __C__

The word *visionary* in this sentence means

person who sees the future
_____

9. The Christian *creed* spread rapidly to the rest of the world. _____

The word *creed* in this sentence means

belief
_____

10. The press asked the president to *clarify* his last statement. _____

The word *clarify* in this sentence means

explain
_____

11. His *credulity* never failed to surprise his friends; there was nothing he was not ready to believe. __C__

The word *credulity* in this sentence means

willingness to believe
_____

12. The *spectators* were not pleased with her performance. __C__

The word *spectators* in this sentence means

audience, observers
_____

13. Unfortunately, his speech lacked *clarity* and didn't do much to straighten out the confusion. __C__

The word *clarity* in this sentence means

clearness
_____

14. Because of the strange things that happened when she was present, they believed she had *supernatural* powers. __C__

The word *supernatural* in this sentence means

beyond human, ghostly

___

15. The *video* portion of this performance will undergo a short interruption. _____

The word *video* in this sentence means

visual

___

Each of the following chapters (beginning with Chapter 3) will end with a section titled "Working with Words." There you'll find more prefixes, suffixes, and roots that commonly appear in English words. Be sure to add them to the ones you already know.

Knowing What to Expect from Your Dictionary

Dictionaries aren't all the same. The formats of entries vary, and some dictionaries contain more information than others. A good way to decide on the dictionary you like best is to look up the same word in different dictionaries.

It is also important to buy a current dictionary. Don't rely on the one that has been in your family for twenty years. After about ten years, dictionaries become dated as new words enter the language. The word *biodegradable*, for example, means "capable of decomposing naturally." But it wouldn't appear in any dictionary published prior to the late sixties. The word entered the language when Americans became increasingly concerned about the environment.

Any one of the following dictionaries would be a good choice.

- ☐ *The American Heritage Dictionary of the English Language*. Boston: Houghton Mifflin, 1985.
- ☐ *The Random House College Dictionary*. New York: Random House, 1986.
- ☐ *Funk and Wagnalls Standard Desk Dictionary*. New York: Funk and Wagnalls, 1984.
- ☐ *Webster's New World Dictionary*. New York: Simon and Schuster, 1983.
- ☐ *Webster's Ninth New Collegiate Dictionary*. Springfield, Mass.: G. & C. Merriam Company, 1983.

We suggest, too, that you purchase not only a hardbound college dictionary but also a paperback edition. You can use the hardbound edition for working at your desk and carry the paperback edition to class.

Reading Entries: Starting Small

Although they may not look it, even very brief dictionary entries contain a good deal of information. Consider this example[1]:

> **bi·o·ta** (bī-ō′tə) *n.* The animal and plant life of a particular region considered as a total ecological entity. [NLat. < Gk. *biotē*, way of life.]

The first thing we learn from this entry is that the word *biota* has three syllables: bi·o·ta. We know this because *The American Heritage Dictionary* uses dots to separate syllables. It uses spaces to separate words, as in *boxing glove.*

The entry also tells us that there is only one acceptable spelling for the word *biota.* If there were others, they would follow the entry word.

The parentheses that follow contain letters and symbols (bī-ō′tə).* The symbols over the letters are called *diacritical* marks. They tell you how the word is pronounced. If, for example, you did not know how to pronounce the *i,* the *o,* or the *a,* you could look at the bottom of the dictionary page and find the following key.

ă pat / ā pay / âr care / ä father / b **bib**
ch **church** / d **deed** / ĕ pet / ē be / f **fife**
g **gag** / h **hat** / hw **which** / ĭ pit / ī pie
îr **pier** / j **judge** / k **kick** / l **lid**, needle
m **mum** / n **no**, sudden / ng thing / ŏ pot
ō toe / ô paw, for / oi noise / ou out
o͝o took / o͞o boot / p pop / r roar
s sauce / sh ship, dish . . .

The key informs us that the *i* is pronounced like the *i* in *pie,* the *o* is pronounced like the *o* is *toe,* and the final *a* sounds like the *a* in *about.* We learn which syllable to stress from the heavy black mark (′) that follows the second syllable.

---

1. This entry and all other dictionary entries in this chapter are from *The American Heritage Dictionary of the English Language* (Boston: Houghton Mifflin, 1985).

* The symbol ə is called a *schwa.*

The letter *n.* that follows the parenthesis tells us that the word is used as a noun. If it could also be used as a verb, adverb, adjective, or interjection, that information would also appear in the entry (*v., adv., adj.,* or *interj.*).

Although dictionary entries can include several definitions, the one for *biota* contains only one: "The animal and plant life of a particular region considered as a total ecological* entity.†"

The following exercise will give you some practice reading and analyzing brief dictionary entries.

Exercise 3

Directions: Read each entry. Then answer the questions that follow.

1.
    bed·roll (bĕd′rōl′) *n.* A portable roll of bedding used esp. by campers and others who sleep outdoors.

a. Is the entry word spelled as one word or two? <u>one</u>

b. Can the word be used as a verb? <u>no</u>

2.
    fore·bear also **for·bear** (fôr′bâr′, fōr′-) *n.* A forefather; ancestor. [ME : *fore-*, fore- + *been*, to be.]

a. What is an alternative spelling for the entry word? <u>forbear</u>

b. What part of speech is it? <u>noun</u>

3.
    lor·gnette (lôrn-yĕt′) *n.* Eyeglasses or opera glasses with a short handle. [Fr. < *lorgner*, to leer at < OFr. < *lorgne*, squinting.]

a. When the word *lorgnette* is pronounced, do you hear the *g*?

    <u>no</u>

b. From what word is the word *lorgnette* derived?

---

* ecological: having to do with the relationship between organisms and their environment.

† entity: being, single unit.

lorgner: to leer at
_____

and lorgne: squinting
_____

4.   **hence·forth** (hĕns′fôrth′) also **hence·for·ward** (hĕns-fôr′-
ward) *adv.* From this time forth; from now on.

a. Is the entry word spelled as one word or two? __one____

b. What is the alternative spelling for this entry word?

henceforward
_____

Reading Longer Entries

The previous dictionary entries were fairly simple, with one definition per word. Some entries, however, are more detailed. The
following is a good example:

> **bra·zen** (brā′zən) *adj.* **1.** Made of brass. **2.** Resembling brass
> in color, quality, or hardness. **3.** Having a loud, resonant
> sound like that of a brass trumpet. **4.** Impudent; bold.
> —*tr.v.* **-zened, -zen·ing, -zens.** To face or undergo with bold
> self-assurance: *brazened out the crisis.* [ME *brasen* < OE
> *bræsen* < *bræs,* brass.] —**bra′zen·ly** *adv.* —**bra′zen·ness** *n.*

The four definitions make this entry considerably longer than
the first. But the number of definitions is not surprising. As you
know, words can have different meanings depending on how we
use them. A good dictionary takes this fact into account and offers
several possible meanings. It's up to you to match the correct
definition to the context in which the word appears.

However, keep in mind that not all dictionaries organize the
definitions of a word in the same way. Some give the oldest meaning of the word first; others give the most common meaning of the
word first. Check the opening pages of your dictionary to see which
method has been used.

Following the list of definitions is the abbreviation *tr. v.* It tells
us that the entry will now give the meaning of *brazen* when it is
used as a transitive verb.* The entry also shows the different forms
of the word *brazen* when it's used as a verb: -zened, -zening, -zens.

According to the entry, there is only one meaning for the word
brazen when it is used as a verb: to "brazen something out" means

_____

*   Transitive verbs take objects: He *drank* the *coffee.*
                               t.v.   obj.

"to face or undergo [it] with bold self-assurance." Note that we also learn that *brazen* is used with the word *out.*

At the end of the entry stands a brief history of the word.

[ME *brasen* ⟨OE *bræsen* ⟨*bræs,* brass.]

Here we learn that the modern word *brazen* can be traced back to the period when Middle English was spoken (1100–1500) and even further back, to when Old English was spoken (800–1100).

Finally, the entry gives two additional parts of speech formed from the word *brazen: brazenly,* which is an adverb, and *brazenness,* which is a noun.

Dictionary Labels

Clearly, the second sample entry was longer than the first. But some entries contain even more information. Many contain labels that tell you more about precisely how and when a word can be used. Here is a list of the most important labels:

1. *Nonstandard* or *Substandard.* If either one of these labels follows a word, you know that the use of that particular word is not considered correct by most speakers of the English language. Words like *ain't* and *nowheres* are examples of nonstandard English.
2. *Informal, Colloquial,* or *Slang.* All three of these labels tell you if a particular meaning of a word is appropriate in casual conversation or writing but inappropriate in a more formal setting. For example, one meaning of the word *bug* is "to annoy or irritate." However, in most dictionaries that meaning is labeled *slang.* The label indicates that this particular use of the word is appropriate for casual conversation but inappropriate in formal speeches or essays.
3. *Archaic.* If this label appears, it signals that a word or meaning is rarely seen and belongs to a style of language no longer in use. The word *shouldst,* for example, appears in Shakespeare's plays, but it is almost never seen in anything written today.
4. *Vulgar.* If this label appears next to a word or expression, it means that you should be very cautious about using the word since many people are shocked or insulted when they hear it. The word *snot,* for example, is usually labeled "vulgar."
5. *Usage.* This label introduces an explanation of usage problems involving the entry word. For example, the entry for the word *between* usually contains a usage label because, for many speakers of English, there is some confusion about when it is correct to use the word *between* rather than the word *among.*

6. *Music, Logic, Mathematics (Math), Linguistics (Ling.).* Labels like these indicate that a given definition applies only when the word is used in connection with a particular field of study. The meaning of the word *base*, for example, differs depending on whether it is used in relation to architecture, chemistry, or baseball.

7. *Obsolete* or *Obs.* When one of these labels follows a definition, it indicates that this meaning of the word is no longer in use. The word *prevent*, for example, when it means "to precede" is usually labeled "obsolete."

8. *Synonyms.* This label introduces words similar in meaning. For example, the entry for *brave* often introduces several synonyms, among them the words *courageous, fearless,* and *intrepid.*

9. *Old English (OE), Middle English (ME), Latin (Lat.), Greek (Gk.), French (Fr.)* are all labels identifying word origins.

The information provided here should enable you to understand an entry fairly easily, but if you need more, check the table of contents in your dictionary to see if there is a section titled "Guide to the Dictionary" or "Explanatory Notes." Most good dictionaries include explanatory sections that help identify all terms and symbols contained in the entries.

The following exercises will give you more practice in working with a dictionary.

Exercise 4

Directions: Answer the following questions based on the dictionary entries that accompany them.

1.

cell (sĕl) *n.* **1.** A narrow, confining room, as in a prison or convent. **2.** A small, one-room abode, such as a hut. **3.** A small religious house dependent on a larger one, as a priory within an abbey. **4.** The primary organizational unit of a movement, esp. of a political party of Leninist structure. **5.** *Biol.* The smallest structural unit of an organism that is capable of independent functioning, consisting of one or more nuclei, cytoplasm, various organelles, and inanimate matter, all surrounded by a semipermeable plasma membrane. **6.** *Biol.* A small, enclosed cavity or space, such as a compartment in a honeycomb or within a plant ovary or an area bordered by veins in an insect's wing. **7.** *Elect.* **a.** A single unit for electrolysis or for conversion of chemical into electric energy, usually consisting of a container with electrodes and an electrolyte. **b.** A single unit that converts radiant energy into electric energy: *a solar cell.* **8.** *Computer Sci.* A basic unit of storage in a computer memory that can hold one unit of information, as a character or word. —*v.* **celled, cell·ing, cells.** —*tr.* To store in a honeycomb. —*intr.* To live in a cell. [ME *celle,* partly < OE *cell,* and partly < OFr., both < Lat. *cella,* chamber.]

a. Give two general meanings for the word *cell*.

(1) a narrow, confining room;   (2) a small one room house;

(3) a small religious house;   (4) the unit of a larger movement

b. What does *cell* mean when used in the context of biology?

(1) the smallest structural unit of an organism

(2) a small enclosed cavity or space

c. In what other fields besides biology is this word used?

electronics, computer science

d. From what language does this word derive?

Latin

2.

bun·dle (bŭn′dl) *n.* **1.** A group of objects tied, fastened, wrapped, or otherwise held together. **2.** Something wrapped or tied up for carrying; package. **3.** *Biol.* A cluster or strand of specialized cells. **4.** *Bot.* A vascular bundle. **5.** *Slang.* A large sum of money. —*v.* **-dled, -dling, -dles.** —*tr.* **1.** To tie, wrap, or fasten together. **2.** To dispatch quickly and with little fuss; hustle: *bundled her off to school.* **3.** To dress warmly: *bundled them up in winter clothes.* —*intr.* **1.** To leave hastily and unceremoniously. **2.** To sleep in the same bed while fully clothed, a custom practiced by engaged couples in early New England. [ME *bundel,* prob. < MDu. *bondel.*] —**bun′dler** *n.*

a. What is the meaning of *bundle* when it is used in the context of biology?

a cluster or strand of specialized cells

b. When used as a slang term, what does *bundle* mean?

a large sum of money

3.

knowl·edge (nŏl′ĭj) *n.* **1.** The state or fact of knowing. **2.** Familiarity, awareness, or understanding gained through experience or study. **3.** That which is known; the sum or range of what has been perceived, discovered, or inferred. **4.** Learning; erudition: *men of knowledge.* **5.** Specific information about something. **6.** *Obsolete.* Sexual intercourse; copulation. Now used only in the phrase *carnal knowledge.* [Middle English *knowlege, know(e)lech,* from *cnawlechen, know(e)lechen,* to confess, recognize, Old English *cnāwlǽcan* (unattested), from *cnāwan,* to KNOW.]
   Synonyms: *knowledge, information, learning, erudition, lore, scholarship, wisdom, enlightenment.* These nouns refer to cognitive or intellective mental components acquired and retained through study and experience. *Knowledge* includes both empirical material and that derived by inference or interpretation. *Information* is usually construed as narrower in scope and implies a random collection of material rather than orderly synthesis. *Learning* usually refers to what is gained by schooling and study, and *erudition* adds to this the idea of profound knowledge often in a specialized area. *Lore* is knowledge gained by tradition or intuition rather than formally. The remaining terms refer to qualities possessed by persons rather than directly to what is stored in their minds. *Scholarship* is the distinctive mark of one who has mastered some area of learning, as reflected in the quality of his work, especially with respect to scope, thoroughness, and care. *Wisdom* involves sound judgment and the ability to apply what has been acquired mentally to the conduct of one's affairs. *Enlightenment* is the state of possessing knowledge and truth.

a. What is an obsolete meaning of the word *knowledge?*

sexual intercourse

b. Explain the difference between *learning* and *lore,* two synonyms for *knowledge.*

Learning refers to what is gained by going to school, whereas lore is

knowledge gained from intuition and tradition.

4.

as·sure (ə-shoor′) *tr.v.* **-sured, -sur·ing, -sures. 1.** To inform confidently, with a view to removing doubt. **2.** To cause to feel sure; convince. **3.** To give confidence to; reassure. **4.** To make certain; ensure: *"Nothing in history assures the success of our civilization"* (Herbert J. Muller). **5.** To make safe or secure. **6.** *Chiefly Brit.* To insure, as against loss. [ME *assuren* < OFr. *assurer* < Med. Lat. *assecurare,* to make sure : Lat. *ad-,* to + *securus,* secure.] **—as·sur′a·ble** *adj.* **—as·sur′er** *n.*
   Usage: *Assure, ensure,* and *insure* all mean "to make secure or certain." Only *assure* is used with reference to a person in the sense of "to set the mind at rest": *assured the leader of his loyalty.* Although *ensure* and *insure* are generally interchangeable, only *insure* is now widely used in the commercial sense of "to guarantee persons or property against risk."

a. Give two different meanings for the word *assure.*

(1) to inform and remove doubt; (2) to convince; (3) to make certain;

(4) to reassure; (5) to make secure; (6) to insure against loss

b. According to the entry, are the words *assure* and *insure* always interchangeable?

no

c. How is the entry word spelled when it is used as an adjective?

assurable

d. According to the entry, the word *assure* is derived from what Latin prefix and root.

*ad:*to, and *securus:*secure

Exercise 5

Directions: Read the sample sentence. Then read the accompanying definitions and write out the definition that *best* fits the context of the word italicized in the sentence or passage.

Example: When he pushed his *secretary* into the center of the room, the room looked much smaller.

> **sec·re·tar·y** (sĕk′rĭ-tĕr′ē) *n., pl.* **-ies. 1.** A person employed to handle correspondence, keep files, and do clerical work for an individual or company. **2.** An officer who keeps records of the meetings, stock transfers, and legal transactions of a company or other organization. **3.** An official presiding over an administrative department of state. **4.** A desk with a small bookcase on top.

Meaning number __4__ fits the context of the sentence.

Explanation: When we think of the word *secretary*, most of us think of definition 1. But obviously that definition does not fit the context, which suggests an object, not a person. In this case, only meaning number 4 would be appropriate.

Now it's your turn to choose the appropriate definition.

1. In his mind, the deathbed promise he had made to his mother was as *binding* as any legal contract. There was no way he could fail to fulfill his promise and still consider himself a truly moral being.

bind (bīnd) *v.* **bound** (bound), **bind·ing, binds.** —*tr.* **1.** To tie or secure, as with a rope or cord. **2.** To fasten or wrap by encircling, as with a belt. **3.** To bandage. **4.** To hold or restrain with or as if with bonds. **5.** To compel, obligate, or unite, as with a sense of moral duty. **6.** *Law.* To place under legal obligation by contract or oath. **7.** To make certain or irrevocable: *bind a bargain.* **8.** To hold or employ as an apprentice; indenture. **9.** To cause to cohere or stick together in a mass. **10.** To enclose and fasten (a book) between covers. **11.** To furnish with an edge or border for reinforcement or ornamentation.

Meaning number __5__ fits the context of the sentence.

2. He had been *blessed* with good looks, but he didn't let that go to his head. He worked hard to achieve success.

bless (blĕs) *tr.v.* **blessed** or **blest** (blĕst), **bless·ing, bless·es.** **1.** To make holy by religious rite; sanctify. **2.** To make the sign of the cross over so as to sanctify. **3.** To invoke divine favor upon. **4.** To honor as holy; glorify: *Bless the Lord.* **5.** To confer well-being or prosperity upon. **6.** To endow, as with talent. [ME *blessen* < OE *blētsian.*] —**bless'er** *n.*

Meaning number __6__ fits the context of the sentence.

3. Many people claim that after his *stint* in the army, Elvis Presley was never the same.

stint¹ (stĭnt) *v.* **stint·ed, stint·ing, stints.** —*tr.* **1.** To restrict or limit, as in amount or number; be sparing with. **2.** *Archaic.* To cause to stop. —*intr.* **1.** To subsist on a meager allowance; be frugal. **2.** *Archaic.* To stop or desist. —*n.* **1.** A fixed amount or share of work or duty to be performed within a given period of time. **2.** A limitation or restriction.

Meaning number __1__ fits the context of the sentence.

4. Her *pathetic* attempts to explain her absence strained all credibility. She obviously did not have an adequate explanation.

pa·thet·ic (pə-thĕt'ĭk) also **pa·thet·i·cal** (-ĭ-kəl) *adj.* **1.** Of, pertaining to, expressing, or arousing pity, sympathy, or tenderness; full of pathos: *a pathetic tale of hardship.* **2.** Distressing and inadequate: *a pathetic attempt to appear worldly.*

Meaning number __2__ fits the context of the sentence.

5. It was the *peak* of winter. Snow was on the ground; the trees were bare, and the birds spent their days hunting for stray seeds.

> **peak** (pēk) *n.* **1.** A tapering, projecting point; pointed extremity: *peak of a cap; peak of a roof.* **2. a.** The pointed summit of a mountain. **b.** The mountain itself: *Pikes Peak.* **3. a.** The point of a beard. **b.** A widow's peak. **4.** The point of greatest development, value, height, or intensity: *a novel written at the peak of his career.* **5.** *Physics.* The highest value attained by a varying quantity: *a current peak.* **6.** *Naut.* **a.** The narrow portion of a ship's hull at the bow or stern. **b.** The upper after corner of a fore-and-aft sail. **c.** The outermost end of a gaff.

Meaning number __4__ fits the context of the sentence.

Identifying Specialized Vocabulary

One important goal of textbook authors is to teach you the **specialized vocabulary** of their subject matter or discipline. They try to identify the words or terms essential to their field of study.

Some of those words will be totally unfamiliar because they are seldom used except in reference to a particular field of study. Students of meteorology, for example, use the word *foehn* to refer to a warm, dry wind. But no one outside the field of meteorology would use it to describe windy weather.

Then there are the words and terms that might seem familiar yet take on surprising meanings when they appear in textbooks. In general conversation, for example, the word *unstable* usually means unreliable. But within the context of meteorology, the word refers to air that tends to rise upward because it is warmer and less dense than its surroundings.

To master the specialized vocabularies in your textbooks, be alert to the ways in which authors signal the appearance of key words. Italics, boldface type, marginal annotations, explicit definitions, and repetition are all ways of highlighting specialized terms.

Look, for example, at how these authors emphasize the definition of the term *craft union.*

craft union an organization of skilled workers in a single craft or trade

Until the middle of the nineteenth century, there was very little organization of labor in this country. Groups of workers did occasionally form a **craft union**, which is an organization of skilled workers in a single craft or trade. These unions were usually limited to a single city, and they often did not last very long. The first known strike in the United States involved a group of Philadelphia printers who stopped working over demands for higher wages. When the printers were granted a pay increase by their employers, the group disbanded. (Pride, Hughes, and Kapoor, *Business*, p. 285.)

Here the authors use three different devices to highlight the term *craft union*. They introduce it in boldface, provide an explicit definition, and repeat that definition in the margins. Whenever a word or phrase gets this much attention, it's important, and you should jot down the definition in the margins or in your notes. **Jotting down the definition when you first see it is crucial.** Usually, authors introduce the definition of a key term the first time they introduce the word. From then on you are expected to know it. The definition will not be repeated.

Pay attention, too, when an author takes the time to define words you think you already know. Here is a good example:

Describing Earthquakes

The *magnitude* of an earthquake is the total amount of energy released. The magnitude is not measured directly, but is expressed on an arbitrary scale independent of the place of observation. At the present time the magnitude of an earthquake is most often expressed in terms of the Richter scale. . . . In contrast, the *intensity* of an earthquake is the amount of shaking of the earth's surface at any given locality, and may vary with the degree of consolidation of the geological materials at that locality. (Young, *Geology: The Paradox of Earth and Man*, p. 218.)

In this case the author knows that words like *magnitude* and *intensity* appear outside the particular context of his field. Therefore he carefully specifies the definition for those words when they are used in a geological context.

Be on the lookout, too, for paragraphs devoted solely to defining a key term. Here's a good illustration:

Fixed-asset investments require a specific amount of money to be invested for a certain amount of time. You can be reasonably certain of receiving periodic income (often interest received quarterly or semiannually) as well as getting back the amount you originally invested. For this small financial risk you usually earn a relatively low total yield, particularly when compared with the typically higher total returns earned on investments in common stocks and real estate. Examples of fixed-asset investments are savings accounts, certificates of deposit, government bonds, corporate bonds, and annuities. (Garman and Forgue, *Personal Finance*, p. 597.)

If an author devotes an entire paragraph to defining and illustrating a word or phrase, you can bet that it is important and should be recorded in your notebook. Think, too, about recording one or two of the examples offered, maybe even making up your own. Examples help fix the definition in your memory.

In addition to defining words within the text, some authors also list specialized vocabulary at the end of every chapter. Here is an example of one such a list drawn from a psychology textbook:

Key Terms

altruism	hostile aggression
anal stage	identification
attachment	identity
conventional level	identity crisis
erogenous zones	instrumental aggression
fixation	internalization
gender identity	latency period
gender roles	Oedipal conflict
genital stage	

(Bootzin, et al. *Psychology Today*, p. 342.)

Many authors also include a **glossary** at the end of their books. The glossary lists all technical or specialized terms, along with their definitions. If a definition is vague or unclear within the text, refer to the glossary to double-check the meaning of a word.

Exercise 6

Directions: Read each of the following selections. Then, on the blank lines that follow, write the words and definitions you think the authors want you to learn.

1. *Rule ethics* are exhaustive principles intended to guide people in their moral decision making in all situations. These principles are explicit, specific, and all-encompassing. People who hold to the letter of the law and proponents* of religious dogmas† are rule ethicists. *Situation ethics*, on the other hand, are based on the premise that all situations are unique and therefore no one set of rules is applicable in all cases. Consequently a situation ethicist faced with a moral decision will carefully review, analyze, and evaluate each specific situation to determine which ethics are applicable; a rule ethicist will apply a given principle, regardless of the specific circumstances. As an example consider a rule ethicist

---

* proponents: supporters

† dogmas: systems of belief

who believes killing to be wrong. For this person killing is wrong in all situations; thus, he or she could be expected to conclude that war is never justified. A situation ethicist, on the other hand, would study each particular war to decide whether or not it was justified. This person could deem a war to be just or unjust and might, within the same war, judge Hitler's killing of the Jews unjust while holding the Allies' killing of German soldiers to be just. (Coreenberg et al. *Sexuality*, p. 72.)

rule ethics : principles intended to guide people in their moral
_____

decision making
_____

situation ethics : based on the premise that no one set of
_____

rules applies in all cases
_____

2. We think of the sun as the bright ball of gas that appears to travel across our sky every day. We are seeing only one layer of the sun, part of its atmosphere; the properties of the solar interior below that layer and of the rest of the solar atmosphere above that layer are very different. The outermost parts of the solar atmosphere even extend through interplanetary space beyond the orbit of the earth.

The layer that we see is called the *photosphere*, which simply means the sphere from which the light comes (from the Greek *photos*, light). As is typical of many stars, about 94 per cent of the atoms and nuclei in the outer parts are hydrogen, about 5.9 per cent are helium, and a mixture of all the other elements make up the remaining one-tenth of one per cent. The overall composition of the interior is not very different. (Pasachoff, *Contemporary Astronomy*, p. 123.)

photosphere : spheres from which light comes
_____

_____

_____

_____

3. **Organizational demographics**—the age, sex, education, race, ethnic background, country of national origin, and experience of the work force—have begun to change. The more obvious aspects of

Organizational demographics refers to the age, sex, education, race, ethnic background, country of national origin, and experience of the work force.

that change are reflected in the increasing presence of women and minority-group members in management. Many aspects of organizational culture have arisen in a white, male, Protestant social culture and hence reflect images, expressions, and attitudes from that social culture. Clearly, those aspects of organizational culture will have to undergo massive change. (Van Fleet, *Contemporary Management*, p. 608.)

Organizational demographics : age, sex, education, race, ethnic

background, national origin, and experience of the workforce

_____

_____

4. To the casual observer the face of the earth may appear to be without change, unaffected by time. For that matter, less than 200 years ago most people believed that mountains, lakes, and deserts were permanent features of an earth that was thought to be no more than a few thousand years old. Today, however, we know that mountains eventually succumb to weathering and erosion and are washed into the sea, lakes fill with sediment and vegetation or are drained by streams, and deserts come and go as relatively minor climatic changes occur.

The earth is indeed a dynamic body. Volcanic and tectonic activities are elevating parts of the earth's surface, while opposing processes are continually removing materials from higher elevations and moving them to lower elevations. The latter processes include:

1. **Weathering**—disintegration and decomposition of rock at or near the surface of the earth.
2. **Erosion**—incorporation and transportation of material by a mobile agent, usually water, wind, or ice.
3. **Mass wasting**—transfer of rock material downslope under the influence of gravity. (Lutgens and Tarbuck, *Essentials of Geology*, p. 69.)

weathering : disintegration and decomposition of rock near surface

of earth; erosion: incorporation and transportation of material by water,

wind, or ice; mass wasting: transfer of rock downslope

_____

DIGGING DEEPER

Imagine that a rule ethicist and a situation ethicist were members of the same jury. They both have to decide whether a woman who killed her abusive husband is guilty of murder. What do you think each one would say?

How do you define yourself? Are you a situation ethicist or a rule ethicist? Or are you somewhere in between?

Learning New Words

Beginning with your first reading assignment, you should use a vocabulary notebook to list and define words essential to an understanding of each subject. Divide the notebook into sections of about twenty pages and label each section according to your courses—algebra, bookkeeping, composition, and so on. Then periodically—at least twice a week—review the words so that they become a part of your vocabulary. During your reviews, make use of the following strategies.

1. **Separate the words and their definitions.** Put the word and the page number on which it appears on the left side of the page. Then put the definition on the right, like this:

   hardware, p. 6 • computer and machinery attached to it, like plotters and printers

   software, p. 6 • computer programs

   To review, cover the definition of each word and see if you can recall it. Once you define the word, check your definition against the definition in your notebook and go on to the next item on your list. This kind of a review—in which you try to remember the definitions *without* looking at them first—will prove more effective than simply reading the list over and over.

2. **Find a visual image.** To remember the definition of *software* for example, picture a floppy disk. To remember what *intensity* means in the context of meteorology, evoke an image of the earth shaking.

3. **Make a map of words sharing a common root.** Periodically, go through your notebook looking for words derived from a common root. Then use mapping to highlight their common origin.

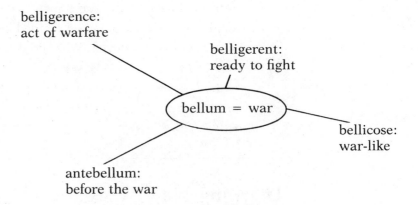

belligerence:
act of warfare

belligerent:
ready to fight

bellum = war

bellicose:
war-like

antebellum:
before the war

4. **Record antonyms.** To learn the word *endogamy*, meaning marriage restricted to members of the same group, learn as well the antonym *exogamy*, meaning marriage restricted to those outside a particular group.
5. **Create your own definitions.** If, for example, the author defines the word *hypothesis* as a "tentative explanation," see if you can translate that definition into your own words—say "initial guess" or "unproven theory." Then record the author's definition as well as your own. The more you use your own language to recreate word meaning, the easier it will be to remember new words.

When you think of learning new words, don't think of memorizing them. That's what parrots do, not people. Instead *create a web or chain of associations that will anchor new words firmly in your memory.* Keep in mind, too, that all the strategies outlined here can be used to learn any new words, not just those drawn from your textbooks.

Stories Behind the Words

Many words in the English language have an interesting story behind them. They are derived from ancient myths, historical events, or famous people. Learning the stories behind words is one of the easiest ways to remember their definitions.

Hiroshima, two months after the atomic bomb was dropped.

To get you started collecting words with a colorful past, here are five derived from Greek myths.

1. *Chaos.* According to an ancient myth, before earth, sea, and heaven were created, all things were in confusion. Earth, sea, and air were all mixed up together in a shapeless mass called *chaos.* Today when we talk about *chaos,* we are referring to a situation in which disorder rules.

   Sample sentence: On August 6, 1945 an atomic bomb exploded over the Japanese city of Hiroshima and engulfed the city in death and *chaos.*

   Definition: disorder, complete confusion

   Other forms: chaotic

2. *Tantalize.* Tantalus was a king who was cruelly punished by the gods. He was forced to stand in a pool of water that dried up whenever he tried to drink. Over his head was a luscious fruit tree that always rose higher than he could reach. Today when we are *tantalized* by something, we are attracted to what is just out of reach.

Sample sentence: The half-starved prisoners were driven mad by the *tantalizing* smell of fried potatoes.

Definition: to tease, torment by holding out of reach

Other forms: tantalizing, tantalized, tantalizes

3. *Nemesis.* Nemesis was a goddess who punished those who had misbehaved, especially those who were overly proud and challenged the gods. Today when we say that someone or something is our *nemesis,* we mean that we are faced with someone or something that will bring about our downfall.

Sample sentence: Oral tests are my *nemesis;* I always fail them.

Definition: source of failure, cause of destruction, an unbeatable rival

Other forms: nemeses

4. *Odyssey.* An ancient book, *The Odyssey,* tells of the voyages of Odysseus, a Greek king who was forced to wander far from home for ten years. During that time he had many adventures. Today the word *odyssey* describes someone's long and adventurous journey through strange territory. The trip, or *odyssey,* may be real or imagined.

Sample sentence: After his long *odyssey* abroad, he no longer felt he could go home.

Definition: an extended trip or adventure

Other forms: odysseys

5. *Titanic* and *Titan.* According to the Greek myth, the Titans were members of a gigantic family of gods who inhabited the earth before people did. Today, when we describe something as *titanic,* we mean that it is enormous. When we say that someone is a *titan,* we mean that he or she has a great deal of power or is outstanding in some field.

Sample sentence: She made a *titanic* effort to move the huge rock.

Definition: powerful, huge, great

Sample sentence: Mozart is a *titan* in the world of music.

Definition: a person of great achievement or note

Exercise 7

Directions: Using the five words you have just learned, fill in the blank lines. Be careful to use the correct form of each word.

1. The __tantalizing__ smell of fried chicken from my neighbor's kitchen made my mouth water.

2. After my long __odyssey__ abroad, I'm not the same.

3. Two small children at home on a rainy day can turn the house into complete __chaos__.

4. I know that course will be my __nemesis__; I have never been good in languages.

5. Einstein is a __titan__ in the world of science.

    More words with a past appear at the end of the following chapters.

Review Test: Chapter Two

Part A: Answer the following questions.

1.   Define the term *word analysis*.

Analyzing parts of a word to discover meaning

2.   What is the *context* of a word?

The sentence, paragraph, or passage in which it appears

3.   If the term *archaic* follows a word in a dictionary, what does that mean?

The word or meaning is rarely used today.

4.   What are the two kinds of words in a specialized vocabulary?

(a) Words that are totally unfamiliar

(b) Familiar words that take on new meanings

5.   What is the glossary in a textbook?

A list of key terms appearing at the end of a textbook

Part B: Fill in the blanks with one of the following words. Some sentences may require you to change the endings of words. For example, you may want the word *eloquently* rather than the word *eloquence*. Be sure to change the ending whenever necessary.

intervention	spectacular	inscription	clarity
circumspect	circumvent	interloper	video
circumference	circa	brevity	chaos
circumscribed	eloquence	credible	tantalize
script	circumnavigate	credence	nemesis
circumlocution	elocution	evident	odyssey

1. It was <u>evident</u> that she had been working hard on her writing. Her words had a kind of <u>clarity</u> they had lacked earlier in the semester when she had tended toward <u>circumlocution</u>. Now she managed to combine <u>brevity</u> of expression with completeness. As every writer knows, this is no minor accomplishment.

2. Mediocre in appearance the speaker still managed to compel the audience with his <u>eloquence</u>. Although the room had been in <u>chaos</u> when he first began to speak, the noise and confusion quickly subsided. The effect of his words was <u>spectacular</u>. Everyone in the audience seemed spellbound as he told of the long <u>odyssey</u> that had brought him so far from home and so close to death.

3. The private club would allow only members whose behavior was polite, quiet, and subdued. Quite naturally then the members were appalled by the possibility that a female mud wrestler might be allowed to join. They considered such a person to be an <u>interloper</u> whose outrageous behavior was anything but <u>circumspect</u>. Still powerful people had <u>intervened</u> on her behalf claiming that attempts to <u>circumvent</u> her entry would be met by a lawsuit.

4. The sight of the chocolate was enormously _tantalizing_.
But if he gave in, his claims to a diet would no longer be
credible and his friends would make fun of him.
Chocolate, in particular, was his _nemesis_. If he took
a bite, all was lost. He wouldn't stop eating for a week, and
his _circumference_ would gain yet another inch.

Relating the General to the Specific

Throughout this book, the terms "general" and "specific" are used to describe various reading strategies. This chapter will define those two terms and show how they relate to one another within the context of reading. After reading this chapter, you'll be able to do all of the following:

☐ See the difference between general and specific words, phrases, and sentences.
☐ Distinguish between various *levels of specificity*.
☐ Understand the function of *modifiers*.
☐ Recognize the connection between general and specific sentences.

New Vocabulary

The following words will be introduced in this chapter. Watch for them as you read and record their definitions for review. However, before you look at the definitions, see if you can derive their meaning from context.

discrimination	extant	irrational
obesity	literally	collaborate
genetically	dupe	superimpose

General and Specific Words

Think about the words *apples* and *fruits*. The word *fruits* is more general than the word *apples*. The question is why?

67

To find the answer, write the two words on a piece of paper. Now using the two words as headings, list all the items that can be included underneath each word. Your lists should look something like this:

Apples

McIntosh
Northern Spy
Golden Delicious
Granny Smith
Macoun
Gravenstein
Jonathan
Winesap
Opalescent

Fruits

apples	cherries
pears	blueberries
bananas	strawberries
grapes	blackberries
apricots	raspberries
plums	kiwis
oranges	kumquats
tangerines	peaches
grapefruits	pineapples

Apples is a more specific word because the items to which it refers are all varieties of the same fruit. They are all about the same size and shape, although they do vary in color and taste. *Fruits* is the more general word because the items to which the word refers are all different. They have very different sizes, shapes, colors, and tastes. The list on the right is clearly much longer than the one on the left.

With this illustration in mind, we can answer the question we raised before: **general words** refer to a greater number of things, and the things referred to are more dissimilar than similar. **Specific words** refer to a lesser number of things, and the things referred to are more similar than dissimilar.

Using what you have just learned about general and specific words, look at the two words *vegetables* and *lettuce*. Decide which word you would call more general and which one you would call more specific. If you have any trouble deciding, make two lists like the ones we made before. Your lists will resemble the following:

Vegetables

tomatoes	lettuce
carrots	cabbage
potatoes	spinach
eggplants	beans
squash	corn
broccoli	cauliflower

Lettuce

romaine
iceberg
Boston
endive

Notice that the list of items appearing under the heading "vegetables" is a great deal longer than the one following the heading "lettuce." The items under "vegetables" are very different from one another; they have different sizes, shapes, and tastes. The items under "lettuce" resemble one another in size, shape, and color. Clearly, *vegetables* is the more general word.

At this point, you are ready to test your understanding of general and specific words.

Exercise 1

Directions: After each general word, list at least three more specific words that could be included under that heading.

Example: communication
speech
signs
television

Explanation: Because all three topics are a specific type of communication, we can include all three under the more general heading.

1. feelings

   Sample responses: anger
   _____

   love
   _____

   gratitude
   _____

2. music

   Sample responses: opera
   _____

   jazz
   _____

   rock and roll
   _____

3. machinery

   Sample responses: cars
   _____

   trucks
   _____

   clocks
   _____

4. illness

Sample responses: schizophrenia

_____

measles

_____

mumps

_____

Exercise 2

Directions: Find one word or term *general enough* to include all the other words listed.

Example: *academic subjects*

_____

American history

English composition

sociology

algebra

Explanation: In this case, all four items can be included under the heading "academic subjects."
   Now it's your turn.

1.   books, novels

_____

The Scarlet Letter

Pet Sematary

Gone With the Wind

The Joy Luck Club

2.   kinds of wood

_____

maple

oak

dogwood

pine

3. things to write with _____

pens

pencils

typewriters

computers

4. comicstrip characters _____

Snoopy

Superman

Lucy

Batman

5. magazines _____

Time

Newsweek

Look

Vogue

6. people who wear masks _____

surgeons

burglars

trick or treaters

welders

7. <u>athletes</u>

Jimmy Connors

Michael Jordan

Jennifer Capriati

Jim Kelley

8. <u>soap operas</u>

"General Hospital"

"One Life to Live"

"Guiding Light"

"All My Children"

9. former presidents

Lincoln

Washington

Jefferson

Truman

10. kinds of music

rap

jazz

classical

country and western

Exercise 3

Directions: In the following word pairs, underline the more specific word.

Example: a. entertainment, <u>movies</u>
b. *Newsweek*, magazines

Explanation: The word *movies* is more specific than the word entertainment. It refers to a lesser number of things, and the things to which it refers are more alike than unlike. The word *Newsweek* is more specific than the word *magazines*. It refers to one particular publication rather than to a variety of different ones.
   Now you pick the more specific word in each pair.

1. architecture, <u>synagogues</u>

2. crimes, <u>robbery</u>

3. directors, <u>Spike Lee</u>

4. <u>Congress,</u> government

5. documents, <u>Constitution</u>

6. creature, <u>person</u>

7. earth, planets

9. phobia, claustrophobia

8. pollution, smog

10. symbol, cross

Levels of Specificity

In Exercise 2, we compared only two words at a time. However, we can expand our comparison to include three terms or more. Take, for example, the words *movie, Western,* and *Shane* (title of a famous Western). To illustrate the relationships among these three words, we can draw a ladder and put each word on a rung to show how general or specific one word is when compared to the other two. Each term will be located on a **different level of specificity.** The word on the top level, or rung, will be the most general, and the one on the lowest level will be the most specific.

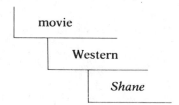

This diagram illustrates that *Shane* is clearly the most specific word of the three. It refers to one particular movie. The word *Western* is more general than the word *Shane* because it refers to many different movies. However, it is more specific than the word *movie.* The word *movie* refers to all kinds of movies, not just Westerns.

We can also include more than three words on our ladder. We can, for example, use a ladder with six rungs, as shown in the diagram on page 75, which illustrates the relationships among the words: animals, quadrupeds, dogs, pedigrees, collies, and *Lassie.*

Whenever we speak, think, or write, we use words that if diagrammed would fall on different levels of specificity. We use general words when we want to refer to a great number of things. We use specific words when we want to put limits around the number of things discussed. When we use general words, we include more things. When we use specific words, we exclude more.

Note that **words can be more or less specific only in relation to other words.** By itself, for example, the word *dogs* seems to be fairly general. However, when the word is compared with the word *animals,* it is more specific than general.

animals | The word *animals* refers to all kinds of living beings. Members of the group called *animals* are very different from one another; they are more dissimilar than similar.

quadrupeds | The term *quadrupeds* refers only to those animals having four legs; all other animals are excluded. Members of the group are more dissimilar than similar.

dogs | The word *dogs* refers to one particular group of animals. Members of the group called *dogs* are more similar to one another than are members of the group called four-legged animals.

pedigrees | The word *pedigrees* now includes only dogs whose parentage is clear; all mixed breeds have been excluded.

collies | The word *collies* refers to one particular pedigree. The members of this group look alike. At this level all other breeds are excluded.

Lassie | The word *Lassie* refers only to collies bearing the name Lassie. All other collies are excluded from this level.

Exercise 4

Directions: Arrange each of the three words according to specificity. The letter representing the most general word goes on the top level. The letter for the most specific goes on the bottom level.

Example: a. musician

b. artist

c. violinist

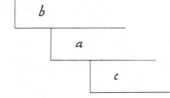

Explanation: The word *artist* can refer to many different kinds of people, for example, painters, sculptors, writers. It is the most general word and therefore goes on the top level. *Musician* is somewhat more specific than *artist.* It excludes all people not concerned with music. Therefore it goes on the middle rung. *Violinist* is the most specific word because it refers to only those people who play the violin.

Do the rest of the exercise in the same manner.

1. a. Children's Hospital

   b. building

   c. hospital

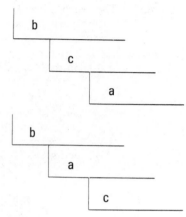

2. a. flu

   b. disease

   c. Hong Kong flu

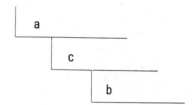

3. a. water

   b. Indian Ocean

   c. ocean

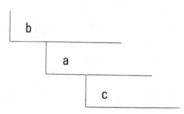

4. a. detergent

   b. product

   c. Tide

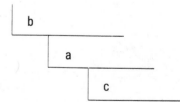

5. a. continent

   b. land mass

   c. South America

Exercise 5

Directions: In the following exercise, write an *s* after the two words that are on the same level of specificity.

Example: church _____

building _____

St. Peter's in Rome __*S*__

St. Mark's in Venice __*S*__

Explanation: *Building* is more general than *church,* but the names of the churches are equally specific.

1. object _____

   knife __S__

   weapon _____

   gun __S__

2. clothing _____

   dress __S__

   coat __S__

   wedding dress _____

3. product _____

   soap _____

   Ivory __S__

   Coast __S__

4. machine _____

   automobile __S__

   Ford _____

   motorcycle __S__

5. creature ____

buffalo __S__

animal ____

deer __S__

The Use of Modifiers

Single words or groups of words, called **phrases,** are frequently needed to help increase specificity. These words or phrases are called **modifiers.**

Take, for example, the word *war.* Alone, the word can refer to many different kinds of conflicts. But if we add the word *civil,* we are talking about a particular kind of war, one in which the people of the same country fight one another. If we further add the word *American,* to form the phrase *American Civil War,* we have made it clear that we are talking about one particular war in U.S. history.

As the preceding example illustrates, modifiers help increase specificity by eliminating all those things not under discussion. Suppose, for instance, that you were registering for spring semester and saw that a course called "Drawing" was offered. Because the word *drawing* can refer to drawing people or objects, you might not be sure if you wanted or needed the course. But if the word *drawing* were changed to the phrase "Advanced Mechanical Drawing," you would have a much clearer idea of what the course offered, and you would know whether or not you wanted to take it.

Phrases, like words, can be more or less specific, as you can see from the following example:

1. students in school
2. students in college
3. Mexican American students

Phrase 1 is more general than phrase 2. It refers to all students in school: The students could be five years old or fifty. The second phrase is more specific because it eliminates all those students who are not attending college. The third phrase eliminates any students who are not Mexican American.

Exercise 6

Directions: Underline the more specific phrase.

Example: a. health risks
b. <u>a high-fat diet</u>

Explanation: Phrase *b* is more specific than phrase *a*. Phrase *a* can refer to a variety of situations that could prove damaging or dangerous to one's health. Phrase *b*, however, restricts phrase *a*, limiting those risks to eating too much fat.
　　　Now it's your turn to choose the more specific phrase.

1. a. <u>cerebral cortex</u>
b. parts of the brain

2. a. the woman carrying traveler's checks
b. <u>the woman carrying American Express checks</u>

3. a. religious ceremonies
b. <u>Holy Communion</u>

4. a. veterans of the war
b. <u>veterans of the Vietnam War</u>

5. a. prison conditions
b. <u>overcrowding in prisons</u>

6. a. brainwashing techniques
b. <u>prolonged isolation</u>

7. a. <u>Friday the 13th</u>
b. old superstitions

8. a. <u>I.Q. tests</u>
b. educational tests

9. a. the card game
     b. <u>the poker game</u>

10. a. the male walking from the room
      b. <u>the boy stomping out of the room</u>

Exercise 7

Directions: Fill in the blanks on each line of this exercise.

Example: a. <u>*academic subjects*</u>   psychology   abnormal psychology

           b. problems   <u>*health problems*</u>   heart disease

Explanation: In example *a,* the blank required words more general than the other two. Since *academic subjects* includes the subject psychology *and* abnormal psychology, it is the correct answer. Example *b,* however, required a phrase more specific than *problems* and more general than *heart disease,* making *health problems* the appropriate answer.

    Make sure the word or phrase you choose is general or specific enough to fit the blank.

1. <u>emotion</u>   fear   fear of flying

2. leaders   <u>presidents</u>   George Washington

3. <u>document</u>   Constitution   Fourteenth Amendment

4. <u>battles</u>   World War II   Battle of the Bulge

5. animals   mammals   <u>dogs, cats, cows, etc.</u>

6. theories   <u>scientific theories</u>   Einstein's theory of relativity

Einstein's theory of relativity revolutionized the scientific world.

7. <u>snacks, junk food</u>   popcorn   caramel corn

8. <u>water</u>   oceans   Atlantic

9. environmental problems   <u>air pollution</u>   smog

10. addictions   <u>drug addiction</u>   cocaine

General and Specific Sentences

This chapter has dealt with individual words and phrases. But that was only preparation for work with complete sentences. Sentences, like individual words or phrases, can be more general or more specific. Take, for example, these two:

1. People are affected by the presence of others.

2. In the presence of a large group, many people are afraid of asking questions.

Sentence 1 announces that people are affected by groups. But it does not tell us *how* they are affected—positively or negatively. Nor does it tell us anything about the size of the groups. Sentence 2, however, answers these questions by providing more specific details: we are dealing with larger groups that tend to intimidate.

The next pair of sentences also illustrates the relationship between general and specific sentences:

1. The ancient Egyptians were experts at preserving the bodies they embalmed.
2. When unwrapped, sometimes after thousands of years, the feet of Egyptian mummies were still soft and elastic.

Sentence 1 makes a claim about the Egyptian skill of embalming. That claim, in turn, raises a question: How do we know that the Egyptians were so skillful? Sentence 2 provides an answer. It gives a specific example of just how skillful the ancient Egyptians were.

Use the following exercise to think about the difference between general and specific sentences.

Exercise 8

Directions: Circle the letter of the sentence that is more specific.

Example:
1. a. Anger can take many forms; people do not all get angry in the same way.
   ⓑ. Some people withdraw when angry; others scream and shout.

2. a. Air pollution can do serious, even fatal, harm to your health.
   ⓑ. High levels of radon gas in the home may cause lung cancer.

Explanation: The sentences following the letter *b* are both more specific. In the first item, sentence *b* tells us two forms anger can take. Sentence *b* in item 2 tells us exactly what kind of pollution can endanger health. Both sentences following the letter *a* are more general; they are open to several interpretations.

The Japanese have the highest life expectancy in the world.

Complete the remaining exercises.

1. ⓐ. The detergent called "Spic and Span" derived its name from the Dutch expression *Spiksplinterneuw* meaning brand new.
   b. The American detergent "Spic and Span" actually has a Dutch origin.

2. a. The Japanese have the highest life expectancy in the world.
   ⓑ. In Japan the average life expectancy is seventy-four for men and eighty for women.

3. a. The story of Cinderella has a long history; it has probably existed for hundreds of years.
   ⓑ. The earliest known version of the Cinderella story appears in a collection of Chinese folktales written in the ninth century A.D.

4. a. The sight of a uniform has a strange effect on many people.
   ⓑ. Many people are frightened by the sight of a uniform and behave like children in front of a stern parent.

5. (a). While Robert E. Lee graduated at the top of his class, Ulysses S. Grant barely graduated.
    b. Prior to the Civil War, Ulysses S. Grant was a failure at everything he tried while Robert E. Lee knew only success.

The Relationship Between General and Specific Sentences

Most of the readings in your textbooks combine different levels of specificity. Authors use **general sentences** to draw a conclusion based on a number of different, yet in some way related, events, ideas, people, or objects. But those general sentences usually suggest more than one interpretation and could, by themselves, cause confusion. Look, for example, at this sentence drawn from a psychology text:

> People usually do not trust other persons who try to influence them.

By itself this sentence raises some questions. Does it mean that we generally do not trust *anybody* who influences us in any way? And how does the author know this is true? What support does he offer for this claim?

As you might expect, our sample sentence does not stand alone. It is followed by more **specific sentences** designed to answer questions readers might raise.

> People usually do not trust other persons who try to influence them. Researchers have demonstrated this experimentally by comparing the effect of messages delivered in various ways. A message was delivered by a person who was obviously trying to persuade the subject. The same message was "accidentally" overheard from a "private" conversation. When the results of these messages were compared, the "accidentally" overheard message was markedly more effective in producing attitude change. (McNeil, *The Psychology of Being Human*, p. 72.)

Do you see how the specific sentences clarify and support the more general one? We don't mistrust everybody who influences us. We mistrust those people who openly try to persuade us. Someone who influences us without meaning to is not subject to the same kind of suspicion.

But the specific sentences do more than clarify the opening statement. They also make it convincing by citing a study that supports the author's claim.

The writing in your textbooks will constantly shift from one level of specificity to another. Your job as a reader is to recognize those shifts and make connections between them by asking yourself questions like the following:

1. Where are the author's more general statements?
2. What questions do they raise?
3. Where are the more specific sentences that answer those questions?

DIGGING DEEPER

Do you agree with the author's claim that people react with suspicion if someone directly tries to influence them? How does this statement fit with your own experience?

Exercise 9

Directions: We have provided three specific sentences. After reading them, decide which general sentence they could support. Circle the number of the general sentence.

Example:
a. Teeth in the front of the mouth are called *incisors;* they cut large pieces of food into smaller ones.
b. The molars crush and grind food.
c. We use our canine teeth when we eat the meat off bones.

General sentences:
1. Teeth are subject to decay.
2. With the correct dental care, human beings can keep their teeth until the day they die.
③. The teeth are important because they prepare food for digestion.

Explanation: The correct answer is 3. Sentence 1 is not a possible answer because none of the sentences mentions decay. Sentence 2 is not a possible answer because none of the sentences mentions dental care.

Now it's your turn to select the appropriate general sentence.

1. a. The tradition of using candles at funerals began with the Romans who used them to frighten away evil spirits.
    b. Tombstones originated as a way of keeping the dead in the underworld.
    c. The original purpose of coffins was to keep the dead safely underground.

General sentences: 1. Anthropologists have found evidence that funeral traditions existed during the Neanderthal age.*
    2. Different cultures have different ways of mourning their dead.
    ③. Many of the modern customs associated with mourning originated from a fear of the dead and what they could do to the living.

2. a. The citizens of Sparta, a city-state of ancient Greece, were not allowed to become farmers; they were made to train as warriors and nothing else.
    b. Family life in Sparta was severely limited because both boys and girls spent long hours in physical training.
    c. From the ages of seven to thirty, boys received instruction in the art of waging war.

General sentences: 1. The Spartans were obedient to the laws of their land.
    ②. The Spartan life was hard and devoted to war.
    3. Spartan men and women were known for their heroism in war.

3. a. During World War II, German invaders devastated some of Russia's richest agricultural regions.
    b. According to official reports, more than seven million Russians were killed while defending their country against German attacks.
    c. Many Russians lost their lives in concentration camps.

General sentences: ①. The Russians suffered heavy losses in World War II.
    2. The Russians suffered more losses than any of the other great powers.
    3. Russia was not prepared for the Germans' attack.

4. a. During World War II the War Department finally approved the training of African-American pilots.

---

* Neanderthal age: 100,000–40,000 B.C.

In January of 1944, Benjamin O. Davis Jr.'s 99th Pursuit Squadron shot down twelve German fighter planes.

    b. In 1941 Benjamin O. Davis Jr. became the first African-American to lead a squadron of pilots.

    c. President Roosevelt's Executive Order 8802 required employers in defense industries to make jobs available "without discrimination* because of race, creed or color."

General sentences ①. For many African-Americans, World War II offered a chance to break down racial barriers.

    2. During World War II, racial violence broke out on several military bases.

    3. World War II brought out the best in Americans.

5. a. Heredity plays an important role in the obesity† of children.

    b. Children tend to consume a high fat diet.

    c. Children are genetically‡ programmed to produce more weight than muscle.

---

* discrimination: to show prejudice in favor of or against a particular group.

† obesity: extreme heaviness.

‡ genetically: by nature, naturally.

General sentences   1. American children are in poor condition.

                       ②. Several factors can contribute to obesity in children.

                       3. American children are terribly out of shape.

Exercise 10

Directions: We have provided one general sentence. Read it and decide which of the specific sentences that follow help clarify and support that statement. Circle the letter of each sentence you choose.

Example: The 1981 eruption of Mount St. Helens was one of the largest volcanic eruptions the world has ever seen.

    ⓐ. The Mount St. Helens eruption was more powerful than any nuclear device ever exploded.

    b. Mount St. Helens has erupted at least twenty times over the past four thousand years.

    c. Mount St. Helens is one of the most active volcanoes in the world.

    ⓓ. Only two eruptions have ever surpassed that of Mount St. Helens, the eruption of Krakatoa in Indonesia and of Katmai in Alaska.

    ⓔ. The power of the Mount St. Helens eruption was more than the total output of all the electric power stations in the United States.

    f. Experts predict that the volcano may erupt again before the end of the century.

Explanation: Sentences *a, d,* and *e* are correct choices because they clarify and support the claim that the eruption of Mount St. Helens "was one of the largest volcanic eruptions the world has ever seen."

    Finish the remaining exercises by selecting the appropriate specific sentences.

1. In 1981, the appointment of the first woman justice of the Supreme Court of the United States was an event of extraordinary importance.

    ⓐ. For 191 years, women had been excluded from the Supreme Court.

    ⓑ. Judge Sandra Day O'Connor from Arizona was appointed to the Supreme Court.

c. *First Monday in October* was a hit play about the conflict between two Supreme Court justices, one a male liberal, the other a female conservative.

d. John Jay was the first chief justice of the Supreme Court.

(e). Prior to Judge O'Connor's appointment to the bench, women's issues like sex discrimination and affirmative action* were decided by an all-male court.

f. Judge O'Connor is the mother of three sons.

2. The fear of rabies is well-founded.

(a). In its final stages, rabies produces hallucinations.

(b). Few people recover from the disease once the symptoms have appeared.

c. Rabies has an ancient history, and there are references to it as early as 700 B.C.

(d). Once the disease takes hold, the victim can neither stand nor lie down comfortably.

e. Recently, scientists have begun to improve upon the painful treatment for rabies, and the new vaccine requires only six doses rather than the standard twenty-one.

f. In the early stages of rabies, a dog is likely to appear tired and nervous. It will try to hide, even from its master.

3. Many people believe that mystery stories are a product of modern times, but the mystery story actually has a long history.

(a). Historians of the detective story claim to have found elements of mystery fiction in the Bible.

b. Dorothy Sayers was for some years an enormously popular mystery writer.

(c). Poe's "The Murders in the Rue Morgue," published in 1841, presented the classic mystery problem of a dead body found in a room that was completely sealed.

d. Mystery historians are continually haggling over what books may or may not be classified as mystery stories.

(e). In the nineteenth century, Charles Dickens created a highly amusing character, Inspector Bucket, who, in a general way, resembles many modern-day detectives.

f. Many mystery writers do not use their real names.

---

* affirmative action: policies employers must follow in order to encourage the hiring of women and minorities and to discourage discrimination.

4. Mohammed, spiritual leader of the Moslems,* had an enormous influence on world history.

  a. Mohammed was born somewhere around the year A.D. 570.
  ⓑ. Mohammed founded a religion, Islam, which was to become Christianity's greatest rival.
  c. Until his fortieth year, Mohammed lived the ordinary life of a well-to-do merchant.
  ⓓ. Mohammed's teachings were the source of the Koran, the sacred text of the Moslems, which is still accepted by Moslems as the final authority on all spiritual matters.
  ⓔ. Mohammed founded an empire that included lands in Syria, northern Africa, and Spain.
  f. Mohammed was born in Mecca.

5. In the twenties, female blues singers addressed a wide variety of themes.

  ⓐ. The song "Poor Man's Blues" tells the story of men and women forced into crime by poverty.
  b. The appearance of radio dramatically diminished the sale of records.
  ⓒ. In "Dead Letter Blues" Ida Cox sang about losing the man she loved.
  ⓓ. But in "Wild Women Don't Have the Blues," she depicted the "new" woman who refused to let men run her life.
  e. Many blues singers who had been popular in the twenties faded during the Depression when few could afford records.
  f. Victoria Spivey was an exception; when the Depression hit, she started a movie career.

Exercise 11

Directions: Create a general statement you think could sum up all three specific statements.

Example: *Americans have had a great influence on German society.*

  a. Everywhere you go in Germany, you hear American music, particularly rock and roll.

---

* Moslems: believers in Islam, a religion based on the teachings of Mohammed. Moslems believe in one God (Allah). They also believe in paradise and hell.

b. Like many Americans, the Germans wear Calvin Klein blue jeans and Reebok running shoes.
c. In most of the big cities, you'll find not just McDonald's, but Burger King and Wimpy's as well.

Now it's your turn to create the appropriate sentences.

1. Sample sentence: Pregnant women who smoke can do long-term damage to their children's health.

   a. As infants, the children of mothers who smoke tend to weigh less than the average baby.
   b. They have more respiratory problems.
   c. Even as grown-ups, the children of mothers who smoke have more colds and allergies than is normal.

2. Sample sentence: Pit bulls can be dangerous animals.

   a. Pit bull terriers have been raised to be aggressive.
   b. They are known to attack without warning or provocation.
   c. The majority of deaths due to dog bites have been caused by pit bulls.

3. Sample sentence: Abusive parents were often abused themselves as children.

   a. As children, abusive parents were often the target of mental and verbal abuse.
   b. Abusive parents are particularly aggressive with the child who bears the strongest resemblance to themselves.
   c. Men and women who abuse their children are often the product of violent homes where physical and mental cruelty was accepted as normal.

4. Sample sentence: Being a professional athlete is difficult and demanding.

a. Men and women who wish to become successful professional athletes must be ready to spend long hours in rigorous training.
b. Professional athletes have to watch their diets constantly; they cannot afford to be either too fat or too thin.
c. Many professional athletes find that they have little time for a personal life because their profession demands too much time and energy.

Exercise 12

Directions: One general sentence is provided. On the blank line that follows the general sentence, write a more specific version of the same sentence.

Example: After the war ended, Vietnam veterans found it hard to come home.

Unlike veterans of previous wars, they were not welcomed with

open arms; they were treated with suspicion and contempt.

Explanation: The second sentence is more specific than the first. It tells us why Vietnam veterans "found it hard to come home."

Now it's your turn to compose the appropriate specific sentences.

1. Dieting can be dangerous.

    Sample sentence: People who lose weight too fast can harm

    their health.

2. Peer pressure is a powerful force in adolescent development.

    Sample sentence: Teen-agers desperately want to fit in and be part

    of a group.

3. AIDS patients frequently face discrimination in their place of work.

Sample sentence: Some employees may refuse to work with them.

4. The blind learn to compensate for their lack of sight.

   Sample sentence: Many blind people have an acute sense

   of hearing.

5. Some people use their automobiles to take out their anger at the world.

   Sample sentence: There are drivers who will start honking their

   horns madly if they have to wait at a light.

DIGGING DEEPER

Do you think AIDS patients have been discriminated against? What would your reaction be if an AIDS patient worked or studied with you?

WRITING SUGGESTION

Write a paragraph in which you give specific examples of how peer pressure can affect teen-age behavior.

Exercise 13

Directions: We have provided one general sentence. Your job is to write two specific sentences that clarify and support the general sentence.

Example: The freshman year in college is almost always a frustrating one.

Specific sentences: a. *Many freshmen have to get used to living with a roommate;*

they may even have to get used to living with a roommate they

don't like.

b. *For many freshmen, the workload seems to be impossibly*

heavy.

Explanation: The general sentence can be interpreted in many ways, but the specific sentences that follow explain exactly what the author means by maintaining that freshman year is frustrating. The specific sentences also help convince us that the first year is frustrating.

Now try your hand at writing two specific sentences for each exercise item.

1. Although they are said to be humanity's best friend, dogs are not always treated that way.

Specific sentences: a. Sample sentence: Sometimes owners leave them outside in

freezing cold temperatures.

b. Sample sentence: Like children, dogs can be the object of

physical abuse.

2. Baby sitters should be prepared for emergencies.

Specific sentences: a. Sample sentences: They should know how to help a child who is

having difficulty breathing.

b. They should know which doctor to call in an emergency.

_____

3. Some teachers don't know how to give lectures.

Specific sentences: a. Sample sentences: They don't make enough eye contact with

their students.

b. They speak too quickly.

_____

4. For some people, taking a vacation can be more stressful than staying at home.

Specific sentences: a. Sample sentences: They spend hours packing and unpacking.

b. They worry about getting sick in a strange city or town.

_____

_____

Working with Words

Here are seven more prefixes and roots you should know. Use them to figure out the meaning of the italicized words, then fill in the blanks in the practice sentences.

1. ad   (Latin prefix)   to, toward
2. ab   (Latin prefix)   away from
3. dis   (Latin prefix)   apart from, not
4. extra   (Latin prefix)   outside, beyond
5. sect   (Latin root)   cut, divide
6. hyper   (Greek prefix)   over
7. anti   (Greek prefix)   against

Practice

1. They could not find an *antidote* for the snake's poison and were afraid the patient would die.

    a remedy against poison

2. The boy refused to *dissect* the frog.

    cut up

3. When strange lines began to appear in the fields overnight, some people called them the work of *extraterrestrial* beings.

    coming from outside of earth

4. She had tended to be *disdainful* of anyone who used coupons to shop, but then she too was forced to pinch pennies, and her contempt for coupons vanished.

    contemptuous, scornful, critical

5. Now that he was running for office he wanted to *disavow* his earlier membership in the Communist Party, but his enemies were not so willing to forget.

    disown, forget, ignore

6. Many people justify the *vivisection* of animals by claiming that human welfare is simply more important than the lives of animals.

    cutting up or operating on living animals for the purpose of research

7. He was such a *hyperactive* child that his mother considered giving him tranquilizers.

    excessively active

8. Because of criminal charges against him in his own country, the doctor was *extradited*.

to surrender or give up to another authority

9. She *abhorred* the idea of going into debt, but the economy was so bad, she could not avoid it.

hate, despise

10. His *discontent* was obvious to anyone who could see his face.

unhappiness

Stories Behind the Words

Here are five more words with stories in their past. Learn those stories, and you will remember the words.

1. *Adonis.* Adonis was a Greek youth famous for his extraordinary physical beauty. He was so beautiful that even Aphrodite, the goddess of love and beauty, fell madly in love with him. Today we use the word *Adonis* to refer to a very good-looking man.

   Sample sentence: The Secretary of State was no *Adonis,* but the power he wielded made him attractive to women.

   Definition: a man of great personal beauty

2. *Quisling.* Vidkun Quisling was a Norwegian statesman who openly collaborated* with the Nazis during World War II. As a result the word *quisling* has come to mean traitor.

   Sample sentence: The quisling who betrayed our country has gone into hiding.

   Definition: traitor, collaborator

---

* collaborate: to cooperate with an enemy (in this case).

3. *Pyrrhic victory.* In the third century B.C., the Greek general Pyrrhus won a victory against King Epirus. But the battle was won at such a great cost that a *Pyrrhic victory* now refers to a victory made meaningless by terrible losses.

    Sample sentence: For the general it was a *Pyrrhic victory.* He had won the battle but lost most of his soldiers.

    Definition: a victory won at a terrible cost

4. *Lethargy.* In Greek mythology, the waters from the river *Lethe* produced deep sleep and forgetfulness. Inspired by this myth, the Greeks gave the name *lethargia* to feelings of extreme sleepiness. Today when we a talk about *lethargy,* we refer to fatigue, so extreme that the person can barely stay awake.

    Sample sentence: Feelings of *lethargy* often accompany clinical depression.

    Definition: drowsiness, lack of energy

    Other forms: lethargically, lethargic

5. *Stigma.* Greek slaves who tried to escape were usually caught and returned to their owners. As a result of their escape attempts, the slaves were considered a high risk. It was correctly assumed they would try to escape again and to ensure against this, slave owners developed a cruel practice. They would brand the potential runaways with a mark on the forehead. That mark was called a *stigma.* From that inhumane practice, we inherited the word *stigma* which refers to any sign of shame or disgrace.

    Sample sentence: The *stigma* of being an ex-convict followed her wherever she went, making it impossible for her to get a job.

    Definition: a sign of shame or disgrace

    Other forms: stigmas

The following pages will test your mastery of Chapter Three.

Review Test: Chapter Three

Part A: Answer the following questions.

1. The word *television* is more specific than the word *media*. How would you describe the difference between the two words?

   Media refs to many different forms of communication,

   whereas television designates one particular form or

   method and excludes all others.

2. Here are four words: people, Geronimo, Native Americans, Seminole. Arrange them according to specificity. Place the most general word on the top level and the most specific word on the bottom level.

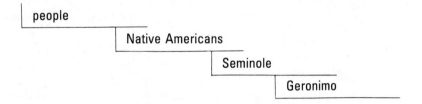

3. Describe the function of modifiers.

   Modifiers increase specificity by eliminating those

   things *not* under discussion.

4. Describe the relationship between general and specific sentences.

   General sentences draw conclusions or make statements about

   a number of different but in some way related events, objects,

   things, or people. Specific sentences help to answer questions

   raised by general sentences. They limit possible interpretations.

   In each group of sentences, there is one sentence that is more general than all the others. The rest of the sentences explain or support the idea contained in the more general sentence. Circle the letter of the general sentence.

5. a. In A.D. 1486, Pope Gelasius outlawed the traditional February festival devoted to the pagan god Luperus; in its place, he decreed a celebration of the martyred St. Valentine.
   b. The earliest extant* valentine was written in 1415.
   (c). St. Valentine's Day has been celebrated for centuries.
   d. By the sixteenth century, it had become a tradition for lovers to exchange gifts on St. Valentine's Day.
   e. It was also in the sixteenth century that the image of Cupid became associated with St. Valentine's Day.
   f. In 1797, a British publisher put together *The Young Man's Valentine Writer*, a collection of verses for young men who were incapable of writing their own valentines.

6. a. Users of amphetamines mistakenly believe that all their problems have been solved.
   b. People who use large doses of amphetamines have trouble sleeping.
   c. Those who use amphetamines often find that they are unable to stop talking.
   d. Under the influence of amphetamines, people usually feel they are working more efficiently; unfortunately, this impression is seldom accurate.
   (e). Amphetamines, also known as *speed*, are dangerous drugs, but not enough people are aware of their effects.
   f. Loss of appetite is another common side effect.

7. a. In the African country of Dahomey, music historians were carefully trained to preserve important records.
   (b). African music literally† sings the history of the African people.
   c. Men followed soldiers to war and recorded great actions in song.
   d. In the not so distant past, many African countries trained men and women to be living books who could record important events in song.
   e. If the songs contained important information, the musicians had to learn them in secret.

---

* extant: known to be in existence, not destroyed.

† literally: really, actually, in reality.

f. In Sudan, singers recited the history of the nation.

8.   a. An intelligent and gifted man, Arthur Conan Doyle, the creator of Sherlock Holmes, was duped* into believing that the spirit world really existed.
   (b). Sometimes even the most sophisticated and knowledgeable people can behave in foolish and irrational† ways.
   c. In late nineteenth-century England, photographs of fairies had become something of a fad.
   d. Doyle was convinced he had found two such photographs; he was also convinced they were authentic.
   e. The "fairies" were actually cardboard cutouts that had been superimposed‡ on the photographs.
   f. Doyle was so taken with the photographs that he published an article about them, which earned him the ridicule of the scientific community.

9.   a. John Merrick could not go into the street without being mobbed by curious strangers who stared at and ridiculed him.
   b. Before he came under a doctor's care, John Merrick was exhibited in the circus, like an animal.
   c. The victim of a terrible disease, Merrick could not sleep like other people; he had to sit up with his heavy head resting on his knees.
   d. The head of the Elephant Man was enormous and misshapen.
   (e). John Merrick, also known as the Elephant Man, had a short and painful life.
   f. Although the last years of his life were spent in pleasant surroundings, Merrick never forgot the brutal beatings and terrible humiliation of his life in the circus.

10.   a. It took a while for Frank Baum, author of *The Wonderful Wizard of Oz,* to find just the right title for his masterpiece.
   b. While the book was in production, Baum changed the title to *From Kansas to Fairyland.*
   (c). Sometimes choosing the title of a book is the hardest part.
   d. When Baum first submitted his manuscript in 1899, it was called *The Emerald City.*

---

* duped: fooled.

† irrational: not based on reason.

‡ superimpose: put on top of something else.

e. But ultimately the book was published in 1900 as *The Wonderful Wizard of Oz.*

f. Just before the book appeared in print, Baum changed the title again, this time to *The City of the Great Oz.*

Part B:
Vocabulary
Review

Here is a list of words drawn from the chapter. Some actually appear in the chapter. Some have been derived from the prefixes and suffixes introduced on page 95. Your job is to match words and blanks.

In some cases, you may have to change the endings of words to make them fit the context. If you need to, consult your dictionary to decide which ending to use. *Note:* You may use some words more than once and others not at all.

hypersensitive	abstain	dissect	quisling
adhere	literally	abhorrent	stigma
antithetical	hyperactive	collaborate	advocate
antidote	dispense	anti-vivisectionists	irrational
lethargic	extraneous	Pyrrhic victory	disdain

1. Tranquilizers are not the ___antidote___ for ___hyperactive___ children. They do more than calm a child down. Very likely they will make him or her ___lethargic___.

A better idea is to alter the child's diet so that he or she ___abstains___ from junk food. In some cases reducing the sugar content in a child's diet can ___literally___ produce a transformation. The child who could not sit still becomes capable of self-control and concentration.

2. Eldridge Danforth was a writer who ___adhered___ to the principle "more is always better." He liked to write pages and pages and could not seem to eliminate one ___extraneous___ detail. When one of his contemporaries suggested he write a little less, he insisted that his art required fullness of expression. From his point of view, brevity was ___antithetical___ to great art. Although editing could have greatly improved his work, he was ___hypersensitive___ to criticism and would immediately ___dispense___ with any editor who suggested he change

a word. Perhaps that is the reason his books have never been published.

3. During World War II, French women who had affairs with German soldiers were considered _quislings_____. To punish the _collaborators_____, opponents of the Germans would kidnap the women and shave their heads. A woman's shaven head was a _stigma_____ of her dishonor, and she was shunned by the rest of the community. Even after the war was over, women who had befriended the Germans were _disdained_____ by their friends and family. The crime of aiding and abetting the Germans was considered too _abhorrent_____ to be forgiven even in peacetime.

4. _Antivivisectionists_____ are opposed to the _dissection_____ of living animals in the name of scientific research. For years they have been _advocates_____ of animal rights, who _abhor_____ the notion that the suffering of animals is acceptable if it benefits human beings. Winning a battle against human disease is a _Pyrrhic victory_____ for them if it costs the lives of thousands of animals. True to their cause, many of these people also _abstain_____ from eating meat and do not wear leather shoes. Although the movement used to be stronger in England than in the United States, it appears to be gaining ground here as well.

Discovering Topics and Main Ideas

This chapter offers a step-by-step strategy for understanding paragraphs. Read it and learn how to do all of the following:

☐ Identify the *topic*
☐ Discover the *main idea*
☐ Recognize or *infer* main idea statements
☐ Understand the purpose of *introductory sentences*
☐ See the value of *transitions*
☐ Use questions to guide your reading

New Vocabulary

The following words appear in this chapter. Watch for them as you read. But before looking at the definitions on the bottom of the page, see if you can derive word meaning from context. Don't forget to record both words and definitions in your vocabulary notebook or file.

instrumental	skewer	contemporary
consolidate	metamorphosis	comprehensive
comprehensible	reanimate	degenerate
momentum	archaeology	wax
prevalent	cloistered	heresy
simile	austere	nationalists
metaphor		

Identifying the Topic

Identifying the **topic** is the first step you need to take toward discovering the message of a paragraph. *The topic is the subject or* *focus of the paragraph. It is the person, place, event, idea, object, or happening under discussion.*

You can usually identify the topic by asking two questions:

1) What word or phrase does the author mention or refer to the most?*
2) Is that word or phrase, by itself, specific enough to express the topic of the paragraph or does it need to be modified?

The following paragraph will help illustrate:

> The origin of the Shakers can be traced to a small Quaker group that originated in Great Britain sometime around 1750. Members of the sect believed that Christ would come to earth again, only this time in the form of a woman rather than a man. Thus when Ann Lee of Manchester, England, claimed to have had sacred visions, members of the group were willing to follow her to Watervliet, New York, where she established a Shaker community. Membership grew to around six thousand by the time of the Civil War, and then rapidly declined. The name "Shakers" is derived from the trembling and shaking form of worship members engaged in during religious ceremonies. First they were called the "Shaking Quakers" and then simply Shakers.

What word or phase does the author mention or refer to the most? "Shakers" is the answer. Just look what happens when we circle all the references to this religious group:

> The origin of the (Shakers) can be traced to a small Quaker group that originated in Great Britain sometime around 1750. (Members) of the sect believed that Christ would come to earth again, only this time in the form of a woman rather than a man. Thus when Ann Lee of Manchester, England, claimed to have had sacred visions, (members of the group) were willing to follow her to Watervliet, New York, where she established a (Shaker) community. Membership grew to around six thousand by the time of the Civil War, and then rapidly declined. The name ("Shakers") is derived from the trembling and shaking form of worship (members) engaged in during religious ceremonies. First (they) were called the "Shaking Quakers" and then simply Shakers.

Is that word or phrase, by itself, specific enough to express the topic of the paragraph, or does it need to be modified? Before you answer, look carefully at each sentence in the paragraph. Those sentences do not explore the many sub-topics that could fall under the head-

---

* Excluding, of course, articles like *a, an,* or *the* and prepositions like *on* or *of.*

ing *Shakers*—organization, customs, membership, etc. Instead, they focus on the *origins of the Shakers*, making this phrase the appropriate topic of the paragraph. Lacking any modifiers, the word *Shakers* would be too general. The paragraph just does not cover all the subjects that come under that heading.

Identifying the topic, then, is a two-step process. **Step 1:** Look for the word or phrase most often mentioned or referred to in the paragraph. **Step 2:** Decide if that word or phrase reflects the specific focus of the paragraph. If it does not, add the necessary modifiers.

To illustrate, here's another example:

> In the last two decades, many American women have chosen to keep their maiden name. In the United States, this seems to be a woman's natural right or prerogative. But in Japan things are not so simple. Women are often penalized for keeping their maiden name. While there is no specific law explicitly stating that women cannot keep their family name, Japanese civil law penalizes them for doing so. A woman who does not take her husband's name is not entitled to inherit his property. Their children are considered illegitimate. For women who, nevertheless, persist in using their maiden name, there can be additional penalties. Grants may be denied, raises withheld, and promotions delayed, sometimes indefinitely.

In this paragraph the phrase most frequently mentioned or referred to is *maiden name*. However, by itself, that phrase remains too general. After all, the paragraph does not discuss women in different countries who keep or change their maiden name. It focuses on the phrase, *Japanese women who keep their maiden name*. This phrase expresses the specific topic of the paragraph.

Most of the time you will be able to find the appropriate modifier somewhere in the paragraph. But occasionally there will be times when you have to **infer** or create your own. Here's an example:

> A bicycle consists of two wheels and a simple steel frame equipped with handles, pedals, cranks, and a saddle. The rider sits on the saddle, grasping the handlebars. The pressure of the rider's foot on the pedal turns the cranks. This action drives a chain over the front and rear sprockets, causing the rear wheel to revolve and setting the bicycle in motion.

The word *bicycle* appears repeatedly in the paragraph. Still that word, by itself, is too general. The paragraph does not focus on the many sub-topics that could fall under that heading like the bicycle's history or popularity. Three out of the four sentences in the paragraph **imply** or suggest the act of *riding a bike*. But that specific phrase does not appear in the paragraph. We have to **infer** it. By using the clues in the sentences, we can draw the appropriate conclusion: *riding a bike* is the topic of the paragraph.

If you cannot find the specific modifier to express the focus of a paragraph, don't be afraid to infer one. **Making inferences is an essential part of reading,** and it is not unusual for authors to give readers just enough information to draw the necessary conclusion.

The following exercises will give you practice identifying topics.

Exercise 1

Directions: Read each paragraph. Then select the topic that you think best identifies the author's subject.

Example: In some societies, primarily agricultural ones, there is a custom known as the *couvade.* This is a ceremony in which the husband acts as if he is suffering from labor pains while his wife actually gives birth. Although no one seems able to fully explain the significance of the couvade, there are some theories about its meaning. According to one theory the couvade ritual is a method of warding off evil spirits. In effect the husband directs attention away from his wife and toward himself. Another theory speculates that the ceremony is a way of publicly proclaiming fatherhood so that paternity will not be in doubt.

   a. ceremony and ritual
   (b). theories about couvade
   c. evil spirits

Explanation: Topic *a* is too general. This paragraph does not cover all of the many events that could fall under the heading *ceremony and ritual.* It does, however, focus on *theories about couvade,* what it is and what it means. Therefore *b* is the correct answer. Topic *c* does not qualify as an appropriate answer because *evil spirits* are mentioned only once in the paragraph.

1. In 1951 Henrietta Lacks died of cancer. Her cells, however, are still alive today and studied in cancer-research laboratories all over the world. Rarely do cells continue to grow once they are separated from a living body. But the cancer cells which killed Henrietta Lacks only eight months after the disease was detected were so potent, they survive today. HeLa cells—the name is derived from the first two letters of Henrietta's first and last names—

were instrumental* in the development of a vaccine against polio. Ultimately researchers hope that the HeLa cells will lead them to a cure for cancer.

a. Henrietta Lacks
b. cancer cures
©. HeLa cells

2. On April fourth of 1989, Joyce Palsa told a House Panel in Washington how her heart had been damaged as a result of cosmetic surgery on her abdomen. Mrs. Palsa, however, called herself "lucky" to be alive. According to her testimony, a woman who had had similar surgery had not survived the same complications. During that same hearing, Joyce Brown testified that a cosmetic procedure called *liposuction*, designed to remove excess fat, had left her unable to walk properly. A group of medical officials also pointed out that not all doctors who practice cosmetic surgery have the same qualifications. They testified that any medical school graduate with a state license can perform cosmetic surgery, and they agreed that there was a need to toughen the regulations governing cosmetic surgery.

a. cosmetic surgery
ⓑ. problems with cosmetic surgery
c. liposuction

3. You have probably heard about firms whose policy is to "promote from within." This simply means that, whenever a position needs to be filled, the firm makes a genuine effort to promote someone from a lower level in the firm to that position. This approach has two advantages. First, the person promoted from within is already familiar with how the organization operates, its strategy, its people, and most other facets of the organization. Second, promotion from within may increase job motivation for all employees. That is, if employees recognize that good work can lead to a promotion, they are more likely to work harder and better and to stay with the company rather than seek advancement elsewhere. (Pride, Hughes, and Kapoor, *Business*, p. 150.)

a. Promotions
b. job motivation
©. "promote from within" policy

---

* instrumental: crucial, important.

4. When Americans think of the Wild West, they don't usually imagine it inhabited by black cowboys. Yet this image of the West—without the presence of African-Americans—is completely inaccurate, fostered by Hollywood rather than reality. In truth, thousands of African-Americans helped settle the West, even though few commercial films have acknowledged their existence. In the forties, for example, Hollywood released a movie called *Tomahawk*. The white actor Jack Oakie played a character named James Beckworth. Beckworth was actually a black cowboy who became famous during the California gold rush. Similarly, Oklahoma, the location for many Westerns, was the site of several African-American communities, none of which has ever appeared on film. Fortunately, Hollywood has begun to acknowledge its historical error, and more recent films do show African-Americans riding the range.

    a. the Wild West
    (b). African-American cowboys
    c. *Tomahawk*

5. Because it was once the practice of ruling European monarchs to consolidate* their empires through marriage alliances, hemophilia came to be transmitted throughout the royal families. **Hemophilia** is a sex-linked condition in which the blood does not clot properly. Any small injury can result in severe bleeding and, if the bleeding cannot be stopped, in death. Hence, it has been called the "bleeder's disease." Hemophilia has been traced back as far as Queen Victoria, who was born in 1819. One of her sons, Leopold, Duke of Albany, died of the disease at the age of thirty-one. Apparently, at least two of Victoria's daughters were carriers, since several of their descendants were hemophilic. Hemophilia played an important historical role in Russia during the reign of Nikolas II, the last Czar. The Czarevich, Alexis, was hemophilic, and his mother, the Czarina, was convinced that the only one who could save her son's life was the monk Rasputin—known as the "mad monk." (Wallace, *Biology*, p. 161.)

    a. Rasputin
    (b). hemophilia
    c. diseases

---

* consolidate: strengthen, combine.

Dian Fossey endured a year of sickness and solitude in order to study the great apes of Africa.

D I G G I N G   D E E P E R

Paragraph 3 describes the advantages of a "promotion from within" policy. What might be some disadvantages?

Exercise 2

Directions: In the blank that follows each paragraph, write the word or phrase you think best expresses the topic.

Between 1963 and 1978, Dr. Dian Fossey spent her days and nights almost completely alone in a camp high in the Virunga Mountains of Africa; her goal was to study, at close range, the behavior of mountain gorillas. Because the gorillas lived in remote rain forests where only poachers would go, no one before Fossey had ever gotten close to them. To achieve her goal, Fossey endured heavy rains, waded through mud, fought off poachers, and survived multiple bouts of disease. In order to make the gorillas accept her, she spent years imitating gorilla behavior. If one of them grew angry and approached her, she would mimic the crouching posture of weaker, more submissive gorillas and thereby save her life. When finally one of the male gorillas reached out and touched her—without making a threatening gesture or sound—Fossey knew she had been accepted. In 1983, Fossey wrote about her life among the great apes in a book called *Gorillas in the Mist*. It eventually became the basis for a movie that recounted her life and death in Africa.

Dian Fossey's observation of the mountain gorillas

Explanation: In this paragraph, the name Dian Fossey receives the most references. However, the paragraph does not detail her life, her death, or the movie based on both. The majority of the sentences focus on her "observation of the mountain gorillas," making that phrase the specific topic of the paragraph. *Note:* Here again the modifier had to be inferred. It did not appear in the paragraph.

Now it's your turn to identify the topic.

1. Current voter registration figures strongly suggest that Hispanic voters are becoming a force to be reckoned with. In California alone, 1.4 million Hispanics are registered to vote. There are 600,000 Hispanic voters registered in New York and 500,000 registered in Florida. The Hispanic vote is particularly important in the Southwest. Texas, for example, has 1.1 million registered voters. The high turnout of Hispanic voters for Ann Richards was one reason why she became governor of Texas.[1]

Hispanic voters

2. In the summer of 1988, America's Yellowstone Park was the site of a huge fire which blazed through almost a million acres of forest. That fire and its charred aftermath brought to a head an ongoing debate about park policy and the handling of fires. From the late nineteenth century until the nineteen seventies, Yellowstone Park officials had routinely put out each and every fire. But when experts claimed that putting out all fires simply loaded the forest with dry kindling, the policy changed. Under close supervision, nature would be allowed to take its course. Fires ignited by lightning would be allowed to burn as long as they posed no serious threat. Thus in 1988 when lightning touched off several small fires,

---

1. Source of statistics: *USA Today*, January 13, 1992, p. 13 A.

park officials did not immediately extinguish them. Unfortunately, by the time efforts were made to put out the fires, the situation was out of control. Yellowstone was ablaze.

the 1988 fire in Yellowstone

---

3. One rule regarding sexual behavior seems to be found in almost all cultures. This rule is the *incest taboo*, a rule that forbids sexual intercourse between parents and their children, between brothers and sisters, and frequently between other designated kin as well. There are a few cultures in which exceptions to this rule exist. For instance, the Hawaiian royalty, the kings and queens of ancient Egypt, and the Inca emperors were expected to perpetuate their lineages by brother-sister marriages. These persons were regarded as sacred and were therefore set apart from ordinary people by the expectation that they violate the incest taboo that applied to all others. Thus, their behavior was regarded as exceptional even in their own societies. Some studies have suggested that brother-sister and father-daughter marriages in ancient Egypt were not limited to the royal family but were actually common in the general population (Hopkins, 1980; Middleton, 1962) and that father-daughter, mother-son, and brother-sister mating and marriages may have been acceptable in ancient Persia as well (Slotkin, 1947). Even so, the incest taboo is the most nearly universal of all human cultural rules. (Crapo, *Cultural Anthropology*, p. 144.)

incest taboo

---

4. In courts all over the country, fathers in divorce cases are growing more assertive about demanding custody rights over their children. Because more mothers are now working outside the home, judges no longer automatically assume children would be better off with their mother. In addition, the fact that fathers often have higher incomes can work in their favor. While mothers win custody in about 90 per cent of all divorce cases, the statistics are far lower in those that are contested. In these cases, fathers win sixty-eight per cent of the time. Divorce lawyer Harriet Cohen says she now tells women to be wary of forcing the issue of custody because "there is more of a chance now they could lose.[2]"

custody rights for fathers

---

2. Elizabeth Grillo Olson. "Why More Dads are Getting the Kids." *Business Week*, November 28, 1988.

5. The Catherine Genovese case has long been cited as one of the most tragic examples of public apathy and indifference toward the suffering of others. In March of 1964, Catherine Genovese was stabbed to death over a period of twenty-five minutes. During that time, thirty-five people watched from the safety of their apartments as the killer hunted his victim down. No one called the police. But instead of assuming an almost horrifying degree of public unconcern in this case, we could consider another interpretation. Catherine Genovese's neighbors may have failed to call the police *not* because they didn't care but because they assumed someone else would call. Every person watching could have assumed that someone else was going to help the screaming woman. Therefore, each person was willing to abdicate his or her personal responsibility, apparently believing that there was safety in numbers. This interpretation, while hardly favorable to the thirty-five onlookers, at least makes their behavior comprehensible.*

a new interpretation for the Catherine Genovese case

Discovering the Main Idea

Identifying the topic is the first step toward understanding a paragraph. The next step is to discover what the author wants to tell you *about* that topic. You need, that is, to discover the main idea. This is the general thought or message of the paragraph. It is the point the author hopes to communicate to an audience.

To make the reader's task easier, authors—especially authors of textbooks—frequently express the main idea in a sentence or two. Such sentences are called **main idea statements.** They have the following characteristics:

1) Main idea statements are more general than other sentences in the paragraph.
2) They can be used to sum up the message of the paragraph.
3) They raise questions that are answered by the more specific sentences in the paragraph.

To illustrate let's look again at the paragraph on page 107 dealing with Japanese women who keep their maiden name. The question now is: What point does the author wish to make *about* that topic?

In the last two decades, many American women have chosen to keep their maiden name. In the United States, this seems to be

---

* comprehensible: understandable.

a woman's natural right or prerogative. But in Japan things are not so simple. Women are often penalized for keeping their maiden name. While there is no specific law explicitly stating that women cannot keep their family name, Japanese civil law penalizes them for doing so. A woman who does not take her husband's name is not entitled to inherit his property. Their children are considered illegitimate. For women who, nevertheless, persist in using their maiden name, there can be additional penalties. Grants may be denied, raises withheld, and promotions delayed, sometimes indefinitely.

Re-read the paragraph, and it's clear that most of the sentences offer specific examples of how Japanese women are sometimes punished for keeping their maiden names. Taken together those specific examples suggest one main idea:

Women in Japan are often made to suffer for keeping their maiden names.

Is there a general sentence in the paragraph that makes that point, one that sums up the more specific sentences? Yes, there certainly is:"Women are often penalized for keeping their maiden name." Does that sentence raise questions answered by the remaining sentences? Again the answer is yes. Upon reading that sentence, you would undoubtedly ask: How are they penalized? The rest of the sentences in the paragraph provide an answer. Clearly we have found the main idea statement in the paragraph.

In the next sample paragraph, the topic is "theories about couvade." But again we need to know what the author wants to say about that topic. We need, that is, to discover the main idea.

In some societies, primarily agricultural ones, there is a custom known as the *couvade*. This is a ceremony in which the husband acts as if he is suffering from labor pains while his wife actually gives birth. Although no one seems able to fully explain the significance of the couvade, there are some theories about its meaning. According to one theory the couvade ritual is a method of warding off evil spirits. In effect the husband directs attention away from his wife and toward himself. Another theory speculates that the ceremony is a way of publicly proclaiming fatherhood so that paternity will not be in doubt.

Because most of the sentences in the paragraph focus on conflicting theories about this mysterious ritual, we can formulate this main idea: No one really knows for sure what the couvade means. Is there a main idea statement that expresses that point? Yes indeed. The third sentence makes exactly this point.

To find the topic, ask:

a. Who or what is repeatedly mentioned or referred to in the paragraph?
b. Does that word or phrase by itself reflect the focus of the paragraph, or do I need to add any modifiers?

To find the main idea, ask:

a. What does the author want to say about that topic?
b. What is the general message or point of the paragraph?

To find the main idea statement, ask:

a. Is there a general sentence that could be used to sum up the message of the paragraph?
b. Do the other more specific sentences answer questions raised by this main idea statement?

Locating Main Idea Statements

Within the following sample paragraph, the first sentence sums up the main idea: "By the mid-fifties, the civil rights movement in Alabama was gaining momentum." The remaining, more specific sentences further explain precisely how the civil rights movement was "gaining momentum."

By the mid-fifties, the civil rights movement in Alabama was gaining momentum*. In December 1955 Rosa Parks refused to give up her seat to a white passenger on a public bus in Montgomery, Alabama. Jim Crow practices required that blacks sit at the back of the bus, and, when asked, surrender their seats to whites. Mrs. Parks's arrest ignited a year-long black boycott of the city's bus system. Blacks walked or carpooled. "My feets is tired," remarked an elderly black woman, "but my soul is rested." With the bus company near bankruptcy and downtown merchants hurt by declining sales, city officials began harassing tactics to frighten blacks into abandoning the boycott. But the black community's leader, Martin Luther King, Jr., urged them to perse-

---

* momentum: increase in speed or strength.

vere. "This is not a war between the white and the Negro," he said, "but a conflict between justice and injustice." (Adapted from Norton et al. *A People and a Nation*, p. 861)

However, don't let examples like this one lead you astray. **Main idea statements can appear anywhere.** They can appear at the beginning, the end, or the middle of a paragraph.

In one common pattern, authors will open with an **introductory sentence** or two. These are sentences that spark interest in or provide background for the main idea statement. However, they themselves are not developed in the paragraph. Their sole purpose is to pave the way for the main idea, for example:

Introductory sentence:
Main idea statement:

The behavior of human beings can be very complicated. To find out how we learn, scientists often study the activities of animals. Sometimes they see how long it will take for a mouse to reach food in the center of a maze. Sometimes pigeons or other animals are taught to obtain food by pressing buttons. In the first experiments in space flight, trained chimpanzees and dogs were sent into orbit. They proved that living things could carry out certain activities while whirling about in space. In the same way, experiments with animals help us understand how we learn. (Tanzer, *Biology and Human Progress*, p. 42.)

 # 1

The first sentence of this paragraph suggests the author will talk about human behavior. But, in fact, the paragraph is not concerned with developing that sentence. That first sentence functions purely as an introduction to the real point of the paragraph, which appears in the second sentence.

In a variation of this particular pattern, authors sometimes open with an introductory sentence and then present a main idea statement that contradicts the point of that opening sentence. In this pattern, authors frequently use a **transition** to signal a reversal in their initial train of thought.

Transitions are words, phrases or sentences that help readers make connections between sentences and paragraphs by signaling how an author's train of thought will develop. While transitions can serve numerous functions—see the chart on pages 161–162—one of their primary functions is to modify, reverse, or contradict an introductory sentence. The following paragraph provides an example of a transitional sentence that contradicts an author's opening statement:

Introductory sentence:
Transitional sentence:

Most Americans are accustomed to thinking of lie detectors as foolproof, as machines that can, without error, separate the guilty from the innocent. But in fact, nothing could be further from the truth.

#2

Main idea statement:

Lie detectors can and do make mistakes. For one thing, the people in charge of lie detectors are not necessarily experts. Many states do not employ licensed examiners who have been trained to read and interpret the lie detector's print-out. In addition, many subjects react to a lie detector test by becoming anxious. As a result their bodies behave as if they were lying even when they are telling the truth. Just the opposite, some subjects are smart enough to use relaxation techniques or tranquilizers to maintain the appropriate calm, even when they are telling a string of lies.

The opening sentence of this paragraph introduces a common belief about lie detectors: they are foolproof. The second sentence, however, is a transitional sentence. It reverses the author's initial point: "But in fact, nothing could be further from the truth." The real main idea appears in the third sentence: "Lie detectors can and do make mistakes." All the remaining sentences serve to illustrate this point.

Transitions signaling difference, change or reversal.

however
unfortunately
but
even so
yet
still
on the contrary
just the opposite
in opposition
in contradiction
on the other hand
nevertheless
despite that fact
nonetheless

Then too, for emphasis, authors sometimes open a paragraph with a question. Read for the answer and you'll discover the main idea statement.

No one disputes that aggression, so tragically prevalent* among human beings, is also found among members of the animal kingdom. *But what about cooperation? Is there any evidence that it*

---

* prevalent: common, widespread.

Main idea
statement:

exists among animals? **The answer is an undisputed yes; coopera-tive behavior appears between and within species.** For example, groups of porpoises will encircle a female ready to give birth. They will drive away any sharks who might approach. If one of their members is wounded, they will bring it to the surface to get air. Similarly wild oxen found in the Arctic form a protective circle around the young if they sense the approach of danger. Even if hunters approach and start shooting they will not break the circle. They will stand and let themselves be shot one by one, determined to save their young.

On occasion, authors—particularly authors of science texts—will delay the main idea statement until the very last sentence. Here is a good example:

One early theory likened human memory to a muscle that had to be regularly exercised in order to function properly. This the-ory was eventually replaced by the notion that remembering was like writing, with experience the pen and the mind a blank page. But eventually this theory was also rejected. In its place came another hypothesis—that human memory functioned like a complex and well-stocked library catalogue. With access to a key word, you could look up any piece of stored or catalogued information. But over time that theory has also been discarded. **Human memory may, in fact, be too sophisticated and too complex to be explained through any one single simile* or met-aphor.†**

Main idea
statement:

\# 4

The author opens his paragraph with several examples of how human memory has been compared to other experiences. It is not until the last sentence that he introduces the main idea statement: "Human memory may, in fact, be too sophisticated and too com-plex to be explained through any one single simile or metaphor."

The following exercises will give you some practice discovering the sentences used to express main ideas.

DIGGING DEEPER

Do you think married women should or should not keep their maiden names? Why or why not?

---

* simile: a comparison using *like* or *as*, for example: He had a smile like a croc-odile.

† metaphor: implied comparison, for example: The woman was a human com-puter.

Exercise 3

Directions: Read each paragraph. Then circle the statement that best expresses the main idea.

Example: The elderly in America will no longer let themselves be ignored. As older Americans have become a larger percentage of America's total population, they have become increasingly aggressive in demanding their rights. The American Association of Retired Persons and the National Council of Senior Citizens have influenced the passage of laws against discrimination in employment on the basis of age and laws providing better health, housing, social security, and other benefits for older people. The Gray Panthers, led by Maggie Kuhn, is a smaller but more militant organization. In the U.S. House of Representatives, Claude Pepper of Florida was successful in securing passage of laws prohibiting mandatory retirement before age seventy in private employment or at any required age level in federal employment. (Adapted from Harris, *American Democracy*, p. 175.)

   ⓐ. As elderly Americans have increased in population, they have become more ready to demand their rights openly.

   b. The American Association of Retired Persons and the National Council of Senior Citizens have influenced the passage of laws against discrimination in employment on the basis of age.

Explanation: Sentence *a* could be used to sum up the point of the paragraph. Sentence *b* could not. Sentence *b* provides a specific answer to the question raised by sentence *a*. In what ways have the elderly become more ready to demand their rights?

1. Experienced divers know that beneath the sea lies an enchantingly beautiful world. But divers know, too, that the sea has its dangers. Among them are members of the family Dasyatidae, more commonly known as stingrays. Stingrays are responsible for a high number of underwater injuries. Lying almost completely covered by sand on the ocean floor, the stingray reacts immediately to the touch of a human hand or foot. The tail whips around and plants a sharp spine in the diver's flesh. Because that spine contains poison-filled glands, a wound from a stingray can cause nausea, diarrhea, decreased blood pressure, occasionally even death. Although there have been cases of stingrays becoming accustomed to and tolerating human beings who feed them, this is the exception, not the rule. Where stingrays are concerned, the best rule is "Divers Beware!"

a. Experienced divers know that beneath the sea lies an enchantingly beautiful world.
ⓑ. Divers know that the sea has its dangers, among them are members of the family Dasyatidae, more commonly known as stingrays.

2. Who was Will Rogers? Will Rogers was the cowboy-philosopher who won America's heart in the 1920s. Rogers began his career on stage with the Ziegfeld Follies. But his widely quoted wisecracks about the American political scene soon made him famous nationwide as he skewered* politicians of every stripe: "I am not a member of any organized party—I am a Democrat."[3] By the time he died in a plane crash in 1935, Rogers had made over twenty films, and quotes from his newspaper column had even appeared on the front page.

   a. Will Rogers liked to good naturedly make fun of politicians and presidents alike.
   ⓑ. With his mixture of down-home humor and political savvy, Will Rogers became one of the most popular men in America.

3. That money represents the satisfaction of different kinds of needs becomes apparent if we speculate a moment on what people would do if they could not obtain social position and power by means of money. In such a case, these needs might most readily be satisfied by service to society. The success of a person then would become a matter of social, rather than financial, status. Instead of competing with one another for money chips, people would compete for other socially recognized indicators of merit. In the Bennington College community, where liberal leanings became associated with prestige, women developed nonconservative values, the most capable leaders showing a greater degree of liberalism than the less capable ones. Prestige is not inevitably associated with wealth; rather, our culture has given money a prestige value. (Maier and Verser, *Psychology in Industrial Organizations*, p. 322.)

   a. We should define as successful those people who work for the benefit of the community rather than for commercial gain.
   ⓑ. By itself money has no value; our society has given money its social importance.

---

3. "Amazing Americans," *People*, January 20, 1992, p. 40.

* skewer: literally to pierce with a long piece of metal or wood; used metaphorically as it is here, to tease with pointed or biting humor.

Any person who lives through a tornado doesn't soon forget its physical and visual impact.

4. When a tornado struck Gainesville, Georgia, in April of 1939, a student at Brenau College was studying for an exam. It was a hot day (tornadoes are often preceded by still, stifling heat), and she was sitting in a tubful of water on the top floor of a dormitory. She heard a noise which she described later as sounding like a speeding freight train. The building began to shudder, there were cracking, wrenching noises, and the roof of the dormitory was peeled off. (The dormitory next door was untouched.) The violent updraft picked up the student, along with other objects—clothing, furniture, books—and carried her a distance of a block. She landed in thick shrubbery, which cushioned her fall, so that she walked away with only cuts and bruises, although she lost the braces from her teeth. The worst part of her ordeal was seeing a baby blown through the air, and being unable to help. Any person who lives through a tornado carries such terrifying memories in the mind's eye for years. (Weisberg, *Meterology*, p. 221.)

   a. In April 1939 a tornado struck Gainesville, Florida.
   ⓑ. Survivors of a tornado usually have frightening memories for years to come.

Getting a perspective on nature's grandeur—including a person for scale—became a Jackson specialty as shown in this 1880s view of Lower Yosemite Falls.

5. In the 1870s, pioneer photographer William Henry Jackson explored vast areas of the West. Through his photographs, he made Americans aware of the beauty to be found in places like the Colorado Rockies and the Grand Teton mountains. Yet despite Jackson's undisputed talent, his success was almost a coincidence, a result of chance rather than planning. When his sweetheart, Caroline Eastman, rejected his proposal of marriage, Jackson was so distraught he packed up his camera and went West. But he never forgot Caroline, keeping her picture with him until his death at ninety-nine. Hidden inside the frame were these words, "For Caddie's now a blooming bride/With Willie standing by her side,"[4] —words commemorating a wedding that never took place.

    a. The photographer William Henry Jackson made Americans aware of their glorious country.

    ⓑ. Although William Henry Jackson was a talented photogra-

---

4. Rowe Findley, "The Life and Times of William Henry Jackson," *National Geographic*, February 1989, p. 225.

pher, he might never have become famous if his sweetheart had not rejected him.

WRITING SUGGESTION

Write a paragraph in which you offer your definition of what it means to be successful. Be sure to give some specific examples.

Exercise 4

Directions: After you finish reading each paragraph, write the topic in the first blank and underline the main idea statement. *If* there is an introductory sentence (or sentences), fill in the second blank. *If* a transitional sentence reverses the opening train of thought, write the number of that sentence in the third blank. *If* the author uses a transitional word or phrase instead, write that word in the fourth blank. (If you need to, review the list of transitional words and phrases on page 118.)

Example: [1] As a relatively young man, Bela Lugosi became rich and famous. [2] Taken by his performance as the blood-drinking Count Dracula, audiences willingly paid to see his particular brand of elegance and evil. [3] But all that changed as Lugosi grew older. [4] <u>By the late forties, Lugosi's fame and fortune had vanished.</u> [5] Because he had become so closely identified with the figure of the count, producers were hesitant to cast him in other roles. [6] In addition, his thick Hungarian accent, so effective in *Dracula*, was a handicap for normal roles. [7] As a result, Lugosi was reduced to making ridiculous, low-grade thrillers like *Bela Lugosi Meets a Brooklyn Vampire* and *Mother Riley Meets the Vampire*. [8] By the late fifties, Lugosi was all but forgotten by Hollywood and his fans. [9] By 1956, he was dead, a victim of drugs and drink.

Topic: *The rise and fall of Bela Lugosi*

Introductory sentence(s): 1, 2

Transitional sentence: 3

*Transitional word
or phrase:* _____

Explanation: This paragraph opens on a positive note. Early in his career, Bela Lugosi was a successful film star. But sentence 3, a transitional sentence, changes the direction of the paragraph and paves the way for the main idea statement: "By the late forties, Lugosi's fame and fortune had vanished." The remaining more specific sentences then tell why his fame and fortune vanished. They also give readers some idea of just how badly off Lugosi was in later years.

Now it's your turn to read and analyze each of the following paragraphs.

1. [1] Did you ever ask yourself just how much truth there is to the eerie legend of Count Dracula? [2] You may be surprised to discover that centuries ago there did exist a Prince Vlad, said to be the source of the Dracula legends. [3] Prince Vlad, however, did not spend his time seeking out fresh young victims; instead he had disobedient members of the villages he ruled brought to his castle, where he decided on their punishment, which was usually death. [4] On one occasion, Vlad became furious because some visiting Turkish diplomats failed to remove their turbans. [5] They meant no disobedience; it was simply not their custom to do so. [6] As punishment for this supposed insult, Vlad had the turbans nailed to their heads.

Topic: Prince Vlad _____

*Introductory
sentence(s):* _____1_____

*Transitional
sentence:* _____

*Transitional word
or phrase:* _____

2. [1] In the film *An American Werewolf in London*, movie audiences watch breathlessly as the charming young hero turns into a grizzly werewolf, bent on the destruction of the human population. [2] Similarly, a high point in the film *Cat People* is the moment when the exquisitely beautiful Nastassia Kinski slowly and horribly changes into a monstrous, bloodthirsty leopard. [3] If older horror films, like the 1940 original version of *Cat People*, lack such grue-

The process of meta-morphosis is a key element in many horror films.

some scenes, it is because their creators did not have the technical sophistication to produce them. [4] But to the best of their ability, even the makers of early horror films tried to put the mysterious moment of metamorphosis* on film, as movies like *Dr. Jekyll and Mr. Hyde* readily attest. [5] <u>Clearly there is something strangely compelling about the idea of human metamorphosis that makes such scenes a crucial ingredient in horror films.</u>

Topic: metamorphosis in horror films
_____

Introductory sentence(s):   _____

Transitional sentence: _____

Transitional word or phrase: _____

_____

*   metamorphosis: marked change in appearance.

3. [1] The old horror movies attempted to create an atmosphere of terror. [2] The same cannot be said, however, of modern films. [3] <u>Modern movies ignore atmosphere and specialize in blood and gore.</u> [4] In the early films starring Boris Karloff and Bela Lugosi, the right atmosphere was created by the sound of wild screams in the background. [5] Open windows revealed a pair of shadowed eyes or the weird smile of a madman. [6] Modern films concentrate on filling the screen with buckets of blood. [7] The audience doesn't hear screams anymore; instead, it witnesses brutal murders. [8] The old shots of wild eyes and crazy smiles are gone. [9] Now there are long close-ups of someone being stabbed to death.

Topic: atmosphere of terror _____

Introductory sentence(s): _____1_____

Transitional sentence: _____2_____

Transitional word or phrase: _____

4. [1] Lydia Sherman's life was never the subject of a horror film. [2] But it could have been. [3] <u>In the late nineteenth century, Lydia Sherman, a demure housewife, committed crimes worthy of the most gruesome horror films.</u> [4] She poisoned three husbands and six children. [5] Her crimes went undetected until she tried to murder a fourth spouse. [6] To modern eyes, her ability to escape detection may seem incredible. [7] But, in the nineteenth century, when diseases like typhus, cholera, small pox, tuberculosis, and dysentery were both prevalent and deadly, it was possible to attribute the deaths to natural causes. [8] Eventually, however, the authorities grew suspicious of Lydia's "bad luck," and she was tried and convicted of murder.

Topic: Lydia Sherman _____

Introductory sentence(s): _____1_____

Transitional sentence: _____2_____

Transitional word or phrase: _____

5. [1] The director George Romero has made a number of horror films. [2] <u>But none of them has ever achieved the fame won by *The Night of the Living Dead,* perhaps the most horrible of all horror movies.</u> [3] Made on a low budget with inexperienced actors, the film tells the story of technology gone wrong. [4] Radiation in the atmosphere has caused the dead to come back to life and attack the living. [5] Not only have the dead come back to life, they have become cannibals as well. [6] Even worse, the living corpses are practically indestructible. [7] Only a bullet through the head can stop them, a discovery not made until the film is half over and the audience has been properly horrified. [8] Not surprisingly, Romero's film has become a cult classic, and true horror fans know the dialogue by heart.

Topic: The Night of the Living Dead

Introductory sentence(s): 1

Transitional sentence: _____

Transitional word or phrase: But

6. [1] George Romero's 1988 film *Monkey Shines: An Experiment in Terror* has a human hero, a young man crippled from the neck down. [2] <u>But the real hero of the film is Ella, a Capuchin monkey who answers his phone, turns out his light, holds his straw, and changes his cassettes.</u> [3] Although Ella eventually turns murderous, in the opening scene she is an angel of mercy. [4] What audience members may be surprised to learn is that the clever Ella is not just a product of Romero's imagination. [5] For the last decade monkeys have been used to help severely disabled men and women resume their lives. [6] Expensive to train, the monkeys are well worth their price because they make excellent companions.

Topic: the character of Ella in *Monkey Shines*

Introductory sentence(s): 1

Transitional sentence: _____

Transitional word or phrase: But

7. [1] During 1888 and 1889, the city of London was horrified by a series of grisly murders involving prostitutes. [2] Perhaps because the murders were never solved, the murderer, nicknamed Jack the Ripper, has never been forgotten. [3] On the contrary, his legend lives on. [4] <u>Over the years, he has been the central figure in numerous horror films.</u> *The Lodger* (1944), *The Man in the Attic* (1953), *Jack the Ripper* (1958), *A Study in Terror* (1965), *Hands of the Ripper* (1972), and *Jack's Back* (1987) are just a few of the films that have exploited the Ripper murders. [5] Although serial murders are an obvious source for horror films, what may make the Ripper murders especially compelling are the persistent rumors that the murderer held a high place in the English court. [6] It has even been speculated that the killer's prestigious post was one reason why he was never caught. [7] In short, Jack the Ripper may have had friends in high places, friends who protected him from the law.

Topic: Jack the Ripper

Introductory sentence(s): 1, 2

Transitional sentence: 3

Transitional word or phrase: _____

8. [1] Most people know the gruesome story of Baron Frankenstein, the mad doctor who created a living monster from the bodies of corpses. [2] Certainly the story has been told and retold. [3] <u>What many people don't know, however, is that the chilling story of Frankenstein and his creature was written by a nineteen-year-old girl named Mary Shelley.</u> [4] As a young bride, Shelley liked to participate in story telling competitions with her husband Percy Bysshe Shelley and his friend George Gordon Byron.* [5] On one particularly boring evening, Byron suggested that everyone write a ghost story. [6] The young bride, inspired by discussions of elec-

---

* Percy Bysshe Shelley, George Gordon Byron: two of the nineteenth century's greatest poets.

trical current and its alleged ability to reanimate* the dead, created for her listeners a story titled *Frankenstein, a Modern Prometheus.* [7] The rest, as they say, is history.

Topic: <u>story of Frankenstein</u>

Introductory
sentence(s): <u>   1, 2   </u>

Transitional
sentence: <u>   </u>

Transitional word
or phrase: <u>however   </u>

9. [1] As early as 1908, Thomas Alva Edison shot a picture of Frankenstein, and a film about a manmade monster (*The Golem*) appeared prior to World War I. [2] Throughout the twenties, a number of German directors produced some classic horror films, among them *Nosferatu*, a brilliant interpretation of Bram Stoker's *Dracula.* [3] By 1930, the German horror film was in decline, and Hollywood producers discovered that the public would pay to be frightened. [4] In 1930, Tod Browning directed *Dracula*, a box-office blockbuster. [5] <u>The history of horror films is almost as long as the history of film itself.</u>

Topic: <u>history of horror films</u>

Introductory
sentence(s): <u>   </u>

Transitional
sentence: <u>   </u>

Transitional word
or phrase: <u>   </u>

10. [1] <u>*Wieland*, one of the first novels written in America, could easily have been the basis for a horror film.</u> [2] Written by Charles Brockden Brown and published in 1798, the book describes the mental·

---

* reanimate: revive, bring back to life.

Throughout the twenties, a number of German directors produced some classic horror films.

collapse of Theodore Wieland. [3] Wieland, a resident of Philadelphia, leads a normal life until the day a ventriloquist comes to town and decides to make him hear voices. [4] The ventriloquist succeeds in his game but soon tires of it. [5] His victim, however, does not. [6] He starts to hear his own voices, heavenly ones, who command him to slay his family. [7] Obedient, Wieland murders his wife and children and is preparing to murder his sister when the ventriloquist, appalled by what he has caused, tells him to "hold." [8] Once Wieland comes to his senses and realizes what he has done, there is nothing left for him but death.

Topic: _Wieland_____

Introductory
sentence(s): _____

Transitional
sentence: _____

Transitional word
or phrase: _____

Inferring the Main Idea

While it would be convenient if they did, authors do not always explicitly state the main idea in a sentence or two. Like topics, main ideas occasionally have to be inferred. Readers have to use the clues in the paragraph to figure out a main idea that is implied but not explicitly stated. Look, for example, at this paragraph:

> It is comforting to believe that scientific knowledge has progressed step by step from ancient times until now. We would like to think that knowledge and understanding have steadily increased until we reached the current level of scientific thought, all to the benefit of mankind. Unfortunately, this is not an accurate picture of scientific expansion.

Here the topic is scientific knowledge, and the author opens the paragraph by telling us what is *not* true about that knowledge—that it has steadily advanced and accumulated. But in telling us what is not true the author also suggests what is: scientific knowledge has advanced by fits and starts. In this case it is clearly up to you to read between the lines and draw the appropriate inference. The same is true of the next paragraph:

---

* For one man's answer to this question, read the essay by John Russo called " 'Reel' Vs. Real Violence," p. 416.

As a young man, British soldier and writer T. E. Lawrence took part in an archaeological* expedition in the Middle East. The work fascinated him, as did the land, and he became possessed by a dream: the Arabs would overthrow the Turks and rule their own country. During World War I, Lawrence saw a chance to make his dream become reality when the British showed an interest in helping the Arabs revolt. Lawrence quickly seized on the idea and brought about a meeting between British and Arab leaders. Supplied by British arms and aided by Lawrence's military strategy, the Arabs rose up and captured several major Turkish strongholds. By 1919 the war was over, and the Turks had been defeated. Thrilled by the Arab victory, Lawrence was called to the Paris Peace Conference, where he learned for the first time that the British did not intend to give up their control in the Middle East.

Here the author repeatedly returns to Lawrence's dream for Arab freedom. We learn what the dream was, how he became possessed by it, and how he hoped to realize it. "Lawrence's dream of Arab freedom" is obviously the topic of the paragraph.

If we ask what the author wanted to say about that topic, the answer is equally clear: "Lawrence's dream of Arab freedom was only partially realized." This is the main idea even though it is not stated but implied by the other sentences in the paragraph. Sentence 2, for example, described Lawrence's dream of Arab independence. In turn, sentences 3–6 explain how he hoped to make the dream a reality. By sentence 7, it is clear that Lawrence was only partially successful: although the Arabs revolted, they did not gain control of their country.

As our illustrations show, you will not always find a main idea statement in paragraphs. Sometimes you will have to *infer the main idea implied by the paragraph.*

This does not mean, however, that you are free to draw any inference you choose. Your inferences must be *logical.* They must follow from or be based on the information supplied by the author.

We'll use the following paragraph to demonstrate this point.

When Annie Sullivan first arrived to teach her young pupil, Helen Keller, she found a little girl who could not see, hear, or speak. Because she was cut off from the world, the child behaved like a savage. She would bite, kick, and spit if anyone approached her. Yet in less than a month, Sullivan had taught her little charge to name objects. Even more astonishing, she had taught Helen to speak, giving her access to language and speech. With Sullivan as her teacher, Keller went on to read Braille in

---

* archaeology: study of ancient cultures.

English, Latin, Greek, French, and German. In her adult years, these accomplishments in the face of her handicaps made her a source of inspiration, and she became a figure of international importance.

The seven sentences in this sample paragraph all describe how Annie Sullivan changed Helen Keller's life for the better. Based on these sentences, we can infer a main idea statement like the following: "With the help of Annie Sullivan, Helen Keller was able to escape the unhappiness imposed by her handicaps and lead a productive life." Because it is based on the information provided by the supporting sentences, we call this a **logical inference.**

But what if we inferred another main idea statement: "Throughout her life, Helen Keller showed the greatest love and respect for her teacher, Annie Sullivan." Initially, this inference seems reasonable enough. After all, personal experience tells us that human beings are usually devoted to those who help or aid them in times of great distress. However, that is precisely the problem. The second inference is based solely on personal experience or common sense. Yet the supporting sentences do not describe how Keller felt about her teacher. That means the second inferred main idea is an illogical or inappropriate inference.

Whenever you infer the main idea of a paragraph, you are not free to draw any conclusion you choose. On the contrary, you must **check your inferred main idea against the information in the supporting sentences.** You should be able to explain how the information in those sentences led you to your final inference.

Exercise 5

Directions: Read each paragraph. Then circle the letter of the inference which best expresses the main idea implied by the paragraph.

Example: An expectant mother has to avoid alcohol during her pregnancy. Too much alcohol in her blood can deprive the fetus of necessary nutrition, and the baby will be born underweight. There is also mounting evidence that smoking during pregnancy can permanently damage the child's health, and children of smokers tend to have a higher incidence of respiratory infection throughout their lives. Clearly, mothers-to-be who smoke should try to cut back or quit. They should also be careful about the type of exercise they do, and very vigorous exercise should be avoided. During pregnancy, medication must be carefully monitored as well. Too often drugs not harmful to the mother can do serious, even irreparable, damage to the child.

    a. Unfortunately many expectant mothers do not take the necessary precautions in order to care for their unborn child.

    ⓑ. To have a healthy baby, expectant mothers must take special precautions.

Explanation: Sentence *a* is not a logical inference. The paragraph does not express any opinion as to whether or not expectant mothers do or do not take precautions. It only explains what expectant mothers must do to ensure a healthy baby. Therefore *b* is the logical inference.

1. Siberia extends from the Ural Mountains to the Pacific Ocean and embraces over five million square miles. Although some native Siberians deny their country is cold, morning temperatures can be as low as 60°F below zero. Layers upon layers of clothing are needed to survive the brutal temperatures. Without them, death by freezing is common. For those Russians who volunteer to live and work in Siberia, there are definite monetary rewards. They can increase their salaries by 30–40 percent. In addition, foods that are in short supply all over Russia—fruit, fish, and game—are plentiful in Siberia. Nevertheless, the shivering population of Siberia remains small and shows no signs of future increase.

    ⓐ. Siberia's extreme cold is one reason why its population does not grow.

    b. Political dissent in Russia is punishable by exile to Siberia.

2. One afternoon in Greenville, South Carolina, when I was 9 years old, my father was raking leaves. The man came outside to offer us a drink of water, and when he left I asked, Why does that man speak differently from us? "He's German," said my father, and he stopped and leaned on his rake. "He's German. I fought in Europe so they could have freedom. I'm proud to be a veteran of that war." His eyes clouded over. "But now he's here, and he can vote, and I cannot. I helped free his people, now I'm raking his leaves." (Jesse Jackson, *The Nation*, July 15, 1991, p. 100.)

    ⓐ. The father feels he has not been justly treated by the country he served.

    b. The father does not like Germans because of what happened during World War II.

3. According to the rules of their order, Carmelite nuns must be cloistered* from the world. They are not allowed to eat meat, and from September until Easter, they can have no milk, cheese, or eggs. Their days begin at 5:30 a.m., when they sing a cycle of psalms. The rest of the day is spent doing chores or saying prayers. Conversation is forbidden, even at mealtimes. Visitors are not permitted, although occasionally the nuns will speak to outsiders through an iron grill that emphasizes their separation from the world.

    ⓐ. Carmelite nuns lead an austere† life of prayer and silence.
    b. The rules of the Carmelite order are far too rigid.

4. Left on his own at a young age, Charlie Chaplin quickly learned how to survive on London's city streets. Living in part from money earned as a mime, he also charmed friends and strangers alike into giving him food and shelter. Above all, he learned how to outwit the police, who were not fond of a young boy without a home or a job. After arriving in the United States in 1910, Chaplin quickly got work in silent films. After that, it did not take him long to develop the character that made him famous—the "little tramp." Dressed in shabby clothes, begging money and food wherever he could find it, the "little tramp" spent most of his twenty-five years on screen avoiding the police, who pursued him in one hilarious scene after another.

    ⓐ. Charlie Chaplin used the experiences of his youth to mold the character that made him famous on screen.
    b. Charlie Chaplin's youthful experience with hunger and unemployment made him bitter throughout his life.

5. Abortion first became illegal in the United States in the nineteenth century. At that time, it was ruled dangerous to the prospective mother. Recently, courts have upheld the right of a woman to undergo abortion on request, but the decision has caused heated debates, animosity, and even violence. The groups opposing abortion have coined the term "right to life," but others argue that pregnancy is a very personal matter and that the decision to accept this condition and the ensuing years of responsibility are primarily the woman's since she must bear the brunt of any pain, risk, and responsibility. One argument has revolved around the question of when a developing embryo becomes a "person." Some believe that

---

*   cloistered: confined, secluded.
†   austere: strict, stern, without luxury.

the fertilized egg is a human being and has a "right" to develop and be born. Others argue that abortion does not actually destroy "life" until later, such as when the heart (still a tubular muscle) begins to beat, or when the embryo begins to stir or "quicken," or the time when it becomes capable of surviving after birth. (Wallace, *Biology, the World of Life*, pp. 297–298.)

ⓐ. The decision to make abortion legal has produced a heated debate.
  b. Prior to the nineteenth century, abortion was not illegal.

DIGGING DEEPER

It has been argued that women should be held legally responsible if, during pregnancy, they consciously act in a way that harms the unborn child. Explain why you think this idea is fair or unfair.

WRITING SUGGESTION

Write a paragraph or two explaining why you personally do or do not approve of abortion.

Working with Words

Here are seven more prefixes and roots you should know. Use them to figure out the meaning of the italicized words and fill in the accompanying blanks. Then add them to your vocabulary notebook for regular review.

1. syn, sym	(Greek prefix)	together, alike
2. pre	(Latin prefix)	before
3. de	(Latin prefix)	removal, down from, reduce, away

4.	dic, dict	(Latin root)	speak
5.	capit	(Latin root)	head
6.	popul	(Latin root)	people
7.	plen, plet	(Latin root)	full

Practice

1. It had once been a *populous* city. But the years had turned it into a ghost town. Its streets were now empty except for an occasional tourist coming to see what the wild West had once been like.

   filled with people

2. She had read several articles about the role of fairy tales in a young child's life. But she was having a hard time *synthesizing* the different points of view. They were all so different; there seemed to be no way of connecting or relating them.

   combining, relating

3. As a manager, she was annoyingly *dictatorial*. From her perspective no one could do anything on their own. They had to follow her orders or face the consequences.

   bossy, demanding

4. The *per capita* income in the village was only about a thousand dollars a year and now even that pitiful amount was being threatened by the loss of the forests. The trees were being destroyed on a daily basis.

   per head, per person

5. Many people believe in *predestination*. They are convinced that their lives are mapped out by God or fate and nothing can alter the pattern of events.

   everything is decided in advance by God or fate

6. His energy had been seriously *depleted* by the illness. He no longer had any interest in those sports he had once loved.

reduced
_____

7. The meal was *replete* with the fattening foods she loved to eat. It began with a hot creamy soup and ended with a cold creamy dessert.

complete
_____

8. The dancers made an effort to *synchronize* their movements. But they had been poorly trained and everyone was moving in a different direction while the choreographer pulled out her hair.

bring together in time
_____

9. As a *prelude* to the speaker's lecture, he described the man's life and work. But the audience was not interested. They were there to see the man himself, not to hear about his past.

introduction
_____

10. At the sight of the king, the ragged *populace* began to scream for his blood. He had kept them starving and ragged for too long. They were not about to show him any mercy.

people
_____

Stories Behind the Words

Here, too, are five more words with stories in their past. Learn the story, and you will remember the word.

1. *Mentor.* Mentor was the trusted friend and teacher of Odysseus. While Odysseus was away, a goddess came down to earth to protect his family. To do so, she disguised herself as Mentor, a friend of the family, and took over his role as teacher and counselor. Today we use the word *mentor* to mean someone we consider a teacher and counselor.

   Sample sentence: My older brother has always been my *mentor* in life.

   Definition: teacher, counselor, guide

2. *Atlas.* Atlas was a Titan who, according to Greek mythology, held up the earth on his shoulders. The image of Atlas with the earth on his shoulders was historically used on map collections. Today when we talk about an *atlas*, we are usually referring to a bound collection of maps.

    Sample sentence: Fascinated, she studied the *atlas*.

        Definition: book of maps, book of tables and charts

      Other forms: atlases

3. *Herculean.* Hercules was a Greek hero who possessed extraordinary strength. It was said that he could perform fantastic feats. Today when we use the word *herculean*, we are talking about something that demands a great deal of effort or strength.

    Sample sentence: Before he became president, he completed the *herculean* task of reorganizing the office.

        Definition: difficult, demanding in mental or physical strength

4. *Flora* and *fauna.* Flora was the Roman goddess of flowers, and Faunus was the Roman god of nature and fertility. Today we use the terms *flora* and *fauna* to mean the plants and animals of a particular region.

    Sample sentence: We spent three days studying the *flora* and *fauna* of New Zealand.

5. *Narcissism.* Narcissus was a beautiful young man who loved no one until the day he saw his own reflection in a pool of water and fell madly in love. Today when we talk about *narcissism*, we are talking about excessive love or admiration for oneself.

    Sample sentence: Only his incredible *narcissism* allowed him to ignore all the insulting remarks directed his way.

        Definition: self-love, admiration for oneself

      Other forms: narcissist, narcissistic

Review Test: Chapter 4

Part A: Read each paragraph. Then write the topic in the first blank. If there is an introductory sentence, fill in the second blank. Write the number (or numbers) of the main idea statement in the third blank. If a transitional sentence reverses the opening train of thought, write the number of that sentence in the fourth blank. If, instead, the author uses just a transitional word, write that word in the last blank.

1. [1] Rabies is a disease of animals that secrete saliva. [2] The **host range** (the diversity of species affected by an agent) of this virus includes members of the canine family, such as dogs and foxes [3]. The disease is also found in skunks, opossums, bats, and many other species. [4] When one considers all these different hosts and the fact that many of them are wild animals, it might appear that *any* measures taken to control the disease would be insignificant. [5] Fortunately, this is not the case. [6] There is one factor that is extremely important in the transmission of rabies infection to humans: The vast majority of human cases involve dogs and cats. [7] It is difficult to arrive at even a reasonably accurate estimate of the number of dogs and cats in the United States, but it is certainly a large number. [8] People are exposed to the infectious agent largely through close association with these animals. [9] If there were some means of controlling the disease in dogs and cats, its incidence in humans would decline. (Buffalo and Ferguson, *Microbiology*, p. 407.)

Topic: transmission of rabies

Introductory sentence(s): 1–4

Main idea statement: 6

Transitional sentence: 5

Transitional word:

2. [1] How did men and women limit their families in the early nineteenth century? [2] Many married later, thus shortening the period

of childbearing. [3] And women had their last child at a younger age, dropping from around forty in the mid-eighteenth century to around thirty-five in the mid-nineteenth century. [4] More important, however, was the widespread use of birth control. [5] The popular marriage guide by the physician Charles Knowlton, *Fruits of Philosophy; or, the Private Companion of Young Married People* (1832), provides us with a glimpse of contemporary* birth control methods. [6] Probably the most widespread practice was *coitus interruptus,* or withdrawal of the male before completion of the sexual act. [7] But medical devices were beginning to compete with this ancient folk practice. [8] Although animal-skin condoms imported from France were too expensive for popular use, cheap rubber condoms were widely adopted when they became available in the 1850s. [9] Some couples used the rhythm method— attempting to confine intercourse to a woman's infertile periods. [10] Knowledge of the "safe period," however, was uncertain even among physicians. [11] Another method was abstinence, or less frequent sexual intercourse. (Norton, et al. *A People and a Nation,* p. 279.)

Topic:	birth control in the early nineteenth century
Introductory sentence(s):	1–3
Main idea statement:	4
Transitional sentence:	
Transitional word:	however

3. [1] In Benjamin Franklin's day, lightning was one of the most feared of all natural phenomena. [2] It especially struck terror in the hearts of people who lived and worked in buildings made of wood and other combustible materials. [3] At the time Franklin performed his famous experiment with the key and the kite, scientists knew very little about electricity or lightning. [4] They did not know what caused lightning to be attracted to objects at the Earth's surface. [5] After his experiment, Franklin went on to invent the lightning rod, which over the past 200 years has undoubt-

---

* contemporary: belonging to the same time.

edly saved hundreds of lives and millions of dollars in buildings that otherwise would have been damaged. (Weisberg, *Meteorology*, p. 327.)

Topic: lightning in Benjamin Franklin's day

Introductory sentence(s): _____

Main idea statement: 1 _____

Transitional sentence: _____

Transitional word: _____

4. [1] Americans love children, but they do not necessarily want them living next door, and couples with children have difficulty getting and keeping apartments. [2] Many landlords, for example, will not allow children in their buildings. [3] In some cases, they even insist that young couples who move in without children sign "adults only" leases. [4] The leases require couples to move if they decide to have children. [5] Resentful of such clauses, some couples who decided to have children after all have taken their landlords to court—with mixed results. [6] Although the parents have won a few cases, most judges have agreed that barring children under the age of twelve is a reasonable way to decrease property damage.

Topic: housing problems for couples with children

Introductory sentence(s): _____

Main idea statement: 1 _____

Transitional sentence: _____

Transitional word: _____

5. [1] For centuries earthquakes were considered warnings from the gods; both the suddenness of the quakes and the amount of damage they left behind were enough to convince even the unbelieving that such things must be the work of supernatural beings. [2] It is only fairly recently that a comprehensive* theory of the cause of earthquakes has been developed. [3] According to this theory, called *plate tectonics*, the earth's surface consists of about a dozen huge seventy-mile-thick rock plates. [4] Propelled by unknown forces, the plates are constantly in motion. [5] Sometimes the plates meet and become temporarily locked together. [6] The locking together of the plates causes stress to build up on the edges of the rocks. [7] Eventually the rocks fracture, and the plates resume their motion, but the sudden release of energy causes the quakes.

Topic: cause of earthquakes

Introductory sentence(s): 1 _____

Main idea statement: 2 _____

Transitional sentence: _____

Transitional word: _____

Directions: For the next set of paragraphs, circle the letter of the sentence that best expresses the inferred main idea.

6. Mark Twain the writer was a genius. The same cannot be said, however, of Mark Twain the businessman. Twain lost money trying to market pre-gummed scrapbooks and a more efficient pants button. But it was a typesetting machine invented by James W. Paige that brought Twain near bankruptcy. After pouring thousands of dollars into the machine's development, Twain gathered together a group of potential investors for a trial demonstration. Shortly after the machine was turned on, the typesetter began to clank ominously. When a piece of the machine flew out the win-

---

* comprehensive: thorough, complete.

dow, the would-be investors flew out the door. Still Twain didn't give up, and he kept on pouring money into the machine until his losses came to almost $200,000.

    ⓐ. As a businessman, Mark Twain was not very successful.
    b. Mark Twain loved to invent new gadgets, some of which were surprisingly modern.

7.   Because fat requires less energy than lean tissue, and because people usually become less active in their later years, the need for calories declines each decade after the age of twenty—which means that a person who does not eat considerably less at sixty than was eaten at twenty will gain weight. At the same time that the need for calories lessens, the requirement for basic nutrients remains about the same; more nutrients obviously have to be packed into less food, and there is less room in the diet for junk foods that are high in calories and low in nutrition. Although the ability to taste salt, which gives flavor to food, also diminishes with age, the receptivity to sweetness does not diminish, and this may tempt the elderly into the consumption of junk foods. By the age of sixty, the salivary glands have degenerated,* and a decrease in the secretion of saliva is noticeable. (Farb and Armelagos, *Consuming Passions*, p. 108.)

    ⓐ. Age brings with it the need for changes in diet and nutrition.
    b. As people get older, they eat more sweets.

8.   The drug called cocaine was formally identified in 1855. By the 1870s, surgeons used it as an anesthetic for minor surgery. In the 1880s it was used to treat opium addiction and alcoholism. The drug came to the notice of the young Sigmund Freud† when he read reports of how small doses could restore exhausted soldiers. Trying it out on himself, Freud waxed‡ enthusiastic, calling cocaine a wonder drug. So enthusiastic was he that he prescribed it for a young colleague who was addicted to morphine. The drug, however, did not effect a cure. Instead, the young man began hallucinating wildly. Believing that snakes were crawling under his skin, he committed suicide.

---

*   degenerate: decline, grow worse.

†   Sigmund Freud: Viennese doctor and founder of psychoanalysis, a theory of the mind that has been highly influential.

‡   wax: become, grow.

(a). Sigmund Freud was badly mistaken about the benefits of cocaine.

b. In the nineteenth century, cocaine was not considered dangerous.

9. Joan of Arc was born in 1412 to a family of poor peasants. In 1425, at the age of thirteen, Joan claimed to hear voices, voices she believed belonged to the early Christian martyrs. Four years later, in 1429, those same voices told her to help the King of France fight the British, who were trying to take control of France in the Hundred Years War. When the king believed her story and gave her troops to command, Joan put on a suit of armor and led her soldiers to a glorious victory. Yet when Joan was captured by the British in 1430 and tried for heresy* and wearing masculine dress, the French king refused to help her, even when the British court condemned her to death. On May 30, 1431, Joan was burned at the stake, still proclaiming her loyalty to the King of France.

a. Joan of Arc is the patron saint of France.
(b). Although Joan of Arc was loyal to the King of France, he betrayed her.

10. During World War I, India supported Britain; and its 300 million inhabitants remained loyal to the "Emperor" in London. After a victory was achieved in 1918, Indian nationalists† hoped that the British would show their gratitude by granting India the privileges of responsible self-government that Canada, South Africa, Australia and New Zealand already enjoyed. Instead, the Parliament at Westminster enacted a compromise, the Government of India Act of 1919, which provided for an all-India parliament of two chambers and promised legislative councils for the provinces. Matters of less and local importance were to be entrusted to these bodies, but decisions on major problems and policies would continue to be made by the British viceroy and his advisors. (Herzstein, *Western Civilization*, p. 725.)

(a). The dreams of Indian nationalists were shattered by British actions after World War I.
b. During World War I, India was deeply loyal to the British government.

---

* heresy: opinion or doctrine that differs strongly with established beliefs.

† Nationalists: people devoted to the cultural and political independence of their country.

Part B:
Vocabulary
Review

Here is a list of words drawn from the chapter. Some actually appear in the chapter. Some have been derived from the prefixes and suffixes introduced on pages 137 and 138. Your job is to match words and blanks.

In some cases you may have to change the endings of words to make them fit the context. If you need to, consult your dictionary to decide which ending to use. *Note:* You may use some words more than once and others not at all.

archaeologist	dictator	cloister	austere
populace	reanimate	comprehensible	nationalist
prevalent	metamorphosis	instrumental	predestine
synonymous	mentor	herculean	
momentum	atlas	consolidate	

1. Opposition to the _____dictator_____ was gaining _____momentum_____ in every segment of the _____nationalist_____ movement. Every week there was a new incident and violent protest was spreading throughout the country. Nevertheless he continued to behave as if he had been _____predestined_____ to rule and nothing could harm him. He had _____consolidated_____ all of the armed forces under his control and believed, therefore, that no one could touch him.

2. The _____archaeologist_____ discovered the mummy _____cloistered_____ in a small closet. Next to the bandaged corpse was a small bowl of burnt leaves and the ashes of what had obviously been a fire. When he questioned the guide, he was told that the leaves were tanna leaves and that someone had been trying to _____reanimate_____ the corpse by burning the leaves. Such superstitions were not _____comprehensible_____ to the _____archaeologist_____ who laughed contemptuously. But for the guide, who came from a country where such superstitions were _____prevalent_____, it was no laughing matter. He feared for his life.

3. The scientist's weird hypotheses had made his name __synonymous__ with the word "crackpot." No one except the most credulous believed his crazy theories. While it would be wonderful if drinking a bottle of vinegar per day could produce a __metamorphosis__ from youth to age, there was absolutely no scientific proof that this was even remotely possible. Even Dr. Eggo's __mentor__, the esteemed Dr. Ava Sophia, worried about the ravings of her once talented pupil who clearly believed he could accomplish __herculean__ tasks simply by consuming huge doses of garlic daily.

4. According to former N.F.L. lineman, Lyle Alzado,* drugs were an __instrumental__ part of his training program during his years as an athlete. Alzado also believed that his long-term use of steroids plus his recent use of human growth hormones in 1990 when he was trying to __reanimate__ his career as a football player took a deadly toll. He developed an inoperable brain tumor. Alzado claimed that the use of such drugs is more __prevalent__ among athletes than most people realize. Athletes whose careers __dictate__ the need for big, muscled bodies are often desperate enough to take steroids. Although former teammates have been quick to express sympathy for Alzado, no one yet has supported his claim that "80 percent of National Football League players are taking human growth hormone or steroids."[5] A spokesman for the N.F.L. has labelled the claim a "wild and inaccurate guess."[6]

---

5. *New York Times*, July 4, 1991, B10
6. Ibid.
* Lyle Alzado died in May of 1992.

The Function of Supporting Sentences

While Chapter Four concentrated on general sentences that convey the main idea, this chapter focuses on the more specific sentences that develop or imply a main idea statement. When you are through reading this chapter, you will be able to:

☐ Locate support for the main idea.
☐ Distinguish between *major* and *minor supporting sentences*.
☐ Take complete notes.
☐ *Paraphrase* with accuracy.

New Vocabulary

As you read, watch for the following words in this chapter. However, before you check the definitions at the bottom of the page, try to derive a meaning from context.

progressive	fervidly	exalted
euphemism	rampant	propagation
idioms	ecology	socialize
incubation	elation	exonerate
reiterate	complacently	authenticity
alienate	travesty	autonomy
resilient		

Supporting Sentences Develop the Main Idea

Writers know that, by themselves, general statements are subject to misinterpretation. Therefore to avoid any confusion or misun-

149

derstanding, they provide **supporting sentences.** These are more specific sentences that help clarify the main idea and make it persuasive. When used effectively, supporting sentences anticipate and answer questions readers might pose about the main idea statement. If there is no main idea statement, supporting sentences combine to suggest one.

To illustrate just how important supporting sentences are, imagine you were confronted with a one-sentence paragraph.

Prolonged unemployment can create serious psychological problems that, in the long run, actually contribute to continued joblessness.

By itself, the sentence tells us that long-term unemployment can do psychological damage. But what does the author mean by the phrase *prolonged unemployment*? Is she talking about six months or six years? Exactly what kind of psychological problems does she have in mind? After all, that phrase covers a great deal of ground. Also, how is it possible for these problems to contribute to continued joblessness? In isolation, that sentence raises a number of questions. The supporting sentences should provide the answers.

[1] Prolonged unemployment can create serious psychological problems that, in the long run, actually contribute to continued joblessness. [2] In a society that stresses the relationship between productive work and personal value, it is easy enough to equate long-term unemployment with personal worthlessness. [3] That is, in fact, precisely what many unemployed men and women begin to do. [4] Out of a job for a year or more, they begin to see themselves as worthless human beings, without any value to their society. [5] In what amounts to a vicious cycle, their sense of personal worthlessness further diminishes their chances of gaining employment. [6] Sometimes they stop looking for work altogether, sure in their despair that no one would hire them. [7] Or else they go to interviews, but they present themselves in such a defeated and hopeless way that the interviewer cannot help but be unimpressed and reject their application.

Notice how the second and third supporting sentences explain the main idea statement. They define the psychological problem unemployment can create—a sense of worthlessness. Sentence 4, in turn, defines the phrase *prolonged unemployment.*

Sentence 5 explains the second half of the main idea statement by telling us that a sense of personal worthlessness can contribute to continued joblessness. Sentences 6 and 7 offer specific illustrations of just how this can happen.

In this paragraph, the supporting sentences explain the general phrases *prolonged unemployment* and *serious psychological damage.* They also anticipate and answer an important question readers might raise after reading the main idea statement: "How can unemployment possibly contribute to continued joblessness?"

Supporting sentences can define technical terms, offer reasons, quote statistics, cite studies, mention exceptions, list dates, present examples, or give expert testimony. The form they take all depends on the main idea they develop. To understand the relationship between the general main idea and the more specific support ask yourself these questions:

1. What kind of specific support does the author supply? Examples, statistics, dates, studies, reasons?
2. How do the more specific statements contribute to the main idea? What words or phrases do they define? What questions do they answer?
3. If there is no general main idea statement that seems to sum up the paragraph, what main idea do the supporting sentences imply?

Exercise 1

Directions: Choose the two specific statements that could support the general statement.

Example: In the 1980s the city of Los Angeles underwent dramatic changes.

    a. Twenty years after the Watts riots,* some of the burned out buildings have still not been rebuilt.
    (b). In 1985 Los Angeles became the second largest city.
    (c). In 1960 only one out of nine county residents was Hispanic; by the 1980s one-third of all county residents was Hispanic.[1]

Explanation: Sentences *c* and *b* are circled because these two sentences further define the "dramatic changes" Los Angeles experienced. Letter *a*

---

1. Carter Vaughn Findley and John Murray Rothney, *Twentieth Century World,* (Boston: Houghton Mifflin, 1986), p. 458.

* Watts riots: The riots took place in 1965 and lasted six days. At the end, 34 people were dead and 1000 injured.

is not circled because that sentence does not explain how the city has changed.

1. With varying degrees of success, hypnosis has been put to a number of uses.

   ⓐ. In some cases, hypnosis can alleviate, even eliminate, pain.
   b. To some degree, a hypnotized person is always aware of what he or she is doing.
   ⓒ. Hypnosis has been used to evaluate eyewitness testimony.

2. The first year of marriage can be a stormy time in a couple's relationship.

   ⓐ. Suddenly two people discover that they are no longer responsible only to themselves; instead, they have to consider the feelings and needs of another.
   b. No one should make the mistake of rushing into marriage.
   ⓒ. In the first year of marriage, both partners have to learn to accept the annoying little habits that each is bound to possess.

3. Students who joined a fraternity twenty years ago underwent the humiliating and painful process called hazing.

   ⓐ. New members were often subjected to beatings with thick wooden paddles.
   ⓑ. They were asked to do chores and run errands until they were physically exhausted.
   c. As painful and humiliating as hazing is, many who have endured it are willing to inflict the same punishment on others.

4. The AIDS virus is particularly deadly because it skillfully disguises itself.

   ⓐ. The AIDS virus usually enters the body hidden within a T-cell; these are the cells that initiate a response to disease.
   b. Outside of the body, the AIDS virus is extremely weak and fragile.
   ⓒ. The defending T-cells immediately attack the infected T-cell, but when they do, the virus simply slips into one of the defending cells and immobilizes it.

WRITING SUGGESTION

Write a paragraph explaining why you would or would not participate in hazing in order to join a fraternity or sorority.

Exercise 2

Directions: Read each paragraph and underline the main idea statement. Decide whether all the supporting sentences explain that statement. If they do, leave the line that follows the paragraph blank. If, however, you find a sentence that does not explain the main idea statement, write the number of that sentence on the blank line.

Example: [1] Relatively unknown two decades ago, Alzheimer's disease now ranks as the fourth most common cause of death in the United States. [2] <u>Because of its serious nature, the disease has been highly publicized in the hope that publicity will increase public awareness and make people more likely to contribute money for research.</u> [3] To raise the necessary funds, the Alzheimer's Disease and Related Disorders Association (ADRDA), a nationwide organization, has even placed an ad in the *New York Times*. [4] The ad outlines the specific areas where research is needed. [5] What is really criminal about Alzheimer's disease is that insurance companies will not pay for care of the victims. [6] Given sufficient funds, ADRDA hopes to raise enough money so that better methods for diagnosing and treating the disease will be made available. _____5_____

Explanation: In this paragraph, the first sentence introduces the topic, "Alzheimer's disease." The second sentence is the main idea statement. It explains the purpose behind the increased publicity about Alzheimer's disease. With the exception of sentence 5, the remaining sentences clarify and explain the main idea statement. They explain what kind of publicity is being used and what it should accomplish. Sentence 5, however, does not fulfill the function of a supporting sentence; it does not add to our understanding of the main idea statement.

Do the rest of the exercise in the same manner.

Snakes are feared, hated, and frequently mistreated for no valid reason.

1. [1] <u>The abuse of a child can take several forms.</u> [2] Sometimes the child is injured physically and may suffer from an odd or disturbing combination of cuts, burns, bruises, or broken bones. [3] Usually the parents or guardians may claim that the child "had an accident," even though no normal accident could cause such injuries. [4] But child abuse may also take the form of emotional neglect; the parents will simply ignore the child and refuse to respond to bids for attention. [5] Children suffering from this kind of neglect often show symptoms of the *failure to thrive syndrome,* in which physical growth is delayed. [6] In still other cases of maltreatment, the child may be abused emotionally. [7] One or both parents may ridicule or belittle the child. [8] In this case, physical problems may be absent, but the child's self-esteem will be seriously undermined. _____

2. [1] Most people run or scream in terror when they see a snake. [2] But, in fact, most snakes are hated and feared for no rational reason. [3] <u>If they are examined without prejudice, snakes prove to be fascinating and, for the most part, relatively harmless members of the reptile family.</u> [4] Like other reptiles, they are cold-blooded, and their temperatures change with the environment. [5] Although most people think that snakes are slimy creatures, the opposite is true. [6] Their skins are cool and dry, even pleasant to the touch. [7] The Hopi Indians perform ritual dances with live rattlesnakes in their mouths. [8] Most snakes do more good than harm, helping

to control the rodent population. [9] In reality, very few snakes are actually dangerous to human beings. __7__

3. [1] On January 30th, 1889, young Crown Prince Rudolf of Austria was found dead in his hunting lodge in Mayerling, near Vienna. [2] Lying next to him was the body of his lover, seventeen-year-old Baroness Mary Vetsera. [3] She had been shot through the left temple. [4] Because Rudolf's family quickly removed all traces of the tragic event, <u>no one knows what really happened that night.</u> [5] Some people claim that Rudolf, depressed over a terminal illness, shot himself. [6] According to this theory, when Mary found him, she too took her life. [7] Others insist, however, that Rudolf was murdered by members of the court who feared his progressive* beliefs would become public policy when the young man came to the throne. [8] But according to the most widely accepted theory, Rudolf had been depressed for a long time and proposed a suicide pact. [9] Mary, who adored him, immediately accepted. _____

4. [1] When sportscasters talk about aggressive play on the football field, they often say that a team or player is "getting physical." [2] The term is a euphemism† and sounds harmless enough. [3] <u>But in fact, "getting physical" can leave players seriously injured.</u> [4] Darryl Stingley is a case in point. [5] A decade ago Stingley was a highly touted football player, said to have a brilliant career ahead of him. [6] But Stingley was knocked unconscious during a game. [7] When he awoke, he was a paraplegic who would probably never be able to walk again. [8] In the movie *The Men*, Marlon Brando played a paraplegic who had lost the use of his legs through a war injury. __8__

DIGGING DEEPER

What are some other euphemisms you can think of? What kinds of situations typically give rise to euphemisms?

---

* progressive: liberal, interested in bringing about reform.

† euphemism: substitution of an inoffensive term for one considered too crude or obvious.

A brief reminder. As you know, supporting sentences sometimes imply the main idea. When they do, be sure that the main idea you infer matches the author's explicit statements. The next set of exercises will give you more practice thinking about logical and illogical inferences.

Exercise 3

Directions: Each group of sentences suggests one main idea. Based on these supporting sentences, choose the main idea statement you think is a logical inference.

Example: a. During the nineteenth century, factory owners hired young orphans, whom they could force to work fifteen hours a day.
  b. Many factory owners preferred to hire women, who could move quickly among the machinery and were easily frightened if threatened with dismissal.
  c. Whenever possible, the employers increased their profits by reducing the workers' wages.
  d. Workers who complained about the hours or poor working conditions were promptly fired; and whenever possible, employers saw to it that rebellious workers were thrown in jail.

Inferences: 1. In the nineteenth century, employers did not tolerate union activity. They fought it with every weapon at their disposal.
  (2). Factory owners in the nineteenth century thought nothing of exploiting their work force.

Explanation: The first four sentences give examples of the way nineteenth-century employers abused their employees. The sentences combine to suggest one main idea: factory owners in the nineteenth century cruelly exploited the men, women, and children who worked for them. Sentence 1 is not a logical inference. None of the supporting sentences mentions union activity, and only one sentence touches on the rebelliousness of the workers.

1. a. In 1975 Vietnam was the war America wanted to forget, but more than a decade later, posters and T-shirts bearing the image of Frederick Hart's memorial to fallen Vietnam soldiers are in great demand.

b. Oliver Stone's 1986 movie *Platoon* was a runaway hit at the box office.

c. In 1988 Empire Press published its first issue of *Vietnam* magazine.

d. By 1989 even television was ready to tackle Vietnam and two new series dealing with the war premiered: *Tour of Duty* and *China Beach.*

Inferences: 1. Veterans returning in 1975 were badly treated by a public who wanted only to forget the war in Vietnam.

②. If in 1975 America wanted to forget the war in Vietnam, by the eighties the public was willing to remember.

2.   a. During the six years that World War II raged, an estimated fifteen million men died in battle.

b. Ferocious air attacks reduced many European cities to little more than rubble.

c. Six million Jews were murdered by the Nazis.

d. Millions of men and women lost their lives in German concentration camps.

Inferences: ①. World War II was a tragedy of catastrophic proportions.

2. At the end of World War II, the Germans tried to hide the gruesome evidence of their crimes.

3.   a. Elvis Presley has been dead for over a decade.

b. He still gets mail, at least a letter per day.

c. His home in Mississippi, "Graceland," draws more than 500,000 visitors a year.

d. There are still 300 Elvis fan clubs active around the world.

Inferences: ①. Even after death Elvis Presley lives on as an American legend.

2. The fascination with Elvis Presley is bizarre and morbid.

4.   a. During the Middle Ages, most men and women found it impossible to travel because roving bands of robbers attacked all but the large and heavily armed traveling parties.

b. If illness swept the land, the rich could close their doors or journey to another country, but the men and women who were not rich—and that was the majority of the population—could only suffer and die.

c. Since there was no knowledge of flood control, floods were more frequent in the Middle Ages, and entire villages were swept away.

d. Villages were constantly prey to starvation because too much or too little rain would wipe out crops needed for survival.

Inferences:
1. The Middle Ages were like any other time; the rich thought only of their own welfare.
②. In the Middle Ages, the general population led a hard and hungry life.

Exercise 4

Directions: Read the supporting sentences. Then, in the accompanying blanks write out the implied main idea.

Example: *Supporting Sentences*

1. In what has become a famous experiment, children watched an adult attack a large rubber doll.
2. The adult sat on the doll, punched, kicked, and hit it with a hammer.
3. Later the children were frustrated by having their favorite toys taken away.
4. Allowed to play with their own rubber doll they behaved like the adult they had observed; they punched, hit, and kicked the doll.

Inference: *There is evidence that children readily mimic the*

aggressive behavior of adults.

Explanation: The supporting sentences describe children who engaged in aggressive behavior after seeing adults be aggressive. The logical inference is that children *learn* aggressive behavior.

1.   *Supporting Sentences*

a. Until he was fifteen, the famed psychologist Jean Piaget *remembered* that his nurse had fought off an attempt to kidnap him when he was only two.
b. But many years after the supposed kidnapping had taken

half-serious article debating an important question is published: did Holmes go to Cambridge or to Oxford?

The main idea statement in this paragraph claims that some people take the character of Sherlock Holmes seriously. The first supporting sentence follows up this idea with a specific illustration of how people believe in Holmes's existence. To indicate that the opening train of thought will continue, the author begins sentence 3 with the transitional phrase *in addition.*

In the next example, however, the transitions have a different function. They help readers identify the individual stages in a sequence or chain of events.

Creative thinking usually involves five stages. *In the first stage* the problem is defined. *In the second stage* creative thinkers saturate themselves with as much information as they can find. *Then* comes the incubation* stage. *At this point* problem solving moves to an unconscious level and the mind ponders different possible, or even impossible, solutions. The incubation stage is followed by illumination, a period of sudden understanding or insight. *Finally* there is the verification stage when solutions or answers are critically evaluated.

The author uses transitions here to help readers understand each step that occurs in creative thinking.

Transitions are important clues to an author's train of thought. They help you make connections between statements. That way you don't end up wondering why one sentence follows another. **To understand and re-create an author's intended message, pay close attention to transitions and the signals they convey.**

Transition	Function
moreover, likewise, too, furthermore, again, also, similarly, in addition, in the same vein, by the same token, then too, in fact	These transitions indicate that the writer will continue to develop an idea already introduced.
but, and yet, nevertheless, still, on the other hand, on the contrary, although, though, however, in spite of that fact, unlike, granted that, to be sure, instead, in reality, in truth	These transitions usually indicate that the writer is modifying or reversing the train of thought previously introduced.

---

* incubation: maintaining something in a favorable environmental condition for development.

Transition	Function
in support of, for example, first, first of all, as an example, for instance, to illustrate	These transitions usually indicate that the author is going to give specific reasons or illustrations to support an idea already introduced.
thus, therefore, as a result, consequently, ultimately, then, for this reason, hence, in response	These transitions usually indicate that the author is going to describe results or consequences.
in summary, in brief, in short, on the whole, to sum up, finally, in conclusion, ultimately	These transitions usually indicate that the author is drawing the paragraph or essay to a close and is going to summarize briefly what has already been said.
again, as I have said, as has already been mentioned, as I have noted, to reiterate*, in other words, in effect, in fact, in short, indeed, even	These transitions usually indicate that the author wants to repeat or emphasize a point already made.
first, second, third, at this point, then, finally, afterward, during, at this stage, next, following, earlier, as soon as, at this time, later on, eventually, at that time, at present, by the time, since then	These transitions help separate ideas or describe a sequence of events.

Exercise 5

Directions: Use the transitions on the following list to fill in the blanks and clarify the relationship between sentences. *Note:* As the preceding chart shows, several different transitions can signal the same relationship. If you think the blank could be filled by more than one transition on the list, write down both possibilities.

still	as a result	however
for example	for instance	nevertheless
consequently	as we have said	moreover

---

* reiterate: repeat.

Example: There was a time when no one aspiring to political office would admit to being a homosexual. <u>*Nevertheless, However*</u>, there are signs that this attitude is changing. Today, <u>*for instance, for example*</u>, there are approximately fifty openly gay elected officials across the country.

Explanation: In the first blank, we need a transition that reverses the opening train of thought because the author wants to show how the original attitude toward homosexuals in public office has changed. The second blank requires a transition that signals illustration because in this sentence the author offers a specific example of her claim. Now it's your turn to fill in the blanks with the appropriate transition.

1. Dr. Jack Krevorkian has publicly admitted to giving assistance to people who have committed suicide. <u>As a result, Consequently</u>, he has been called a saint by some, a murderer by others.

2. The earthquake in Guatemala reduced hundreds of buildings to rubble. <u>Consequently, As a result</u>, millions of dollars were needed for reconstruction.

3. George Washington was much admired as a soldier. In his private life, <u>however</u>, it has been claimed that he was proud and demanding.

4. Thomas Jefferson was a great statesman. <u>Moreover</u>, he was a talented architect and inventor.

5. Amnesty International is a worldwide organization dedicated to helping men and women who have been unjustly imprisoned. <u>For example, For instance</u>, the organization regularly publishes the names and addresses of political prisoners and asks that letters requesting the prisoners' release be addressed to the proper authorities.

6. <u>As we have said</u> in the preceding paragraphs, Ralph Ellison's *Invisible Man* is a work of genius, and time will not decrease its importance.

7. When Rachel Carson first wrote in *Silent Spring* that human beings were destroying the environment, she was laughed at. Time, <u>nevertheless, however</u>, has proved her right.

8. At one time, some federal officials treated the Indian reservations as if they were federal colonies subject to federal rule rather than self government. <u>Consequently, As a result</u>, Congress had to pass the Indian Self-Determination Act of 1975.

9. AIDS cannot be spread by casual contact. <u>Still, Nevertheless</u>, some people shun those who carry the virus.

10. He had been continuously abused as a child. <u>Consequently, As a result</u>, he grew up to be a bitter and violence-prone adult.

11. In general, early American architecture was developed by men who had little formal training in architecture. Samuel McIntire,

    for example, for instance
    _____, one of the earliest and finest architects, was a woodcarver, and Thomas Jefferson, the designer of Monticello, was educated as a lawyer.

Exercise 6

Directions: Circle the transitions in the following paragraphs. Then explain the function of each transition.

Example: In 1986 journalist Betty Rollin published *Last Wish,* an account of her decision to help her mother, Ida Rollin, commit suicide. In 1981 Ida Rollin fell victim, at the age of seventy-four, to ovarian cancer. But after an operation and a brutal round of chemotherapy treatments, she appeared to have beaten the disease. (Unfortunately, however) the cancer returned. This time the tumor was inoperable, and Ida was too weak for chemotherapy. Because the tumor was growing and she was in terrible pain, Ida Rollin decided to commit suicide. Her daughter agreed to help her. In October of 1983, Ida swallowed the pills her daughter had gotten for her and died in her sleep. (Today) Betty Rollin openly mourns her mother. (Still) she has no regrets about her actions. For her, death was her mother's "last wish."[4]

"But" reverses the sad note of the previous sentence.

"Unfortunately" and "however" reverse the more hopeful note of the previous sentences.

"Today" helps the reader understand the movement in time.

"Still" helps modify the point made in the previous sentence.

1. When robotics, the science of building robots, first emerged in the 1950s, it was thought that robots could do just about anything. (In

---

4. Karen S. Schneider and Sue Carswell, "Love and Death" (*People,* January 20, 1992), p. 58.

(fact) many factory workers were nervous about losing their jobs to robots, who couldn't ask for more money and who never went out on strike. But it hasn't been that easy to develop the sophisticated robots needed to perform assembly line tasks. Those that have been designed are expensive and prone to breakdowns. (In) (addition) most robots are still far from seeing or hearing like humans. The best they can do is detect general shapes and forms while their sensors respond only to the smell of smoke. (At present) (at least) plans for using robots to revolutionize industry will have to be scaled back.

(1) *In fact* suggests the sentence will further emphasize a point already made.

(2) *But* signals a reversal or change in the previous train of thought.

(3) *In addition* signals a line of thought similar to the previous one.

(4) *At present at least* helps the reader follow the sequence in time created by the author.

2. Movie stars were never more adored or more imitated than they were in the thirties and forties. When a beautiful platinum-blonde woman named Jean Harlow became a star, women all over the country dyed their hair platinum blonde in imitation of their heroine. (By the time the forties rolled around), women were no longer sporting platinum hair; they were wearing a peek-a-boo hair style just like the one Veronica Lake had worn in the film *The Glass Key*. (And women were not the only ones who imitated their favorite stars.) Sales of T-shirts dropped when a barechested Clark Gable appeared in the 1934 film *It Happened One Night*. Men (even) began lighting their cigarettes differently after seeing Paul Henreid in a film called *Now Voyager*. It was considered the height of sophistication for a man to put two cigarettes into his mouth, light them both, and hand one to the woman he was with, all the while looking deeply into her eyes.

(1) *By the time the forties rolled around* helps the reader keep track of the author's time sequence.

(2) *And women were not the only ones who imitated their favorite*

stars signals that the previous thought will be modified.

(3) *Even* suggests that the following sentence will emphasize a

point already made.

3. In order to exercise the freedom of the press guaranteed by the First Amendment, the media must first acquire information to print or broadcast. (In response to this need) the media have claimed that the First Amendment guarantees them a special right of access to information—particularly information possessed by the government. The courts have not agreed. (For example) in the 1972 case of *Branzburg* v. *Hayes*, the Supreme Court states: "It has generally been held that the First Amendment does not guarantee the press a constitutional right of special access to any information not available to the public generally." Without guaranteed *rights*, access to information or events becomes a constant struggle. Political actors try to limit what the media know, while the media constantly try to acquire information that the government doesn't want them to have. (However) attempts to deny media access totally are rare. When the Reagan administration launched its invasion of Grenada in 1983, the government restricted the flow of information by denying the media access to the island. The action raised a storm of protest, and reporters were soon on the scene. Because the politicians who run the government depend on the media to communicate their side of political conflicts, they must avoid alienating* the media too much. (Adapted from Aldrich, *American Government*, p. 311.)

(1) *In response to this need* indicates that what follows is an

effect of events previously described.

(2) *For example* signals a specific illustration of what has already

been said.

(3) *However* indicates a reversal in the previous thought.

---

* alienate: to make hostile.

4. In August of 1986, thirteen-year-old Deanna Young attended a deputy sheriff's lecture given at her church. That lecture, on the effects of drugs, had far-reaching consequences for both her and her family. (Following the lecture) Deanna took a bag containing marijuana, cocaine, and tranquilizers to the local police station. She claimed that her parents had ignored her pleas to stop using drugs, and she had, (therefore,) decided to take a more drastic approach. (As a result,) the girl's mother and father were arrested and charged with illegal possession of drugs. Deanna herself was temporarily placed in a juvenile home.

    (1) *Following the lecture* helps the reader follow the

    sequence of events.

    (2) *Therefore* signals a cause and effect relationship.

    (3) *As a result* signals that what follows is the

    effect of a cause described in the previous sentence.

5. For centuries the Mexican-American family has withstood political and economic hardships in Mexico and in the United States; it has been resilient* enough to survive and to grow. (For example,) at the end of the war with Mexico in 1848, there were only about 74,000 Mexicans in Texas, New Mexico, Arizona, and California combined. (Today) California alone has a population of about 5 million Mexican-Americans and Mexicans. The Mexican-origin population in this nation approached 9 million in 1980. (Since then,) this has been the fastest-growing ethnic group in America. (Kephart and Jedlicka, *The Family, Society and the Individual*, p. 119.)

    (1) *For example* signals an illustration of the previous

    statement.

    (2) *Today* helps the reader follow the sequence of time.

    (3) *Since then* also helps the reader see the time

    relationships.

---

* resilient: strong, capable of recovering quickly from disease or illness.

DIGGING DEEPER

If someone you loved who was terminally ill and suffering asked for your help to commit suicide, how would you respond and why?

WRITING SUGGESTION

Write a paragraph explaining why you would or would not have behaved like Deanna Young if you had been placed in the same situation.

Major and Minor Supporting Sentences

Until now we've talked generally about supporting sentences. However, it's time to be more specific. You need to know that there are two kinds of supporting sentences. **Major supporting sentences** provide information that clarifies and reinforces the main idea. **Minor supporting sentences** flesh out or further explain what's already been said in the major supporting sentences.

For an illustration look again at the following paragraph about unemployment. The major supporting sentences appear in bold-face, the minor ones in italics.

[1] Prolonged unemployment can create serious psychological problems that, in the long run, actually contribute to continued joblessness. [2] **In a society that stresses the relationship between productive work and personal value, it is easy enough to equate long-term unemployment with personal worthlessness.** [3] **That is, in fact, precisely what many unemployed men and women begin to do.** [4] *Out of a job for a year or more, they begin to see themselves as worthless human beings, without any value to their society.* [5] **In what amounts to a vicious cycle, their sense of personal worthlessness further diminishes their chances of**

gaining employment. [6] *Sometimes they stop looking for work altogether, sure in their despair that no one would hire them.* [7] *Or else they go to interviews, but they present themselves in such a defeated and hopeless way that the interviewer cannot help but be unimpressed and reject their application.*

Within this paragraph, sentences 2, 3, and 5 are major supporting sentences. They introduce new information designed to explain and develop the main idea statement. Sentences 4, 6, and 7 are all minor supporting sentences. They fill out, or modify, points already made in the major supporting sentences.

Not all paragraphs contain both kinds of supporting sentences. The following paragraph, for example, contains only major supporting sentences.

Many people believe that the famous Loch Ness monster really exists. They maintain that the monster must exist because several witnesses claim to have seen it emerge from the lake in which it allegedly lives. Their position has been further strengthened by the appearance of what seem to be actual photographs of the creature.

The main idea statement tells us that some people really do believe in the Loch Ness monster. The supporting sentences supply reasons why some people believe in the monster's existence: (1) there are witnesses, and (2) there are photographs.

Both reasons help explain why men and women living in the twentieth century could believe in the Loch Ness monster. They are of equal importance; that is, both are necessary to make the main idea statement more convincing. Diagrammed, the paragraph would look like this:

Diagram 1

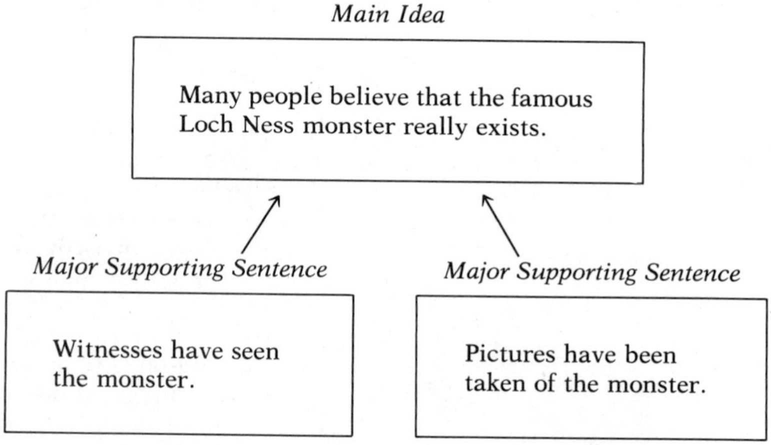

Main Idea

> Many people believe that the famous Loch Ness monster really exists.

Major Supporting Sentence

> Witnesses have seen the monster.

Major Supporting Sentence

> Pictures have been taken of the monster.

Now let's expand the paragraph to include minor supporting sentences.

Many people believe that the famous Loch Ness monster really exists. They maintain that the monster must exist because several witnesses claim to have seen it emerge from the lake in which it allegedly lives. *Believers in the monster's existence emphasize that eyewitness reports are strikingly similar in their description of the monster.* Their position has been further strengthened by the appearance of what seem to be actual photographs of the creature. *The photographs show a large creature that resembles an ancient sea serpent.*

The italicized sentences in the sample paragraph are minor supporting sentences. They expand what was said in the major supporting sentences. Diagram 2 below illustrates their relationship.

Diagram 2

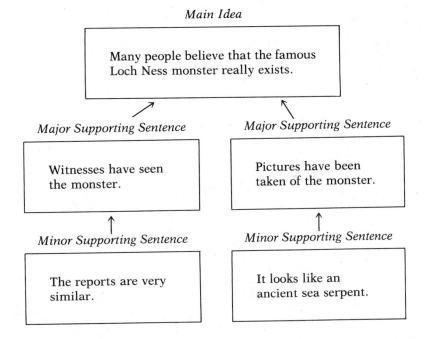

Main Idea

Many people believe that the famous Loch Ness monster really exists.

Major Supporting Sentence

Witnesses have seen the monster.

Major Supporting Sentence

Pictures have been taken of the monster.

Minor Supporting Sentence

The reports are very similar.

Minor Supporting Sentence

It looks like an ancient sea serpent.

Before we introduce the exercises, here is one more illustration and diagram:

From the perspective of some people, the Bermuda Triangle is an area to be avoided. On July 3, 1947, a United States C-54 Superfortress bomber vanished while flying near the region known as the Bermuda Triangle. The plane was never heard from again. On January 30, 1948, a British airliner, the *Star*

MAJOR AND MINOR SUPPORTING SENTENCES   **171**

Tiger, disappeared while flying over the same region. Nothing was ever heard from either crew or passengers. In 1968, the *Scorpion*, a nuclear submarine, disappeared, and months went by without a trace of it. After a lengthy search, it was found in the waters located on the fringes of the Triangle. There was no trace of the one hundred men who had been on board.

Diagram 3

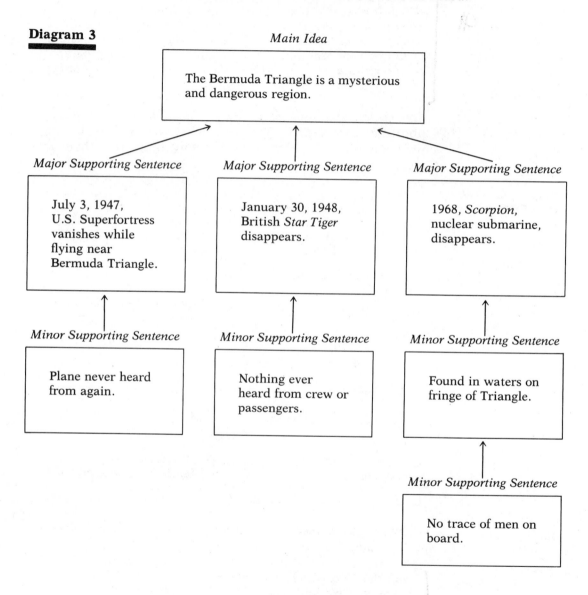

Main Idea

The Bermuda Triangle is a mysterious and dangerous region.

Major Supporting Sentence

July 3, 1947, U.S. Superfortress vanishes while flying near Bermuda Triangle.

Major Supporting Sentence

January 30, 1948, British *Star Tiger* disappears.

Major Supporting Sentence

1968, *Scorpion*, nuclear submarine, disappears.

Minor Supporting Sentence

Plane never heard from again.

Minor Supporting Sentence

Nothing ever heard from crew or passengers.

Minor Supporting Sentence

Found in waters on fringe of Triangle.

Minor Supporting Sentence

No trace of men on board.

The first sentence of this paragraph is the main idea statement. The major supporting sentences then answer a question readers might raise: why should the Bermuda Triangle be avoided? Because major supporting sentences can contain only a limited amount of information, the author has followed each one with a minor supporting sentence. The minor supporting sentences fill out, or modify, what was said in previous sentences. Diagrammed to show the relationship between major and minor supporting sentences, the paragraph looks like Diagram 3.

As the diagram shows, minor supporting sentences can also modify other minor supporting sentences. But the relationship between the sentences remains the same: one minor sentence follows another in order to develop further a point already made.

The following exercise will give you practice seeing the relationship between major and minor supporting sentences.

Exercise 7

Directions: Read the following paragraphs and then fill in the boxes that follow. You do not have to use complete sentences from the paragraphs; you can rephrase or shorten them.

Note: Not every paragraph will contain exactly the same number of major and minor supporting sentences. For example, one paragraph may have one major supporting sentence and two minor ones; another might have two major supporting sentences and no minor ones. Therefore you will not always be able to fill in all the boxes in the diagram.

Example: It is impossible that large prehistoric creatures could have remained on land to this day without being discovered. On the other hand, there is a possibility that huge creatures from the dinosaur age still exist beneath the sea. After all, as fossil remains show, dinosaurs had relatives who lived in the sea. They were huge, had long necks and snake-like heads. Those who maintain that monsters from the time of the dinosaurs still live point out that accounts of strange creatures seen in the sea fit the description of ancient sea monsters. According to reports, the modern-day sea creatures have long necks and snake-like heads.[5]

See Diagram 4 on next page.

Explanation: The main idea statement makes the claim that huge creatures from the dinosaur age might still exist beneath the sea. Two major supporting sentences help make that statement more convincing. Each major supporting sentence is followed by a minor one that adds some more information.

---

5. DeWitt Miller, *Impossible, Yet It Happened* (New York: Ace Books, 1947), p. 30.

Diagram 4

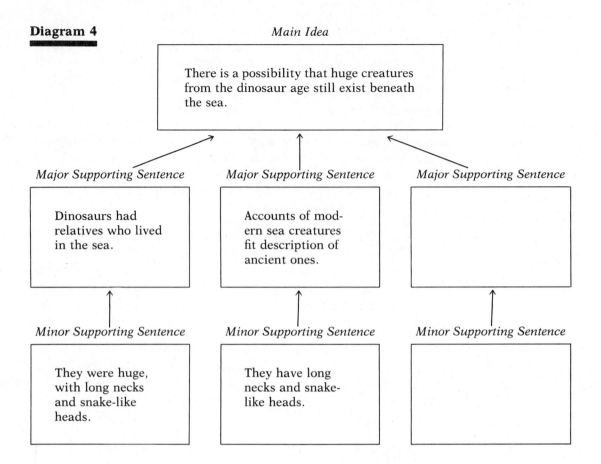

Main Idea

There is a possibility that huge creatures from the dinosaur age still exist beneath the sea.

Major Supporting Sentence

Dinosaurs had relatives who lived in the sea.

Major Supporting Sentence

Accounts of modern sea creatures fit description of ancient ones.

Major Supporting Sentence

Minor Supporting Sentence

They were huge, with long necks and snake-like heads.

Minor Supporting Sentence

They have long necks and snake-like heads.

Minor Supporting Sentence

Complete the rest of the exercise by filling in the diagram that accompanies each paragraph.

1. The word *Poltergeist* is German, and it means "noisy ghost." To many people the word is a joke, but to others poltergeists are no laughing matter. They exist! In 1935 Dr. Hereward Carrington collected 318 cases of poltergeist phenomena to prove their existence.[6] His cases included reports of nails, pieces of tile, stones, and walnuts being mysteriously thrown into the air.

---

6. Miller, *Impossible, Yet It Happened*, p. 57.

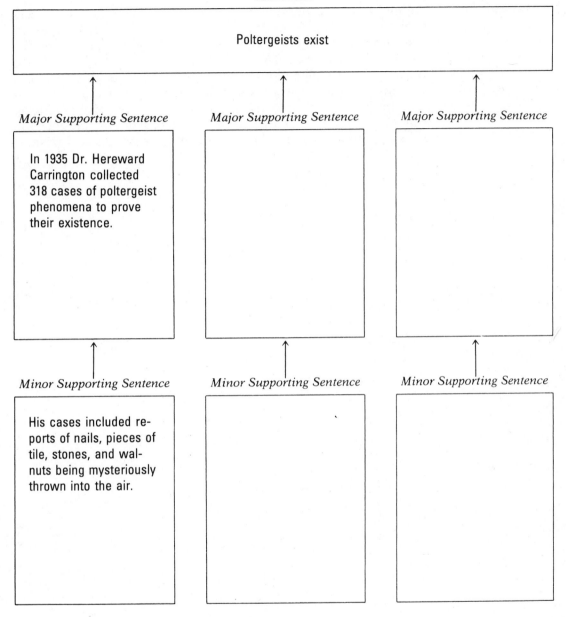

Main Idea

Poltergeists exist

Major Supporting Sentence

In 1935 Dr. Hereward Carrington collected 318 cases of poltergeist phenomena to prove their existence.

Major Supporting Sentence

Major Supporting Sentence

Minor Supporting Sentence

His cases included reports of nails, pieces of tile, stones, and walnuts being mysteriously thrown into the air.

Minor Supporting Sentence

Minor Supporting Sentence

2. In the nineteenth century, Margaret and Kate Fox made a fortune duping a gullible public, who fervidly* believed that the sisters could communicate with the dead. Traveling throughout America and Europe, the sisters would ask questions of the spirits, and the spirits would answer. They would rap once for "no" and three times for "yes."[7] The public was impressed and willingly paid to see the Fox sisters at work. What the public did not know was that the raps came from the sisters, not the spirits. Margaret and Kate could crack the joints of their toes and ankles at will, and they did so every time they needed an answer from their spiritual friends.

---

7. Carl Sagan, *Broca's Brain* (New York: Ballantine Books, 1979), p. 57.
* fervidly: with great emotion or excitement.

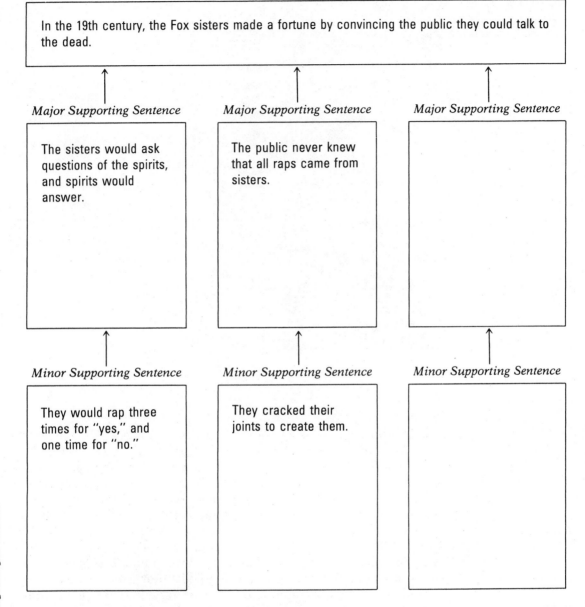

Main Idea

In the 19th century, the Fox sisters made a fortune by convincing the public they could talk to the dead.

Major Supporting Sentence

The sisters would ask questions of the spirits, and spirits would answer.

Major Supporting Sentence

The public never knew that all raps came from sisters.

Major Supporting Sentence

Minor Supporting Sentence

They would rap three times for "yes," and one time for "no."

Minor Supporting Sentence

They cracked their joints to create them.

Minor Supporting Sentence

Some people believe that Big Foot is alive and hiding in the Cascade Mountains.

3. The creature called Sasquatch or Big Foot belongs to the ancient legends of Indian tribes living on the Northwest coast. However, some people claim that Sasquatch is not legend but a living, breathing creature roaming the thick forests of the Cascade mountains. In 1957 a Canadian lumberjack claimed he had been kidnapped by a tribe of huge ape-like creatures resembling Sasquatch. According to his story, he was held captive for a week but escaped. Once this story surfaced, many people claimed to have seen Big Foot. There were more than three hundred separate reports of sightings.[8] Currently the Big Foot Information Center examines all claims by sending out a team of volunteers. Although most turn out to be hoaxes, the center lists ninety-four credible sightings.[9]

---

8. *The World Almanac Book of the Strange.* (New York: Signet, 1977), p. 306.
9. *Almanac,* p. 306.

Main Idea

Some people still believe that Sasquatch or "Big Foot" is alive and living in the Cascade Mountains.

Major Supporting Sentence

In 1957 a lumberjack claimed to have been kidnapped by a tribe of huge creatures.

Major Supporting Sentence

Others made similar claims.

Major Supporting Sentence

The Big Foot Information Center examines all claims.

Minor Supporting Sentence

The lumberjack claimed to have been held captive until he escaped.

Minor Supporting Sentence

There were more than 300 separate reports.

Minor Supporting Sentence

The center lists 94 credible sightings.

4. Although Harry Houdini, the world-famous magician, could have benefited from the public's belief in the supernatural, he spent much of his time trying to expose the fraud and trickery behind supposed supernatural happenings. Over the years, Houdini collected a huge file of all the frauds and hoaxes he had managed to expose. On his death, the file was turned over to the famous magician Joseph Dunninger, who was to make sure the evidence would not be lost.[10] Houdini also spent much time and energy trying to convince Arthur Conan Doyle, creator of Sherlock Holmes, that most of the miracles Doyle believed in were simply tricks. Unfortunately, Doyle remained unconvinced and was made a fool of on at least one well-known occasion: he assumed that pictures of fairies perched upon leaves were actually unretouched photographs.

---

10. Miller, *Impossible, Yet It Happened*, p. 87.

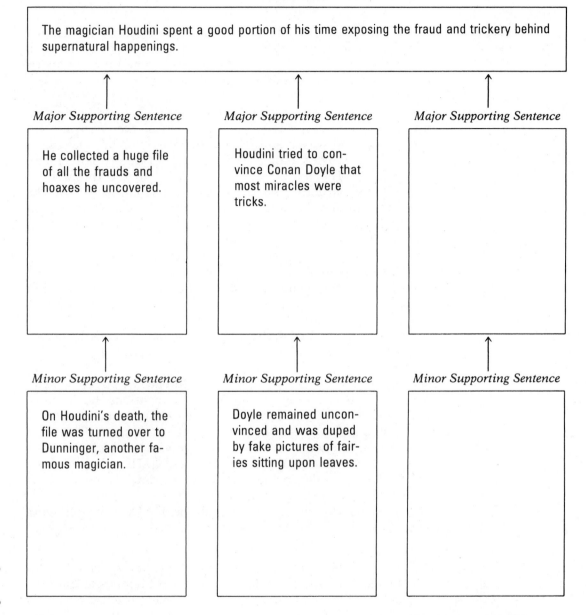

Main Idea

The magician Houdini spent a good portion of his time exposing the fraud and trickery behind supernatural happenings.

Major Supporting Sentence

He collected a huge file of all the frauds and hoaxes he uncovered.

Major Supporting Sentence

Houdini tried to convince Conan Doyle that most miracles were tricks.

Major Supporting Sentence

Minor Supporting Sentence

On Houdini's death, the file was turned over to Dunninger, another famous magician.

Minor Supporting Sentence

Doyle remained unconvinced and was duped by fake pictures of fairies sitting upon leaves.

Minor Supporting Sentence

Exercise 8

Directions: All the paragraphs in this exercise lack some minor supporting sentences. Read each one. Then look at the sentences below each paragraph, and write the letter of the appropriate minor supporting sentence on each blank line in the paragraph.

Example: [1] The human ear is a complicated structure that can be divided into three main parts. [2] First of all, there is the outer ear. [3] It collects sound waves and directs them to the auditory canal. [4] __c__ [5] The middle ear contains three small bones. [6] __a__ [7] The middle ear is connected to the throat by a small tubelike structure known as the Eustachian tube. [8] The inner ear contains the actual hearing apparatus, a small, shell-like organ filled with fluid and nerve endings. [9] It is called the cochlea. [10] __b__

    a. These are called the hammer, anvil, and stirrup.
    b. When the nerve endings receive vibrations from the fluid in the cochlea, they transmit them directly to the hearing portion of the brain.
    c. At the very end of that canal is a membrane called the eardrum, or tympanum.

Explanation: Choosing the correct minor supporting sentence will be easy if you use context clues. Sentence 3, for example, mentions the auditory canal. Therefore we put sentence *c*, which refers to the canal, into the first blank. Sentence 5 mentions three small bones. Therefore the next sentence logically should be sentence *a*, which identifies those bones. Sentence 9 introduces the cochlea. Therefore sentence *b*, which mentions the cochlea, is the appropriate choice to follow it as a minor supporting sentence.

    Complete the exercise by filling in all the blanks in the following paragraphs.

1. [1] In October 1957 the Russians leaped into the space age with the launching of a satellite that became world famous as *Sputnik*. [2] Awed by this breakthrough, America made intense efforts to improve its satellite technology. [3] Since that time, the United States has rivaled Russia by launching its own share of satellites. [4] Hundreds of American satellites have been successfully propelled into the air. [5] As our technology improves, scientists expect that many more satellites will be used. [6] __b__ [7] The military, which already makes extensive use of satellites, will also continue to do so in the future. [8] __c__ [9] Although they pos-

sess no satellites of their own, Third World countries have already laid claim to precious space. [10] __a__

a. If they gain the technology to launch satellites in the future, Third World governments do not want to discover that all usable orbits have been taken.
b. Certainly the use of satellites in global communication will increase.
c. Military satellites are essential to intelligence gathering.

2. [1] More than fifty years ago, John Steinbeck wrote a novel called *The Grapes of Wrath*. [2] In it, he depicted the sorrows and trials of the Joads, a family of migrant workers. [3] When Steinbeck wrote the book, there were no laws protecting migrant workers, and they were almost uniformly mistreated by their employers. [4] Public response to the book was strong, and reforms were undertaken. [5] Unfortunately, most of the reforms never took effect, and even today most migrant workers still live under terrible conditions. [6] Every year the Department of Labor receives numerous complaints about improper recruitment procedures and failure to pay proper wages. [7] __b__ [8] In addition, housing provided for migrant workers is often substandard. [9] __a__ [10] Meals are equally inadequate, and poor nutrition makes disease rampant.* [11] Owners of farms employing migrant workers are often absent, leaving them in the hands of crew leaders. [12] __c__

a. They are given little more than shacks, and overcrowding is the norm.
b. But the charges are hard to prove, and workers are often intimidated into dropping them.
c. Unfortunately, many crew leaders, paid according to the amount they harvest, abuse their authority.

3. [1] The Galápagos are volcanic islands located about six hundred miles from South America's Pacific coast. [2] With their barren landscape, the islands do not seem the ideal spot for a summer vacation. [3] Nevertheless, they have begun to attract growing numbers of tourists, and that increase in tourism has created a variety of problems. [4] Some tourists, planning a long stay, have brought their pets with them. [5] __b__ [6] In addition, many tourists have decided that the tortoises inhabiting the island make splendid souvenirs. [7] __a__ [8] Even the tourists who bring no

---

* rampant: widespread.

Many migrant workers are still forced to live and work under the worst conditions.

pets and steal no tortoises have still managed to injure the island's fragile ecology.* [9] They did not realize that killing a stray spider can actually harm the environmental balance. [10] __c__

   a. Hundreds of them have been captured and taken off the island.

   b. Unhappily, those pets have helped destroy vegetation needed to support the wild population.

   c. Spiders are needed in great numbers to keep numerous island pests under control.

4. [1] For years medical researchers have known that athletes who take steroids risk damaging their liver or kidneys. [2] But now it appears that taking steroids can hurt the mind as well as the body. [3] In one study of forty-one athletes, two Harvard researchers found that five of their subjects showed signs of psychosis. [4] __b__ [5] Nine others suffered from severe mood swings. [6] __a__ [7] Apparently, the mental side effects disappear once the steroids are eliminated. [8] __c__

---

* ecology: environmental balance.

a. Periods of violent elation* were followed by periods of deep depression.
b. They heard voices, had delusions of grandeur, and exhibited symptoms of paranoia.
c. But in a few cases the damage has already been done, and some steroid users have had to pay for crimes committed while under the drugs' influence.

5. [1] Progeria is a genetic disorder that strikes children. [2] Victims of the disease experience rapid aging. [3] __c__ [4] First mentioned at the turn of the century, progeria is extremely rare. [5] __a__ [6] Usually the disease goes undetected until just past infancy when children suddenly stop growing. [7] __b__ [8] Death usually occurs in the teens, often from a disease associated with aging like hardening of the arteries.

a. It occurs about one in eight million births.
b. They seldom reach a weight of more than fifty pounds.
c. For every one year, their bodies age ten.

DIGGING DEEPER

What do you think motivates athletes to continue taking steroids despite the dangers they pose? Would you take them if you were an athlete?

Taking Notes: Recording the Essential Elements

Your ability to see relationships between the general and specific sentences in a paragraph is central to taking good notes. When you can decide which sentences provide major support for the main idea and which ones provide minor support, you're capable of deciding what should be included in your notes and what can be left out.

---

* elation: feeling of well-being.

The bog people were so well preserved that workers thought they had uncovered a recent murder.

Look, for example, at the following paragraph:

The very name "bog people" sounds like the title of a horror movie. Despite that name, however, the bog people are not the main figures in a new film. The name "bog people" refers to corpses discovered in the Scandinavian bogs sometime at the end of the nineteenth century; the corpses were thousands of years old, yet perfectly preserved. The bodies had changed so little that workmen, upon finding a corpse, thought that a recent murder had been committed. According to research following the discovery of the corpses, the bog people were human sacrifices who had been offered up to an earth goddess. After they had been strangled or stabbed, their bodies had been deposited in the bogs; and the soil acids contained in the waters of the bogs had preserved them for thousands of years. Some specimens were so well preserved that it was possible to see the stubble of a beard on their faces. Initially the bog people were thought to be limited to Scandinavia, but archaeologists have also uncovered similar corpses in the swamps of South America.

Here the first sentence is an introductory sentence. The second sentence makes a transition and points to the real direction the paragraph will take. We do not reach the main idea statement until the third sentence, where we learn that chemicals in the Scandinavian bogs helped preserve corpses that were thousands of years old. The rest of the paragraph consists of major and minor supporting sentences that develop this point.

To take notes on this paragraph, we needn't record each and every sentence. As our analysis of the sample paragraph showed, not every sentence contains new or significant information. The introductory sentence, for example, is not developed throughout the paragraph, so there is no reason to include it in our notes.

Instead, we can **condense** or reduce the original text by recording information only from the six sentences that convey the **essential elements** of the paragraph: the main idea and supporting details. Here is an informal* outline which does precisely that:

Main Idea: "Bog people" refers to perfectly preserved corpses found in Scandinavia at the end of the 19th century.

Support: 1. Bodies have changed very little.
2. Bog people had been used in rituals of human sacrifice.
3. Soil acids in the bog waters preserved the bodies so well that beard stubble could still be seen.
4. Corpses similar to the bog people have been discovered in South America.

As you can see, the main idea statement has been **paraphrased** or reworded. Numbered and indented underneath are the four pieces of information offered in support of that main idea. *That indention is important.* It's a way of showing relationships between ideas and serves the same function as letters or numbers. In any format for note-taking, indention plays a crucial role.

Notice, too, that sentence 3 of our notes combines the information from two different sentences in the sample paragraph—one major, one minor. This is important. Do not assume that you have to record the contents of each sentence exactly as they are presented in the original paragraph. Whenever you can combine two sentences and still retain the sense of the paragraph, you should do so.

For the sake of clarity, you may also decide to separate information that was originally presented in one sentence. This, too, is a good organizational strategy, as long as you do not distort or change the author's original message.

In taking your own notes, you may decide to use fewer sentences and more phrases. That's fine. Just be sure to *abbreviate with care.* Do not abbreviate too much and leave yourself with notes that are meaningless unless you refer to the original text. Good notes should free you from having to check the author's original words.

---

* "informal" because it does not follow the established rules for outlining.

To illustrate how abbreviating too much can cause problems, here is a sample paragraph followed by some overly brief sample notes:

For centuries human beings complacently* considered themselves superior to their ancestors, the apes. Their reasoning was simple and straightforward. Humans could communicate with one another while the best the apes could do was produce mating calls or howls of pain. That position of superiority, however, was profoundly challenged in the 1970s by research at the Institute of Primate Studies in Norman, Oklahoma, where talented chimpanzees were taught to use the sign language of the deaf. The chimps could express their emotions and ask questions. Some even managed to invent words. Upon seeing two swans, for example, one bright chimp who didn't know the word *swan* promptly invented the phrase *water birds*. Unfortunately, despite the promising nature of the research at the institute, federal funds have not been forthcoming; and the research has been discontinued, except on a very small scale.

Main Idea: Chimps talk.

Support: questions
        words
 water birds
 Research continues.

Imagine trying to use these notes three or four weeks after you had read the paragraph. Wouldn't you be puzzled about the relationship between the terms *words* and *questions*? Could you be sure that they are both examples of the chimp's speech? Or would you think that *questions* refers to critical comments about the research? Particularly puzzling would be the role of the water birds.

The point is this: do not leave out crucial information and thereby lose clarity or completeness. For example, the notes above have condensed the last sentence of the paragraph to two words—"Research continues." Yet the point of that sentence is that research continues on a very small scale because funds have been greatly reduced. In this instance, the original meaning has been distorted.

Whatever form they take—sentences or phrases—your notes should identify the essential elements of the paragraph *and* show their relationship to one another, as in the following example.

Main Idea: In the 1970s, chimps at the Institute of Primate Studies in Norman, OK, learned to speak using sign language of the deaf.

---

*   complacently: in a self-satisfied manner.

Support: 1. Expressed emotions, asked questions
2. Invented words
—Seeing a swan, one chimp invented the name *water bird*.
3. Lack of federal funds has made continued research all but impossible, except on a very small scale.

Exercise 9

Directions: Read and take notes on each of the following paragraphs.

Example: The most widespread way in which Native Americans altered their environment was through fire. All across the continent, Indians regularly burned large tracts of land. Cabeza de Vaca, the Spanish explorer who crossed much of the Southeast during the 1530s, noted that the Ignaces Indians of Texas went about "with a firebrand, setting fire to the plains and timber so as to drive off the mosquitoes, and also to get lizards and similar things which they eat, to come out of the soil." Plains Indians used fires for communication: to report a herd of buffalo or warn of danger, as well as to drive off enemies in war. In California, where grass seeds were an important food, Indians burned fields annually to remove old stocks and increase the yield. In fact, in 1602 the Spanish explorer Vizcaino reported that near San Diego the Indians "made so many columns of smoke on the mainland that at night it looked like a procession and in the daytime the sky was overcast." (Adapted from Davidson and Lytle, *After the Fact*, p. 122.)

Topic: Native Americans' use of fire

Main Idea: Native Americans used fire in a variety of ways that changed the environment.

Support: 1. set fires to drive off mosquitoes and get lizards to eat.

2. fires to communicate; report herd of buffalo; warn of danger and drive off enemies of war.

3. burned fields to remove old stocks of grass and increase yield.

1. A. Philip Randolph (1889–1979), born in Crescent City, Florida, was to emerge as one of the most significant African-American leaders of the twentieth century. In a very long life, his participation in various civil rights activities spanned a period of over fifty years. The son of James Randolph, an African Methodist Episcopal Church preacher, A. Philip moved to New York and joined the Socialist party in 1911. He was fired from successive jobs as an elevator operator, maintenance man, and waiter for having tried to start unions with his fellow workers. Along with fellow socialist Chandler Owens, Randolph condemned the war in the *Messenger* and traversed the country making speeches in opposition to it. He declared in the *Messenger*, "Lynching, Jim Crow, segregation, and discrimination in the armed forces and out, disfranchisement of millions of black souls in the South—all these things make your cry of making the world safe for democracy a sham, a mockery, a rape of decency, and travesty* of common justice." (Adapted from Cashman, *African-Americans and the Quest for Civil Rights* 1900–1990, p. 28.)

Topic: The accomplishments of A. Philip Randolph

Main idea: A. Philip Randolph became one of the most important

African-American leaders in the 20th century.

Support: (1) Participation in civil rights movement spanned 50 yrs.

(2) Fired for trying to start unions

(3) Condemned W.W.I

— Speech in *Messenger* called fighting for freedom

abroad a mockery when there was lynching and

segregation at home.

*   travesty: a ridiculous imitation.

2. In both Christian and Jewish culture, the family has always occupied an exalted* station. It represents the chosen instrument of God for the reproduction of the species, the nurturing of the young, and the propagation† of moral principles. But as the French social historian Philippe Aries has noted, the family as a tightly knit group of parents and children is a development only of the last two hundred years. Prior to the eighteenth century, the community was more important in determining an individual's fate than was his family. In pre-Napoleonic Europe, about 75 percent of the populace lived in squalid hovels, which were shared with unrelated individuals and with farm animals. Another 15 percent lived and worked in the castles and manor houses of the rich and powerful, where any notion of the nuclear family (father, mother, and children in isolation) was impossible. In cities each household was a business—a bakery, hotel, livery stable, countinghouse—and apprentices, journeymen, servants, and retainers lived there along with assorted spouses and children. Much of life was inescapably public; privacy hardly existed at all. Even the word *home* referred to the town or region rather than to a particular dwelling. (Adapted from Jackson, *Crabgrass Frontier*, p. 47.)

Topic: The family throughout history

Main idea: The notion of family is a fairly recent historical development.

Support: (1) Pre-Napoleonic Europe 75% of populace lived in poor housing with people who were not related.

(2) Another 15% worked for the wealthy and any notion of the nuclear family was impossible.

(3) In cities households were businesses where workers lived together.

— privacy hardly existed

(4) Even word "home" referred to town or region, not a particular dwelling.

---

* exalted: high.

† propagation: making more widely known.

_____

_____

_____

_____

3. The pursuit of success breeds imitation, and it's not uncommon for employees to mimic their bosses' behavior. If he rocks back and forth in his chair, so do they. If she taps her finger while talking, so do they. According to psychologists, the tendency to such mimicry already begins in childhood, when we imitate our parents in the hopes of pleasing them and winning their favor. As adults, such mimicry is often unintentional. Without realizing it, we may unconsciously nod or doodle like our superiors. However, some employees use mimicry consciously as a way of winning approval and promotions. They assume their employers will view imitation as a form of flattery and bask in such obvious evidence of their power.

Topic: Employee mimicry
_____

Main Idea: In order to be successful, employees will sometimes mimic their
_____
bosses' behavior.
_____

Support: (1) Psychologists think the tendency begins in childhood when we
_____
    please parents by imitating them.
_____

(2) Some employees do the same thing as adults.
_____
    — assume employers will view imitation as flattery.
_____

_____

_____

_____

_____

_____

_____

_____

4. Just as we have been socialized* to believe that getting married is part of being an adult, we also tend to believe that having children is part of being married. We have been taught that children are a sign of the love between a woman and a man and that children make the couple happier. But some research suggests the opposite is true. Although having children may increase personal happiness (particularly the wife's), children tend to decrease positive marital interactions. In a study comparing couples who intentionally had children with those who intentionally were child-free, the latter reported having more "positive marital interactions" such as fun away from home, working together on a project, and having sexual relations (Feldman, 1981, p. 597). Spouses are happiest before children come and after they leave home. This negative effect of children on marriage is true for both spouses of all races, major religious preferences, educational levels, and employment status (Glenn & McLanahan, 1982). (Knox, _Choices in Relationships_, p. 299.)

Topic: Having children
_____

Main Idea: Some research suggests having children may not improve
_____

a marriage.
_____

Support: (1) In one study (Feldman 1981) child-free couples reported
_____

more fun together.
_____

— spouses were happiest before
_____

children came and after they left home
_____

(2) Another study (Glenn & McLanahan 1982) found the effect
_____

of children on marriage true for groups of all races, religions,
_____

professions, and educational levels.
_____

* socialize: to teach the particular values and attitudes of a culture.

_____

_____

_____

_____

_____

5. It remained for Robert Koch, a German scientist, to prove that a human disease was caused by bacteria. Koch found rod-shaped bacteria in large numbers in the blood of animals suffering from a disease called **anthrax** [ann'-thrax], which also attacks humans. These bacteria had been seen before. But no one could prove that they were the cause of the infection. Most scientists of the time believed that they were in the blood merely by accident. Koch grew these bacteria outside the body of the animal in pure unmixed form. He watched them grow under his microscope. Then he injected these bacteria into mice. The mice died of anthrax, and in their blood were great numbers of the same bacteria. The bacteria could be grown outside the body of the mouse once again, and again they could cause anthrax. Thus Koch proved that bacteria were the cause of anthrax. (Tanzer, *Biology and Human Progress*, p. 249.)

Topic: Bacteria
_____

Main Idea: German scientist Robert Koch was the first to prove

bacteria caused disease.
_____

Support: (1) Koch grew anthrax bacteria outside body of animal and

   injected them into mice.
_____

(2) Mice died of anthrax and blood was filled with bacteria.
_____

(3) Bacteria could grow outside body of mouse and again

   caused anthrax.
_____

   — Proof that bacteria caused anthrax.
_____

A Word on Paraphrasing

As we pointed out on page 187, our notes paraphrased the original material. We took the author's words and translated them into our own. Because **paraphrasing is an excellent way of checking comprehension,** you should paraphrase whenever you read or take notes. If you can translate an author's words into your own, then you have certainly understood the meaning of those words.

Paraphrasing also ensures remembering. As you mentally search for words to replace the author's, you are rethinking what you've read. During that period of review, the new information is being transferred to your **long-term memory** where information is stored over time, perhaps forever.

When you paraphrase, you can change the author's words, sentence length, and even word order. However, you cannot distort the original meaning. Compare these examples:

Original: The name "bog people" refers to corpses discovered in the Scandinavian bogs at the end of the nineteenth century; the corpses were thousands of years old, but perfectly preserved.

Accurate paraphrase: In the late nineteenth century, perfectly preserved corpses dating back thousands of years were discovered in the Scandinavian bogs. The corpses came to be called "bog people."

As you can see, the paraphrased version changes words, word order, and sentence length. But it does not alter the original meaning. Unfortunately, the same is *not* true of the next paraphrase.

Inaccurate paraphrase: In the nineteenth century, archaeologists discovered that chemicals had preserved the corpses of men thousands of years old.

In this example the original meaning has been distorted. The time of the discovery has become more vague, "the nineteenth century" instead of "late" nineteenth century. "Archaeologists" supposedly discovered the corpses although the original paragraph does not say that. This is clearly the reader's unsupported inference as is the notion that the corpses were all men.

It's worth mentioning here that paraphrasing someone else's words does not mean that you do not have to cite or mention the source of those words. If you are describing a theory or interpretation unique to a particular person, you need to make it clear that the theory or interpretation belongs to someone else, not to you.

Four Pointers for Good Notes

1. Reduce the original text to its essential elements: main idea and supporting details.
2. Show relationships through indention and symbols like dashes, letters, and numbers.
3. Reorder and abbreviate information carefully so that you do not distort meaning or eliminate crucial information.
4. Paraphrase rather than copy.

Exercise 10

Directions: Choose the most accurate paraphrase for each original passage.

Example: *Original text:*
Some years ago, a Canadian neurosurgeon named Penfield made a surprising discovery. During an operation he found that memories of previous events were recalled when the brain of a patient was accidentally stimulated by a mild electrical current.

Paraphrase: ⓐ. During an operation performed several years ago, a neurosurgeon named Penfield made an unexpected discovery. When, by chance, he stimulated the brain of a patient with a mild electric current, that patient would recall previous events in his life.

Paraphrase: b. Two years ago a Canadian surgeon experimented with one of his patients and discovered that electrical stimulation could cause the patient to remember events forgotten since childhood.

Explanation: Paraphrase *a* changes the words but not the meaning of the original passage. In contrast paraphrase *b* alters the original meaning in significant ways. "Some years ago" has become "Two years ago"—even though the original does not specify the amount of time passed. In addition, the surgeon's name has been omitted. Perhaps most important, it sounds as if Dr. Penfield had planned the experiments. Yet the original text indicates his discovery was unintentional. Finally, the paraphrased version claims the memories recalled were from childhood. But no such claim is made in the original.

1. The extent to which rates of physical diseases, such as coronary heart disease, can be controlled or reduced through such means as reducing serum cholesterol levels has not been conclusively established. (Carson et al. *Abnormal Psychology and Modern Life,* p. 257.)

    a. There is no evidence that reducing cholesterol will reduce the chances of coronary heart disease.
    (b). It has not been proven without a doubt that reducing serum cholesterol will eliminate or even diminish the risk of illnesses like coronary heart disease.

2. In 1845 and 1846 potatoes—the basic Irish food—rotted in the fields. From 1845 to 1849 death in the form of starvation, malnutrition, and typhus spread. In all 1 million died and about 1.5 million fled, two thirds of them to the United States. (Norton et al. *A People and a Nation,* p. 283.)

    (a). Between 1845 and 1846, Ireland's potato crop failed. Because potatoes were a nutritional staple, starvation, disease, and death were widespread forcing about 1.5 million people to flee, with two-thirds of that number coming to the United States.
    b. In the nineteenth century, Ireland's potato crop was destroyed and many people were forced to go hungry. When typhus began to increase the death toll, millions of people emigrated to the United States and found a safe haven.

Exercise 11

Directions: Underline the main idea statement. Then decide which sentence offers the most accurate paraphrase.

Example: *The Boomerang Effect* has been defined as a phenomenon in which attempts to change people's attitudes lead to the exact opposite: They become more convinced of their original point of view. No one knows for sure what causes the boomerang effect. Sometimes it occurs, sometimes it does not. But some psychologists believe it is likely to occur when strong emotional feelings are involved. Feeling emotionally attacked, the person or group addressed becomes defensive and stubbornly insists on doing the opposite. Parents who don't approve of a child's choice of friends would do well to remember the boomerang effect and not criticize those friends too harshly. If they do, the child may respond by liking them all the more. (Adapted from Goldberg, *The Babinski Reflex*, p. 36.)

a. According to the boomerang effect, you should never tell your children you do not like their friends.

(b). The boomerang effect occurs when we try to change someone's attitude and succeed only in making that person more committed to his or her original point of view.

Explanation: Sentence *a* distorts the original meaning of the main idea statement. It suggests that the boomerang effect applies solely to children. Sentence *b* more effectively sums up the general nature of this phenomenon.

Now it's your turn to choose the most accurate paraphrase.

1. Three days before Christmas in 1894, Captain Alfred Dreyfus, a Jewish officer in the French army, was found guilty of treason and sentenced to life imprisonment on Devil's Island. In 1906 Dreyfus was completely exonerated,* but in those twelve years before Dreyfus was proved innocent, every possible attempt was made to prove him guilty. Key officers in the military gave the newspapers material that supposedly proved Dreyfus's guilt. The newspapers, for their part, printed the stories without questioning their authenticity.† Evidence proving Dreyfus innocent was ignored, and attempts to open the case were blocked because an examination of the Dreyfus case was considered dangerous to the prestige of both the army and the government.

(a). Before Alfred Dreyfus was proved innocent, numerous groups insisted upon his guilt.

---

* exonerate: prove innocent.

† authenticity: trustworthiness.

    b. The Dreyfus case was a clear example of how vicious anti-Semitism can be.

2. The early Americans led hard lives that left little time for the pleasures of the table; at least that is the modern view. Certainly, Europeans who journeyed to America reinforced the idea that the American diet was both limited and tasteless. Journals, letters, and notes from Americans, however, belie this depressing picture of American cooking (or "cookery," as it was then called); on the contrary, Americans seem to have enjoyed a variety of delicious foods. Game, for example, was one of the staples of the American diet, since wild turkeys, passenger pigeons, and canvasback ducks were all plentiful. Food from the sea was also available; and oysters, terrapin, and turtles are mentioned in letters describing American fare. Most families raised vegetables; and broccoli, asparagus, and cauliflower were enjoyed in season.

    a. As usual, Europeans underestimated early American cooking.
    ⓑ. Contrary to traditional belief, early American cooking was both varied and delicious.

3. Robert Falcon Scott (1868–1912) dreamed of being the first man to explore the South Pole. But his dream was not fulfilled. He failed in his attempt, and the Norwegian explorer Roald Amundsen reached the South Pole before him. Scott and his party set out from Cape Evans, a site about nine hundred miles away from the pole, and although the ponies on which they were relying did not take well to the Antarctic conditions, the group thought they were ahead of Amundsen. They did not realize that the Norwegian was four hundred miles in front of them. As the ponies grew weaker and blizzards slowed their progress, Scott and his companions grew steadily more discouraged. Their depression increased when they found traces of Amundsen's party. When they finally reached the pole, they discovered that their fears had been well founded; Amundsen had camped at the pole and was already returning home. Scott's party had no other choice but to turn around and try to make its way back home; the return journey was a nightmare filled with cold weather and hunger. None of the men survived.

    ⓐ. Robert Falcon Scott failed in his dream of becoming the first man to explore the South Pole.
    b. Had Robert Falcon Scott been a better leader, his men might have survived.

When the notice ordering the Seminoles to leave their homeland was presented to Osceola, he speared it with a dagger.

4. In the nineteenth century, many runaway slaves sought refuge in Florida among the Seminole Indians. As a result, the U.S. government ordered the Seminoles to leave Florida. But the Indians refused. They were encouraged in their rebellion by Osceola, the fiery Indian leader who was determined to retain his tribe's autonomy* even if he had to die for it. When the notice of the government's plan arrived in Florida, Osceola speared it with a dagger, announcing, "There, this is the only treaty I will make with the whites!"[11] These were not empty words. When government troops arrived to capture and subdue Osceola, they were all slaughtered, and war began. For two years Osceola outwitted his pursuers. But in 1837 he was captured and placed in prison, where he died the following year. The war raged on. Convinced that their leader had been murdered, the Seminoles were determined to avenge him. By 1842, however, even the memory of Osceola was not enough to

---

11. Jean Craighead George, *The American Walk Book* (New York: E. P. Dutton, 1978), p. 118.

* autonomy: independence.

fuel what had become a bloody and losing battle. Defeated, the Seminoles were moved to Oklahoma.

    ⓐ. When the U.S. ordered the Seminole Indians to leave Florida, the Indian leader Osceola led their fight to stay.

    b. When Indian leader Osceola encouraged his people to fight the government, he was murdered.

DIGGING DEEPER

If you could advance your career by openly mimicking your boss's behavior, would you be willing to do it? Explain why or why not.

Working with Words

Here are seven more prefixes, suffixes, and roots you should know. Use them to figure out the meaning of the italicized words. Then add them to your vocabulary notebook for regular review.

1. pseudo	(Greek root)	false
2. homo	(Greek root)	same
3. psych	(Greek root)	spirit, life
4. crypt	(Greek root)	secret
5. onym	(Greek root)	name, word
6. log, logy	(Greek root)	word, study of
7. ambi	(Latin root)	both

1. Many men and women write mysteries under *pseudonyms* because they do not consider mystery stories to be completely respectable.

false names

2. The group was clearly *homogeneous;* every member came from the same age group and income bracket. Unfortunately, so much similarity produced a boring evening, and they left early.

similar, uniform

3. Physically he had survived the war, but it had severely damaged his *psyche*. He was troubled by nightmares and viewed the future with alarm.

mind, spirit
_____

4. It was hard to tell what she was thinking. Even her smile was *ambiguous*. She could have been happy or sad; I couldn't tell which, and the mystery made me curious.

having more than one meaning
_____

5. During World War II the Germans relied on a complicated code to send their *cryptic* messages. But with the help of the mathematician Alan Turing, the British were able to break the code and decipher those messages.

secret
_____

6. The test required him to give an *antonym* for every word on the list. Dutifully he did. When they said "hot," he said "cold"; when they said "friendly," he said "unfriendly." But he went blank when they said "death."

word opposite in meaning
_____

7. Despite public interest, astrology is not a science. It is a *pseudoscience:* the stars have no influence on our lives.

false science
_____

8. She was astonished at their request that she deliver the *eulogy* for her dead husband. She detested him and everyone knew it. Now they expected her to stand there and praise him?

public speech of praise given when someone dies
_____

9. The words *WAC* and *radar* are both *acronyms;* the word *WAC* comes from Women's Army Corps and *radar* comes from *r*adio *d*etecting *a*nd *r*anging.

words made up of initials from other words
_____

10. On the subject of the president's speech, she was hopelessly *ambivalent*. One moment she was convinced his plan was their only hope. The next she was equally convinced it was a blueprint for disaster.

having two contradictory feelings
_____

Stories Behind the Words

The following words do not have anything to do with mythological figures. They come from the names of people, places, and customs. Learn the meanings of the words and the stories that go with them.

1. *Bedlam.* The St. Mary of Bethlehem hospital in London was used to house the mentally ill. Everyone knew of the hospital, and stories about it were repeated again and again. The name of the hospital was often pronounced "Bedlam" or "Bethlem." Today when we use the word *bedlam*, we are talking about a place or situation that is filled with noise and confusion.

   Sample sentence: When the children were home from school, the house was *bedlam*.

   Definition: place filled with noise and confusion

2. *Martinet.* Jean Martinet was a seventeenth-century French general famous for the way he disciplined his army. Today when we say that someone is a *martinet,* we mean that he or she follows the rules to the letter and expects everyone else to do the same.

   Sample sentence: The new sergeant was a *martinet*.

   Definition: person who demands strict discipline

3. *Quixotic.* Don Quixote is a famous hero of an old Spanish novel that deals with his attempt to do the impossible. Today when we say that someone is *quixotic*, we mean that he or she is not very practical. He or she has a romantic view of life and pursues impossible goals.

   Sample sentence: His *quixotic* nature would not allow him to admit that he might fail.

<dl>
<dt>*Definition:*</dt>
<dd>romantic, impractical, unrealistic</dd>
</dl>

<dl>
<dt>*Other forms:*</dt>
<dd>quixotically, quixotical</dd>
</dl>

4. *Tawdry.* St. Audrey was a queen who died of a throat tumor. After her death, cheap lace neckties were sold in her honor at country fairs. The name of the necktie was shortened from St. Audrey's lace to *tawdry lace.* Today when we say that something is "tawdry," we mean that it looks cheap and gaudy.

<dl>
<dt>*Sample sentence:*</dt>
<dd>The *tawdry* wallpaper added to the ugliness of the apartment.</dd>
</dl>

<dl>
<dt>*Definition:*</dt>
<dd>cheap, vulgar, gaudy</dd>
</dl>

<dl>
<dt>*Other forms:*</dt>
<dd>tawdrier, tawdriest, tawdrily, tawdriness</dd>
</dl>

5. *Chauvinist.* Nicholas Chauvin was a legendary French soldier who was said to be extremely devoted to Napoleon and France. Today when we say that someone is a *chauvinist,* we mean that he or she is prejudiced in favor of his or her country or particular group.

<dl>
<dt>*Sample sentence:*</dt>
<dd>She is a *chauvinist;* for her, American policies are the only right ones.</dd>
</dl>

<dl>
<dt>*Definition:*</dt>
<dd>a person who believes that his or her country or group is better than any other</dd>
</dl>

<dl>
<dt>*Other forms:*</dt>
<dd>chauvinism, chauvinistic, chauvinistically</dd>
</dl>

Review Test: Chapter Five

Part A: Answer the following questions.

1. List the four pointers for taking good notes introduced in the chapter.

   1) Reduce the original text to its essential elements.

   2) Show relationships through symbols and indention.

   3) Reorder and abbreviate with care.

   4) Paraphrase rather than copy.

2. Read the following paragraph. Then identify, by number, the major and minor supporting sentences.

   [1] If the message a person receives does not conform to the clearly stated views of a closely knit *group* to which the person belongs, the receiver is likely to reject it. [2] In one study, several small groups were shown three unequal lines and asked to determine which one was the same length as a fourth line. [3] In each group, however, all the members except one had been coached by the researcher to give an incorrect answer. [4] One third of those who had not been coached changed their correct answer to the incorrect answer of the majority. [5] As we would expect, some groups have more influence on the way we receive and digest information than others. [6] They are called primary groups: family, peers, and specific peer groups. (Harris, *American Democracy*, p. 208.)

   Major supporting sentences: 2 5

   Minor supporting sentences: 3 4 6

3. Explain the difference between major and minor supporting sentences.

   Major supporting sentences introduce reasons, examples,

   studies, etc. that support or develop the main idea.

Minor supporting sentences further expand upon some point or

fact already introduced in the major supporting sentences.

---

4. Explain why paraphrasing is important.

Paraphrasing the author's words forces you to rethink what you

have read and helps store the information in long-term memory.

---

5. Which inference logically follows from the more specific statements supplied by the author?

In a 1980 poll conducted by CBS and the *New York Times,* Americans were questioned about a constitutional amendment concerning abortion. When interviewers asked if abortion should be "prohibited" by the Constitution 62 percent were opposed, 29 percent were in favor, and 9 percent undecided. However, when the question was reworded to ask if there should be an amendment "protecting" the life of an unborn child only 39 percent were opposed, while 50 percent were in favor.[12]

Inferences: a. Americans generally support the idea of a constitutional amendment forbidding abortion.
ⓑ. When polled about a constitutional amendment concerning abortion, people were influenced by the way the question was worded.

Read and take notes on the following paragraphs.

6. The most advanced Native American cultures appeared in Mexico and Central America. The Maya and Toltec peoples built vast cities, formed sophisticated government bureaucracies that dominated large populations, and developed an accurate calendar and a complex form of writing. Their cities were especially impressive.

---

12. Fred R. Harris, *America's Democracy.* (Glenview: Scott, Forsman, 1986), p. 216.

Some were as large as Paris or London, housing several hundred thousand inhabitants. When the Spanish conquerors first saw them, they compared these American cities to Venice, one of Italy's most stunning artistic and engineering achievements. Indeed, so spectacular were the temples and towers of one Mexican city that one explorer proclaimed it "the most beautiful . . . in the world." (Adapted from Divine et al. *America: Past and Present* I, pp. 5–6.)

Topic: Maya and Toltec peoples

Main idea: The Maya and Toltec peoples are examples

of the most advanced Native American cultures.

Support:
1. Built huge cities, formed sophisticated bureaucracies to rule

    large populations

2. Developed calendar and a complex form of writing

3. Built impressive cities

    a. Some as large as London or Paris

    b. Spanish conquerors compared them to Venice

7. It is not at all uncommon for new discoveries or inventions to be treated with skepticism or doubt. When, for example, two unknown young men, Wilbur and Orville Wright, announced that they had succeeded in building a flying machine, the public paid little attention. In 1903, the Wrights' flying machine stayed aloft for 59 seconds and travelled 852 feet. Nevertheless, response to the invention was lukewarm at best. In fact, the army, to whom the machine had been offered, initially showed little or no interest, and officials refused to see a test flight until 1908.[13] When that flight succeeded, the Wrights' spectacular achievement was finally recognized, and they were allowed to manufacture airplanes under their own patent. Oddly enough, however, the Wrights were never accorded the recognition in their own country that they received in Europe. Long after the brothers had achieved an international reputation, American papers still tended to play down their achievements.

Topic: The Wrights' flying machine

Main idea: Wilbur and Orville Wright's flying machine is a good example

of how new discoveries are often treated with skepticism.

Support: 1. 1903 machine stayed aloft for 59 seconds and travelled

852 feet.

— public response lukewarm

2. Army officials refused to see test flight until 1908.

a. achievement finally recognized

b. given patent to manufacture planes

3. Never fully accorded recognition in U.S. that they got in Europe.

_____

_____

_____

_____

_____

8. Entrants in the Little Miss of America beauty contest—girls between the ages of three and six—are not asked to pay a fee. But their parents do have to pay around three hundred dollars to have

13. George Canning, *100 Great Modern Lives.* (London: Souvenir Press, 1972) p. 317.

their child's photographs included in the pageant catalogue. They also have to pay for the singing and dancing lessons that will allow their child to participate in the talent section of the contest. But perhaps even more costly than the lessons are the extensive wardrobes of party dresses that the girls must have in order to participate in the contest and its related functions. Furthermore, traveling expenses for the children and those relatives who must accompany them can easily run into thousands of dollars.

Topic: Entrants in Little Miss of America

Main idea: To be an entrant in the Little Miss of America Pageant is a

costly experience.

Support:
1. Parents pay around three hundred dollars to have child's

    photograph in catalogue.

2. Pay for singing and dancing lessons

3. Extensive wardrobe

4. Traveling expenses can cost thousands.

9. What makes a happy and satisfied life is a hard question to answer. But according to current research, most of the conventional answers—fulfilling a long-held dream, finding the right spouse, being financially successful—are inaccurate. The key factor, for men at least, appears to be temperament. When Berkeley researchers followed a group of men through several decades, those

who were happy, cheerful teenagers were found, when tested again in middle and old age, to be satisfied with their jobs and with the overall course of their lives. On the other hand, those subjects who had been suspicious and unhappy as teenagers, were largely dissatisfied with the course their lives had taken.

Topic: A happy life

Main idea: Temperament appears to be the key factor in having a happy life.

Support: Berkeley researchers followed group of men through several decades.

a. Those happy as teenagers tended to be happy later in life.

b. Those suspicious and unhappy as teenagers were unhappy about direction their lives had taken.

10. Mircea Eliade, in his reports of initiation* experiences in dozens of cultures all over the world, mentions that initiation of boys begins with two events. The first is a clean break with the parents, after which the novice† goes to the forest, desert, or wilderness. The second is a wound that the older men give the boy, which could be scarring of the skin, a cut with a knife, a brushing with

---

* initiation: ceremony that admits one to a group.

† novice: beginner.

nettles, a tooth knocked out. But we mustn't leap to the assumption that the injuries are given sadistically.* Initiators of young men in most cultures make sure that the injuries they give do not lead to meaningless pain. (Adapted from Robert Bly, *Iron John*, p. 28.)

Topic: Initiation ceremonies
_____

Main idea: According to Mircea Eliade initiation ceremonies all over the
_____
world begin with two events.
_____

Support: 1. First there is a clean break with parents and boy goes off alone
_____
to woods or desert.
_____

2. Boy is wounded.
_____

a. Wounds are not sadistic.
_____

b. Injuries have a purpose.
_____

_____

_____

Part B: **Vocabulary Review**
Here is a list of words drawn from the chapter. Some actually appear in the chapter. Some have been derived from the prefixes and suffixes introduced on page 201. Your job is to match words and blanks.

In some cases you may have to change the endings of words to make them fit the context. If you need to, consult your dictionary to decide which ending to use. *Note:* You may use some words more than once and others not at all.

elation	fervidly	rampant	authentic
exonerate	homogeneous	ecology	resilient
quixotic	euphemism	reiterate	complacently
ambiguous	psychic	travesty	pseudoscience
autonomous	progressive	cryptic	

_____

* sadistically: taking pleasure in cruelty.

1. Unfortunately the common response to calls for improving our society and our government tend to be a defeatist version of "you can't fight city hall." We have heard this __reiterated__ so often, we forget how much power people have if they are willing to exert themselves and work together. Throughout American history there have been many __progressive__ movements that have improved our quality of life. Unfortunately a healthy skepticism can too often become an excuse for laziness and __complacency__. Telling ourselves that change is impossible, we allow ourselves to give up and defeatism becomes __rampant__.

2. Far too many people look to a __pseudoscience__ for help with their problems. They believe that the stars can explain their lives or that __psychics__ can decipher __cryptic__ messages by adding up the numbers in their name. Although this particular form of credulity seems particularly prevalent at the present time, it also played a large role at the end of the nineteenth century when tarot readers, psychics, hypnotists, and spiritualists of all kinds were in great demand because they could supposedly communicate with the spiritual world. However, the messages they received from the spirits were so __ambiguous__, no one could tell for sure if they had talked to a spirit or simply made up the ghostly message.

3. Generally the states do not have authority over Indian tribes. The tribes are __autonomous__ and treaties entered into by a particular tribe are held binding by the courts. Although Native Americans can hardly be considered __homogeneous__, they still have managed to work together, particularly where __ecological__ issues are concerned. Indian tribes control up to one half of the water in western streams and they are

___fervidly_____ determined to keep those streams free of industrial pollution.

4. During the campaign, she had been devoted to her candidate and wildly __elated_____ when he won. Once he was in office, she was convinced that his campaign promises would give way to __authentic_____ social change. But she was growing anxious. He had been in office almost a year and little had changed. She was beginning to think her plans for a new world had been little more than a __quixotic_____ dream. Even worse, she could not __exonerate_____ herself from her own nagging sense of guilt. After all, she had helped to elect him.

Beyond the Paragraph

Chapters Four and Five introduced several strategies for reading and taking notes on paragraphs. But now you need to learn how these same strategies can be adapted and applied to longer, multi-paragraph selections like those in textbooks. From reading this chapter, you will learn how to do the following:

☐ Discover the *controlling idea.*
☐ Relate the supporting paragraphs to the *thesis statement.*
☐ Mark pages in preparation for note-taking.
☐ Take effective notes on longer readings.
☐ Write summaries.

New Vocabulary

As you read, watch for the following words in this chapter. However, before you check the definitions at the bottom of the page, try to derive a meaning from context.

indulgently	apprehension	reciprocation
inherent	imperative	pervasiveness
heterogeneous	rationale	misconstrue
constitute	reverence	criterion
documentation	constrain	fluctuations

Moving Beyond the Paragraph

Now that you know how to read a paragraph efficiently, you possess all the skills necessary to read longer multi-paragraph selections, like the ones in textbooks and magazines. Like single paragraphs, these longer readings focus on a specific topic. Only in this case, the title or heading frequently identifies the topic for you or at least gives you a general clue.

If the title or heading does not identify the topic, follow the same two-step process you used to discover the topics of paragraphs: 1) Look for the word or phrase most commonly referred to or mentioned. 2) If that word or phrase by itself does not adequately express the topic, add the appropriate modifier.

Like single paragraphs, longer readings also develop one main point or message. But within longer readings, this message is called the **controlling idea,** because it controls or determines the content of the other paragraphs. While these *supporting paragraphs* all state or imply their own main ideas, they all must serve to develop the controlling idea.

For the most part, controlling ideas within longer readings are stated rather than implied. The sentence or sentences that express the controlling idea are termed **thesis statements,** a phrase you may already be familiar with from composition classes. Like main idea statements in paragraphs, thesis statements give written form to the central message of the reading or article. Unlike main idea statements, however, thesis statements are relatively fixed in location. The thesis statement of an article or reading usually appears somewhere in the first three paragraphs.

Like main idea statements in paragraphs, thesis statements are not very effective by themselves. To communicate their messages clearly and persuasively, they require more specific development. That development comes in the form of **major** and **minor supporting paragraphs.** Major supporting paragraphs introduce the different examples, reasons, studies, statistics, etc. that make the controlling idea clear and convincing, while minor supporting paragraphs further develop or elaborate points already made in the major ones. Like major and minor supporting sentences, supporting paragraphs limit interpretations and answer questions readers might have about the controlling idea and thesis statement.

There is, however, one essential difference between reading single paragraphs and reading longer selections: you have to read with a dual purpose. On the one hand you still have to analyze and understand each paragraph. But you also need to **connect those paragraphs into a unified whole. You need to figure out what each paragraph contributes to your understanding of the controlling idea expressed in the thesis statement.**

For an illustration of what this means, read the following passage. Then look at the accompanying diagram. It shows how the major and minor supporting paragraphs work toward one goal—explaining the thesis statement.

Anorexia Nervosa: The Starvation Disease

Introductory sentences: When their children begin talking about dieting, most parents ₁ smile indulgently* and do not worry. In figure-conscious America, it is quite natural for young people to desire a slim figure. However, for some teenagers, dieting is no laughing matter. *Thesis statement:* <u>It is not a momentary whim that will be pursued and forgotten; instead, it is the symptom of a serious emotional disorder called *anorexia nervosa*, a disease that can have terrible and even fatal consequences.</u>

The disease usually strikes adolescent girls who have no reason ₂ to diet. They are not overweight. They are not preparing to take part in specialized sports activities requiring a slender figure. They have not been told to diet by their doctors. They stop eating because, in spite of all evidence to the contrary, they believe they are fat. Determined to lose the imaginary excess poundage, they refuse to eat more than a few morsels of food. Usually, the weight loss is rapid, sometimes more than fifty pounds in a few months.

Some teenagers who are obsessed with the need to diet seek ₃ psychiatric treatment because they, or their parents, realize that the diet is leading to starvation. Others do not seek treatment but simply begin eating normally again on their own. However, because the disease comes in waves, or bouts, a few victims manage to keep it a secret and so avoid both exposure and treatment. Unfortunately, members of this group are in the most serious danger. Although they may be able to keep their secret right into adulthood, the disease, if untreated, almost always goes out of control, with tragic results. In fact, some victims like singer Karen Carpenter have actually died from the physical effects of prolonged starvation.

To date, the actual cause of the starvation disease has not been ₄ determined. But three possible theories have been widely discussed by therapists and physicians. According to one theory, teenagers may be starving themselves in order to rebel against parental authority. Traditionally, refusal to eat has been a young child's weapon against parental discipline. The parent may plead and even demand that the child eat, but the child can refuse and demonstrate his or her power over the situation. Unconsciously, teenagers who diet to the point of starvation may be attempting to teach their parents the same lesson: control is not in the hands of the parents.

According to another theory, anorexia may indicate a young ₅ girl's deep-rooted fear of growing up. From this perspective, starving the body can be viewed as a way of maintaining its childish

---

* indulgently: leniently.

contours and rejecting adult femininity. Yet another hypothesis views the disease as a form of self-punishment. The victims may have extraordinarily high standards of perfection and punish themselves for failing to meet their goals. □

Diagram

Anorexia Nervosa: The Starvation Disease

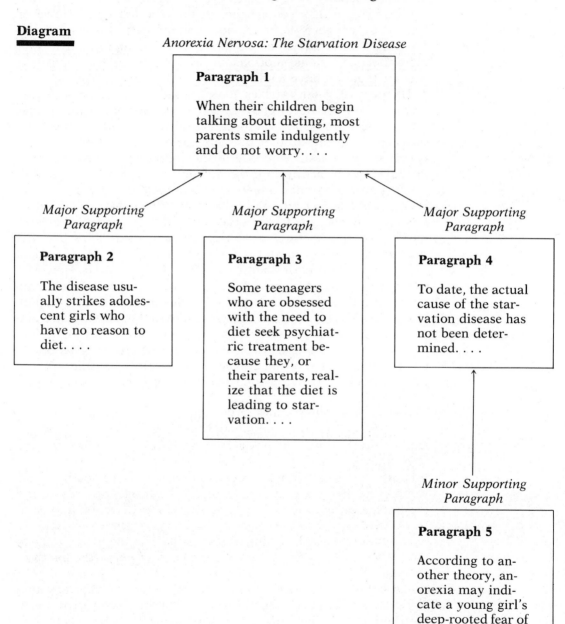

Paragraph 1

When their children begin talking about dieting, most parents smile indulgently and do not worry. . . .

Major Supporting Paragraph

Major Supporting Paragraph

Major Supporting Paragraph

Paragraph 2

The disease usually strikes adolescent girls who have no reason to diet. . . .

Paragraph 3

Some teenagers who are obsessed with the need to diet seek psychiatric treatment because they, or their parents, realize that the diet is leading to starvation. . . .

Paragraph 4

To date, the actual cause of the starvation disease has not been determined. . . .

Minor Supporting Paragraph

Paragraph 5

According to another theory, anorexia may indicate a young girl's deep-rooted fear of growing up. . . .

As the diagram shows, the first paragraph introduces the thesis statement. Then three major supporting paragraphs answer questions like: "What teenagers get this disease? What are its symptoms and causes?" One minor supporting paragraph further elaborates or fleshes out the main idea of the last major supporting paragraph. It discusses two possible theories about the cause of the disease.

Reading multi-paragraph selections like the previous one does not require a brand new set of reading strategies. On the contrary, focus your reading with questions similar to those you used when analyzing individual paragraphs.

To find the controlling idea and thesis statement ask:

What idea is developed in more than one paragraph?
What general statement could sum up the message of the entire reading?
If there is no general statement that sums up the reading, what statement can I infer?

To relate the supporting paragraphs to the controlling idea, ask:

What *kind* of specific information does the author supply? Examples, studies, anecdotes, statistics, quotations, reasons, etc.
What purpose does that information serve?
What does it contribute to my understanding of the controlling idea?

Exercise 1

Directions: The paragraphs in the following excerpt have been scrambled. Read each one separately. Then decide which paragraph expresses the controlling idea and which ones the major or minor support. Write the appropriate numbers in the boxes. *Note:* You may not be able to fill in all the boxes. Some readings, for example, may or may not have introductory paragraphs that introduce the thesis statement.

Example: **Marketing and the Hispanic Community**

1

Despite the inherent* difficulties in reaching the Hispanic market, many companies have recognized the value of doing so, and have organized conscious and culturally sensitive promotional campaigns. Recently, in an annual Hispanic State Fair in San Antonio, Texas, exhibitors included PepsiCo, Miller Brewing Co., Colgate-Palmolive, Del Monte Foods, Avon Products, KMOL-TV San Antonio, area Lincoln-Mercury dealers, McDonald's, Quaker Oats, Old El Paso sauces, and Uncle Ben's rice.

2

According to the U.S. Census Bureau, Hispanics will account for 42 percent of new population growth in the United States between 1990 and 2010. In 2010, there will be nearly 40 million Hispanics in the United States, more than double today's number. Already, U.S. Hispanics have $171 billion in purchasing power—a 27 percent increase from the 1987 figure.

3

Marketers spend billions of dollars every year to promote their goods and services. However, most of these dollars are spent on mainstream American consumers. Some critics charge that advertisers are overlooking or ignoring ethnic consumers. But this is in the process of change as Hispanic purchasing power increases.

4

The numbers are impressive but many firms find it difficult to tap this growing market. The problem is that U.S. Hispanics are a heterogeneous† and geographically widespread group. For example, most Mexican-Americans live in California and the Southwest, Dominicans and Puerto Ricans in New York, and Cubans in Florida.

5

Marketing to the Hispanic community requires a thorough understanding of and respect for its culture. Companies such as Frito-Lay Inc. and Quaker Foods have stopped using negative stereotypes (such as the Frito Bandito), which offend Hispanic consumer groups. (Pride et al., *Business*, p. 277.)

---

*   inherent: natural.

†   heterogeneous: different, varied.

Introductory Paragraph	**Second Major Supporting Paragraph**
	4
Thesis Statement Paragraph	**Minor Supporting Paragraph**
3	
First Major Supporting Paragraph	**Third Major Supporting Paragraph**
2	*1*
Minor Supporting Paragraph	**Minor Supporting Paragraph**
	5

Explanation: Paragraph *3* contains the thesis statement developed throughout the reading: "Some critics charge that advertisers are overlooking or ignoring ethnic consumers. But this is in the process of change as Hispanic purchasing power increases." Paragraph 2, the first major supporting paragraph, offers the first specific example of how purchasing power has increased while paragraph 4 identifies some difficulties encountered in tapping the new markets. Paragraph 1 explains how those difficulties are being overcome by marketers becoming more culturally sensitive. Paragraph 5, a minor supporting paragraph, offers a specific example of this new sensitivity.

D I G G I N G   D E E P E R

Why do you think it is important for advertisers to be "culturally sensitive"?

1. Keep Your Hands, Comments, and Jokes to Yourself!

1

Some think the most effective method to combat sexual harassment is to ask or tell the offender to stop. Threatening to tell or actually telling others, including supervisors and high company officials, is another option. Avoiding the harasser, making a joke of the situation, or entirely ignoring the behavior might make the offender think you are receptive to the questionable actions.

2

In 1980, the Equal Employment Opportunity Commission (EEOC) issued sexual harassment guidelines to Title VII of the 1964 Civil Rights Act. The EEOC stated: "Unwelcome sexual advances, requests for sexual favors, and other verbal or physical conduct of a sexual nature constitute* sexual harassment when submission to such conduct is made either explicitly or implicitly a term or condition of an individual's employment, submission to or rejection of such conduct by an individual is used as the basis for employment decisions affecting such individual, or such conduct has the purpose or effect of substantially interfering with an individual's work performance or creating an intimidating, hostile, or offensive working environment." Currently, 70 percent of all sexual harassment claims filed with the EEOC are "hostile environment" cases.

3

If the offensive behavior persists, there is always legal action. Before contacting a lawyer, though, you should know that these lawsuits are often embarrassing, emotionally difficult, hard to win without careful documentation,† and extremely lengthy.

4

Since the Supreme Court held that an employer is liable for employees who sexually harass, there has been a new drive to educate employees on sexual harassment. A good rule to keep in mind is: If you think it might be offensive, don't do it or say it. If you think you have been sexually harassed, there are several steps you can take. (Pride et al., *Business*, p. 277.)

---

*   constitute: make up, comprise.

†   documentation: proof, evidence.

Introductory Paragraph

```
┌─────────────────────┐
│                     │
│         2           │
│                     │
└─────────────────────┘
```

Second Major
Supporting Paragraph

```
┌─────────────────────────┐
│                         │
│                         │
│                         │
└─────────────────────────┘
```

Thesis Statement Paragraph

```
┌─────────────────────┐
│                     │
│         4           │
│                     │
└─────────────────────┘
```

Minor Supporting Paragraph

```
┌───────────────┐
│               │
│               │
└───────────────┘
```

First Major
Supporting Paragraph

```
┌─────────────────────┐
│                     │
│         1           │
│                     │
└─────────────────────┘
```

Third Major
Supporting Paragraph

```
┌─────────────────────────┐
│                         │
│                         │
│                         │
└─────────────────────────┘
```

Minor Supporting Paragraph

```
┌───────────────┐
│               │
│       3       │
│               │
└───────────────┘
```

Minor Supporting Paragraph

```
┌───────────────┐
│               │
│               │
└───────────────┘
```

2. European Contact

1

Some Indians were greatly attracted to Christianity, but most paid it lip service or found it irrelevant to their needs. As one Huron told a French priest, "It would be useless for me to repent having sinned, seeing that I never have sinned." Another Huron announced very candidly, "We have no such apprehensions* (about punishments after death) as you have, of a good and bad Mansion after this life, provided for the good and bad Souls; for we cannot tell whether everything that appears faulty to Men, is so in the Eyes of God."

2

Nor did the Native Americans show enthusiasm for European clothes, diet, or houses. Even matrimony seldom eroded the Indians' attachment to their own customs and habits. When Native Americans and whites married—unions which the English found less desirable than did the French or Spanish—the European partner usually elected to live among the Indians. Impatient settlers sometimes adopted more coercive methods, such as enslavement, to achieve cultural conversion. Again, from the white perspective, the results were discouraging. Indian slaves ran away or died. But they refused to become Europeans.

3

There is no question that the arrival of white men and women on this continent dramatically altered the lives of the native inhabitants. European colonizers regarded their own cultures as superior to those of the Indians, and whether the newcomers came from England or Spain, it seemed imperative† to introduce "civilization" as quickly as possible to those they regarded as "savages." The attempt was a universal failure.

4

The white settlers' educational system proved no more successful in winning converts to European culture. Young Indian scholars deserted stuffy classrooms at the first opportunity. In 1744, Virginia offered several Iroquois boys a free education at the Col-

---

* apprehension: fear.
† imperative: important, crucial.

lege of William and Mary. The tribe's leaders rejected the idea, said Benjamin Franklin, because boys who had gone to college "were absolutely good for nothing being neither acquainted with the true methods of killing deer, catching Beaver or surprising an enemy." (Adapted from Divine, *America Past and Present*, pp. 7–8.)

Introductory Paragraph

Second Major Supporting Paragraph

2

Thesis Statement Paragraph

3

Minor Supporting Paragraph

First Major Supporting Paragraph

1

Third Major Supporting Paragraph

4

Minor Supporting Paragraph

Minor Supporting Paragraph

DIGGING DEEPER

If you thought you were a victim of sexual harassment, would you take legal action? Why or why not?

Try your hand at paraphrasing the sexual harassment guidelines on page 222.

Inferring the Controlling Idea

Within longer readings, the controlling idea is usually stated rather than implied. Much of the time, it appears somewhere in the first three paragraphs, right after the heading or the introduction.

However, even in textbook readings, authors occasionally imply the controlling idea, leaving it up to their readers to draw the most logical inference. Here's an example:

Attitudes Toward Singles

Married people tend to have a negative view of single women. At least that is the finding of one Australian study (Stolk & Brotherton, 1981) in which 48 spouses were asked how they felt most people would respond when asked to complete the sentence "I think of single women over 30 as . . ." [1]

Seven in 10 husbands and four in 10 wives said that "spinster," "failure," and "hasn't met the right person" would be how most people would respond. But these negative feelings seemed to be a result of other than personal contact with singles—20 percent of the spouses didn't know a single woman and half had never had a single woman in their home. [2]

Americans have their own prejudices against singles. In one study, undergraduate students rated never-married persons as less secure and less reliable than marrieds (Etaugh & Malstrom, 1981). [3]

This prejudice against singles exists for at least two reasons: First is the attitude that singlehood is deviant. Although being unmarried is normative in your teens and early twenties, it becomes deviant when you are 30. Since most people marry, those who don't become somewhat suspect. Then, too, since most singles express a desire to be married and to have children, marrieds assume that since they don't have what they want, they must be frustrated and unhappy. □ (Knox, *Choices in Relationships*, p. 137.) [4]

Initially you might think that the first sentence in the opening paragraph is the thesis statement. But as you continue reading, it's clear that the authors are not talking just about Australians or just about single women. They are talking about a prejudice against single people in general. Yet there is no thesis statement expressing that point. You have to infer one like the following: Studies in Australia and America suggest that single people over thirty are the object of prejudice.

Most longer readings will contain a thesis statement. But if the first three paragraphs do not introduce one, think about inferring a thesis statement that could generally sum up the entire reading.

Exercise 2

Directions: Read each selection. If the controlling idea appears in a thesis statement, underline it. If the controlling idea is implied rather than stated, write your inference in the blanks that follow.

Example: **Extinction and Us**

Should we care if over 150 known species of animals have disappeared from the earth in the last fifty years? Should we be concerned that there are literally thousands of species whose very existence is presently endangered—largely because of our activities? Extinction, after all, is the natural end of populations. Species are born, they mature, and they die. Some live a long time, perhaps millions of years; some die more quickly. We have hastened the extinction of many species we know about, and we have undoubtedly sealed the fate of others. In fact, there are undoubtedly many other species that have lived among us during our time on earth, but that have disappeared as a result of our activities without our ever having known they existed. 1

It is hard to explain the rationale* of many of us who are concerned about such matters. I have never seen a sei whale, yet I don't want them to become extinct. Moreover, I felt this way long before I understood anything about how they might be an important part of an ecosystem. Possibly such feelings merely reflect the cultural attitude that it is "nice" to wish other living things well; thus, the attitude is rewarded. I feel nice. 2

There are, of course, more rational reasons for mourning the extermination of any species. For one thing, the kind of attitude that encourages or sanctions the destruction of other species is a 3

---

* rationale: reason or explanation for something, logical basis.

The gray timber wolf may be in danger of extinction. (Storm Runner—Timber Wolf. © 1991 Bradley J. Parrish.)

threat to our own well-being. If such an attitude exists, we ourselves might fall victim to it. Living things (including us) might be expected to fare better where there is reverence* for life. The extinction of other species could also threaten us indirectly by simplifying the system of which we are a part or by destroying parts of the ecosystem upon which we directly rely. For example, if we continue to poison the oceans because we are willing to believe only a few bottom dwellers are affected, we might eventually overstep some critical threshold and trigger the wholesale death of plankton, thus finding ourselves without a major source of the world's food and with our oxygen supplies dwindling.

This is all very rational, but none of this caused my gut response when I learned that some major whaling nations intended to resist the international ban on whaling. I simply found it very sad. For some reason, I wanted those whales to continue to share the planet. If you had the same reaction and you don't ever expect to see or eat a whale or use its oil, you might try to analyze the roots of your own response. □ (Adapted from Wallace, *Biology: The World of Life,* pp. 503–504.)

---

* reverence: respect.

Inference: <u>There are many reasons why we should care about the number</u>

<u>of species that have disappeared in the last 150 years.</u>

Explanation: Here the author uses a question to open the reading: "Should we care if over 150 known species of animals have disappeared from the earth in the last fifty years?" However, he does not explicitly answer that question. Instead he gives his readers enough information to infer the answer he intended.

1. Executive Celebrities: There's No Business Like Show Business

Executive celebrities are highly visible. They're in commercials, *1* on television shows, at fashionable Manhattan parties. T. Boone Pickens, Jr., Lee Iacocca, Ted Turner, Steven Jobs, Donald Trump, Victor Kiam—these individuals are all as familiar to us as a movie star or a famous athlete.

Lee Iacocca* seems to thrive on his celebrity status. The brash, *2* outspoken head of Chrysler Corp., fired from his position at Ford, personally took the lead in saving his new company. He made the right decisions, collected a competent staff, and even starred in Chrysler commercials. Iacocca has appeared on "Miami Vice" and was instrumental in the restoration effort of the Statue of Liberty. Iacocca has an opinion on everything from taxes to foreign policy, and is more than happy to express these ideas. Iacocca's appearances, candor, and best-selling biography have all made him a business star.

Victor Kiam is the chief executive officer (CEO) and sole share- *3* holder of Remington. He came to struggling Remington and quickly made some major changes. He drastically reduced the number of executives, brought all production plants back to the United States, and aggressively promoted Remington's electric shavers himself. He became Remington's primary salesperson and sales figures soared. Kiam, like Iacocca, has also published a book, and he is marketing it as vigorously as he does his shavers.[4]

Donald Trump, the real estate magnate, is also a celebrity. He *4* can be seen anywhere from his luxury ocean cruiser to his Atlantic

---

* As of December 1992, Lee Iacocca will no longer head the Chrysler Corporation.

City hotel to a major sporting event. Recognized wherever he goes, Trump greatly enjoys the limelight.

These—and others like T. Boone Pickens of Mesa Limited Partnership and Steven Jobs of NeXT Computers—are just some examples of celebrity executives. Celebrity CEOs have naturally drawn public attention to the businesses they control. Chrysler, Remington, and Trump's real estate holdings have all benefited substantially by the attention paid to their CEOs. 5

Other CEOs dread the spotlight. They think that being a celebrity is dangerous and that persons like Iacocca spend entirely too much time away from their desks. Iacocca especially has been criticized for neglecting new car development at Chrysler. Executives also avoid stardom because they think that executive celebrities become overconfident. With constant media exposure, talk-show appearances, and devoted fans, a celebrity executive might have a tendency to feel invincible and infallible. One major bad decision by a CEO could lead to problems or even disaster for an organization. Furthermore, training the successor to a celebrity executive is difficult. The new CEO will probably not be able to fill the shoes of a celebrity predecessor. Celebrity executives also face a security risk. Ambitious kidnappers or fanatical followers pose a potential threat to celebrity executives and their families. 6
□ (Pride, et al. *Business*, p. 143.)

Inference: While some chief executive officers love the spotlight,

others recognize its drawbacks.

2. Daydreams and Fantasies

Two of the most common daydream plots are the **conquering hero** and the **suffering martyr** themes. In a conquering hero fantasy, the daydreamer gets the starring role as a famous, rich, or powerful person: a celebrity, athlete, musician, famous surgeon, brilliant lawyer, or magnificent lover. Themes such as these seem to reflect needs for mastery and escape from the frustrations of everyday life. Suffering martyr daydreams center on feelings of being neglected, hurt, rejected, or unappreciated by others. In such fantasies, others end up regretting their past actions and realizing what a *wonderful person* the daydreamer was all along. 1

Daydreams often fill a need for stimulation during routine or boring tasks. They also improve our ability to delay immediate plea- 2 sures so that future goals can be achieved. And in everyday terms, fantasy can be an outlet for frustrated impulses. If you have a momentary urge to kill the fool in front of you on the highway, substituting fantasy for action may avert disaster (Biblow, 1973).

Perhaps the greatest value of fantasy is its contribution to creativity. In the imaginative realm of fantasy, nothing is impossible—a quality allowing for tremendous fluency and flexibility of thought. For most people, fantasy and daydreaming are associated with positive emotional adjustment, lower levels of aggression, and greater mental flexibility or creativity (Singer, 1974). Perhaps this is why Albert Einstein, one of the world's most celebrated thinkers, was, in his own words, "disorderly and a dreamer." □ (Adapted from Coon, *Introduction to Psychology*, p. 269.)

Inference: <u>Daydreams serve a number of different functions.</u>

And Once Again Transitions

Transitions, those *verbal bridges* writers use to connect sentences, also help connect paragraphs. Here, for example, a transitional sentence pointedly announces the direction the supporting paragraphs will take.

Psychology: A Brief History

Psychology has a long past but a short history. Psychology's past is centuries old because it includes **philosophy,** the study of knowledge, reality, and human nature. In contrast, the history of modern psychology began only about 100 years ago. As sciences go, psychology is the new kid on the block: Easily 9 out of 10 persons to ever work in the field are alive today. Of course, to some students this history is still "not short enough!" Yet, the ideas in psychology's past are intimately tied to the present. *To understand where psychology is now, let's take a brief look at its short history.*

Transitional sentence:

Into the Lab. Psychology's history as a science began in 1879 at Leipzig, Germany. There, the "father of psychology," **Wilhelm Wundt** (VILL-helm Voont), created the first psychological laboratory so that he could study *conscious experience.* How, he wondered, are sensations, images, and feelings formed? To find out, Wundt observed and carefully measured **stimuli** of various kinds (lights, sounds, weights). He then used **introspection,** or "looking inward," to examine his reactions to them. Wundt called this approach **experimental self-observation** (Blumenthal, 1979). Over the years, he used it to study vision, hearing, taste, touch, reaction time, memory, feelings, time perception, and many other subjects.

Experimental self-observation was a highly developed skill, much like the skill needed to be a professional wine taster. Wundt's subjects had to make at least 10,000 practice observations before they were allowed to take part in a real experiment (Lieberman, 1979). By using such careful observation and measurement, psychology was truly off to a good start. ▫ (Coon, *Introduction to Psychology,* p. 8.)

Then, too, transitional words can tell readers when one major supporting paragraph ends and another begins.

Thirst

Transition: You may not have noticed, but there are actually two kinds of thirst. The *first* kind, **extracellular thirst,** occurs when water is lost from the fluids surrounding the cells of your body. Bleeding, vomiting, diarrhea, sweating, and drinking alcohol cause this type of thirst (Houston, 1985). When a person loses both water and minerals in any of these ways—especially by perspiration—a slightly salty liquid may be more satisfying than plain water.

The reason is that before the body can retain water, minerals lost through perspiration (mainly salt) must be replaced. In lab tests, animals greatly prefer salt water after salt levels in their bodies are lowered (Stricker & Verbalis, 1988). Similarly, some nomadic people of the Sahara Desert prize blood as a beverage, probably because of its saltiness. (Maybe they should try Gatorade?)

Transition: A *second* type of thirst occurs when you eat a salty meal. In this instance your body does not lose fluid. Instead, *excess* salt causes fluid to be drawn out of cells. As the cells "shrink," **intracellular thirst** is triggered. Thirst of this type is best quenched by plain water. ▫ (Coon, *Introduction to Psychology,* p. 290.)

Transitions can also prepare readers for a shift or change in thought as the author moves from one paragraph to another:

In 1922, Lord Carnarvon and Howard Carter made a discovery that shocked and delighted the entire world of archaeology: they found the fabulous tomb of King Tutankhamen. Two rooms of the tomb had been attacked by grave robbers, but the third room had been left untouched for thousands of years. The room contained not only the mummy of the eighteen-year-old king but

The discovery of King Tutankhamen's tomb shocked and delighted the archaeological world.

also hundreds of priceless objects that provided valuable information about the ancient Egyptian culture.

Transitional sentence:

Unfortunately, the story does not end with the discovery. Following the opening of the tomb, stories of the "curse of the Pharaohs" began to circulate, and many believed that the curse was beginning its awful work. Lord Carnarvon died suddenly, and for some that was proof enough. But even more amazing, as time went on more than twenty people connected with the tomb died under mysterious circumstances.

In the first paragraph, the author explains what was so significant about the opening of Tutankhamen's tomb. However, by the second paragraph, he shifts gears and describes why many people believed those who opened the tomb were cursed. To help his readers move smoothly from point to point, he provides a transitional sentence that signals a shift in the direction of his thought.

Transitional sentences can also end a chapter section and pave the way for what follows.

Most experts predict that in the future computers will affect every aspect of human life. As a result, computers will be as common as the toaster, the television, and the automobile. While we have tried to describe the most obvious technological trends and how computers affect business, the advances in medicine, transportation, conservation of natural resources, and all other areas of human life as we know it today are just as spectacular. It is safe to say that every aspect of your life will be affected by the changes that will take place in the development of computer technology.

Now that we understand how computers transform data into information, it is time to examine a management information system (MIS). (Pride et al. *Business*, p. 468.)

Transitions between paragraphs are valuable signals. They help clarify relationships between paragraphs, and enable you to make connections between individual sections of a chapter. It's worth your while to watch for them as you read.

Exercise 3

Directions: Fill in the blanks with the number of the appropriate transition.

Transitions: 1. For additional material about landmarks and shrines founded more in myth than reality, read the following section on "Plymouth Rock."
2. Then, too,
3. But, in fact,
4. for example
5. However, under close examination, the legend of the Liberty Bell does not hold up well.
6. Finally,

Of all American landmarks, perhaps none is more sacred than the Liberty Bell. Every year thousands of tourists trek to Philadelphia to get a closer look and to hear how the legendary bell was rung when independence was declared on July 4, 1776. ___5___

According to Richard Shenkman, author of *Legends, Lies, and Cherished Myths*, many of the stories surrounding this famous landmark are more fiction than fact. There is no evidence, ___4___, that the bell's inscription "Proclaim Liberty throughout all the Land unto the Inhabitants Thereof" was a consequence of the American Revolution. The bell was cast in 1753, twenty-three years before the Revolution. The motto was inscribed at that time, long before America had won her independence from England.

___2___ there is no support for the claim that the bell was rung when independence was declared. According to the legend, the bell was rung by an old man with white hair who kept shouting "Liberty throughout the land." ___3___ there is no written record of the old man's existence.

___6___ the very name "Liberty Bell" was not coined by the American revolutionaries. The name was coined in 1839 by anti-slavery activists, and the word "liberty" referred to liberty for America's slaves. ___1___

Marking Your Text

As you learned in Chapter Five, **good notes selectively paraphrase, condense** and **abbreviate** the original text. Good notes do not copy the original text word for word.

Not surprisingly, these general principles of good note-taking apply even more to longer readings. However, to apply them effectively, you should first mark your text and highlight the *relevant* or essential information.

To help you do precisely that, here are four pointers for marking pages in preparation for note-taking:

1. **Annotate the text in the margins:** Jot key words or phrases in the margins. Your jottings should identify the controlling idea and list any major or minor support necessary to your understanding of the controlling idea.
2. **Highlight content and structure:** Make up your own code and use it to make the essential elements—controlling idea and support—stand out during later reviews. Be sure, too, to highlight underlying patterns of organization.* For example, use arrows to indicate cause and effect or numbers to identify steps in a sequence.
3. **Underline sparingly:** Research suggests that underlining aids remembering.[1] Therefore it's a good idea to spend some time underlining sentences you think contain particularly important information. However, do underline carefully. Imagine you are sending a telegram. Then mark only those words that are essential to your message.
4. **Respond personally:** Don't restrict yourself only to understanding what the author says. See if you can **integrate** or combine it with your own experiences. If the author talks about celebrity executives, see if you can think of additional examples. If the author claims that the public is generally misin-

---

1. Linda Johnson, "Effects of Underlining Textbook Sentences on Passage and Sentence Retention." (*Reading Research and Instruction*, Fall, 1988, p. 18.)

* For more on these patterns, see Chapter 7.

formed about the transmission of AIDS, consider if you are an exception to that general rule. In short, make connections between what you read and what you already know. Those connections are the keys to remembering what you read long after you have put down your textbook.

To illustrate how those four pointers can be put into practice, here is a page marked in preparation for note-taking.

Mnemonics—Memory Magic

Mnemonics or memory systems are the key to having a magic memory

Various "memory experts" entertain by giving demonstrations in which they memorize the names of everyone at a banquet, the order of all the cards in a deck, long lists of words, or other seemingly impossible amounts of information. Such feats may seem like magic, but if they are, you can have a magic memory too. ★★ These tricks are performed through the use of **mnemonics** (nee-MON-iks). A mnemonic is any kind of memory system or aid.

Def.

Exs. of mnemonics

Fall backwards, spring forwards to remember how to set clock

Some mnemonic systems have become so common that almost everyone knows them. If you are trying to remember how many days there are in a month, you may find the answer by reciting, "Thirty days hath September. . . ." Physics teachers often help their students remember the colors of the spectrum by giving them the mnemonic "Roy G. Biv": **R**ed, **O**range, **Y**ellow, **G**reen, **B**lue, **I**ndigo, **V**iolet. The budding sailor who has trouble telling port from starboard may remember that port and left both have four letters or may remind himself, "I *left* port." And what beginning musician hasn't remembered the notes represented by the lines and spaces of the musical staff by learning "F-A-C-E" and "**E**very **G**ood **B**oy **D**oes **F**ine."

superior to rote learning or learning by simple repetition

Why only one example then?

Mnemonic techniques are ways of avoiding *rote* learning (learning by simple repetition). The superiority of mnemonic learning as opposed to rote learning has been demonstrated many times. For example, Bower (1973) asked college students to study 5 different lists of 20 unrelated words. At the end of a short study session, subjects were asked to recall all 100 items. Subjects using mnemonics remembered an average of 72 items, whereas a control group using simple, or rote, learning remembered an average of 28. □ (Coon, *Introduction to Psychology*, p. 250.)

Exercise 4

Directions: The following chart shows some of the symbols commonly used to mark textbook pages. Read the chart to decide which symbols you think you could use. Then mark the following excerpt. Feel free to invent new symbols or modify those given.

Symbols for marking your text:

Brackets for thesis statements	[ ]
Underlining for main idea statements and supporting details	—— —— ——
Abbreviations to show the type of support: examples, studies, reasons, exceptions, statistics	Ex, Stu, R, Exc, Stat.
Numbers to itemize examples, reasons, steps or studies	1, 2, 3
Stars for particularly important statements or quotations	★★
Boxes for transitional words or key terms	▭
Circles for key names, dates, terms	◯
Exclamation points to show surprise	!!
Question marks to indicate an unclear sentence or passage	??
Connected arrows to highlight related statements	⤢
Vertical marks to emphasize a key passage	‖
Marginal notes to record comments and questions	*I don't believe this.*
Equal signs to indicate definitions	=

Now mark the following passage.

Alex Joseph with the members of his polygamous family.

Polygyny

Polygyny, the marriage of one man to several women, is more wide-spread and more acceptable than any other form of marriage. It is practiced throughout Africa, the Middle East, and South and Southeast Asia. If it were not prohibited by law, it would probably flourish in China and among some ethnic groups in the United States. Even after these legal restrictions are taken into account, polygyny is still preferred in about 70 percent of all societies.

At this point, it is important to distinguish between normative forms of marriage and actual marriages. Although most societies approve and even encourage some form of polygyny, in reality it is often unattainable by most people. Individual preferences, the expenses involved in supporting more than one wife, and the limited availability of partners constrain* polygyny.

One of the most interesting exceptions to this pattern is found in the mountains of Ecuador and Peru. This region is inhabited by some 20,000 aborigines called Jivaro (Hee-varo). Jivaros are probably known best for their ability to shrink human heads to the size of an orange, and for their prowess in battle. Jivaros also are proud of the fact that they have never been conquered by the white man. In addition, they are known as a society where some 90 percent of the females share husbands. It has been speculated

---

*   constrain: limit, restrict.

that the Jivaro males run a great risk of being killed in feuds and wars; thus polygyny is a highly adaptive form of marriage. □ (Adapted from Kephart and Jedlicka, *The Family, Society and the Individual*, pp. 21–22.)

Taking Notes

If you are reading material that is relatively familiar and fairly uncomplicated, mark the text and use the marked pages for review. But if you are trying to read and remember material that is both difficult and unfamiliar, you also need to takes notes. By marking the text *and* taking notes, you are re-thinking and re-working the material at least twice. This double processing of new information will ensure better understanding *and* better remembering.

With a little modification, the same principles for taking notes on paragraphs apply to taking notes on longer readings.

1. **Be selective:** Your notes should certainly identify the controlling idea. They should also identify main ideas from major and minor supporting paragraphs. But with the supporting paragraphs, *be selective*. Perhaps a major supporting paragraph offers an example that seems obvious to you. If so, don't include the example in your notes.

   Be equally selective with minor supporting paragraphs. Don't take notes on them unless they add to your understanding of the major supporting paragraphs. If they repeat or further illustrate a point that is already clear to you, ignore them.

2. **Create easy-to-remember chunks of information:** Good note-takers do not necessarily follow the author's original order or placement of information. Instead they separate and combine information into manageable chunks they can readily remember. Let's say, for example, that an author lists three causes and three effects of one event. Although the author might present them individually, cause, effect, cause, effect, etc., you could combine them in your notes under two headings: *Causes* and *Effects*. Those two "chunks" of information will be easier to remember.

3. **Show relationships:** When you took notes on paragraphs, you used indention, letters, and numbers to show relationships. You need to do the same with longer readings that contain more information to organize and connect.

4. **Paraphrase, condense, and abbreviate:** Be sure to translate the author's words into your own. Eliminate any words you don't need and use abbreviations whenever possible.

To give you a concrete illustration of how to apply these principles, here are sample notes for the reading on page 236:

Topic: Mnemonics

Controlling idea: Mnemonics—memory systems or aids—are the keys to a good memory.

Support:
1. Some mnemonics systems are common to almost everyone. Examples:
   a. "Thirty days hath September"
   b. "Roy G. Biv" for colors of the spectrum
   c. "FACE" for lines of the music staff
2. Mnemonics help avoid rote learning (simple repetition)
   — superiority of mnemonic learning has been repeatedly demonstrated. Example: Bower (1973) showed that subjects using mnemonics remembered on average 72 out of a hundred items; those using rote learning remembered 28.

Exercise 5

Directions: Read and mark each of the following selections. Then take notes in the blanks provided.

Example: **The Rule of Reciprocation†**

A few years ago, a university professor tried a little experiment. He sent Christmas cards to a sample of perfect strangers. Although he expected some reaction, the response he received was amazing—holiday cards addressed to him came pouring back from people who had never met nor heard of him. The great majority of those who returned cards never inquired into the identity of the unknown professor. They received his holiday greeting card, *click,* and, *whirr,* they automatically sent cards in return.

Rule of reciprocation: we try to repay in kind

While small in scope, [this study nicely shows the action of one of the most potent of the weapons of influence around us—the rule of reciprocation. The rule says that we should try to repay, in kind, what another person has provided us.] If a woman does us a favor, we should do her one in return; if a man sends us a birthday present, we should remember his birthday with a gift of our own;

---

* When you are taking notes on your own, you would not be labeling each element. The labels used here are purely for explanation and illustration.

† reciprocation: mutual giving and receiving.

if a couple invites us to a party, we should be sure to invite them to one of ours.

By virtue of the reciprocity rule, then, we are *obligated* to the future repayment of favors, gifts, invitations, and the like. So typical is it for indebtedness to accompany the receipt of such things that a phrase like "much obliged" has become a synonym for "thank you," not only in the English language but in others as well.

What's impressive about the rule of reciprocation is its pervasiveness* in human culture. It is so widespread that, after intensive study, Alvin Gouldner (1960), along with other sociologists, reports that all human societies subscribe to the rule. Within each society it seems pervasive also; it permeates exchanges of every kind. Indeed, it may well be that a developed system of indebtedness flowing from the rule of reciprocation is a unique property of human culture.

A widely shared and strongly held feeling of future obligation made an enormous difference in human social evolution because it meant that one person could give something (for example, food, energy, care) to another with confidence that the gift was not being lost. For the first time in evolutionary history, one individual could give away any of a variety of resources without actually giving them away. □ (Adapted from Cialdini, *Influence*, pp. 21–22.)

Topic: Rule of reciprocation

Controlling idea: The rule of reciprocation plays a powerful role in human society

Support:

1. Reciprocity rule obligates us to return or repay gifts, favors, and invitations

2. Very pervasive, appears all human societies subscribe to this rule in one form or another

   — Alvin Gouldner and other sociologists claim all human societies subscribe.

3. Made a big difference in social evolution

   — meant giving would not be penalized

---

* pervasiveness: being present throughout.

Explanation: Although the selection contains five paragraphs, we need to take notes on only four. The first paragraph is an introduction to the thesis statement appearing in paragraph 2 and contains no essential information.

Paragraphs 3, 4, and 5, however, do contain essential information. Each one further explains the thesis statement introduced in paragraph 2. Note how the main idea of each supporting paragraph has been numbered and indented beneath the controlling idea of the entire selection.

Information from supporting sentences has been placed under the main ideas and preceded by a dash.

Now it's your turn to apply those four principles of note-taking.

1. **AIDS: A Devastating New Problem**

Not long ago, an accused murderer was led into a courtroom by a *1* sheriff's deputy who was wearing rubber gloves. The jurors facing the accused did not include the fourteen people who asked to be excused because of the medical condition of the accused. The unusual circumstances arose because the defendant was guilty of having AIDS.

The fear of AIDS now probably surpasses the fear of flying. *2* People with the disease, or those in high-risk groups, are often shunned, even by those in the health services community. The argument regarding the contagion of the disease seems to be more vigorous outside the medical community, however, because most researchers in the area seem to agree that the disease is not particularly contagious *if* certain simple safeguards are taken. But what is AIDS? What is the problem? And what are the safeguards?

AIDS is an acronym for **acquired immune deficiency syndrome.** *3* Essentially, it acts by suppressing the victim's immune system. People with AIDS are susceptible to virtually any disease. In fact, the appearance of rare diseases such as Kaposi's sarcoma (a skin cancer) and pneumocystic pneumonia frequently occur with the disease. Early signs of AIDS include a series of lingering, simple colds, "night sweats," persistent fever, swollen glands, and coughing. (Immediately upon learning this, of course, everyone detects just those symptoms in themselves.) More serious conditions follow, including at least three forms of cancer and destruction of the lungs and brain.

By some accounts, the first case of AIDS in the United States *4* appeared in 1979, followed by a half-dozen cases reported in Los Angeles in 1981. By early 1986, the number of AIDS victims had passed 15,000 in the U.S., with the number of known victims doubling every nine months. Many people carry antibodies to AIDS, showing that they have been exposed to it, and some may carry the disease in its early stages without developing the symptoms. It is feared that such people may be able to transmit the disease, nonetheless.

The disease, once full-blown, is believed to be incurable and to *5* virtually always cause death within a few years (fewer than fourteen percent of victims survive past three years). Because so much is unknown about the disease, much of what is known is misconstrued,* often by sensationalist media. □ (Wallace, *Biology*, pp. 387–390.)

Topic: AIDS

Controlling idea: People are terrified of getting AIDS.

Support:

1. Acronym for acquired immune deficiency syndrome

  a. suppresses victim's immune system

  b. victims susceptible to any disease

    — even rare diseases like Kaposi's sarcoma

2. Early signs: a series of lingering colds, persistent fever, swollen glands, and coughing

    — later on cancer and destruction of brain

3. By some accounts first appeared 1979

4. By 1986 number of victims 15,000 with number doubling every 9 months.

5. Once full-blown, there may be no cure

    — fewer than 14% of victims survive after 3 years

* misconstrued: misinterpreted, misunderstood.

2. Finding a Date or Mate

Because two people suited for each other may never meet by [1] chance, formal mate selection networks have developed to make such people aware of each other. The following advertisements are typical of those designed to seek a particular type of partner or to offer one's self for someone who may be looking. They might appear in national magazines such as *Intro* and the *Mother Earth News* or in local newspapers.

MALE, 32, attractive, professional looking for single, white, female, for fun and frolic. Must be herpless but not hopeless, helpless, or hapless. Mike, P.O. Box 24, Arcola, In. 46704

LADY, 28, seeks gentle Paul Bunyan for loving, working, the rest of my life. Nancy, Route 2, Box 54B Republic, Wash. 99166

SINGLE mother, 34, 135, two biracial adopted children, former model now technical writer, humorous, handy, desires correspondence with same type person. Mary Mitchener, 228 Culpepper Ave., Dothan, Ala. 35226

Whereas these ads give the information necessary for the parties [2] to contact one another, other magazines function as go-betweens in which parties can contact each other only through the publisher of the magazine. "An interested reader makes contact by writing letters in response to one or more advertisements. Each letter is sealed and identified by a number. These are then mailed to the publisher who, for a fee, addresses and forwards each letter" (Jedlicka, 1980). Suzanne Douglas, publisher of *Intro* magazine, says one advertisement results in an average of 14 replies. As to the truthfulness of the advertisements, she said that men tend to lie about their age and women tend to lie about their weight.

Dating Service Organizations

A number of organizations exist for the purpose of finding mates [3] for their members. Although many of these are for the general public, some are specialized. Examples include Jewish Dating Service (to match Jewish singles), Preferred Singles (to match singles who are overweight), and Execumatch. The latter, for a fee of $100,000, finds a marriage partner for the wealthy.

Computers

The computer revolution has introduced another way to meet a [4] dating partner. Campus bulletin boards and newspapers often feature advertisements for computer-matched dates. Titles such as "Pick A Date," "Computer Match," and "Why Be Lonely?" are followed by the promise to find the "right" date for the person who completes the questionnaire. The information requested is designed to help the computer match respondents on the basis of social background, personal attitudes, and complementary needs. The individual's profile is matched with similar profiles in the computer and he or she is given a list of several names, usually three.

The suitability of the partners for each other will depend on how accurately they completed the questionnaire. For example, individuals may indicate they are more physically attractive than they actually are for fear that otherwise they may be paired with the son or daughter of Frankenstein's monster.

Video Cassettes

The newest method of partner finding is having yourself inter- 5 viewed on videotape and letting others watch your cassette in exchange for your watching those already on file. If you like what you see, you can contact the person directly for a date. Great Resources (New York), Great Expectations (Los Angeles), and Couple Company (Boston) offer to make a videotape of you and permit you to view the tapes of others. The price at Great Resources is $350 for a six-month membership. □ (Knox, *Choices in Relationships*, p. 165.)

Topic: Finding a mate

Controlling idea: Nowadays there are a number of mate selection networks that help people find a mate or date.

Support:
1. Advertisements help people make contact.

2. Dating services find mates for members

 — some for general public; others, like the Jewish Dating Services and Execumatch, specialize

3. Computers matchmake based on answers to questionnaires.

4. Video cassettes let people view potential dates for a price.

_____

_____

_____

_____

_____

_____

_____

DIGGING DEEPER

If you knew that a classmate of yours carried the AIDS virus, how would you respond and why?

WRITING SUGGESTION

Write a paper in which you give reasons why you would or would not use a dating service.

Writing Summaries

If you are working with a fairly detailed text, one with lots of dates and key terms, informal outlines, like the ones we've been using, are an excellent tool for note-taking. But if you are reading a chapter that is not rich in definitions and details, you might consider making **summaries** of those sections you think need additional attention, but do not require detailed notes.

Summaries are easy to write if you keep these four points in mind.

1. Good summaries reduce the text to about one quarter of the original length. Generally marking your text before writing your summary will help you sift out the information most essential to your summary: (a) the controlling idea of the entire reading and (b) the main ideas in major supporting paragraphs. These elements are the building blocks of your summary.

2. The first sentence of your summary should paraphrase the controlling idea. The first paragraph should include any important background information presented in the introduction.

3. The remaining sentences or paragraphs should paraphrase any support essential to making the controlling idea clear and convincing. Obviously the definition of what is essential will change with the reader. Someone familiar with the material will create a summary quite different from that of someone who encounters the information for the first time.

4. Transitions help you create links between statements that appeared paragraphs apart in the original text, but in the summary are next to one another.

The following article has been marked and summarized to illustrate how to put these four points into practice.

Can We Trust You?

"integrity tests"

tests supposedly predict lateness, abuse of sick leave, strike participation

6,000 companies use test

Types of questions Why would blushing or not blushing predict ★★ honesty?

More and more employers are using written psychological tests to screen job applicants. The exams, often dubbed honesty or integrity tests, are supposed to predict tendencies toward theft and a range of potentially troublesome behaviors, including lateness, abuse of sick leave, even an inclination to participate in strikes. Since the 1988 federal ban on polygraphs, or lie detectors, the government's Office of Technology Assessment (OTA) estimates that as many as 6,000 companies give the tests to about 5 million people per year, most of them applicants for low-skilled jobs such as shop clerks. One type of test asks direct directions, such as "How honest are you?" and "Do you think it's stealing to take small items home from work?" Other tests are subtle: "How often do you blush?" and "Do you make your bed?"

Most experts say the tests' value is questionable at best, and the American Psychological Association recently joined the OTA in

one of experts

Reason why
questionable

good!

prohibit use as only
criterion

issuing a warning of their potential misuse. Much of the problem centers around the interpretation of the results. Paul Sackett, a professor of industrial relations at the University of Minnesota, says the tests can be useful but the results, usually summarized in a simple comment such as "recommended" or "not acceptable," are gross oversimplifications of a complex psychological exam.

Some states have already taken steps to prevent discrimination based on the new tests. Massachusetts has outlawed them, and Rhode Island prohibits their use as the only hiring criterion.* □ (Adapted from Allstetter, *American Health*, November 1991, p. 27.)

Sample Summary: A number of employers, perhaps as many as 6,000 per year, have started using exams, nicknamed "honesty tests," to screen employees. The tests ask questions like "How honest are you?" and "Do you make your bed?" The answers to these questions are supposed to reveal potentially troublesome employees. However, many experts say the tests may be less useful than some employers think. According to Paul Sackett, a professor of industrial relations, interpretation of the tests cannot be so easily reduced to simple labels like "recommended" or "not recommended." Several states have tried to prevent discrimination based on the tests. Massachusetts and Rhode Island do not accept them as the only standard for hiring people.

DIGGING DEEPER

Why do you think these tests ask questions like: Do you make your bed? Do you blush? What do you think the answers to these questions are supposed to reveal?

Exercise 6

Directions: Mark and then summarize each of the following selections.

---

* criterion: standard of judgment.

Example: Power

*power is
hard to measure*

therefore

source of debate

Look up

*1. Sociologists like
C. Wright Mills
believed only a few
people had real
power*

I agree with Mills

*2. Others believe
many different
groups wield power*

*Agreement that
power not always
where it seems.*

★★

*Ex. many mayors
don't have real
power.*

Sociologists use the term **power** to refer to the capacity of people or groups to control or influence the actions of others, whether those others wish to cooperate or not. Sociologists study power to determine not only who exercises it, but also why it is exercised and who benefits from its use.

Of the three main types of desirables—wealth, power, and prestige—power is the hardest to measure. Most studies of power are nothing more than an average of guesses about where power is found. Many forms of power are so well hidden that only the power holders know their source. Because it is so hard to measure, and because it is so tied to questions of ideology, the subject of power—who holds it and how it is used—is a source of much debate in sociology. [1] Some sociologists maintain that power in America is concentrated in the hands of a few people who have a common background and who tend to act together (Domhoff, 1983, 1978). C. Wright Mills (1956) suggested that America is run by a "power elite" and set its total number at no more than 300 people. [2] Other sociologists believe that power in America is divided among many groups and people (Rose, 1967; Riesman, 1961).

Sociologists do agree that real power may not always lie where we think it does. The mayors of some cities, for example, are sometimes mere figureheads who simply look impressive. The actual decisions are made by a handful of business leaders who stay behind the scenes. And some decisions are made at the lowest level, where the work is really carried out. Such is the case with the police officer on the beat or the teacher in the classroom.

Clearly, power may exist without wealth: Not all the rich are powerful, and not all the powerful are rich. But the two categories are closely related. Wealth can sometimes buy power. In national politics, for instance, candidates for office are often wealthy. The Kennedy brothers, the three Rockefeller governors, the Roosevelts, and Ronald Reagan are only a few men of wealth who have become powerful in politics. Moreover, power is often used to acquire wealth. How many lawmakers, generals, or labor union heads retire in poverty?   □   (Poponoe, *Sociology*, pp. 218–219.)

Summary:

According to sociologists, power is the capacity of some people or groups to decide the actions of others. Unfortunately power is easier to define than measure. For some, like C. Wright Mills, power in America is possessed by a very few, perhaps 300 people. Others, however, believe that power is divided among several groups.

But on one point there is agreement: Power is not always where it seems to be. Sometimes seemingly powerful people are nothing more than figureheads; they only appear to have power. Then, too, there are people who outwardly don't seem to have much authority but actually exert a lot of control over others. Although not all the rich are powerful, there does seem to be a relationship between money and power, particularly in politics.

Explanation: In this summary the opening paragraph defines power and introduces the controlling idea: Measuring power is a tricky business. The remaining paragraph explains why this is true.

Now it's your turn to mark and summarize the following articles.

1. Japanese Techniques Come to America

In a total of six states in the middle of America, 15,000 assembly-line workers are putting Japanese cars together. These autoworkers are assembling Hondas in Ohio, Toyotas in Kentucky, Mazdas in Michigan, and Nissans in Tennessee. Mitsubishi and Chrysler are jointly making cars in Illinois, and Subaru and Isuzu have set up shop in Indiana. The Japanese have brought more than their technology to their auto plants—they have also brought their own way of doing things. *1*

Using Japanese management techniques, managers at these plants have motivated American workers to produce cars of the same high quality as those made in Japan. There is a definite Japanese philosophy of all-for-one and one-for-all running through the day-to-day operations of these plants. For example, there are no narrow job classifications: No one is a welder or a painter. Instead, a visitor finds "technicians" at Nissan, "associates" at Honda, and "team members" at Mazda and Toyota. *2*

Employees at these manufacturing plants work in small, highly coordinated groups. Every worker on an assembly line is responsible for his or her particular job, for inspecting the overall quality of the product at hand, and for improving the production process. Management tries to make all workers feel equally important. Assembly-line workers actively participate in decisions on scheduling overtime and rotating jobs. *3*

In the Japanese-managed plants in the United States, an air of equality appears to be present. There are no private offices for those in management—even senior executives share large, simple offices. Executives do not have reserved parking spots; they eat in the same cafeterias and even wear the same uniforms as line workers. No office workers can drink coffee at their desks because line workers are not allowed to. *4*

The Japanese managers spend a great amount of time and energy building the morale of workers and trying to ensure company harmony. Toyota encourages its "personal touch program," an effort to promote after-hours socializing between Japanese and American workers. All the cheerleading that goes on in these plants must work very well: Nissan has the best attendance record in the U.S. auto industry, and it does not use time clocks.

For the Japanese management system to be effective, the Japanese companies need highly skilled and motivated workers. Japanese car companies spend weeks testing potential employees and training recently hired ones. The Japanese companies sometimes send workers to training sessions in Japan.

Team participation and strong interpersonal skills are definite requirements for workers in Japanese companies. Workers are rewarded for the impact they have on their "job team," and not for any personal performance. Many autoworkers love the Japanese system; others say it is too stressful. □ (Pride et al. *Business*, p. 225.)

Summary: Sample summary: The Japanese have their own way of doing things in the auto industry. First of all, they have done away with limiting job classifications like "welder" or "painter." Workers are now "associates" or "technicians." In the Japanese plants, more decisions are shared by management and employees. There are also fewer distinctions made between executives and workers. For example, executives eat in the same cafeteria as workers. Overall, Japanese employers spend a lot of time building morale among workers. But the Japanese methods are not popular with everyone: Some workers find them too stressful.

2. Yo-Yo Dieting May Be Hard on Your Heart

Losing and regaining weight, otherwise known as yo-yo dieting, may be hazardous not only to your wardrobe but also to your heart, according to a major report. [1]

Over a 14-year period, researchers analyzed the weight fluctuations* and health of 3,130 participants in the Framingham Heart Study. They found that those adults whose weight shifted the most had about a 50% increased risk for developing heart disease than those whose weight remained more stable. Death rates were also higher for those with marked weight shifts. [2]

For now the researchers are unsure how weight fluctuations are linked to health problems, but they speculate that people who diet frequently may develop a preference for high-fat foods. (Increased risk for heart disease has been associated with high-fat diets.) Yo-yo dieting, the researchers further speculate, may also cause an unhealthful distribution of body weight. Dieters may lose pounds from their legs, for example, only to regain the weight in an area such as their stomach, which puts them at increased risk for developing heart disease. [3]

Of the nearly 50 million American adults currently dieting (about 50% of American women and 25% of American men), less than 10% will be able to maintain their weight loss for at least a year. The researchers suggest that people approach weight control more seriously. "Going on a diet because it's New Year's, or because your spouse teases you about your weight, is a poor reason," says Dr. Kelly Brownell, a professor of psychology at Yale University. Instead, he recommends that people first make sure they really *need* to lose weight (by consulting their doctor), and then ask themselves if they are willing to make behavioral changes that help maintain weight loss, such as exercising and adopting healthful eating patterns. □ (Munnings, *American Health*, November, 1991, p. 93.) [4]

Summary: Sample summary: Researchers in the Framingham Heart Study have spent 14 yrs. analyzing weight fluctuations of 3,130 people. They discovered that adults whose weight shifted the most from diet to diet increased their chances of getting heart disease. Although researchers are not sure why this happens, they think those who repeatedly diet may eat more high-fat

---

* fluctuations: changes.

food, which has been linked to the development of heart disease. Dieters

may also lose weight in other places but put it back on in their stomachs,

another factor that encourages heart disease.

_____

_____

_____

_____

_____

_____

Working with Words

Here are seven more prefixes and roots you should know. Use them to figure out the meaning of the italicized words. Then fill in the accompanying blanks. Be sure, too, that you add these prefixes and roots to your vocabulary notebook.

1.	contra	(Latin prefix)	against
2.	ante	(Latin prefix)	before
3.	mort	(Latin root)	death
4.	phil	(Greek root)	love
5.	anthrop	(Greek root)	human, man
6.	chron	(Greek root)	time
7.	ist	(suffix)	person who does what is described in the rest of the word

1. When the Supreme Court convened, the justices all agreed on the decision, except for Justice Oliver Wendell Holmes. Not *contradictory* by nature, Holmes was still more liberal than his colleagues. And he frequently disagreed with other members of the court, earning himself the nickname "The Great Dissenter."

argumentative, ready to disagree _____

2. In the poem "Tithonus," the hero is granted *immortality*. But he quickly discovers that immortality without youth is a curse, not a blessing. As an old man, he wanders the earth and longs for death. In the end, immortality becomes a terrible burden.

the ability to live forever
_____

3. The American *anthropologist* Margaret Mead died in 1978. Widely known for her studies of different cultures, Mead had varied interests. She conducted research in child care, problems of adolescence, and sexual behavior. Two of her books, *Coming of Age in Samoa* and *Male and Female*, are considered classics.

person who studies human culture and history
_____

4. When they arrived at the door, they thought they were in the wrong place. The *anterior* portion of the hotel was so poorly lit. But when they entered the main ballroom, they found the room ablaze with light and full of people dancing. The party had definitely begun.

front
_____

5. In 1868, at the age of thirty-three, the industrialist Andrew Carnegie had an annual income of $50,000 and decided to interest himself in the welfare of others. He gave more than $350 million to various schools and institutes and endowed nearly two thousand libraries. By the end of his life, most people had forgotten Carnegie's reputation as a tough industrialist who grew rich by making others work hard for little money. He was remembered only as a generous *philanthropist*.

lover of humanity
_____

6. The novelist James Baldwin grew up in Harlem. But when a fellowship gave him the money to live and work in France, he quickly moved to Paris. Although Baldwin maintained a passionate interest in the country of his birth, he became a devoted *Francophile* who adored the acclaim and acceptance he found in his adopted country.

lover of France
_____

7. Lyme disease usually begins as a harmless rash followed by typical flu symptoms—fatigue, headache, and nausea. If the disease is not treated with antibiotics at this stage, it becomes serious. It can damage the heart and the brain, leaving the victim with *chronic* and often untreatable pain.

recurrent, continuing over time

_____

8. The *mortality* rate for those under thirty is extremely high in non-industrialized countries. Children are particularly at risk. Lacking the proper nutrition, their bodies are weak and cannot withstand disease.

death

_____

9. When the police interviewed him, he tried to recount the events of the robbery in *chronological* order. But he couldn't keep the events straight, and he continually contradicted himself. As a result, the police asked him to start over. Clearly, they did not find his account credible.

according to time, in sequence

_____

10. The conquest of Mexico by the Spanish *antedated* the conquest of Peru. In 1519 Hernando Cortez brutally conquered the Aztec Indians and stole from them huge quantities of silver and gold. Inspired by those riches, Francisco Pizarro began the conquest of Peru, taking from the Incan Indians more wealth than even Cortez had managed to steal.

came before

_____

Stories Behind the Words

1. *Ostracize.* The word *ostrakon* is Greek for "shell." When in times of crisis or conflict the Athenians of Greece wanted to send someone out of the city for a period of years, everyone would write a name on a piece of shell. The person receiving the most votes would have to leave the city. Today when we say that we *ostracize* someone, we mean that we are excluding

or shutting out that person from our group. (No vote is necessary to ostracize someone.)

Sample sentence: They *ostracized* him because of his political
views.

Definition: exclude, banish, shun

Other forms: ostracism, ostracizing

2. *Utopian* and *utopia*. Utopia was an imaginary island that
served as the subject and title of a book. The island was the
perfect place to live because the people of the island used reason to guide their lives. Today when we talk about a *utopia*,
we are talking about a condition, situation, or place that is
socially and politically perfect. When we say that an idea is
utopian, we mean that it is excellent but too impractical to be
put into actual use.

Sample sentence: Anita's a fool; she thinks that if she works
hard enough she can make this society into
a *utopia*.

Definition: place of perfection

Sample sentence: When will he stop trying to put those *utopian* schemes into practice?

Definition: unrealistic, excellent but impractical

3. *Jingoist.* In the eighteenth century, there was a music hall song
sung by those who were ready to go to war. The song contained
the words *by jingo*. Today when we say that someone is a *jingoist*, we are talking about a person who is always ready to go to
war. A jingoist is almost eager to begin a war.

Sample sentence: Long before he was called into action, he
was a proud *jingoist* who was ready to pick
up a gun.

Definition: person who is eager for war

Other forms: jingoism, jingoistic

4. *Mesmerize.* In the eighteenth century, an Austrian named Franz
Anton Mesmer used hypnosis to put people into a strange,

sleeplike state. People were fascinated by his skills and gathered to watch him. Today we still use the word *mesmerize* to indicate that someone is being put under hypnosis. However, frequently we use it to mean that we are fascinated by what we see.

Sample sentence: The audience seemed *mesmerized* by the sheer beauty of the ballet.

Definition: fascinate, hypnotize

Other forms: mesmerizing, mesmerist

5. *Laconic.* The Laconians were a Greek tribe who were known for their simple ways and brevity of speech. The legend goes that a Laconian general was once threatened by a rival. The rival claimed that if his army came to Laconia, his men would reduce it to ashes. The Laconian general is said to have answered with one word, *if.* Today when we say that someone is *laconic,* we mean that he or she doesn't use a great many words; someone who is laconic comes straight to the point.

Sample sentence: The heroes of old Westerns were nothing if not *laconic;* they hardly ever said more than "yep" or "nope."

Definition: brief and to the point

Other forms: laconically

Review Test: Chapter 6

Part A: Answer the following questions.

1. According to the chapter, what's the main difference between reading individual paragraphs and reading longer multi-paragraph selections?

    With longer readings, you have to connect the paragraphs into a

    unified whole.

2. List the four pointers introduced for effectively marking a text:

    (1) Annotate in the margins.

    (2) Highlight content and structure.

    (3) Underline sparingly.

    (4) Respond personally.

3. List the four pointers the author suggests for taking good notes:

    (1) Be selective.

    (2) Create easy-to-remember chunks of information.

    (3) Show relationships.

    (4) Paraphrase, condense, and abbreviate.

4. Read, mark, and take notes on the following selection. Circle all transitions.

Parents Are Only One Influence in Their Children's Development

Although parents often take the credit and the blame for the way their children turn out, they are only one among many influences. Peers, siblings, teachers, relatives, and the mass media are (also) influential. Although parents are the first significant influence, peer influence becomes increasingly important and remains so into the college years. The values and behaviors of our friends and age-mates are likely to be mirrored in our own.

Siblings are not necessarily peers, but they too have an important and sometimes lasting effect on each other's development. (For example,) an older sibling who is required to take care of a younger sibling may resent such responsibility and be careless about fulfilling it. "I really didn't care if my younger sister fell down the steps or not," said one sibling. "She did and limps today because of it." Sibling influences may also be positive. "I've always been close to my sister," remarked one woman. "She's the best friend I have." 2

Relatives may also be significant childrearing agents, especially grandmothers and aunts. One graduate student remarked, "My grandmother is the one that reared me. She was a very polite person and although I resented her nagging me to be polite when I was a kid, I am very much the way she would have wanted me to turn out." 3

Teachers become influential once a child begins school, and they remain so as long as the child is exposed to the educational system. Since most teachers are middle class, they tend to stress the values of achievement and discipline. (But) teachers have another effect on their students. They may teach offspring things parents do not want them to know. One conservative parent told his son that he was more concerned about his getting a B.A. as a born-again Christian than a B.A. from the university he was attending. "You've got some liberal professors down there that are threatening your very soul," he said. 4

Children don't need to go to school to be exposed to influences their parents may not approve of. Television is a major means of exhibiting to children language, values, and life-styles that may be different from those of the parents. □ (Knox, *Choices in Relationships*, pp. 490–491.) 5

Notes

Topic: Influences on children

Controlling idea: In addition to parents, children are influenced by other sources.

Support: 1. Siblings have a powerful effect, both positively and negatively.

2. Relatives, especially grandmothers and aunts

3. Teachers encourage the values of achievement and discipline.

— may also teach children things parents don't like

4. Television can also expose children to values, language,

and life-style parents don't approve of.

_____

_____

_____

_____

_____

5. Read, mark, and summarize the following selection.

Voodoo Death

Few events are more bizarre than sudden death caused by "voodoo" or "magic." Yet, many scientists have witnessed this strange spectacle. Here is an account of what happens in one tribe when a man discovers that he has been cursed by an enemy:

> He stands aghast, with his eyes staring at the treacherous pointers, with his hands lifted as though to ward off the lethal medium. . . . His cheeks blanch and his eyes become glassy and the expression of his face becomes horribly distorted. . . . His body begins to tremble and the muscles twist involuntarily. He sways backwards and falls to the ground. . . . From this time onwards he sickens and frets, refusing to eat and keeping aloof from the daily affairs of the tribe. Unless help is forthcoming in the shape of a countercharm, death is only a matter of a comparatively short time. (Basedow, 1925; cited in Cannon, 1942).

At first glance, voodoo deaths seem to require belief in the power of magic. Actually, all they require is belief in the power of emotion. Walter Cannon (1942), a well-known physiologist, studied many voodoo deaths and concluded that they are explained by changes in the body that accompany strong emotion. Specifically, he believed that the fear of cursed victims is so intense that it causes a heart attack or other bodily disaster.

More recent research suggests that Cannon's explanation was only partly correct. It now appears that such deaths are caused not by fear itself, but by the body's delayed reaction to fear. Normally, the parasympathetic nervous system reverses the bodily changes caused by strong emotion. For example, during intense fear, heart rate is dramatically increased; to counteract this increase, the parasympathetic system later slows the heart. It is now believed that the cursed person's emotional response is so intense that the parasympathetic nervous system overreacts and slows the heart to a stop (Seligman, 1974). Emotions are not only the spice of life. For some, they may be the spice of death as well. □ (Coon, *Introduction to Psychology*, pp. 308–309.)

Summary:

Sample summary: Recent research suggests that sudden deaths caused

by voodoo or magic may be caused by the body's reaction to fear.

Under normal conditions, the parasympathetic system reverses the bodily

changes resulting from strong emotional reactions. It will, for example,

slow down a heart that is beating too fast in response to fear. But if

a cursed person's response is extremely intense, the parasympathetic

nervous system may overreact and stop the heart, thereby

causing death.

Part B: Vocabulary Review

Here is a list of words drawn from the chapter. Some actually appear in the chapter. Some have been derived from the prefixes and suffixes introduced on page 253. Your job is to match words and blanks.

In some cases you may have to change the endings of words to make them fit the context. If you need to, consult your dictionary to decide which ending to use. *Note:* You may use some words more than once and others not at all.

anthropology	chronic	imperative
apprehensive	ostracize	laconic
indulgence	revere	criterion
documentation	rationale	misconstrue
mesmerism	philanthropy	inherent

1. __Apprehensive__ that their children will not grow up to be healthy and happy human beings, some parents become overly __indulgent__. They constantly try to fulfill their children's every wish or whim. Unfortunately this kind of over-__indulgence__ seldom produces a happy child. More often than not it produces one who is __chronically__ dissatisfied and envious of others.

2. While it may seem incredible to us, __anthropologists__ have repeatedly studied and __documented__ cultures that make the seemingly mad or insane their healers or shamans. The __rationale__ for this choice is not clear. But one hypothesis suggests that madness is __revered__ because it is considered a form of religious power. The more a person's behavior deviates or differs from normal behavior, the closer he or she may be to the gods.

3. At the end of the eighteenth century, __mesmerism__ flourished in Vienna, Austria. According to its founder and chief practitioner, Anton Mesmer, a variety of ills—from migraines to insomnia—could be cured by those who understood the workings

of animal magnetism. Mesmer claimed that the entire universe was permeated by a mysterious fluid. He also claimed that he could bring about miraculous cures by manipulating the movement of that fluid.

Although there was little __documentation__ for his claims, patients began flocking to Mesmer's door. What undoubtedly aided his popularity was the knowledge that Mesmer did not always charge his clients. In the eyes of the public that made him a __philanthropist__ as well as a healer.

But if the public loved him, the medical establishment preferred to __ostracize__ him. Other doctors considered his methods at best useless, at worst dangerous. Ultimately the refusal of Vienna's medical establishment to accept him led Mesmer to France where he became the rage of Paris and was surrounded by fervid admirers.

4. The mysterious disease called __Chronic__ Fatigue Syndrome has been widely __documented__. But as of yet no one knows what causes it. This mysterious illness strikes its victims suddenly without warning, leaving them almost too exhausted to speak. It can disappear just as suddenly, but it almost always recurs to once again make its victims __chronically__ bedridden. It is __imperative__ that those suffering from the disease dramatically alter their lifestyle. They must limit all physical activity and give themselves plenty of time to rest. Although some medical authorities have suggested the disease might have a genetic basis, that hypothesis has not been adequately tested.

Recognizing Patterns of Development

This chapter introduces five common **patterns of development** used to organize both individual paragraphs and longer readings. Recognizing an author's method or pattern of development can help you decide what is important and what to record in your notes.

- ☐ Pattern 1 traces a *sequence of dates and events.*
- ☐ Pattern 2 follows a *sequence of steps.*
- ☐ Pattern 3 shows *comparison and contrast.*
- ☐ Pattern 4 connects *cause and effect.*
- ☐ Pattern 5 describes a system of *classification.*

This chapter also shows you how to respond to paragraphs and readings that mix or combine different patterns.

New Vocabulary

As you read, watch for the following words in this chapter. However, before you check the definitions at the bottom of the page, try to derive meaning from context.

conservative	genes	abstract
liberal	hierarchically	diversion
trounced	coercive	elixir
entourage	stint	spate
abolitionist	monarchy	paradox
ratification	debilitating	sedentary
capital	gregarious	marginal
chromosomes		

Pattern 1: Sequence of Dates and Events

Dates and events appear in all kinds of writing; however, they are particularly characteristic of history and government textbooks. Authors of articles or books on history and government frequently outline a **sequence of dates and events** to explain or argue their claims. Usually they list a series of dates and events according to the order in which they occurred. Here is a good example:

> [1] The years between 1918 and 1945 brought violence and upheaval to the newly formed Polish nation. [2] In 1918, Poland was declared independent, and army officer Józef Pilsudski took control of the government. [3] After 1926, the government became a dictatorship, first under Pilsudski and later, after his death in 1935, under officers loyal to him. [4] The officers, however, did not rule for long. [5] In 1939, Germany and Russia invaded Poland, and both powers divided up the country. [6] During the war years that followed, the Germans murdered anywhere from three to five and a half million Polish Jews. [7] They killed more than half of the population of Warsaw, and the capital itself was completely destroyed. [8] Warsaw, once one of the most beautiful capitals in Europe, was reduced to rubble.

The topic of the above paragraph is "Poland between the years 1918 and 1945." The main idea is contained in the first sentence: Poland underwent violence and upheaval during the years between 1918 and 1945. The supporting sentences, with the exception of the fourth and last sentences, use specific dates and events to support that main idea. The fourth sentence is a transitional sentence that helps us move from the idea contained in sentence 3 to the idea contained in sentence 5. The last sentence is a minor supporting sentence that further develops sentence 7.

Although the paragraph contains eight sentences, only six are crucial to our notes:

Topic: Poland between 1918 and 1945

Main idea: Poland experienced violence and upheaval between the years 1918 and 1945.

Support:
1. 1918: Poland declared independent; Pilsudski took control.
2. 1926: government became dictatorship.

---

* When you take notes on your own, you need not include labels like *topic* and *main idea*. They are here purely for illustration and explanation.

3. 1935: Pilsudski died; loyal officers maintained dictatorship.
4. 1939: Germany and Russia invaded Poland and divided up the country.
5. 1939–1945: Germans murdered 3 to 5.5 million Polish Jews.
6. Warsaw destroyed.

As the sample notes indicate, complete notes on a paragraph organized around a sequence of dates and events should clearly identify the following:

1. the dates and events mentioned by the author
2. the order in which they occurred
3. the main idea they develop

Words and Phrases Commonly Used to Organize Dates and Events*

In the year _____

By the year _____

Afterwards

After _____

At this time

On the day, afternoon, evening of _____

From _____ to _____

_____ years later

Between _____ and _____

Then

Then in _____

By the end of the year

In the spring, summer, fall, winter of

In the century following

During that time, period

In the years since

Finally

---

* Blanks represent specific years that would appear in an actual text.

Look again at the sample notes, and you'll see that one date does not appear in the original paragraph: the date for the end of World War II. The author assumes his readers know when the war ended. As you read, if it becomes clear that the author expects you to know certain dates, be sure to include those dates in your notes, even if you have to look them up.

Practice reading and taking notes on these paragraphs that describe a sequence of dates and events.

Exercise 1

Directions: Read and take notes on each of the following paragraphs. *Note:* Occasionally paragraphs organized around a sequence of dates and events do not develop a main idea; instead the sequence of dates and events is the point of the paragraph. If this is the case, leave the main idea blank empty.

Example: The son of a Spanish immigrant, Fidel Castro was educated at a Roman Catholic school in Santiago, and from 1945 to 1950, he attended the University of Havana. In 1947 he participated in an unofficial raid on the Dominican Republic, and in July 1953 he organized an attack on the army barracks in Santiago. The attack was not successful, and Castro was sentenced to fifteen years in prison. In 1955 Castro was released from prison, and the following year he went to Mexico to build a Cuban revolutionary movement. In December 1959 he returned to Cuba, and in January 1960 he led a successful attempt to overthrow dictator Fulgencio Batista. Since that time, Castro has ruled Cuba with an iron hand.

Topic: Fidel Castro's rise to power

Main idea: _____

Support:
1. 1945–1950: attended University of Havana

2. 1947: took part in unofficial raid on Dominican Republic

3. July 1953: organized attack on army barracks in Santiago

4. 1955: released from prison

5. Went to Mexico to organize Cuban revolution

6. December 1959: returned to Cuba

7. January 1960: overthrew Batista

8. Since 1960, ruled with iron hand

Explanation: The purpose of this paragraph is to generally outline the dates and events in Fidel Castro's rise to power. There is no main idea. Thus the sample notes briefly record all the significant dates and events in his rise to power.

Now it's your turn.

1. Because it was a while before they produced it themselves, American colonists were dependent upon England for their tea. The first tea shrub was planted in the early nineteenth century. In 1848 more extensive experiments with tea production were carried out, and ten years later, plans were made to distribute tea seed throughout the South. These experiments, however, were cut short by the Civil War, and it was not until 1880 that the United States Department of Agriculture resumed tea production. In 1890 Charles U. Shepard of Summerville, South Carolina, devoted his private fortune to growing tea, and by 1900 he had planted sixty acres and harvested 5,000 pounds of tea.

Topic: Tea production in America

Main idea: It took a while for Americans to stop being dependent on England

for tea.

Support: 1. Early nineteenth century, first tea shrub planted

2. 1848—more experiments with tea production

3. 1858—plans to distribute throughout South

    —cut short by Civil War

4. 1880—Dept. of Agriculture resumes tea production

5. 1890—Charles Shepard of S. Carolina devoted own fortune to

   growing tea

6. 1900—had planted 60 acres, harvested 5,000 lbs.

_____

_____

_____

_____

2. Langston Hughes was born at the turn of the century in 1902. Shortly after his birth in Joplin, Missouri, Hughes's father, James Nathaniel Hughes, moved to Mexico in an effort to escape racial prejudice, but his mother, Carrier Mercer Langston, could not bear the idea of settling in a foreign country. She stayed in the United States but was forced to move constantly in order to stay employed and support her family. Despite the continual moving, Hughes developed a strong interest in poetry, and was good enough to be elected class poet when the family settled for a time in Lincoln, Illinois. Upon entering high school in 1916, Hughes was still interested in poetry and began working on the school newspaper. After graduation, he enrolled at Columbia University in 1921 but was still not sure what he wanted to do. Anxious for adventure, he signed on with a cargo vessel and, in 1923, sailed for Africa. After his return to the States in 1924, Hughes got a job as a busboy in the Waldman Park Hotel. As luck would have it, poet Vachel Lindsay visited the Waldman in 1925 and sat at Hughes's table. The young poet-busboy was able to slip several poems under Lindsay's plate. The next day Lindsay announced that he had discovered a poetic genius, and less than three years later, Langston Hughes was publishing his work in *Vanity Fair*, *Poetry*, and *The New Republic*.

Topic: Life and career of Langston Hughes
_____

Main idea: _____

_____

Support: 1. 1902—born in Joplin, Missouri
_____

2. Shortly after, family moves to Mexico to avoid racial prejudice.
_____

3. Mother and son return to U.S.

4. Hughes developed interest in poetry.

5. 1916 enters high school

6. 1921 enters Columbia University

7. 1923 sails for Africa

8. 1924 returns to America and gets job as busboy

9. 1925 slips poems under Vachel Lindsay's plate and Lindsay declares him poetic genius.

10. Less than three yrs. later he was a published poet in *Vanity Fair, Poetry* and *New Republic.*

Dates and Events in Longer Readings

As you might expect, the sequence of dates and events pattern can also exist in longer reading selections. Here, for example, the author uses dates and events to illustrate how the number of people calling themselves Democrats has shifted with the popularity of party leaders:

Party Identification and Voting

There are a number of things which can be said about party identification. First, since 1940, a large and remarkably stable percentage of Americans—usually between 42 and 48 percent—have identified themselves as Democrats.

This self-identification seemed to be affected by the relative popularity or unpopularity of leaders associated with the party. For example, in 1946, when Harry Truman's public approval was at a low point (before he bounced back to win reelection against Thomas E. Dewey in 1948), the Gallup poll found that the percentage of Americans who called themselves Democrats was down to 39. By 1948, that figure was back up to the more usual 45 percent. Democratic self-identifiers hit the high of 53 percent in 1964, when former President Lyndon Johnson was winning big over highly conservative* Republican Senator Barry Goldwater of Arizona. Then in 1972, when the very liberal† Democratic Senator George McGovern of South Dakota was being trounced‡ by Richard Nixon, the percentage of Americans who called themselves Democrats ebbed to 43, but rose back up thereafter.

Some observers thought that the election of Ronald Reagan as President in 1980 signaled a party realignment, a permanent shift in the ratio of Democratic and Republican identifiers. This proved false. As had happened so often in the past, the percentage of Democratic self-identifiers did drop to 42 in 1981, but, by 1982, the percentage was back up to 45, a level which continued to hold in Gallup polls the following year, 1983. □ (Harris, *American Democracy*, p. 275.)

Like the notes on single paragraphs using this pattern, notes on longer selections describing a sequence of dates and events should include three basic elements: (1) the dates and events identified by the author, (2) the order in which they occurred, and (3) the controlling idea they develop.

Topic: Americans identified as Democrats

Controlling idea: Since 1940 a large number of Americans have identified themselves as Democrats. However, that figure has shifted with party leaders.

Support:
1. 1946 Truman's public approval low, only 39% of Americans called themselves Dem.
2. 1948 Truman re-elected and 45% called themselves Dem.
3. 1964 Lyndon Johnson winning over the more conservative Barry Goldwater and 53% called themselves Dem.
4. 1972 liberal McGovern being beaten by Richard Nixon and percent drops to 43%
5. 1980 Ronald Reagan succeeds and figure drops to 42%
6. 1982–3 figure back up to 45%

Here again the sample notes clearly identify the dates and events that support the controlling idea. In the following exercise, make sure your notes do the same.

---

* conservative: tending to oppose change and favoring the preservation of the existing order or conditions.

† liberal: supportive of change and in favor of government playing a role in social and economic problems.

‡ trounced: beaten.

Exercise 2

Directions: Read and take notes on the following selections.

Example: **The Rise and Fall of Rasputin**

Grigori Rasputin, the Russian monk, was an influential member *1*
of the czar's court from 1907 until 1916, and during that time he
managed to discredit not only himself but the czar's authority as
well, thereby contributing to the onset of the Russian Revolution.
Rasputin first acquired prominence in 1907, when it was discovered that Alexei, the czar's son, suffered from hemophilia, a mysterious blood disorder. Because he appeared able to heal the boy,
Rasputin became the czarina's closest friend. She relied on him
for every decision, making him the most influential member of her
entourage.*

By 1909, with the help of the czarina, Rasputin dominated the *2*
Holy Synod, the supreme body in the Russian Orthodox Church.
But he had not abandoned the riotous ways of his youth, and
rumors still circulated concerning his drunken orgies. Rasputin,
however, did not seem to care, responding with his personal brand
of religious credo: "Sin in order that you may obtain forgiveness."

In 1911 Rasputin was so sure of his powers that he began to *3*
meddle openly in political affairs. Although Russian aristocrats
had at first found him a willing instrument, they soon realized
that his power had grown beyond their control. Because he was
standing in the way of reforms needed to divert the impending
revolution, it was clear that something had to be done.

In December 1916, a group of his former supporters waylaid and *4*
assassinated the monk. But if they hoped to ward off the revolution
by killing Rasputin, their efforts were in vain. By 1917 the peasants were in revolt, and the Russian Revolution had begun. □

Topic: The rise and fall of Rasputin

Controlling idea: Between 1907 and 1916, Grigori Rasputin was an influential

member of the czar's court who managed to discredit both

himself and the czar.

Support: 1. 1907 Acquired power because he appeared able to heal the

---

* entourage: train or group of followers.

czar's son who had hemophilia.

— the czarina relied on him for every decision

2. *1909 With the help of the czarina, Rasputin gained control of*

    Holy Synod, supreme body of Orthodox church.

    a. *did not abandon riotous ways*

    b. *personal creed seemed to be "Sin in order to be forgiven."*

3. *1911 Began to meddle in political affairs*

    a. *aristocrats used him at first*

    b. *then got nervous that his power was beyond their control*

4. *1916 group of supporters assassinated him*

5. *1917 peasants revolt; revolution begins*

Explanation: Since all the dates and events seem essential to explaining how Rasputin came to power and ultimately discredited himself, they have all been included in our notes.

Now it's your turn to take notes.

1. **The Movement for Women's Rights**

The civil rights, student, and antiwar movements of the 1950s and 1960s produced large numbers of young women activists. Like the women in the earlier abolitionist* movement, they began to call attention to their own inequality in America. By the late 1970s,

---

* abolitionist: person who opposed slavery

Controversy over the Equal Rights Amendment has kept it from being ratified.

they had helped to establish what came to be known as the Women's Liberation Movement.

Responding to increased lobbying by women, former President *2* John F. Kennedy created a Commission on the Status of Women in 1961. The Commission's report deplored the fact that women continued to be second-class citizens in America, and it led to the establishment of similar commissions at the state level and a national advisory council. The Equal Pay Act was passed in 1963.

In 1966, Betty Friedan, author of *The Feminine Mystique*, led a *3* movement to form the first important national feminist organization in America since Susan B. Anthony's National Woman Suffrage Association. The new organization was called the National Organization for Women (NOW). It continues to be a vocal and visible force in America on such issues as equal employment opportunity for women, full legal equality, and the rights of lesbians.

In 1967, pressured by NOW, Lyndon Johnson formally prohib- *4* ited sex discrimination in federal employment and by those doing business with the federal government. Richard Nixon extended this order and also applied it to the military. The 1964 Civil Rights Act was also amended to include sex as a prohibited ground for discrimination in private employment.

In 1969, Nixon set up another presidential task force on the *5* status of women. It found that women had not achieved equality. In higher education, for example, less than 12 percent of the doctoral degrees that were awarded that year in the United States went to women. Only 8 percent of the medical students were women. Less than 6 percent of the law students were women.

In 1972, Congress proposed the **Equal Rights Amendment (ERA)** [6] by a two-thirds vote in each house, as required by the Constitution, and referred it to the states with March 1979 set as the deadline for ratification.*

The Equal Rights Amendment had first been proposed in the [7] Congress nearly fifty years before it was finally approved by the two houses. It states: "Equality of rights under the law shall not be denied or abridged by the United States or by any state on account of sex." The words seem fairly plain, but they have caused many conflicting arguments that have kept the amendment from ratification. □ (Adapted from Harris, *American Democracy*, pp. 170–171.)

Topic: Women and equality

Controlling idea: In the 50's and 60's, the civil rights, student, and anti-war movements

produced women activists who called attention to their own inequality.

Support: 1. 1961 Kennedy responded to lobbying by women and created Commission

on Status of Women.

— Commission's report deplored women's status and established

similar commissions at state level.

2. 1963 Equal Pay Act

3. 1966 National Organization for Women formed

4. 1967 Under pressure from NOW, Johnson formally prohibited sex

discrimination in govt.

5. 1968 Nixon extended order and applied it to military.

— Civil Rights Act of 64 also amended to include sex as grounds

of discrimination

---

* ratification: the official approval of a treaty or constitution

6. 1969 Nixon set up task force on status of women and found

   women had not achieved equality.

   — Fewer than 12% of doctoral degrees went to women; only

   8% of medical students were women; fewer than 6% of

   law students were women.

7. 1972 Congress proposed Equal Rights Amendment and referred it to

   states for ratification.

8. 1979 deadline for ratification: "Equality of right under the law

   shall not be abridged under the law."

   — Controversy has kept it from ratification

2. The Rise of Samuel Gompers

Samuel Gompers was born in London in 1850. After only four *1*
years of elementary school he was apprenticed to a cigar maker
and learned the trade that he followed for more than a quarter of
a century. But it was as a labor leader rather than a cigar maker
that Samuel Gompers made his mark in history.

When his family moved to America in 1863, Gompers went with *2*
them. In 1864 he became a member of the Cigar Makers' International Union. Young as he was, he took an immediate interest in
the progress of the union and began speaking at the local meetings.
His topic was always the same—the importance of labor unity.

The hard times of the 1870s only strengthened Gompers' belief *3*
in the importance of unions, and he became even more active.
Elected president of the local union in 1874, he was ousted from
that position by the socialist opposition in 1880. But this defeat
left him free to take a prominent role in founding the Federation
of Organized Trades and Labor Unions, established in 1881 to influence legislation on behalf of labor. When the American Federation of Labor (AFL) was founded in 1886, Gompers was elected
president.

From the founding of the federation until his death in 1924, *4*
Gompers was re-elected as president. During that time he stamped
the organization with his own conservative theory. He firmly op-

posed independent politics for trade unions and resisted all social-ist efforts to infiltrate the union and politicize it. Antagonistic to the more militant Industrial Workers of the World, Gompers refused to support their strikes. Instead he advocated greater cooperation between capital* and labor.

Topic:	Rise of Samuel Gompers
Controlling idea:	Samuel Gompers was an important labor leader.
Support:	1. 1859 Apprenticed to London cigar maker

2. 1863 Moved to America

3. 1864 Became member of Cigar Makers' International Union

    a. Began speaking at local meetings

    b. Topic always importance of labor unity

4. 1870s hard times strengthened belief in unions

5. 1874 elected president of union local

6. 1880 ousted by socialist opposition

    — Freed him to take important role in founding new union

7. 1881 Federation of Organized Trades and Labor established

8. 1886 American Fed. of Labor founded and Gompers elected president

9. 1886–1924 stamped organization with own conservative theory

    a. Opposed independent politics for trade unions

    b. Resisted socialist efforts to infiltrate

    c. Antagonistic to more militant Industrial Workers of the World

        — Advocated greater cooperation between capital and labor

*   capital: in this case, owners of businesses.

DIGGING DEEPER

Do you think women still need to struggle for equality or do they have it? Explain your answer.

WRITING SUGGESTION

Go to the library and look up the history of one of your favorite foods—chocolate, pizza, ice cream, hamburgers. Then write a paper in which you describe, through a series of dates and events, how the food came into being and became popular.*

Pattern 2: Sequence of Steps

Authors, particularly those writing in the sciences, often need to explain how something works, functions, or develops. When that is their purpose, they usually employ a **sequence of steps** pattern. Step by step or stage by stage, they guide their readers through some process or development. Here, for example, the author describes the three stages in the growth of identical twins:

> There are three basic stages involved in the development of identical twins. Their growth begins when the father's sperm pierces the egg of the mother. The fertilized egg then splits and divides into equal halves, each half receiving exactly the same number of chromosomes† and genes.‡ The halves of the egg then develop into two babies who are of the same sex and who are identical in all hereditary traits such as hair color and eye color.

---

* See the *American Heritage Cookbook* and *Illustrated History of American Eating, Dictionary of Gastronomy, Encyclopedia of Food, The Wise Encyclopedia of Cookery.*

† chromosomes: bodies within a cell that consist of hundreds of clear, jellylike particles strung together like beads. They carry the genes.

‡ genes: the elements responsible for the transmission of hereditary characteristics, such as hair color and eye color.

The topic of this paragraph is "the development of identical twins." The main idea statement tells us there are three specific stages. The supporting sentences then describe these stages in more detail. Notes on a paragraph like this one should identify the following:

1. the topic
2. the main idea if there is one (Some paragraphs describing a sequence of steps simply describe the sequence of steps and do not develop a main idea.)
3. the specific steps in the sequence
4. the order in which they are presented
5. any specialized vocabulary used to describe the sequence

As you can see, the following sample notes identify all five essential elements of this pattern:

Topic: Development of identical twins

Main idea: There are three stages in the development of identical twins.

Support:
1. Father's sperm pierces mother's egg.
2. Fertilized egg splits and divides into equal halves; each half receives same number of chromosomes and genes.
3. Halves of egg develop into two babies of same sex, identical in all hereditary traits such as hair color and eye color.

The next exercise will give you some practice reading and taking notes on paragraphs describing a sequence of steps or stages.

Exercise 3

Directions: Read and take notes on the following paragraphs.

Example: In spring, the stickleback, a small fish found in both fresh and salt water, goes through a strange courtship ritual. With the coming of the spring months, the male stickleback begins to look for a place where he can build his nest. Once he has found one, he grows aggressive and fights off all invaders. After finishing the nest, he goes off in search of a female. When he finds one, he leads her to the nest, and she enters it. The male then hits the tail of the female, forcing her to deposit her eggs. Once she lays the eggs, the female swims off, and the male enters the nest.

Topic: Courtship of the stickleback

Main idea: In spring, the stickleback goes through a strange courtship ritual.

Support:
1. Male stickleback looks for place to build nest.
2. Finding one, he grows aggressive.
3. After finishing nest, he looks for female.
4. Leads her to nest, which she enters.
5. Male hits female's tail, forcing her to deposit eggs.
6. Once eggs are laid, she swims off, and male enters nest.

Explanation: Since our notes contain the topic, main idea, and all the steps described in the paragraph, we have everything of importance.
Do the rest of the exercises in the same manner.

1. There are three basic stages involved in the growth of fraternal twins. Their growth begins when two different eggs are pierced by two different sperms. The two eggs then develop separately, each with its own individual set of genes and chromosomes. Eventually the two eggs become two babies with different hereditary traits.

Topic: Growth of fraternal twins

Main idea: There are three stages in the growth of fraternal twins.

Support:
1. Two different eggs are pierced by 2 different sperms.
2. Two eggs develop separately.
   — Each has own genes and chromosomes.
3. Two eggs become 2 babies.
   — Each has different hereditary traits.

_____

_____

_____

_____

_____

_____

_____

_____

2. The eggs of the King Salmon hatch in freshwater streams, but within a year after hatching, the young salmon head out to sea. During their journey they are destroyed by their natural enemies, the bear, duck, and raccoon and by the polluted waters containing the wastes of factories and cities. Only a small proportion of the salmon actually reach the sea. Those who do stay anywhere from four to six years and then begin their journey back to a river like the one in which they hatched. Here they lay thousands of eggs that will hatch and go through the same life cycle. Once the adult King Salmon have laid their eggs, life is over for them. They change color and become slimy. Slowly, they float downstream with their tails forward. In a matter of days, they are dead.

Topic: Life cycle of King Salmon

Main idea: Shortly after hatching, young salmon head out to sea on a

threatening journey.

Support:
1. Eggs hatch in freshwater streams.

2. Year later head out to sea

   a. During journey destroyed by pollution and natural enemies

   b. Only small portion reach sea

3. After 6 yrs. begin journey back to river where hatched

   — Lay thousands of eggs

4. Life over, they change color and become slimy

    — Float downstream and die

Sequences of Steps in Longer Readings

Within longer selections organized around a sequence of steps, the author has a chance to explain each step or stage in more detail. The following passage describes five distinct stages or steps in the development of paranoia.

The Development of Paranoia

Paranoia is a psychological disorder in which people believe, for *1* no evident reason, that others are trying to do them harm. The disorder appears to follow a consistent sequence of steps or stages, each one characterized by a specific type of behavior or thinking. In their study of the disorder, researchers have outlined five basic stages.

At the onset of the disorder, victims begin to distrust the motives *2* of others. They are convinced that people are taking advantage of them. They are constantly on the alert and trying to detect ulterior or secret motives in the actions of others.

If suspicion marks the *first* stage, self-protection is central to the *3* *second. At this point* any personal failure is seen as the fault of others. Victims no longer take responsibility for their actions and their consequences. Someone else is always to blame.

As a result of their suspicions, the victims *now* respond to the *4* world with hostility. They are openly angry at their supposed ill-treatment at the hands of others. The period of anger usually leads to a moment of **paranoid illumination.** At this point everything falls into place, and the victims begin to understand the plot or conspiracy which they claim has been directed against them.

Following the period of illumination, the victim may develop *5* **delusions of persecution.** Seeing enemies everywhere, they are now convinced that someone, often a whole group, is trying to do them bodily harm, perhaps even kill them. □

In this case the thesis statement all but announces the author's pattern of organization: "In their study of the disorder, researchers have outlined five basic stages." Statements like these are typical of this pattern as are transitional words like the ones italicized in the sample selection.

Transitions frequently used to organize a sequence of steps:

Once	At this point
First, Second, Third	At this stage
Then	Now
Next	In the beginning
Afterwards	In the initial stages
Finally	At the onset
At this time	In the final stage

Much like notes on paragraphs that describe a sequence of steps, notes on longer readings using this pattern should indicate the topic, the controlling idea (if one is present), and all of the steps in the appropriate order. Naturally your notes should also include any specialized terms used to describe the sequence. Here to illustrate are notes on the above reading:

Topic: Development of paranoia

Controlling idea: In studying paranoia, researchers have identified five distinct stages.

Support:
1. Victims are distrustful and think everyone is taking advantage of them.
2. Self-protection is central.
   a. refuse to take responsibility
   b. somebody else always to blame
3. Hostile response to world
4. Moment of "paranoid illumination"
   — victims claim to understand plot or conspiracy against them
5. Delusions of persecution
   — enemies everywhere

The following exercise offers you a chance to take notes on longer readings describing a sequence of steps.

Exercise 4

Directions: Read each selection. Then take notes on the blanks provided. *Note:* The selection may or may not express a controlling idea.

Example: **The Body's Healing Powers**

Flesh wounds are a common and dangerous injury. Because the skin has been broken, the body is open to infection. However, the body's response to such wounds is remarkably quick and efficient. [1]

The *first* response occurs when the blood begins to clot. *Then* tiny bodies in the blood stream called **platelets** rush to the site of the wound and disintegrate. Fibrous proteins begin to form, and the blood that has already escaped hardens into a scab. [2]

Once the blood flow stops, the body releases chemicals in response to trauma. Those chemicals called **pyrogens** cause the area of the wound to grow warm and blood vessels to open, allowing nutrients, oxygen, and white blood cells to flood the area and encourage the formation of new tissue. ☐ [3]

Topic: Body's response to flesh wounds

Controlling idea: The body's response to flesh wounds is quick and efficient.

Support:
1. Blood clots.

2. Tiny bodies in the bloodstream called platelets rush to wound site and disintegrate.

3. Fibrous proteins begin forming.

4. Escaped blood hardens into scab.

5. Body releases chemicals called "pyrogens."

    a. Area grows warm.

    b. Blood vessels open.

6. White blood cells flood area and encourage formation of new tissue cells.

Explanation: In this case, the author has not identified a specific number of steps. But with the help of the italicized transitions, we could break the process down into six basic steps and record them in the correct order.

Now it's your turn.

1. Volcanic Eruptions

During the eruption of a volcano, *lava* or molten rock within the volcano becomes charged with steam and gas. The lava then shoots upward and falls back to earth in fragments of all sizes. Depending on their size, the fragments are called *bombs, cinders,* or *ash.* The fragments either fall on the slopes of the cone, increasing its size, or they re-enter the volcano's crater and continue the cycle of fiery explosions. ₁

When the lava within the crater builds up to the point that it flows over the crater's rim, the volcano's eruption is at its *crisis* or crucial point. After a final explosion of lava, the volcano begins to cool. ₂

During the cooling stage, the volcano emits gases and vapors. This phase is often followed by the appearance of hot springs or geysers like the ones that can be seen in Yellowstone National Park. Eventually the last traces of volcanic heat disappear, and cold springs may emerge in and around the volcano. □ ₃

Topic: Volcanic eruptions _____

Controlling idea: _____

_____

Support: 1. Molten rock charged with steam or gas _____

2. Lava shoots upward and falls back to earth in fragments.

a. Called bombs, cinders or ash _____

b. Either fall on slopes or enter crater and continue fiery explosions

3. When lava in crater builds up to the point that it flows over rim,

eruption at "crisis"

4. Final explosion and lava cools

 — Emits gases and vapors

5. This phase often followed by appearance of hot spring or geysers

6. Cold springs may appear around volcano after last traces of

volcanic heat disappear.

_____

_____

_____

_____

_____

_____

2. **Laboring to Give Birth**

Within the context of giving birth, the term **labor** refers to a series *1* of uterine contractions that start at half-hour intervals and gradually increase in frequency. During that time, the mother's body undergoes a rather remarkable series of changes.

In the early period of labor, the sphincter muscle around the *2* cervix widens or **dilates.** Then as the contractions grow stronger, the baby's head begins to push through the enlarged cervical canal and into the opening of the vagina. When the baby's head emerges, the contractions become less strong but more frequent. The baby's shoulders then come into view and finally the body.

Once the baby emerges, the **umbilical cord** that had connected *3* the **fetus** to the **placenta** is tied off and cut. However, the contractions continue until the placenta is expelled from the body as **afterbirth.** ☐

Topic: The stages of labor

Controlling idea: During the series of uterine contractions called "labor," the mother's body undergoes a remarkable series of changes.

Support:

1. Sphincter muscle widens or dilates.

2. Contractions grow stronger and baby's head pushes through.

3. Contractions grow weaker but more frequent as baby's head emerges.

4. Once the whole baby emerges, the umbilical cord connecting fetus to placenta is tied off and cut.

5. Contractions continue until placenta is expelled as afterbirth.

WRITING SUGGESTION

Write a paper in which you describe the sequence of steps men and women follow when they try to attract a member of the opposite sex.

Pattern 3: Comparing and Contrasting

Undoubtedly at some point you have **compared**—pointed out the similarities—and **contrasted**—mentioned the differences—between two people, events, animals, or objects. It shouldn't be surprising, then, to *discover* that many writers compare and contrast in print. Take, for example, the following paragraph:

> Much attention, perhaps too much, has been paid to the differences between Japanese and American workers. But perhaps we do need to examine more carefully the differences between Japanese and American management at the highest levels of decision making. In Japan the heads of companies are discouraged from earning more than fourteen times the salary of their highest paid workers. In America the head of a company can be expected to earn as much as fifty times more than the highest salaried worker. In Japan if someone in top management makes a serious blunder, he is in public disgrace. In America if the same thing happens, the company may suffer bankruptcy, but no one would expect the man or woman who erred to take responsibility publicly.

While the introductory sentence suggests a paragraph that will focus on the differences between Japanese and American workers, the transitional word *but* reverses the opening train of thought. The main idea statement—"But perhaps we do need to examine more carefully the differences between Japanese and American management at the highest levels of decision making"—makes it clear that the paragraph will concentrate on differences between Japanese and American management; the supporting sentences, in turn, cite specific differences.

Notes on a paragraph using a comparison and contrast pattern should contain the following:

1. the two topics being compared and/or contrasted
2. the similarities and/or differences mentioned
3. the main idea they explain or support

Here to illustrate are notes on the above paragraph:

Topic: Differences between Japanese and American management

Main idea: We need to look at the differences between Japanese and American management.

Support: 1. In Japan heads of companies discouraged from making more than 14 times highest salary of employees.
2. In America can make 50 times more than employees.
3. Japanese top management publicly disgraced for mistakes.
4. American management not expected to take responsibility publicly.

The next exercise will give you some practice reading and taking notes on paragraphs that use a comparison and contrast method of development.

Exercise 5

Directions: Read and take notes on the following paragraphs.

Example: The Africanized or so-called *killer bees* have finally entered the United States, and their arrival has aroused intense speculation and fear. Yet some of that anxiety may prove to be unfounded. In some ways the African bees resemble ordinary American honeybees. For example, the venom of the African bee is no more toxic or poisonous than the honeybee's. In fact, it is actually less toxic than that of the ordinary American wasp. What does distinguish the African bee from the honeybee is the African bee's determined defense of territory. If disturbed by an intruder, the African bees will mount a frenzied attack and pursue the person who disturbed their nest. Although honeybees also pursue intruders, they quickly give up. Clearly the African bees can be dangerous if disturbed, but it is unlikely that many people are going to approach their nest. Thus their danger can, for the most part, be avoided.

Topic: Similarities and differences between African bees and honeybees

Main idea: The fear of African bees may be exaggerated; they actually resemble honeybees.

Support: 1. Venom is not more toxic.

— Less toxic than wasp

2. Both kinds of bees pursue intruders.

3. Difference is in degree of intensity.

With the film Glory, *Hollywood finally focused on the contribution of African-Americans during the Civil War.*

    a. honeybees give up.

    b. African bees don't.

4. Since most people avoid bees, much of their danger can

    be avoided.

Explanation: In this paragraph the author used both similarities and differences to illustrate how the threat of African bees may have been exaggerated. As you can see, the sample notes clearly indicate how the similarities and differences cited support that main idea.

    Now it's your turn.

1. The Civil War was fought to win equality for all African-Americans. Yet ironically, the Union army did not treat black and white soldiers equally. Although their duties were the same, black soldiers received less money than their white counterparts. Black soldiers earned seven dollars per month, white soldiers earned thirteen. Likewise, it was claimed that black and white soldiers had an equal chance to become officers. But, in fact, very few black soldiers were promoted. What is surprising is that such treatment did not destroy the fighting spirit of African-American soldiers, who were cited, throughout the war, for acts of heroism above and beyond the call of duty. In recent years, historians have begun to focus on these contributions, bringing them to the attention of the American public. Even Hollywood has taken notice of African-American participation in the Civil War, and the movie *Glory* movingly depicted the bravery of the first black regiment allowed to go into battle.

Topic: Differences between black and white soldiers in Civil War

Main idea: Although the Civil War was fought to win equality for African-Americans, the army did not treat black and white soldiers equally.

Support:
1. Duties were the same but black soldiers received less money.

2. Black soldiers did not have the same chance to be promoted.

3. Recently historians have begun to write about heroism of African-American soldiers.

— Even Hollywood has taken notice with movie *Glory*.

2. When Gerald Ford, the thirty-eighth president of the United States, came to office, he was fond of emphasizing his resemblance to one of his famous predecessors, Harry S Truman. Like Ford, Truman had been a vice president who became president only by chance. Truman took over when Franklin Roosevelt died in office, a circumstance that resembled Ford's own ascent to the presidency when Richard Nixon resigned from office. Truman, like Ford, was not an intellectual, and he tended to exaggerate his lack of learning, insisting that he was just a simple man with simple tastes. Ford also liked to emphasize that both he and Truman came to office at a difficult time. Truman led the nation during the final months of World War II, and Ford entered office after the nation had been faced with the Watergate scandals.

Topic:	Similarities between Ford and Truman
Main idea:	Gerald Ford, the 38th president of the U.S., liked to emphasize his resemblance to his predecessor, Harry Truman.
Support:	1. Both became president by chance.
	a. Truman took over when Roosevelt died.
	b. Ford took over when Nixon resigned.
	2. Both played the role of anti-intellectual.
	3. Both came to office at difficult times.
	a. Truman at end of World War II
	b. Ford after political scandal of Watergate

Comparing and Contrasting in Longer Readings

By using the comparison and contrast method of development in longer readings, the author has a chance to describe similarities and differences in greater detail. The following reading is a good example:

Broadcast and Print Media

Political coverage in both the broadcast and print media* is shaped by their need to attract consumers in order to make a profit; however, the two media differ in ways that are worth mentioning.

---

* broadcast and print media: in this case the phrase applies primarily to television and newspapers.

Although both are profit-making enterprises, the lion's share of profit in radio and television comes from entertainment programming. Newspapers, *on the other hand*, make more money on the news. For newspapers, public events are the first priority. To be sure, they do feel pressure to increase sales by being as entertaining and attractive as possible, and that pressure results in sections devoted to sports, comics, human interest, family living, and so forth. Nonetheless, a central purpose of the newspaper remains the news. And, compared with television, newspapers provide far more depth of coverage and report on a broader spectrum of events and people.

By its very nature as a visual, time-limited medium, television news places a high premium on short stories that permit attractive and dramatic pictures. Thus, a story about a candidate in a parade, surrounded by cheering crowds, is more likely to be broadcast than is a story with "talking heads" discussing some policy option at length. Air time is very short (about twenty-two minutes per half hour) and *very* expensive.

By contrast, newspapers have fewer restrictions on content. Their readers can dwell at greater length on a story or reread parts of it or browse and skip around if they wish. This permits the typical daily newspaper to provide a more detailed account of a larger number of stories than can be covered in a half-hour TV news show. □ (Adapted from Aldrich et al., *American Government*, pp. 309–310.)

In this selection the author's thesis statement all but announces a comparison and contrast pattern of organization: "Political coverage in both the broadcast and print media is shaped by their need to attract consumers in order to make a profit; however, the two media differ in ways that are worth mentioning." Additional clues to this pattern are transitions like "on the other hand" and "by contrast."

Transitions frequently used in comparison and contrast:

However	In comparison
In contrast	On the contrary
By contrast	Conversely
In opposition	In a similar fashion
On the one hand	Similarly
On the other hand	Likewise
Just the opposite	

Like notes on paragraphs, notes on longer readings using the comparison and contrast pattern should include the two topics discussed, the similarities and/or differences cited, and the controlling idea they develop. Here to illustrate are notes on the previous reading:

Topic: Differences between newspaper and television

Controlling idea: In their coverage of political events, television and newspapers both want to make a profit, but they differ in important ways.

Support:
1. Television makes more money from entertainment.
2. Newspapers try to be entertaining, but the main focus is public events.
   — Provide more depth of coverage than does television
3. Because it is a visual and time-limited medium, television focuses on short stories and dramatic pictures.
4. In newspapers content is less limited; they can offer more detailed accounts.

In a case like this, in which the author's description of similarities and differences is not extremely detailed, you could consider summarizing as an alternative to informal outlining.

In covering political events, both television and newspapers want to make a profit, but there are significant differences between the two. For television the lion's share of profits come from entertainment while newspapers concentrate on public events. While television is forced to focus on short stories and dramatic pictures, newspapers can provide more depth of coverage and more detail.

In the following exercises, one of the readings will lend itself well to summarizing. You decide which one.

Exercise 6

Directions: Read and take notes on the following selections.

Example: **Cheetahs and Leopards**

It is easy enough to confuse cheetahs with leopards. Even in Africa where people are used to seeing these animals, they are often called by the same Swahili name "ngari." The confusion is understandable. On a superficial level, the two have much in common.

Both have light tan fur and dark spots. Both have about the same body weight, approximately one hundred and ten to one hundred and thirty pounds.

However, upon closer inspection, there are clearly more differences than similarities between the two. The cheetah has longer legs and a much smaller head. The leopard is an agile climber that climbs trees to hunt monkeys; the cheetah, one of the fastest animals on earth, takes its prey on the ground, running it down at full speed. The leopard's diet is varied. When game is scarce, it can subsist on mice and fruits. The cheetah, by contrast, relies primarily on antelope for food. [2]

Their temperaments vary almost as much as their eating habits. Leopards will occasionally hunt in pairs. But cheetahs are solitary animals who hunt alone. The only departure from their solitary life comes when the females raise their young. At that point, they, like leopards, are devoted mothers who keep careful watch over their cubs. □ [3]

Topic: *Cheetahs' and leopards' similarities and differences*

Controlling idea: *Although cheetahs and leopards share some similarities, they are really quite different.*

Support:

1. *Cheetahs and leopards share the same name in Swahili: "ngari."*

2. *They both have light tan fur and dark spots, and both are about same body weight: 110–130 pounds.*

3. *Both good mothers*

4. *Cheetah, however, has longer legs and smaller head.*

5. *Leopard is an agile climber that hunts in the trees while cheetah, one of the fastest animals on earth, hunts down prey.*

6. *Temperaments also vary*

    — Leopards hunt in pairs while cheetahs are solitary and hunt alone.

Explanation: Our sample notes record the similarities and differences cited in support of the thesis statement: Upon closer inspection there are as many differences as there are similarities between the two.

Now it's your turn.

1.   Losing a Spouse

For wives, death of the husband often presents financial difficulties. Life insurance does not carry with it the major benefits that are commonly assumed. Although women are the beneficiaries in the large majority of cases, the stereotype of the rich widow is largely false.

Financial difficulties are not the only—or even the major—problem facing widows. There is the deep emotional shock and the sense of personal loss. In a large number of cases, the wife simply has not been prepared for the death. (For some reason, discussions of impending death—with family or friends—are considered taboo in our society.) And, of course, there is the loneliness and necessity for making new living arrangements—and a new social life.

Despite the problems facing older widows, those facing widowers are at least as formidable, if not more so. In addition to the difficulties mentioned—emotional shock, personal grief, adapting to a new life-style—older men undoubtedly have a harder time taking care of general household chores, laundry, shopping, food preparation, and so on.   □   (Adapted from Kephart, *The Family, Society, and the Individual,* pp. 391–393.)

Topic: Differences between widows and widowers

Controlling idea: Although men and women who lose their spouses face some similar

problems, there are some definite differences between

the two.

Support: 1.   For wives, the death of a husband often presents financial difficulties.

a.   Life insurance does not always carry the kinds of benefits

assumed.

b.   Stereotype of rich widow false

2. Face deep emotional shock and sense of personal loss.

   a. Need to make new living arrangements

   b. Create new social life

3. Men also face emotional shock, personal grief, and need to adapt to

   new life-style.

4. Have a harder time taking care of household chores.

Sample Summary: Widowhood creates problems for both men and women.

Both sexes experience a profound sense of personal grief and loss. Women,

however, tend to experience more financial difficulties while men have trou-

ble keeping up a household by themselves.

2. Rapport-Talk and Report-Talk

Who talks more, then, women or men? The seemingly contradic- *1*
tory evidence is reconciled by the difference between what I call
public and *private speaking*. More men feel comfortable doing
"public speaking," while more women feel comfortable doing "private" speaking. Another way of capturing these differences is by
using the terms *report-talk* and *rapport-talk*.

For most women, the language of conversation is primarily a *2*
language of rapport: a way of establishing connections and negotiating relationships. Emphasis is placed on displaying similarities
and matching experiences. From childhood, girls criticize peers
who try to stand out or appear better than others. People feel
their closest connections at home, or in settings where they *feel* at
home—with one or a few people they feel close to and comfortable
with—in other words, during private speaking. But even the most
public situations can be approached like private speaking.

For most men, talk is primarily a means to preserve independ- *3*
ence and negotiate and maintain status in a hierarchical* social

---

* hierarchical: ordered according to rank.

order. This is done by exhibiting knowledge and skill, and by holding center stage through verbal performance such as storytelling, joking, or imparting information. From childhood, men learn to use talking as a way to get and keep attention. So they are more comfortable speaking in larger groups made up of people they know less well—in the broadest sense, "public speaking." But even the most private situations can be approached like public speaking, more like giving a report than establishing rapport. □ (Tannen, *You Just Don't Understand*, pp. 76–77.)

Topic: Rapport- and report-talk

Controlling Idea: Men feel more comfortable with public or report-talk while women are more inclined to use rapport-talk.

Support:
1. Language of rapport is a way of establishing connections and negotiating relationships.
   a. Emphasis placed on similarity of experience
   b. Even in childhood, girls criticize those who are different.
2. For men, talk is a way of maintaining status in a social order.
   a. Exhibit knowledge
   b. In childhood, men use talking to get and keep attention.

Does your own experience support the differences in male and female speech described in the previous reading? Do you agree that men engage in report-talk while women prefer the language of rapport?

Pattern 4: Cause and Effect

Like the comparison and contrast method of development, the cause and effect pattern can appear just about anywhere. Writers of science texts make use of it, as do writers of history and sociology. Whatever type of reading you do, you are bound to run across passages that explain how one event—the *cause*—leads to or produces another event—the *effect*. Look, for example, at the following paragraph:

> Fear has a profound effect on the human body. When you become frightened, you breathe more deeply thereby sending your muscles more oxygen and energy. In addition, your heart beats faster making your blood circulate more quickly, rushing oxygen to all parts of your body. In response to fear, your stomach and intestines stop contracting and all digestive activity ceases. Your saliva also stops flowing, causing your mouth to become dry. Fear also causes the body's blood vessels to shrink, making your face grow pale and white.

In this paragraph the main idea statement identifies the cause-and-effect relationship under discussion: Fear has a profound effect on the human body. The supporting sentences then describe those effects in specific detail. They also describe *cycles of causes and effects* in which one effect becomes the cause of another. Fear, for example, causes your blood vessels to shrink, which, in turn, produces another effect—your face grows pale.

As you might expect, cycles of causes and effects should be included in your notes. But, in addition, you also need the following:

1. the general cause and effect relationship described by the stated or implied main idea
2. the specific details about causes and/or effects

To illustrate, here are notes on the above paragraph:

Topic: Effects of fear

Main idea: Fear has a powerful effect on the human body.

Support:
1. Breathe more deeply, sending muscles more oxygen and energy
2. Heart beats faster, making blood circulate more rapidly.
   — Blood then rushes oxygen to all parts of body
3. Stomach and intestines stop contractions so that all digestion ceases.
4. Saliva stops flowing and mouth gets dry.
5. Blood vessels shrink.
   — Causes face to get pale

The following exercise will allow you to practice reading and taking notes on paragraphs that describe cause and effect relationships.

Exercise 7

Directions: Read and take notes on the following paragraphs.

Example: It would seem in retrospect that the prohibition laws* of the 1920s actually helped encourage, rather than hinder, illegal activity. Citizens in every section of the country showed nothing but contempt for the laws, and any attempt at law enforcement was met with indifference or hostility. Probably the worst result of the laws was that the control of liquor distribution fell into the hands of organized crime, leading to increased criminal violence throughout the country. Rather than decreasing crime, the prohibition laws actually helped to increase it.

---

* prohibition laws: laws forbidding transportation, sale, and possession of alcoholic beverages.

Topic:	*Effects of Prohibition*
Main idea:	*Prohibition encouraged illegal activity.*
Support:	*1. Citizens showed contempt and hostility for enforcement of the laws.*
	2. Liquor distribution fell into the hands of organized crime causing violence to spread.

Explanation: Effects of prohibition is the topic of the paragraph. The first sentence of the paragraph is the main idea statement. It explains that the prohibition laws led to increased illegal activity. The remaining supporting sentences describe the effects in detail, and we have included all the effects in our notes.

1. No one would deny that several events led up to America's rebellion against British domination. However, it is certain that the Coercive* Acts were an important contributing factor. Designed to punish Americans for the Boston Tea Party, the acts treated Bostonians with great severity. The Port of Boston was closed until the tea that had been destroyed was paid for, and Massachusetts' colonial charter was revoked. In addition, any English officials indicted for capital offenses could no longer be tried in Massachusetts; they were to be tried only on British soil. Moreover, officials could no longer be locally elected; instead, they had to be appointed by the king. Perhaps most offensive to the Americans was the new quartering act. It specified that British troops could be housed in all public inns or empty homes without the owners' permission. Not surprisingly, the Coercive Acts earned a nickname; the colonists called them the Intolerable Acts.

Topic:	Coercive Acts
Main idea:	The Coercive Acts, meant to punish rebels for the Boston Tea Party, actually contributed to the American Revolution.
Support:	1. Port of Boston closed until tea destroyed in Boston Tea Party paid for.

* coercive: forcing someone to do something against his or her will.

2. Colonial charter of Massachusetts revoked. _____

3. English officials had to be tried in England. _____

4. Officials could not be locally elected; had to be appointed by king. _____

5. New quartering act housed soldiers in public inns or empty homes

   without owners' permission. _____

6. Colonists called them Intolerable Acts. _____

_____

_____

_____

2. When Elvis Presley, the acknowledged king of rock-and-roll, died, he was horribly overweight, addicted to countless drugs, and subject to fits of uncontrollable rage. Exactly what caused Presley to degenerate so terribly is still unknown; there seems, in fact, to have been no one cause, but a complicated variety of causes. Throughout his career, Presley longed to be taken more seriously as an actor, but he never made anything but critical disasters. Films like *Blue Hawaii* earned money, but they never made the critics take notice. Devoted to his mother, who protected him throughout his childhood and youth, he was grief-stricken over her death in 1958, and he never quite recovered from her loss. Oddly enough, although he never complained, Elvis's spirit seems to have been broken by his highly publicized stint* in the army. Upon his return to civilian life, he failed to achieve the promise, personally or professionally, of the pre-army years. What is astonishing is that Presley has been dead for almost two decades but he is still idolized by millions of fans.

Topic: Causes of Elvis Presley's deterioration _____

Main idea: No one knows precisely what caused Elvis Presley's deterioration;

there seem to have been several causes. _____

_____

* stint: period of time spent at a particular activity.

Support: 1. Movies were critical disasters.

      — Made money but critics didn't care

2. Grief-stricken over mother's death in 1958

3. Spirit may have been broken by army service

4. Still idolized after almost 20 yrs

Cause and Effect in Longer Readings

In longer readings authors can spend more time describing both causes and effects. Here, for example, the author explains in some detail how having friends and family (cause) can help keep us alive (effect):

Friendlessness: A Major Risk

People who have close ties to their friends and family tend to be better off physically and psychologically than loners. A recent study at the University of Michigan suggests that a lack of social relationships actually puts people at greater risk of dying prematurely. This "major risk factor for health," say sociologist James House and his colleagues, "rivals the effects of well-established health risk factors such as cigarette smoking, high blood pressure, blood lipids, obesity, and physical activity." [1]

A number of studies have tracked health habits and social ties for several years. Their unanimous conclusion: Men and women who keep to themselves, even those in good physical health, are more likely to die younger than are those who have relatively extensive social relationships. [2]

Other research has shown that simply the presence or touch of 3 another person can calm us physiologically—keeping blood pressure and heart rate at low levels, for example. One theory suggests that social contact may keep us healthy by lowering the brain's secretion of stress hormones.

It's still unclear whether these benefits result from the quantity, 4 quality or nature of the bonds we form with others. Researchers speculate that social ties either foster a sense of meaning that promotes health or they motivate people to take care of themselves—to eat right, for example, and to exercise and stay away from drugs. □ (*Psychology Today*, November 1988, p. 8.)

Like notes on paragraphs describing cause-and-effect relationships, notes on longer readings using this pattern should identify the topic, controlling idea, and all causes and effects described.

Topic: Effect of social relationships

Controlling idea: Several studies suggest that people with extensive social relationships tend to live longer and have better health than those without.

Support:
1. As a risk factor, friendlessness rivals effects of established risks like smoking and high blood pressure.
2. Just the presence of others can keep heart rate and blood pressure low.
   — Social contact may also lower brain secretion of stress hormones.
3. Researchers don't know for sure if quantity or quality of ties is crucial.
4. Social ties may also motivate us to take care of ourselves.

The next exercise will give you a chance to take notes on longer readings that connect cause and effect.

Verbs frequently used to link cause and effect

result	cause
increase	begin
produce	foster
stimulate	stop
generate	lead to, lead up to
induce	bring about
introduce	create
contribute	set off

Exercise 8

Directions: Read and take notes on the following selections.

Example: **Farming the Earth's Jungles**

There was a time, not too many years ago, when people believed ₁
that the problem of food shortages could readily be solved by culti-
vating the world's jungles. In Brazil an agricultural colony was
organized with precisely this objective since the Amazon Basin
seemed the perfect site for cultivation. But to the surprise of many,
the project failed and failed badly. However, in retrospect, several
major causes of that failure can readily be identified.

The first and most fundamental cause was the tropical soil itself. ₂
Surprisingly the soil is poor in nutrients, and it is not helped by
the frequent torrential rains that come. Decaying foliage, which
could contribute nutrients to the soil, washes away with the heavy
rains before it can enrich the earth.

Then, too, there is the problem of how quickly the jungle grows.
Workers on the project claimed they would clear a space for plant-
ing one day, return the next, and find it overgrown. The jungle
seemed too powerful for the puny efforts of human beings to make
a lasting imprint.

Yet another cause was the relationship between the sunlight and ₄
soil. In many areas when the soil is exposed to sunlight, it hardens
and turns into laterite, a red, rock-like substance containing high
concentrations of aluminum and iron. Beautiful to look at, laterite
is all but impossible to till. □

Topic: <u>Causes of failure to cultivate the Amazon Basin</u>

Controlling idea: <u>There were several causes for the failure to cultivate the Amazon</u>

<u>Basin.</u>

Support: <u>1. Tropical soil was poor in nutrients.</u>

<u>a. Rains don't help.</u>

<u>b. Wash away nutrients.</u>

<u>2. Jungle grows too quickly</u>

— Workers would clear a space and the next day it would

be overgrown.

3. Sunlight turns soil into hard laterite

— Looks pretty but hard to till.

Explanation: In this reading the author identifies three causes for the failure to cultivate the Amazon Basin. The sample notes, therefore, identify and explain all three causes.

Now it's your turn.

1. Of Comets and Dinosaurs

The causes for the extinction of dinosaurs remain one of science's great mysteries. Although there are several theories as to why the dinosaurs disappeared, only one seems truly sound. According to this theory, dinosaurs became extinct because a comet or asteroid crashed into the earth, producing huge quantities of dust. The dust blocked out sunlight for many months, and plants dependent on photosynthesis* for survival died out. Thus the dinosaurs, who were vegetarians, were left without food. The absence of sunlight would have also caused temperatures to drop sharply, subjecting the dinosaur to twin forces of destruction—freezing and starvation.

The theory of comet collision has been around for a long time, but it earned serious scientific respect in 1979 when Luis and Walter Alvarez collected concrete evidence to support it. Calling on the work of Frank Asaro and Helen Michael, they showed that massive amounts of iridium were present in rocks deposited at the time of the dinosaurs' disappearance.[1] What's important about this fact is that almost no iridium appears naturally in the earth's crust. Almost all of the iridium present on earth comes from meteorites that have crashed into the earth's surface.

True, other theories have been proposed. According to one, dinosaurs could have poisoned themselves by eating the flowering

---

1. Stephen Jay Gould, *The Flamingo's Smile.* New York: Norton, 1985, p. 424.

* photosynthesis: process by which plant cells make carbohydrates and release oxygen as a by-product.

plants that had begun to evolve at the end of their reign. Some of those flowers may have contained toxic substances, which the dinosaurs' bodies could not tolerate. But this new theory, unlike the Alvarezes', has no evidence to support it and must remain in the realm of pure speculation. □

Topic: Theory of dinosaur extinction

Main idea: Only one theory of dinosaur extinction seems sound.

Support: 1. Dinosaurs became extinct because a comet or asteroid crashed into Earth.

    a. Produced huge quantities of dust

    b. Dust blocked out sunlight.

    c. Plants dependent on photosynthesis died, leaving dinosaurs without food.

    d. Absence of sunlight caused temperatures to drop, subjecting dinosaurs to freezing temp.

2. Theory has been around for a long time but earned scientific respect in 1979 when Luis and Walter Alvarez collected evidence.

    a. Showed that massive amounts of iridium present in rocks deposited during dinosaur disappearance

    b. Iridium comes from meteorites that have crashed on Earth's surface.

3. Other theories have been proposed.

    a. Maybe they poisoned themselves by eating toxic plants.

    b. No evidence

2. **The Aftermath of Rape**

Adolescent rape victims seem to have more subsequent behavior problems than other victims. This is probably because the adolescent experiences the attack at the time when she is developmentally trying to maintain a steady self-concept. Immediate reactions may include not trusting herself, turning away from friends, retreating to the protection of the family, and avoiding social activities. Long-term reactions include sustained unrest, sleep disturbances, and abnormal fears. _1_

Adult rape victims experience a shattering effect on personal stability and adjustment. Many do not wish to confide in another person and try to suppress their feelings. Some are hesitant to participate in their usual sexual relations. Personal feelings of privacy, dignity, and trust are undermined, while feelings of vulnerability are common. _2_

Burgess (1985) described a rape trauma syndrome that consists of two phases. The acute phase which can last from months to weeks is characterized by increased irritability, difficulty thinking clearly, and difficulty sleeping. In the second phase the victim has difficulty restoring order to her life and even more difficulty establishing a sense of control over the world. □ (Adapted from Greenberg et al., _Sexuality_, p. 513.) _3_

Topic: Effects of rape

Controlling idea: The effects of rape vary with the age of the victim.

Support:

1. Adolescents seem to have more behavior problems.

   a. Perhaps because attack occurs at a time when adolescent is trying to develop a steady sense of self

   b. Immediate reactions may include not trusting self, avoiding friends, retreating to family, and limiting social activity.

   c. Long-term reactions: unrest, sleep disturbances, and abnormal fears

2. Adults experience a shattering of personal stability and adjustment.

    a. Hesitant about sexual relations

    b. Feelings of privacy and dignity undermined

3. Burgess (1985) described 2 phases.

    a. Acute phase which can last several weeks: irritability, difficulty thinking and sleeping

    b. Second phase: difficulty getting sense of control over life and world

---

DIGGER DEEPER

The reading on pages 304–305 describes some positive effects of having friends. What are some positive effects of spending time alone?

WRITING SUGGESTION

Write a paper describing the person in your childhood who had the most powerful effect on who you are today.

Pattern 5: Classification

The following paragraph discusses the topic "the audience at horror movies." The main idea statement—in this case the first sentence—divides members of the audience into three smaller subgroups. Note how each group is defined and then illustrated. This is a good example of a paragraph devoted to *classification*.

> The theater audience in a horror movie can be divided into three groups. First of all, there are the gigglers. Members of this group may giggle out of nervousness, or they may find the scenes really funny. Then there are the hand grabbers. This group seems to think they can get through anything as long as there is something to hold. The last group contains the talkers. They always have a comment to make. For example, when the horrible-looking monster comes into view, they turn to a neighbor and say something clever, like "He's certainly cute, isn't he?"

To be considered complete, notes on a paragraph describing a system of classification should include the following:

1. the name of the larger group being broken down into smaller subgroups
2. the characteristics of each category
3. the names of each group (if any are given)

Here to illustrate are notes on the above paragraph:

Topic: The audience at horror movies

Main idea: Theater audiences in horror movies can be divided into three groups.

Support: 1. Gigglers:
— Laugh out of nervousness or amusement
2. Hand grabbers:
— Must hold on to something
3. Talkers:
— Always have a comment to make
e.g., "movie monster is cute"

Use the following exercise to practice reading and note-taking on paragraphs that describe a system of classification. Before taking your notes, make sure you identify the larger group being broken down into smaller subgroups or categories.

Exercise 9

Directions: Read and take notes on the following paragraphs.

Example: Studies indicate that human beings use two kinds of memory: short-term and long-term. When we use short-term memory, we retain information for a very brief period of time. For example, we use short-term memory when we look up a phone number and remember it only long enough to dial. When we use long-term memory, we retain information for a considerable length of time. A young child, for example, may memorize a poem and remember it for the next twenty years.

Topic: *Human memory*

Main idea: *Human beings use two kinds of memory.*

Support: *1. Short-term memory: retain information for short period of time*

   — Look up information in telephone book and remember it long enough to dial.

2. Long-term memory: retain information for longer period of time

   — Memorize poem and remember it for twenty years.

Explanation: As you can see, the sample notes contain the essential elements: the larger group being broken down into smaller sub-groups, the names and characteristics of each group.

Now it's your turn.

1. In the human body, blood circulates through elastic, tubelike canals called *blood vessels.* Consisting of three different types, blood vessels are well adapted to their functions. The vessels called *arteries* carry blood away from the heart to all parts of the body. The largest artery in the human body is the *aorta.* Because of oxygen, blood in the arteries appears bright red. In contrast, blood in the *veins,* another type of blood vessel, appears purplish because it is no longer carrying a supply of oxygen. Veins carry blood back to the heart, and they contain small valves that prevent the blood from flowing backward. This is important in those parts of the

body where the blood has to move against the pull of gravity. The third type of blood vessel is the *capillary*. Capillaries are tiny vessels connecting arteries and veins. Their walls are extremely thin. They have to be so that digested food can pass through them to the cells of the body.

Topic: Types of blood vessels

Main idea: Blood vessels, elastic tubelike canals, consist of 3 types.

Support:
1. Arteries carry blood away from heart to all parts of body.

   a. Aorta is largest artery.

   b. Blood in arteries appears bright red.

2. Veins carry blood back to heart.

   a. Blood appears purple because no oxygen.

   b. Small valves prevent blood from flowing backward.

3. Capillaries are tiny vessels connecting arteries & veins.

   a. Walls are thin.

   b. Digested food can pass through to cells of body.

2. Studies indicate that learning can be divided into two categories: incidental learning and intentional learning. *Incidental learning* takes place by chance; there is no clearly defined intention to learn. For example, a student who wants to check if he or she knows the first sixteen presidents of the United States may ask a friend to listen while they are named; during the recitation, the friend may, by chance, also learn the names of the first sixteen presidents. *Intentional learning* takes place when there is a clearly defined purpose present from the very beginning. For example, a student may sit down with a list of the fifty states and their capitals because he or she needs to learn them for a test.

Topic:	Two categories of learning
Main idea:	Learning can be divided into two categories.
Support:	1. Incidental learning takes place by chance.
	— Student who helps a friend learn first 16 presidents of U.S.
	may, by chance, learn them too.
	2. Intentional learning takes place when purpose is present from
	very beginning.
	— Student sits down with intention to learn the capitals of all
	50 states.

Classification in Longer Readings

Longer readings describing a system of classification are organized much like paragraphs based on this pattern. Usually a thesis statement announces the number of categories, and a description of each group follows. Here is a typical example:

Sources of Power

Max Weber (1919/1946) classified the main sources of social authority, or legitimate power, into three major types. [1]

Traditional authority is authority that is conferred by custom and accepted practice. In a hereditary monarchy,* the power of the head of the government is legitimated by birth. The person [2]

---

* monarchy: government ruled by a king or queen who inherits power at birth.

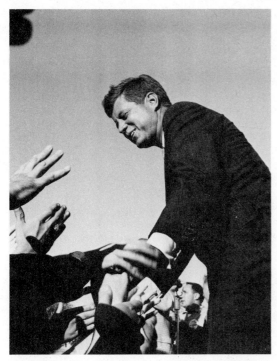

Benazir Bhutto and John F. Kennedy are two examples of leaders with charismatic authority.

who becomes the monarch does so because a parent or some other ancestor reigned before. The ancient Chinese believed that the ruling elite (called the mandarins) of their society received their authority from a heavenly order that permitted them to govern the rest of China in accordance with the ethical rules of the prevailing religion, Confucianism.

Charismatic authority is authority that is generated by the personality or exceptional personal appeal of an individual. The leaders of many movements—George Washington, Martin Luther King Jr., and Iran's Ayatollah Ruhollah Khomeini—are examples of people whose authority was or is based partly on their *charisma*. Literally, charisma is defined as a "gift of grace" from heaven, bestowed upon unique individuals.

Legal-rational authority is authority that rests on rationally established rules—in other words, rules that reflect a systematic attempt to adjust means to ends, to make institutions do what they are supposed to do. The elected and appointed government officials and officers of a formal organization hold this type of authority. In the United States, political legitimacy is based on the ultimate consent of the people through such "rational" mechanisms as the Constitution and popular elections.

Although one type usually predominates—as legal-rational au- *s*
thority does in the United States—all three types of authority are
present in most societies. □ (Poponoe, *Sociology*, pp. 436–437.)

In this excerpt the thesis statement announces the number of
categories while the three supporting paragraphs name and describe them. Typically for this method of development, the author
uses the last paragraph to make some general comment about all
three categories.

An informal outline based on the above reading would look
something like this:

Topic: Sources of social authority

Controlling idea: According to Max Weber, social authority or legitimate power has
three basic sources.

Support: 1. Traditional authority is given through custom or practice.
             a. In a hereditary monarchy power is given through family.
             b. Ancient Chinese believed that the ruling group called man-
                 darins received power from heaven.
          2. Charismatic authority comes from the personality of the indi-
              vidual
             a. Charisma means "gift of grace"
             b. Examples: George Washington and Martin Luther King
          3. Legal-rational authority relies on rules established to make in-
              stitutions function
             a. Elected and appointed officials hold this kind of authority
             b. U.S. is an example
          4. All three types of authority are present in most societies

For those readings that do not contain an enormous amount of
detail, you might also consider making a chart as an alternative
to informal outlining. On the next page, for example, is a chart
based on the above reading.

When you complete the next set of exercises, use the accompanying charts to complete your notes. In addition to informal outlines and summaries, charts are a good note-taking format to have
at your disposal.

Max Weber Classified Three Sources of Authority		
Traditional	Charismatic	Legal-rational

Conferred by custom and established practice
    ex. monarchy
 	
    mandarins in China
	Comes from force of personality
	    ex. George Washington
	
	    M.L. King
	
	    Khomeini
	
	    –charisma means "gift of grace"
		Comes from rules designed to make institutions work
		    ex. elected and appointed officials in U.S.

All three types present in most societies.
    –Pope John Paul's authority comes from all three sources

Exercise 10

Directions: Read and take notes on each of the following selections.

Example: **The Four Forms of Schizophrenia**

Schizophrenia is perhaps the most puzzling of all mental illnesses. [1] Even after years of research, scientists still cannot say for sure what causes the disease. However, they have been able to identify four basic types or forms of schizophrenia.

The type known as *simple dementia praecox* is characterized by [2] progressive mental deterioration, with patients becoming increasingly infantile in their behavior. Left to their own devices, they will pay little or no attention to their personal grooming, remaining dirty and unwashed for days. After a while, even the simplest daily task becomes impossible for them to perform.

Those suffering from a second form of the disease, called *catatonic schizophrenia*, can remain immobile for hours. Mentally [3] withdrawing from their environment, they adopt rigid postures and remain silent for long periods of time. But without reason, they may suddenly become violent and attack anyone who comes near.

Patients suffering from *hebephrenic schizophrenia* are all but in- 4
capable of quiet behavior. They talk and babble constantly. Their
responses are excited and violent, and they suffer from vivid hallucinations, which prevent them from getting proper sleep or rest.

In *paranoid schizophrenia*, the most marked symptom is the 5
presence of delusions. Patients suffering from this form are convinced that someone or something is trying to harm them. They
feel themselves to be surrounded by enemies and may, in response,
become violent.

Although psychiatrists have done extensive research on the 6
causes of schizophrenia, the results of their research have not been
in any way conclusive. Attempts to prove that the disease is the
consequence of some kind of chemical imbalance in the brain have
been only partially successful. Nor is there clear-cut evidence
showing that schizophrenia is the result of mental conflict or mal-
adjustment. At present, scientists simply do not know what causes
this mysterious and debilitating* disease. □

Schizophrenia can take four different forms.			
dementia praecox	catatonic schizophrenia	hebephrenic schizophrenia	paranoid schizophrenia
patients progressively deteriorate become infantile in behavior pay no attention to appearance or cleanliness	can remain immobile for hours mentally with-draw from envi-ronment	incapable of quiet behavior talk and babble constantly hallucinations	delusions, believe someone is trying to get them may become violent
Scientists do not know what causes the disease			

---

* debilitating: exhausting, weakening.

Explanation: As you can see, the sample chart clearly identifies all four types of schizophrenia. It also lists the characteristics that define each one. Information that applies to schizophrenia in general appears at the bottom of the chart.

Now it's your turn.

1. Personality and Body Type

In the 1940s, a number of researchers tried to revive a much-debated theory of human behavior called *constitutional typology*, a theory that views body type as the essential clue to personality. Even today, there are those who claim that body type controls personality, and they use constitutional typology to explain and predict human behavior. Although the theory has been criticized, it still has numerous supporters who insist that human beings fall into three basic categories of physique or body type, with each body type corresponding to a particular set of character traits. 1

According to constitutional typologists, *endomorphs* tend to be round and soft with protruding abdomens. They are said to love gracious living and good food. They have gentle, relaxed temperaments and prefer to keep life uncomplicated. Said to embody the cliché about fat people being friendly, endomorphs like to be surrounded by their friends and are not comfortable being alone for any length of time. 2

The exact opposite of the endomorph, the *ectomorph* is described as all skin and bones, with a flat belly and long legs. Much less gregarious* than the fun-loving endomorph, the ectomorph prefers intellectual pursuits, especially if they can be carried on in relative isolation from people. Less good natured than the endomorph, ectomorphs are nervous and high strung. Given to quick reactions and high-intensity relationships, they suffer from the aftermath of tension and have difficulty relaxing and falling asleep. 3

The *mesomorph* is neither fat nor thin, but broad and muscular with a strong, rugged physique. People who fall into this category are said to love physical activity, the more daring and fast-paced the better. They also enjoy games of risk or chance. Domineering by nature, mesomorphs like to be around people but prefer to be in situations that they can control. □ 4

---

* gregarious: enjoying the company of people.

Controlling Idea:	According to constitutional typology, physique determines personality.			
Endomorph	Ectomorph	Mesomorph		
−round and soft protruding abdomen	−skin and bones, flat belly	−neither fat nor thin		
−loves good living and good food	−less gregarious	−likes adventure and risk		
−relaxed temperament	−high-strung, tense, has difficulty sleeping	−domineering		
−doesn't like being alone	−likes to be alone	−likes to be around people but wants to control them		
	−intellectual			

Even today, there are those who claim that body type can predict personality.

	Endomorphic	Mesomorphic	Ectomorphic
Body Type	Round, soft	Rugged, muscular	Fragile, thin
Temperament	Gentle, relaxed, sociable, and fond of food	Energetic, daring, domineering, assertive	Brainy, nervous, withdrawn

The skills that typify effective managers tend to fall into five general categories: technical, conceptual, interpersonal, diagnostic, and analytic.

Technical Skills

A technical skill is a specific skill needed to accomplish a specialized activity. For example, the skills that engineers, lawyers, and machinists need to do their jobs are technical skills. Lower-level managers (and, to a lesser extent, middle managers) need the technical skills that are relevant to the activities they manage. Although these managers may not have to perform the technical tasks themselves, they must be able to train subordinates, answer questions, and otherwise provide guidance and direction. In general, top managers do not rely on technical skills as much as managers at other levels. Still, understanding the technical side of things is an aid to effective management at every level.

Conceptual Skills

Conceptual skill is the ability to think in abstract* terms. Conceptual skill allows the manager to see the "big picture" and to understand how the various parts of an organization or an idea can fit together. In 1951 a man named Charles Wilson decided to take his family on a cross-country vacation. All along the way, the family was forced to put up with high-priced but shabby hotel accommodations. Wilson reasoned that most travelers would welcome a chain of moderately priced, good-quality roadside hotels. You are no doubt familiar with what he conceived: Holiday Inns. Wilson was able to identify a number of isolated factors (existing accommodation patterns, the need for a different kind of hotel, and his own investment interests) to "dream up" the new business opportunity and to carry it through to completion.

Interpersonal Skills

An interpersonal skill is the ability to deal effectively with other people, both inside and outside the organization. Examples of interpersonal skills are the ability to relate to people, understand their needs and motives, and show genuine compassion. When all other things are equal, the manager who is able to exhibit these skills will be more successful than the manager who is arrogant and brash and who doesn't care about others.

---

*   abstract: in theory rather than concrete practice.

Diagnostic Skills

Diagnostic skill is the ability to assess a particular situation and identify its causes. The diagnostic skills of the successful manager parallel those of the physician, who assesses the patient's symptoms to pinpoint the underlying medical problem. We can take this parallel one step further, too. In management as in medicine, correct diagnosis is often critical in determining the appropriate action to take. All managers need to make use of diagnostic skills, but these skills are probably used most by top managers.

Analytic Skills

Analytic skill is used to identify the relevant issues (or variables) in a situation, to determine how they are related, and to assess their relative importance. All managers, regardless of level or area, need analytic skills. Analytic skills often come into play along with diagnostic skills. For example, a manager assigned to a new position may be confronted with a wide variety of problems that all need attention. Diagnostic skills will be needed to identify the causes of each problem. □ (Pride et al., *Business*, pp. 142, 144.)

DIGGING DEEPER

What do you think of constitutional typology? From your experience, is it a useful system for explaining variety in human personality? Why or why not?

WRITING SUGGESTION

Try your hand at classifying members of some group—the people you work with, your classmates, friends in the neighborhood, people you meet at parties, and so on. For an illustration of the way one author classifies friends, see the reading "Convenience Friends and Historical Friends, Etc." on page 409 in the appendix.

	Topic:	Management skills		
	Controlling Idea:	Managers need at least five key skills		

Technical	Conceptual	Interpersonal	Diagnostic	Analytic
−skills needed for a specialized activity	−ability to think in abstract terms	−ability to deal with other people inside and outside organization	−ability to look at situation and understand causes	−used to identify relevant issues in a situation
−skills lawyers and engineers need to do their jobs	ex. Charles Wilson "dreamed up" Holiday Inns	−ability to relate to people; understand needs and motives	−used most by top managers	−all managers need them
−may not have to use them but need to answer questions	−most crucial at top levels of management			
−Important at every level				

Mixing Patterns

Authors often need to mix or combine patterns in order to fully explain their ideas. The following is a good example of a paragraph that combines two patterns:

Increased spells of warm weather and decreased use of a pesticide called Mirex have resulted in a plague of what laypeople call fire ants. Indeed, pleasant weather and an absence of pesticides have encouraged whole armies of ants to make their homes in farmers' fields, where they can leisurely munch on crops of potatoes and okra. Should a tractor overturn one of their nests, the furious ants swarm over the machine and attack the driver. Using their jaws to hold the victim's skin, they thrust their stingers into the flesh, holding the same position for up to twenty-five seconds. The sting produces a painful burning sensation and frequently produces painful infections, which can last weeks and even months. Some victims who were especially allergic to the ants' poison have not survived a fire ant attack.

The main idea statement in this paragraph describes a cause-and-effect relationship. From it, we learn that warm weather and decreased use of a pesticide called Mirex have resulted in a plague of fire ants. The second sentence, a supporting sentence, describes the same cause-and-effect relationship in more detail. The remaining supporting sentences describe the sequence of steps in a fire ant attack, a disagreeable aspect of the plague. Thus we are dealing with two methods of development: cause-and-effect *and* a sequence of steps.

Our notes look like this:

Topic: Fire ants

Main idea: Increased warm weather and decreased use of the pesticide Mirex have resulted in a plague of fire ants.

Support:
1. Whole armies of ants have moved into farmers' fields and are eating potatoes and okra.
2. If tractor overturns nest, ants swarm over machine and attack driver.
3. Sting produces painful burning sensations and can cause infections.
4. Some especially allergic victims have died following fire ant attacks.

Since the paragraph describes a cause-and-effect relationship plus a sequence of steps, the sample notes include all causes and effects mentioned in the paragraph and list all the steps in the order in which they occur.

· Notes on a paragraph that mixes patterns present no problem once you can identify the patterns that have been combined. Just make sure your notes contain the most important elements of each pattern.

The next exercise gives you some practice reading and taking notes on paragraphs combining different methods of organization.

Exercise 11

Directions: Read and take notes on the following paragraphs. Be sure to circle the letter of the patterns used in each paragraph.

Example: In 1874, Mary Outerbridge brought tennis equipment to American soil. In the same year, a court was laid out in the private club to which Miss Outerbridge belonged. Within seven years, tennis had become quite popular with the upper classes, and Eugene E. Outerbridge decided to organize the United States Lawn Tennis Association. By 1914, interest in tennis increased, and the nature of the game began to change. Prior to 1914, the game had been considered a delightful, if slightly too strenuous, pastime, a game to be played by the wealthy in their leisure moments. However, 1914 saw the entrance of young players like Maurice E. McLoughlin, a tennis champion whose competitive and aggressive playing style helped change the very nature of the game. By 1915, the national tennis championship had been transferred from the privileged environment of Newport, Rhode Island, to the far less sophisticated West Side Tennis Club at Forest Hills, New York, and tennis was beginning to break free of its role as an upper-class diversion.*

- ⓐ. The paragraph outlines a sequence of dates and events.
- b. The paragraph describes a sequence of steps.
- c. The paragraph compares and/or contrasts two topics.
- ⓓ. The paragraph explains a cause-and-effect relationship.
- e. The paragraph classifies people or things into smaller categories.

Topic: Changes in tennis

Main idea: Although tennis began as a pleasant diversion, it changed dramatically when players like Maurice McLoughlin entered in 1914

Support:
1. 1874 M. Outerbridge brought tennis equipment to American soil and laid out a private court.

2. 1881 Eugene Outerbridge organized U.S. Lawn Tennis Assoc.

---

* diversion: pastime, a pleasant activity.

"Big" Bill Tilden (l) helped revolutionize the game of tennis. Andre Agassi's (r) style of play illustrates just how different tennis is today from Mary Outerbridge's time.

3. *1914 Players like Maurice McLoughlin enter and change nature of the game—more aggressive.*

4. *1915 transferred from privileged Newport, Rhode Island to Forest Hills, N.Y.*

Explanation: This paragraph describes a cause-and-effect relationship. It explains how players like Maurice McLoughlin helped change the face of tennis. Our notes clearly indicate that relationship. However, they also include the sequence of dates and events used to show the way in which the game evolved or changed over time.
      Now it's your turn.

1. Anyone who has ever cheered on his or her favorite athlete knows that yelling can produce hoarseness. When a person yells or screams, the vocal cords—two thick, muscular strings—close tightly and create a tremendous amount of air pressure. As they open to let out a sound, the sudden release of air causes the cords to slam together. When the cords hit each other, especially over a long period of time, they can bruise and swell. If this happens, they will not fit together properly. Air then leaks between the cords, and the voice sounds hoarse. Hoarseness is a sign that the vocal cords need rest. Trying to talk to get rid of the hoarseness only makes matter worse, and the cords may begin bleeding. Many vocalists, especially rock singers who shout a lot, suffer from bleeding and irritated cords.

   a. The paragraph outlines a sequence of dates and events.
   b. The paragraph describes a sequence of steps.
   c. The paragraph compares and/or contrasts two topics.
   d. The paragraph explains a cause-and-effect relationship.
   e. The paragraph classifies people or things into smaller categories.

Topic: Cause of hoarseness

Main idea: Yelling can cause hoarseness.

Support:
1. When someone yells, vocal cords, 2 thick muscular strings, close and create air pressure.

2. When cords hit, they can close and swell.

3. Don't fit together properly.

4. Air leaks between and hoarseness results.

   a. vocal cords need rest.

   b. trying to talk makes things worse.

2. Viruses are difficult to classify, and numerous systems have been proposed. One commonly used system classifies them according to their host cells. On this basis, there are three groups of viruses: animal, plant, and bacterial. On the whole, animal viruses are much more complex than plant viruses and have, therefore, been given distinct names like *poxvirus* and *parvovirus*. In contrast, plant viruses are named according to the host they invade, for example, the tobacco virus. Bacterial viruses, also called *bacteriophages*, or *phages*, are usually identified by a system of letters and numbers, like the T-2 bacteriophage.

    a. The paragraph outlines a sequence of dates and events.
    b. The paragraph describes a sequence of steps.
    ⓒ. The paragraph compares and/or contrasts two topics.
    d. The paragraph explains a cause-and-effect relationship.
    ⓔ. The paragraph classifies people or things into smaller categories.

Topic: Types of viruses

Main idea: According to one system of classification, there are 3 groups of viruses: animal, plant, and bacterial.

Support:
1. Animal viruses are more complex than plant viruses.

    — have distinct names like poxvirus and parvovirus

2. Plant viruses named according to host they invade.

    — ex. tobacco

3. Bacteria usually identified by system of letters or numbers.

    — T-2 bacteriophage

_____

_____

_____

_____

Mixing Patterns in Longer Readings

As you might expect, authors don't combine patterns only when composing paragraphs. They also combine them when writing longer, more extended passages. In fact within longer readings, authors may even combine three different patterns, as the following selection illustrates:

A Healthy Dose of Religion

The way that Christians view their relationship with God may affect their health. The view that "God helps those who help themselves" is probably healthier than believing that we're puppets on God's string. 1

Christians can be divided into three very broad categories, according to psychologists Daniel McIntosh of the University of Michigan and Bernard Spilka of the University of Denver: *active Christians,* who derive great meaning from religion and tend to see God as a partner to work with; *passive Christians,* who tend to be less involved in religion and believe that everything is preordained; and *questors,* who are still searching for the truth. 2

McIntosh and Spilka asked 69 Christian college students about their religious beliefs and health history. In general, the active Christians were healthier than the others. They reported having fewer colds, headaches, ulcers, respiratory problems, and other ailments. 3

In contrast to those who believe that health is largely a matter of chance or God's will, active Christians believe that, along with God's helping hand, they have a responsibility to behave in a healthy way. Active Christians are also more likely to pray. McIntosh and Spilka note that prayer has been found to reduce tension, and it is also a means of seeking control over a situation, providing that all-important elixir*: hope. 4

_____

* elixir: medicine believed to cure illness.

Stress reduction, a sense of control over one's life and optimism ₅ have all been linked to better health in a spate* of recent studies. Active and meaningful prayer may be yet another means to these ends. □ (*Psychology Today*, November 1988, p. 13.)

The author's thesis statement identifies a cause-and-effect relationship. "The way that Christians view their relationship with God may affect their health." To make that point convincing, the author uses classification *and* comparison and contrast. He divides Christians into three categories and identifies some key differences (Note the transitional clue *in contrast.*)

Notes on this reading should identify the cause-and-effect relationship described in the thesis statement, explain the system of classification, and list the points of contrast. As you can see, the sample notes contain all three elements:

Topic: Christians and their health

Controlling idea: Study suggests that how Christians view God may affect their health.

1. According to psychologists McIntosh and Spilka, 3 categories of Christians:
   a. *active:* see God as working partner
   b. *passive:* see everything as preordained
   c. *questors:* still searching
2. Unlike passive and questor Christians, active Christians believe that health is not a matter of chance; more likely to use prayer as a source of hope and control.
3. Active Christians reported fewer colds, headaches, respiratory problems than the other 2 groups.

The readings in the following exercise may combine two or even three methods of organization. Remember to identify the different patterns and record the key elements of each one.

Exercise 12

Directions: After reading each selection, identify the patterns of development used to organize the material. Then take notes, making sure to include the key elements of each pattern.

---

*   spate: sudden rush.

Example: **How a Handful of Spaniards Won Two Empires**

The fact of Spanish Conquest raises a question: How did small *1* groups of Spaniards, initially numbering a few hundred men, conquer the Aztec and Inca empires, which had populations in the millions, large armies, and militarist traditions of their own?

Here we have a paradox.* With relative ease the Spaniards con- *2* quered the Aztecs and the Incas, peoples who were organized on the state level, lived a sedentary† life based on intensive agriculture, and were ruled by emperors to whom they owed complete obedience. *On the other hand*, tribes of marginal‡ culture such as the nomadic Chichimec Indians of the northern Mexican plains or the Araucanians of Chile, who practiced a simple shifting agriculture and herding, were indomitable; the Araucanians continued to battle white invaders for hundreds of years until 1883.

A sixteenth-century Spanish soldier and chronicler of uncom- *3* mon intelligence, Pedro Cieza de León, reflecting on the contrast between the swift fall of the Inca Empire and the failure of the Spaniards to conquer the "uncivilized" tribes of the Colombian jungles, found an explanation in the simple social and economic organization of the tribes, which made it possible for people of nomadic tribes to flee before a Spanish advance and rebuild village life elsewhere.

In contrast, the mass of the Inca population, docile subjects, *4* accepted their emperor's defeat as their own and quickly submitted to the new Spanish masters. For these people, flight from the fertile valleys of the Inca to the deserts, bleak plateaus, and snow-capped mountains that dominate the geography of the region would have been unthinkable. □ (Adapted from Keen and Wasserman, *History of Latin America*, p. 75.)

a. series of dates and events
b. sequence of steps
ⓒ. comparison and contrast
ⓓ. cause and effect
e. classification

Topic: Defeat of Aztecs and Incas

Controlling idea: Differences in social organization made it easier for the Spaniards

---

*   paradox: seeming contradiction that can actually be explained and make sense.

†   sedentary: without much movement.

‡   marginal: minimal, limited.

to defeat the Incas and Aztecs than to defeat the smaller

Colombian tribes.

Support: *1. Aztecs and Incas*

    a. Lived sedentary life based on farming

      — Under attack from Spaniards, could not simply flee to

       mountains

    b. Obedient to Emperor

      — Accepted his defeat as their own

  2. Tribes of Colombian Jungles

    a. Nomadic herders

      — Under attack, could simply flee

    b. Obedient to no one

      — Continued to battle white invaders for hundreds of years

Explanation: In this excerpt the authors want to explain how the Aztec and Inca Indians were quickly defeated by the Spanish, while smaller tribes remained indomitable or undefeated. To explain this point, they combine two methods of development: comparison and contrast with cause and effect. The sample notes record the key elements of each pattern.

1. **1986—Chernobyl**

In 1986 the world was initiated, for the first time, to the consequences of a cataclysmic accident at a nuclear power plant. A loss of cooling accident occurred at the Soviet reactor at Chernobyl, and the reactor exploded, dispersing radioactive contamination across several continents. Although many of the details of the accident have been kept secret by the Soviet government, the broad outlines have been revealed.

The disaster started when some sequence of events caused the cooling system to fail at the Chernobyl reactor site. Within a short time the fuel rods overheated, and eventually the rod cladding and the uranium oxide fuel began to melt. Reacting to the meltdown, operators flooded the core with water, but the remedial action came too late. Upon contact, the water instantly turned to steam, and the steam reacted with the graphite core, the molten cladding material, and the uranium oxide to produce a mixture of hydrogen, oxygen, methane, and carbon monoxide. These gases then exploded. (Note that the explosion was a chemical reaction; it was not a thermonuclear explosion.)

The facility had no containment structure, so the walls of the building ruptured and large quantities of radioactive material were injected into the atmosphere. Contaminants continued to be released for several days as the graphite core burned out of control. The fire was eventually contained by smothering it with over 5000 tons of sand, clay, lead, and boron dropped from helicopters. □ (Adapted from Amos and Turk, *Physical Science*, pp. 315–316.)

a. series of dates and events
ⓑ. sequence of steps
c. comparison and contrast
ⓓ. cause and effect
e. classification

Topic: Consequences of Chernobyl accident

Controlling idea: A failure of cooling system at Chernobyl sent radioactive contamination

across several continents

Support:

1. Cooling system failed causing fuel rods to overheat.

2. Rod cladding and uranium oxide fuel began to melt.

3. Reacting to meltdown, operators flooded core with water.

4. Water turned to steam.

5. Steam reacted with graphite core and uranium oxide to produce mixture

of gases that exploded.

6. Facility had no containment structure and large quantities of radioactive material entered atmosphere.

7. Contaminants were released for several days.

8. Fire smothered with sand, clay, lead, and boron dropped from helicopters.

_____

_____

_____

_____

_____

_____

2.   The Dual Nature of Curare

Curare is a blackish, resin-like substance made from the roots and bark of a woody vine that grows in South America. Although many people know that curare is a deadly poison, they do not know that its effects can save life as well as take it. Once known only as the "flying death," curare has become one of medicine's most trusted weapons in the fight against disease. [1]

Reports of curare's deadly powers began to circulate as early as the sixteenth century when explorers returned from the Amazon telling of hostile Indians who could bring down their prey with a single blow from a dart gun. According to the few eyewitness accounts that could be found, the Indians would boil the roots and bark of a woody vine into a heavy syrup and then dip their darts into the thick liquid. Expert hunters, capable of finding their target at over a hundred yards away, would then blow the darts through hollow reeds. Death came almost instantaneously. A bird would die in less than five seconds, a human being in less than five minutes. [2]

But because the jungles were all but inaccessible to everyone but the Indians, no one really understood how curare worked until the mid-nineteenth century when experimenters began to unravel its deadly secrets. It was found that curare, if swallowed, is relatively harmless. But if it penetrates the skin, it is lethal. The poison [3] works to relax all of the muscles in the body, including those that control breathing, and the victim quickly suffocates if not kept alive on a respirator. Once researchers knew how curare worked, they were in a better position to figure out how it might be used to more beneficent ends. However, researchers were reluctant to experiment with curare imported from South America. Its strength varied, and one could never be sure how strong a dosage to use.

Then in 1935, Dr. Harold King identified the paralyzing agent ⏴ that made curare so deadly. Within the same year, Guillermo Klug, a German botanist, tracked down the root that was the source of the poison. During World War II, Daniel Bovet, an Italian pharmacologist, developed the first synthetic form of curare, and the stage was set to discover if curare could prove beneficial to mankind. In 1942, Dr. Harold Griffith successfully used it as an anesthetic during surgery. From that time on, curare was used in many operations because its ability to relax the patient's muscles made the surgeon's work easier. Eventually it was also used to treat rabies and tetanus, diseases which produce severe muscle cramps. ☐

ⓐ. sequence of dates and events
ⓑ. sequence of steps
  c. comparison and contrast
ⓓ. cause and effect
  e. classification

Topic: Beneficial effects of curare
_____

Controlling idea: Many people don't realize that curare, a deadly poison, can also save life.
_____

_____

Support: 1. Reports of curare circulated 16th century:
_____

  a. Explorers from the Amazon described how Indians dipped blow darts

  in syrup made from boiling bark of woody vine.
_____

  b. Hunters brought down prey over one hundred yards away; death

  almost instantaneous.
_____

2. Mid-nineteenth century experiments led to understanding of how poison

  worked:
_____

a. Poison penetrates skin, enters bloodstream, and paralyzes muscles.

_____

b. Muscles controlling breathing are paralyzed and victim suffocates.

_____

3. 1935, Dr. Harold King identifies paralyzing agent, and Guillermo Klug

tracked down root that was source of poison.

_____

4. During W.W. II, Daniel Bovet developed first synthetic form of curare.

_____

5. 1942, Dr. Harold Griffith used curare as an anesthetic.

_____

a. Made surgeon's work easier by relaxing patient's muscles.

_____

b. Eventually used to treat rabies and tetanus.

_____

_____

_____

Working with Words

Here are seven more prefixes and roots you should know. Use them to figure out the meaning of the italicized words and fill in the accompanying blanks. Then add them to your vocabulary notebook for regular review.

1. bi   (Latin prefix)   two
2. mono   (Greek prefix)   one, alone
3. pro   (Latin prefix)   forward, forth, in favor of,
                                 advancing, inclined
4. reg, rec   (Latin root)   straighten, rule
5. gam   (Greek root)   marriage
6. voc   (Latin root)   call
7. mo, mot,   (Latin root)   move
   mob, mov

1. Initially, when the two superpowers met, they could not agree on anything. Neither side seemed willing to compromise, and war seemed unavoidable. But with the arrival of the secretary of state, the situation improved. In just a few hours they were able to come to a *bilateral* agreement.

two-party _____

2. For the most part Americans are *monogamous*, but some religious groups allow a man to take more than one wife. Within these religious communities, a family consisting of one husband and three wives is not considered immoral. Rarely, however, are women encouraged to take more than one husband.

married to one person
_____

3. Prior to World War II, the British Prime Minister Neville Chamberlain claimed that Adolf Hitler would leave the rest of Europe alone if he were allowed to conquer Czechoslovakia. Guided by this belief, Chamberlain signed the Munich Pact, which allowed Hitler to invade Czechoslovakia. But the pact was a mistake. It only encouraged Hitler to think he could gobble up all of Europe, and he went on to invade Poland. Horrified by the mistake he had made, a mistake that could not be *rectified*, Chamberlain resigned in disgrace.

improved, made right
_____

4. *Proponents* of the bill were determined to win Senate support. But the opposition was strong, and in the end the bill was defeated. However it re-emerged in new form as an amendment to a bill that was sure to pass. As one senator explained to the press, "There's more than one way to skin a cat."

people in favor, supporters
_____

5. Richard Burton's riotous nights of drinking and well-publicized affairs all but erased his reputation as an actor. But one has only to hear him recite a *monologue* from Shakespeare's *Hamlet* to know that he was a great actor, whose marvelous voice made words come alive in a unique and powerful way.

speech in a play recited by a single person
_____

6. The shah of Iran's *regime* was hated by his people. Unfortunately, America supported that regime until the shah fell from power. This is one of the reasons why anti-Americanism in Iran remains so strong. The Iranians have not yet forgiven us for supporting the man they hated.

government
_____

7. The Jim Crow laws used to segregate his people *evoked* a righteous anger in Charles H. Houston, the Dean of Howard University. But unlike so many of us, Houston made constructive use of his anger. He gathered around him some of the finest legal minds in America—among them Thurgood Marshall who was to become a Supreme Court Justice—and launched a legal battle that was to bring Jim Crow to its knees.

called up, produced

8. In the nineteenth century, women could not become doctors or lawyers. Those *vocations* were closed to women because the intellectual activity they required was thought to endanger female health. No one today, however, would take such an idea seriously, and many women become doctors or lawyers.

professions

9. In his book *The Autobiography of Malcolm X*, Malcolm X described the painstaking way in which he taught himself to read and write while in prison. His *motivation* for learning was frustration at not being able to express what he wanted to in letters to people on the outside. On the street he had been able to talk to anybody about anything. But in prison he had to rely on the written word.

source of action, reason for behavior

10. He seemed to be a gentleman of the old school, polite, courteous, and well mannered. But if crossed, he had a nasty *propensity* to become verbally abusive.

tendency or leaning

Stories Behind the Words

Each of the following words comes from the name of a person.

1. *Gargantuan*. Rabelais was a sixteenth century French writer who became famous with his tale of *Gargantua and Pantagruel*, two good natured giants who had an enormous appetite. Gar-

gantua has survived in the form *gargantuan* which today means huge or colossal.

Sample sentence: He had a *gargantuan* appetite for life.

Definition: enormous, huge

2. *Machiavellian.* In a book called *The Prince*, Nicolo Machiavelli described how to use trickery and dishonesty to gain power. Because of that work, *machiavellian* has come to mean crafty and deceitful.

Sample sentence: Fortunately her *machiavellian* schemes to gain power had been a complete failure.

Definition: immoral, particularly in the pursuit of political power

3. *Malapropism.* Mrs. Malaprop was a comic character in the play called *The Rivals* by William Sheridan. What made her humorous was her constant misuse of words. Today when we talk about *malapropisms*, we are referring to words used inappropriately by someone who is usually unaware of the error.

Sample sentence: She meant to praise her lawyer when she called him a "supercilious" person; unfortunately it was one of her usual *malapropisms*, and he was neither flattered nor amused.

Definition: the humorous misuse of a word

4. *Bowdlerize.* Thomas Bowdler was a nineteenth-century lover of Shakespeare. But he thought some of the plays too racy, so he published a censored collection of Shakespeare's works, giving rise to the word *bowdlerize* which now means to remove objectionable passages from a written work.

Sample sentence: His father would allow him to read only *bowdlerized* versions of D.H. Lawrence's work.

Definition: to censor or remove any material considered vulgar.

Other forms: bowdlerized, bowdlerizing

5. *Stentorian.* In the *Iliad*, Homer tells the story of Stentor, a Greek herald who could shout as "loud as the cry of fifty men." Not surprisingly, *stentorian* refers to loud voices.

Sample sentence: The coach's *stentorian* tones could be heard throughout the gymnasium, and he wasn't using a microphone.

Definition: very loud or powerful in sound

Review Test: Chapter 7

Part A: Read each selection, identifying the method or methods of development. Then take notes.

1. The Liberation of South America

The Latin American struggle for independence suggests comparison with the American Revolution. Some obvious parallels exist between the two upheavals. Both sought to throw off the rule of a mother country whose mercantilist* system hindered the further development of a rapidly growing colonial economy. Both were led by well-educated elites who drew their slogans and ideas from the Enlightenment.† Both were civil wars in which large elements of the population sided with the mother country. Both owed their final success in part to foreign assistance (although the North American rebels received far more help from their French ally than came to Latin America from outside sources). *1*

The differences between the two revolutions are no less impressive, however. Unlike the American Revolution, the Latin American struggle for independence did not have a unified direction or strategy. This lack was due not only to vast distances and other geographical obstacles to unity but to the economic and cultural isolation of the various Latin American regions from each other. *2*

Moreover, the Latin American movement for independence lacked the strong popular base provided by the more democratic and fluid society of the English colonies. The Creole elite, itself part of an exploitative white minority, feared the oppressed Indians, blacks, and half-castes, and as a rule sought to keep their intervention in the struggle to a minimum. This lack of unity of regions and classes helps to explain why Latin America had to struggle so long against a power like Spain, weak and beset by many internal and external problems. □ (Keen and Wasserman, *History of Latin America*, p. 157.) *3*

    a. series of dates and events
    b. sequence of steps
    ⓒ. comparison and contrast
    ⓓ. cause and effect
    e. classification

---

* mercantilist: an economy that emphasizes shipping and trade.

† Enlightenment: 18th century movement that stressed the power of human reason.

Topic:	Similarities between Latin American and American revolutions

Controlling idea: Although there are a number of similarities between the Latin American and American revolutions, there are also some significant differences.

Support:

1. Both sought to throw off rule of mother country because mercantilist system threatened development.

2. Both led by well-educated upper classes who got slogans and ideas from Enlightenment.

3. Both had civil wars.

4. Both owed final success to foreign assistance.

5. Unlike American Revolution, Latin American did not have unified direction.

   a. Due to vast distances

   b. Economic and cultural isolation of some Latin American regions

6. Latin American revolution lacked strong popular base.

   a. Society was not democratic.

   b. Revolution not supported by elites who feared oppressed

   c. Lack of unity helps explain why revolution against weakened Spain took so long.

2. Styles of Leadership

For many years leadership was viewed as a combination of personality traits, such as self-confidence, intelligence, and dependability. A consensus on which traits were most important was difficult to achieve, however, and attention turned to styles of leadership behavior. In the last few decades several styles of leadership have been identified: authoritarian, laissez-faire, and democratic. The **authoritarian leader** holds all authority and responsibility, with communication usually moving from top to bottom. This leader assigns workers to specific tasks and expects orderly, precise results.

At the other extreme is the **laissez-faire leader,** who waives responsibility and allows subordinates to work as they choose with a minimum of interference. Communication flows horizontally among group members. The **democratic leader** holds final responsibility but also delegates authority to others, who participate in determining work assignments. In this leadership style, communication is active both upward and downward.

Each of these styles has its advantages and disadvantages. For example, democratic leadership can motivate employees to work effectively because it is *their* decisions that they are implementing. On the other hand, the decision-making process takes time that subordinates could otherwise be devoting to their tasks. Actually, each of the three leadership styles can be effective. □ (Pride et al., *Business*, pp. 147–148.)

a. series of dates and events
b. sequence of steps
c. comparison and contrast
d. cause and effect
ⓔ. classification

Topic: Styles of leadership
_____

Controlling idea: In the last few years, three different styles of leadership have been

identified.
_____

Support: 1. Authoritarian: holds all authority in hands
_____

   a. Communication moves from top to bottom.
_____

   b. Leader assigns tasks and demands results.
_____

2. Laissez-faire leader allows employees to do work with minimal

interference.
_____

   — Communication flows horizontally.
_____

3. Democratic leader holds final responsibility but does delegate

   authority.

   a. Employees make decisions.

   b. Communication moves up and down.

4. Each style has advantages and disadvantages.

_____

_____

_____

_____

_____

_____

3. King Philip's War

In the half-century since the founding of New England, white set- *1*
tlements had spread far into Massachusetts and Connecticut. In
the process, the settlers had completely surrounded the ancestral
lands of the Pokanoket Indians of Narragansett Bay. Their chief,
Metacomet (known to the whites as King Philip), was the son of
Massasoit, who had signed the treaty with the Pilgrims in 1621.
Troubled by the impact European culture and Christianity were
having on his people, Metacomet, in late June 1675, led his warriors in attacks on nearby white communities.

By the end of the year, two other local tribes, the Nipmuck and *2*
the Narragansett, had joined Metacomet's forces. In the fall of
1676, the three tribes jointly attacked settlements in the northern
Connecticut River valley; in the winter and spring they devastated
well-established villages and even attacked Plymouth and Providence. Altogether, the alliance totally destroyed twelve of the
ninety Puritan towns and attacked forty others. A tenth of the
able-bodied adult males in Massachusetts were captured or killed;
proportional to population, it was the most costly war in American
history. New England's very survival seemed to be at stake.

But the tide turned in the summer of 1676. The Indian coalition ₃ ran short of food and ammunition, and whites began to use "praying Indians"* as guides and scouts. After Metacomet was killed in an ambush in August, the alliance crumbled. Many surviving Pokanokets, Nipmucks, and Narragansetts, including Metacomet's wife and son, were captured and sold into slavery in the West Indies.

The power of New England's coastal tribes was broken. There- ₄ after they lived in small clusters, subordinated to the whites and often working as servants or sailors. Only on the isolated island of Martha's Vineyard were some surviving Pokanokets able to preserve their tribal identity intact. □ (Adapted from Norton et al. *A People and a Nation*, p. 57.)

(a). series of dates and events
b. sequence of steps
c. comparison and contrast
(d). cause and effect
e. classification

Topic: Metacomet's war

Controlling idea: Upset by the effect European culture and Christianity were having on his

people, Metacomet, chief of the Pokanoket Indians, led his warriors into

battle with nearby white communities.

Support: 1. 1675 joined by Nipmuck and Narragansett

a. 1676 jointly attacked settlements in Connecticut valley, even

attacked Plymouth and Providence

b. Together destroyed 12 of 90 Puritan towns and attacked 40 others

2. 1/10th of able-bodied males were captured or killed: New England's

survival seemed to be at stake.

* praying Indians: Native Americans who had been converted to Christianity.

3. Summer of 76, tide turns

    a. Indian coalition runs short of food

    b. "praying Indians" serve as scouts

    c. After Metacomet was killed in ambush, alliance crumbled

4. Power of N.E. tribes broken

    — Only on Martha's Vineyard were some Pokanokets able to

    preserve tribal identity.

4. Ice Cream's Origins

Ice cream's origins are known to reach back as far as Alexander [1]
the Great, although no specific date or personality has been cred-
ited with its actual invention. Incidents recorded over the centuries indicate that ice cream's evolution was a combination of people's attraction for cool, sweet foods and their creativity in finding
the perfect one.

Biblical references show that King Solomon was fond of iced [2]
drinks during harvesting, and in the Roman Empire, Nero Claudius Caesar (A.D. 54–86) frequently sent teams of runners into the
mountains to get snow, which was then flavored with honey, fruits,
and juices.

Over a thousand years later, Marco Polo returned to Italy from [3]
the Far East with a recipe that closely resembled what is now
called sherbet. Historians estimate that this recipe evolved into
ice cream sometime during the 16th century in Italy. France was
introduced to similar frozen desserts in 1553 by the Italian Catherine de Medici who became the wife of Henry II of France.

England seems to have discovered ice cream at the same time, [4]
or perhaps even earlier than the Italians. "Cream Ice," as it was
called, appeared regularly at the table of Charles I during the 17th
century.

Ice cream was made available to the general public for the first [5]
time at Cafe Procope, the first cafe in Paris in 1670.

Throughout the 18th century, ice cream became more and more 6 popular in Europe. Books were written heralding prize recipes. In 1768, a monumental tribute to the subject appeared in England called *The Art of Making Frozen Desserts*, which was written by M. Emy, who described her frozen delights as "food fit for the gods." □ (*New York Times*, July 17, 1991, C7.)

(a). series of dates and events
b. sequence of steps
c. comparison and contrast
(d). cause and effect
e. classification

Topic: Ice cream's origins

Controlling idea: Ice cream evolved because people liked cool, sweet foods and tried to create the perfect one.

Support:
1. King Solomon liked iced drinks.

2. Nero Claudius Caesar (A.D. 54–86) sent runners for flavored snow.

3. Thousand years later Marco Polo returned Italy with a recipe resembling sherbet.

— Recipe evolved in ice cream in 16th century

4. 1553 Catherine de Medici introduced similar frozen dessert to France.

5. At same time, or even earlier, England discovered ice cream

— Called Cream Ice during 17th century

6. 1670—ice cream made available to general public.

7. 18th century—ice cream became increasingly popular in Europe

— 1768 tribute appears in England: *The Art of Making Frozen Desserts*

5. Harriet Tubman and the Underground Railroad

Even though Harriet Tubman gave several interviews about her life as a child and young woman, the facts are hard to verify. There are, for example, no exact records of her birth, although most history books cite 1820 as the year she was born. However, one item in Tubman's biography needs no verification: because of her efforts, hundreds of slaves found their way to freedom. Inspired by seemingly inexhaustible courage and initiative, Tubman spent ten years of her life guiding bands of men, women, and children to the North and to freedom.

According to Tubman's own account, she decided on her course of action when she was only thirteen years old. Badly beaten and wounded in the head by the man who owned her, she prayed that his guilt would make him repent and see the light. But when he came to visit her, intent only on seeing if she was well enough to sell, the girl realized that prayers were not enough. From that moment on, she knew that she had no choice but to escape to the North and take action against slavery.

Although Tubman married in 1844, she did not forget her vow to fight. Quiet as she seemed to those around her, she was only biding her time until she could escape with her two brothers, and in 1849 the three set out together. Although her brothers eventually gave up, Tubman did not. Hunger and exhaustion could not deter her. From her point of view, death was a better alternative than slavery. Spending long nights alone in the woods, Tubman traveled hundreds of miles until she arrived in Philadelphia, a free woman. The year was 1850, and Tubman was just thirty years old.

Initially, Tubman went to work as a servant in order to feed and clothe herself. But before long she made contact with members of the Underground Railroad, learning through them the names of people and places that could guarantee safety for fleeing slaves. With her knowledge of the underground network, Tubman returned home to bring back her sister and her sister's children. One year later, in 1851, she returned home for her brothers. In the same year, she returned for her husband, only to find that he had a new family and was content to stay where he was.

During the next ten years, Tubman traveled back and forth between the free and slave states, making about twenty secret journeys in all. Ultimately, she was personally responsible for the escape of over three hundred men, women, and children. 5

Because some of the escapes were extraordinary, and because she was subject to strange seizures, there were those who thought Harriet Tubman had magical powers. But those who traveled with her knew otherwise. To them it was clear that Tubman's success came from no magical source. It was the result of brains, daring, and ingenuity.* Magic had nothing to do with it. 6

Tubman's rescues were planned with enormous attention to detail, and she would flatly refuse to take any chances that might endanger her charges. If, for example, wanted notices were posted describing the number and appearance of her group, she would see to it that the composition of the group was changed. If the description said one man and and two women, she would dress one of the women in her party in men's clothes, thus outwitting her pursuers. If she had any doubts about a member of her party, she would refuse to take that person. It was this kind of attention to minute detail that made her so successful in her rescue attempts, earning her the nickname Moses. □ 7

(a). series of dates and events
b. sequence of steps
c. comparison and contrast
(d). cause and effect
e. classification

Topic: Harriet Tubman's fight against slavery

Controlling idea: Because of Harriet Tubman's courageous efforts, hundreds of men, women, and children gained their freedom on the Underground Railroad, a secret network of people who aided fleeing slaves.

Support: 1. In 1833, at 13, Tubman decided on her course.

   a. Wounded by her owner, she prayed for him.

   b. Decided to fight because he could think only about selling her.

* ingenuity: imagination.

2. Married in 1844, but never forgot her vow to escape

3. In 1849, set out for the North with her brothers

   a. They gave up the difficult journey.

   b. But in 1850, at 30, she arrived in Philadelphia.

4. Making contact with the Underground Railroad, she learned about people and places offering safety.

   a. In 1851, helped brothers and sister escape

   b. Also tried to help her husband, but he didn't want to leave

5. From 1851 to 1861, Tubman made about 20 journeys and was personally responsible for the escape of more than 300 men, women, and children.

   a. Rescues planned with enormous attention to detail

     (1) If notices described group too closely, she would use disguises.

     (2) Never took anybody she didn't trust

   b. So successful, nicknamed "Moses"

Vocabulary Review

Part B: Here is a list of words drawn from the chapter. Some actually appear in the chapter. Some have been derived from the prefixes and suffixes introduced on page 336. Your job is to match words and blanks.

In some cases you may have to change the endings of words to make them fit the context. If you need to, consult your dictionary to decide which ending to use. *Note:* You may use some words more than once and others not at all.

motivate	gargantuan	abolitionist	ratification
conservative	capital	marginal	diversion
trounce	monologue	rectify	elixir
propensity	coerce	debilitate	sedentary
bowdlerize	evoke	entourage	

1. The senator had wanted to have the amendment speedily __ratified__, and he, or a member of his __entourage__, had spoken to every influential member of the committee. But in the end his opponents had badly __trounced__ him. An outspoken man, his blunt comments had __evoked__ outrage in too many people, and he could neither entice nor bully anyone into supporting him. He went down in defeat and was too spiritually __debilitated__ to resume the battle.

2. The first seeds for the nineteenth century women's movement were sown at the World Anti-Slavery Convention of 1840. Although for years women had been active in the __abolitionist__ movement, it had been decided that only male delegates would be seated. Women were to be assigned a decidedly __marginal__ role. __Motivated__ by the desire to __rectify__ what to them was an obvious injustice, Elizabeth Cady Stanton and Lucretia Mott planned and organized the Seneca Falls Convention of 1848. Hardly __conservative__ in their demands, the two women composed a Declaration of Principles that openly demanded equal rights and even more shocking—the vote. Having done so, however, both men were nervous about reading their proposals aloud at the conference until the abolitionist, Frederick Douglass, volunteered his support.

3. Orson Welles was a man of __gargantuan__ appetites. When he died in 1985 his face and body were bloated from years of overindulging in fine wine and rich food. But if his appetite was enormous so was his talent. A splendid actor capable of spellbinding dramatic __monologues__ both on and off stage, he was also a gifted producer, director, and writer. To those old enough, his name still __evokes__ memories of the

panic that occurred in 1938 when Welles broadcast his production of H. G. Wells's *War of the Worlds*. It was so realistic, thousands believed an alien attack was in progress and panicked. Yet despite or perhaps because of his talent, Welles had a definite propensity _____ toward insulting and irritating the Hollywood backers he needed to finance his always extravagant projects. Consequently he was seldom able to charm or coerce _____ them into financing his films. In the last years of his life, he spent much of his time in Europe where there seemed to be more appreciation for his particular brand of genius.

4. In 1818 when the Scottish physician Thomas Bowdler brought out his bowdlerized _____ edition of Shakespeare's works, his motivation _____ was to provide a more refined version of Shakespeare that could be a pleasant diversion _____ for the whole family, including women and children. He hoped to rectify _____ Shakespeare's unfortunate propensity _____ for describing immoral behavior and language. Poor Dr. Bowdler believed his removal of the offending passages would only improve Shakespeare's poetry. History, however, has not agreed with him. His name lives on in a word that identifies a particularly prudish and silly form of censorship.

Critical Reading

The previous chapters focused on understanding the author's message. In this chapter you'll learn how to *evaluate* that message by examining the author's use of language and evidence. To that end, we will demonstrate how to do the following:

- ☐ Distinguish between *statements of fact* and *statements of opinion.*
- ☐ Evaluate an author's opinions.
- ☐ Recognize *connotative* and *denotative* language.
- ☐ Look for evidence of *bias.*
- ☐ Identify tone.
- ☐ Analyze arguments.

New Vocabulary

equitable	fallible	indiscriminately
vigilantism	unification	posthumous
annals	emit	ordinance
fraudulent	defray	

Distinguishing Between Fact and Opinion

Experienced critical readers are careful to distinguish between **fact** and **opinion.** The following explanation will help you to do the same.

Facts

Statements of fact describe people, places, and events without benefit of interpretation, inference, or value judgment. "The sun is red," for example, is a statement of fact. "The red sun is beautiful" is a statement of opinion. It offers a value judgment.

Unlike opinions, facts can be **verified** or checked for accuracy through observation or reference to written records. In contrast to opinions, facts can be labelled "true" or "false," "accurate" or "inaccurate."

The language used to state facts is usually **denotative.** It has little or no power to affect our emotions and employs words primarily for their dictionary meanings. The following statements of fact employ denotative language:

Twelve inches of snow fell in Buffalo last night.

The shortest war on record was between the United Kingdom and Zanzibar. It took place on August 27, 1896, and it lasted from 9:02 to 9:40 a.m.

Facts

1. rely on denotative language.
2. can be verified for accuracy.
3. are not affected by a writer's personality, background, or training.
4. frequently employ numbers, statistics, dates, and measurements.

Opinions

In contrast to facts, statements of opinion cannot be verified. They reflect a person's personal response to the world and can't be proven true or false.

However, opinions can be labelled "valid" or "invalid," "sound" or "unsound," "informed" or "uninformed." What those labels identify is the amount and type of support a writer or speaker has used as the basis for the opinion expressed. Yes, everybody has a right to his or her own opinion. But everyone's opinion does not deserve the same degree of attention or consideration. (For more on justifying opinions, see pages 362–364.)

Unlike statements of fact, statements of opinion are very much influenced by a person's background, training, and experience. For an illustration of just how much opinions can vary, read these three opinions about a 1987 Supreme Court decision:

> It's probably the worst affirmative action decision ever issued by the Supreme Court . . . (Linda Chavez, Former Staff Director of the United States Commission on Civil Rights)

> The opinion is very important because it emphasizes the fact that in most job situations, the differences between candidates are rather insignificant. (Drew S. Days, Professor, Yale Law School)

> It's a wonderful decision . . . (Joyce D. Miller, Vice President of the Amalgamated Clothing and Textile Workers Union[1])

Depending on with whom you speak, the decision was "wonderful," "important," or "terrible." And, as is typical, the opinions change from person to person.

In contrast to statements of fact, statements of opinion rely heavily on **connotative** language that plays on our emotions or evokes a mood. Rewritten in more connotative language, the two statements on page 354 would read something like this:

> Last night Buffalo was buried under a sudden avalanche of freezing snow.

> The shortest and probably the least devastating war in history took place on August 27, 1896; it lasted almost a whole hour.

In these examples the language does more than describe the situation. It also interprets it. The first sentence uses words like *buried*, *avalanche*, and *freezing* to encourage readers to feel the harshness of the storm. In the second sentence, phrases like *least devastating* and *whole hour* suggest the war should not be taken too seriously.

Although you might not think statements of opinion appear in textbooks, the following statements are all opinions. Every one of them came from a textbook:

1. A ruthless land grab, the Cherokee removal exposed the prejudiced and greedy side of Jacksonian democracy. (Divine et al., *America Past and Present I*, p. 285.)
2. Despite its mixed economic record, the [Cuban] revolution's achievements in the areas of employment, equitable* distribu-

---

1. *New York Times*, "This Week in Review," March 29, 1987, p. 1.
* equitable: fair.

tion of income, public health, and education are remarkable. (Keen and Wasserman, *A History of Latin America*, p. 457.)

3. Vigilantism,* sparked often by a superpatriotism of a ruthless sort, flourished [during World War I]. (Divine et al., *America Past and Present II*, p. 707.)

Unlike science texts—which rely heavily on statements of fact—history, government, sociology, and psychology texts are likely to include numerous statements of opinion. On the one hand, authors intentionally offer readers the standard interpretations or explanations of events or situations in their field. As writers of textbooks, that is their primary goal or **purpose.** But on the other hand, they may also unintentionally pass on their personal interpretations of those events.

In one text, for example, an author who had opposed the Vietnam War might suggest that government policy during the war years (1964–1973) was mistaken from beginning to end. In a different text, another author—one who had supported the war—might imply that the policy was sound but the leadership inadequate. In short their opinions might well intrude into their descriptions of events.

On the whole, there is nothing wrong with authors including their own personal slant or **bias** in their explanations. Producing a fully unbiased or objective account of any event is difficult, maybe even impossible. Our background, training, even our language influence the way we see the world, what we pay attention to, and what we ignore.

Blending Fact and Opinion

But because, to some degree, bias does influence most writers, critical readers distinguish carefully between fact and opinion. In particular, they notice when fact and opinion blend within the same sentence, as they do in the following example:

Sigmund Freud's *Interpretation of Dreams* was published in 1905, and its revolutionary impact is still being felt today.

Here the date of publication is a matter of fact, but the book's impact is another matter. Although Freud's interpretation of dreams still has its supporters today, there are those who flatly

---

* vigilantism: rule of self-appointed citizens, organized to punish criminals and maintain law and order.

dismiss both Freud and his book, making this sentence a blend of fact and opinion. It is important that you recognize where the one leaves off and the other begins.

Opinions

1. rely on connotative language.
2. cannot be verified for accuracy.
3. are affected by a writer's personality, background, and training.
4. frequently express comparisons using words like "more," "better," "most," and "least."
5. are often introduced by verbs and adverbs that suggest doubt or possibility, "appears," "seems," "apparently," "probably," "potentially," "possibly."

DIGGING DEEPER

Do you support affirmative action? Do you think past discrimination should be taken into account by schools or employers? Explain why or why not.

Exercise 1

Directions: Read each statement carefully. Then write *F* for fact, *O* for opinion, or *B* for both in the blanks that follow.

Example: In 1963 the Supreme Court prohibited the Lord's prayer and Bible reading in the schools. This decision was misguided and should be reversed.
  _B_

Explanation: In response to passages like these, critical readers need to be alert to the place where fact and opinion blend. The first sentence is indeed a fact, one that can be easily verified. The second statement, however, is an opinion that makes a value judgment.

1. Measles has an incubation period of seven to fourteen days.
   F

2. Within ten years, computers are going to replace teachers.
   0

3. From full moon to full moon, the lunar cycle is about 29.5 days.
   F

4. In 1985 Tommy "Muskrat" Green ate 6 pounds of oysters in 1 minute and thirty-three seconds. That's sick.
   B

5. The battle of the Alamo, where frontier hero Davy Crockett died, took place on February 23, 1836. It was a tragic event.
   B

6. Soap operas are pure junk.
   0

7. In 1988 sisters-in-law Jackie Joyner-Kersee and Florence Griffith Joyner both set world records in the U.S. Olympic Trials on the same day. What a talented family!
   B

8. The rap group "DC Talk" got their initials from the words "Decent Christian."
   F

9. Some experts suspect that the universe may be only half as large and half as old as is generally believed.
   B

10. Attorney Morris Dees has used the courts to seriously weaken the power of the Ku Klux Klan.
    B

Exercise 2

Directions: Label each sentence in the following paragraphs *F* for fact, *O* for opinion or *B* for both.

Example: [1] Worse than the common cold, backaches hinder, disable, even cripple millions of people every year. [2] Backache is no respecter of age. [3] It plagues both young and old. [4] Although there are drugs to relieve the pain of backache, they are not a cure; they simply relieve the symptoms. [5] Every year in the hope of the cure, around 200,000 people undergo back surgery. [6] But in 20 percent of all cases, surgery fails completely, and patients are left with their symptoms intact.

(1) __*B*__ (2) __*F*__ (3) __*F*__ (4) __*F*__ (5) __*F*__ (6) __*F*__

Explanation: Every sentence is labeled according to whether it contains a fact, opinion, or mixture of both. Sentence 1, for example, is labeled *B* because it begins with an opinion—not everyone would consider the backache worse than the cold—and ends with a fact—you can check medical records to see if millions of people do indeed suffer. Complete the rest of the exercises in the same manner.

1. [1] Cookbooks produced in America during the early forties and fifties show a varied collection of recipes rich in butter, milk, and eggs. [2] But such cookbooks are clearly a thing of the past since many Americans have become aware of the need to reduce the large amounts of fat they consume. [3] According to a study produced by the American Heart Association, there is much evidence tying fatty foods to diseases of the heart like arteriosclerosis. [4] Saturated fats raise the level of cholesterol in the blood, and cholesterol in turn directly contributes to hardening of the arteries. [5] Aware of the changing times, even such formerly staunch supporters of cream and butter as Chefs Jacques Pepin and Julia Child now publish recipes that limit both.

(1) __F__ (2) __B__ (3) __F__ (4) __F__ (5) __F__

2. [1] There is no sport that can rival the game of soccer. [2] Certainly America's tedious national pastime, baseball, cannot compare with it. [3] Even on its best days, baseball lacks the speed and grace of soccer. [4] Every four years, teams from all over the world

Orcas, or "killer whales," are highly successful predators.

compete for the world cup in soccer. [5] It is time for America to join the rest of the developed nations, like England, France, Germany, and Italy, in the competition for the World Cup. [6] That would be a truly international game of champions, unlike the "World" Series, which contains only North American teams.

(1) __0__ (2) __0__ (3) __0__ (4) __F__ (5) __0__ (6) __B__

3. [1] Orcas, or "killer whales" as they are more commonly known, are extraordinary creatures. [2] Inhabitants of the cold seas, they are huge, black and white mammals with enormous, jagged teeth that make them highly successful predators. [3] In turn, none of the other ocean creatures are capable of preying on them. [4] Some years ago, *Orca, the Killer Whale,* was a financially successful movie starring Richard Harris.

(1) __B__ (2) __B__ (3) __F__ (4) __F__

4. [1] The atmosphere of Venus is approximately ninety times hotter than Earth's. [2] Temperatures near the planet's surface are as

high as 900 degrees Fahrenheit. [3] The planet nearest Earth, Venus, is shrouded in clouds and is, therefore, not highly visible. [4] In the past, several attempts have been made to explore the planet's surface, particularly in Russia. [5] The Russians have landed several robot crafts on Venus, and at least one has been able to collect soil samples and transmit color pictures.

(1) __F__ (2) __F__ (3) __F__ (4) __F__ (5) __F__

5. [1] In the annals* of public health, what some critics now call the "swine flu affair" may go down as one of the federal government's greatest disasters. [2] In 1976, federal health authorities made a concentrated effort to immunize the public against an influenza epidemic they knew might never arrive. [3] The concern was great because the so-called *swine flu* virus seemed to resemble a virus believed to have caused a deadly outbreak of flu in 1918. [4] After the government spent over $100 million, the flu never came. [5] But several people who had the shot to prevent flu came down with a rare illness called the *Guillain-Barré syndrome*. [6] The disease appeared to be linked to being immunized, and more than $9 million in damages was paid to those who contracted the paralytic disease. [7] As a result of the swine flu affair, two high-ranking federal officers were dismissed from their posts.

(1) __0__ (2) __F__ (3) __F__ (4) __F__ (5) __F__

(6) __B__ (7) __F__

W R I T I N G   S U G G E S T I O N

Write a report of your first meeting with someone who proved very important to you—your wife, best friend, child, your boss. Avoid all opinions. Concentrate on getting the facts, and emphasize denotative language.

---

* annals: records.

Evaluating Opinions

While everybody has a right to his or her own opinion, it does not
follow that every opinion deserves the same degree of attention or
respect.

Imagine, for example, that a friend saw you taking an aspirin
for a headache and told you that chewing a clove of garlic was a
far better remedy. When you asked why, he shrugged shoulders
and said: "I don't know. I heard it someplace." Given this lack of
support, you probably wouldn't pay much attention to your
friend's claim. It doesn't appear to represent a **justified opinion,**
one based on relevant facts, reasons, examples, statistics, or other
appropriate evidence.

The following paragraph illustrates the kind of justification critical readers expect authors to provide:

opinion

justification

> *The impact of media on the war in Vietnam went beyond mere
> reporting.* In 1968, the highly respected anchor of the CBS nightly
> news, Walter Cronkite, visited Vietnam. Upon his return, he
> made a rare editorial statement indicating his opposition to a
> continuation of current government policy. According to Presi-
> dential Press Secretary George Christian, when Cronkite made
> his statement, "the shock waves rolled through the Govern-
> ment." President Lyndon B. Johnson, an avid watcher of TV
> news (as well as reader of printed news) believed that, by
> "losing" Cronkite, he had lost the support of the American peo-
> ple.[2] Not long after, Johnson decided not to run for re-election.
> (Aldrich, et al. *American Government,* p. 302.)

In this brief paragraph the authors justify their opinion by offering the factual reports and expert opinions on which it was based:

---

2. Quoted in Herbert Y. Schandler, *The Unmaking of a President: Lyndon Johnson
and Vietnam* (Princeton, N.J.: Princeton University Press, 1977), p. 198.

1. Cronkite's 1968 statement
2. the press secretary's interpretation of what happened as a result
3. Johnson's reaction (Note the footnote referring you to the source for this claim)
4. Johnson's decision not to run shortly after.

Now you may decide that, despite the authors' justification, you still do not agree with their opinion. There's nothing wrong with that. Critical readers do not automatically accept everything they read. However, it's important that you understand how the authors arrived at their conclusion. That understanding gives you a basis for agreement or disagreement. More importantly it allows you to draw your own conclusions and form your own opinion.

To see the difference between justified and unjustified opinions, imagine yourself asking of the next paragraph, "Why should I accept this opinion?" You would be hard pressed for an answer.

> We Americans like to brag about progress, but in fact, life was better in the nineteenth century than in the twentieth. People were happier and more at peace with themselves. There just wasn't the same kind of anxiety and tension that there is today. If we had a chance, we would probably all get into a time machine and go backward in time, rather than forward. All of our highly touted technological progress has not brought us an increased measure of contentment.

The author of this paragraph believes life was better a century ago. However she, like our friend who suggests garlic for headaches, offers no justification for that opinion. In support of her claim, she might have noted that there was hardly any divorce a century ago or that aging parents lived with their children, not in a nursing home. But instead of offering the factual support that could justify her opinion, she repeats the same claim in different words. This tactic, called **circular reasoning,** would prompt critical readers to be skeptical of the opinion being offered.

Such circular reasoning also suggests the author is overly biased or inclined toward her own position. Convinced of her own rightness, she cannot imagine disagreement. Consequently she considers justification unnecessary.

The author of the following paragraph has the same unfortunate tendency towards excessive bias. Convinced of his own rightness, he does not feel compelled to justify his opinion. Instead he simply repeats it, as if repetition by itself were adequate justification.

> The government of the United States should regulate the number of hours a worker can complete on a night shift. It is a disgrace

that this has not been done already. The United States is one of only six industrialized countries that does not regulate night shift hours. This lack of regulation is a dangerous and costly oversight.

It's not hard to determine the opinion expressed in this paragraph: The United States government should regulate night shift hours. What's not so easy to determine is why the author takes this position. Most of the paragraph simply repeats the opening opinion and thereby offers another example of circular reasoning.

The closest the author comes to offering a reason is to say that most other industrialized countries already have such a regulation. But saying that other people do what the author considers correct is hardly good justification. Maybe the other nations are wrong and the United States is right. Claiming that "everybody else is doing it" is not adequate justification for an opinion. In fact, it illustrates a common propaganda technique, called the **bandwagon appeal.** The assumption underlying this appeal is that if everybody else holds a particular opinion, you should too.

But imagine now that the author had recognized his lack of justification and revised the above paragraph to make it more convincing:

> The government of the United States should regulate the number of hours a worker can complete on a night shift. According to studies completed by the National Commission on Sleep Disorders, the loss of sleep, whether voluntary or involuntary, is a dangerous and deadly threat. The commission concluded that literally millions of accidents are caused every year by drivers and workers trying to function normally on too little sleep. Yet another study by the Congressional Office of Technology pointed to the importance that changes in the sleep cycle play in human errors within the work place. Additional studies suggest that people are more likely to make errors of all kinds, if they have not slept seven to eight hours within the last twenty-four hours. These studies strongly suggest that limits be placed on disturbances in the human sleep cycle. While the government cannot determine how many hours employees sleep, it can and should place limits on the number of hours they spend on night shifts.[3]

In this paragraph the author anticipates and answers the question he rightly assumes his readers might pose: "Why should I accept this opinion?" To justify his claim, he provides his readers with some of the studies on which he based his conclusion. While

---

3. Statistics and studies drawn from Merrill M. Miller, "Punch the Clock, Hit the Hay," *New York Times*, Jan. 11, 1992, p. 19.

critical readers might not immediately embrace this author's opinion as their own, they would certainly give it some serious consideration.

To evaluate an author's opinions, ask yourself these questions:

1. Does the author make it clear that he or she is presenting an opinion rather than a fact?
2. What justification does the author provide?
3. Is the justification **relevant** or related to the opinion expressed? Or does it support a different claim altogether?

Exercise 3

Directions: Each exercise opens with an opinion. Label the statements that follow *R* (relevant fact), *I* (irrelevant fact) or *C* (circular reasoning).

Example: Japan, as everyone knows, has accomplished an economic miracle. But in the last few years, the country has come face to face with the dark side of prosperity—greed and corruption.

a. The Recruit scandal of 1989 toppled the regime of Prime Minister Takeshita.
   _R_

b. Gift giving is an accepted tradition among many Japanese businessmen.
   _I_

c. The eighties brought the Japanese prosperity and corruption in equal measure.
   _C_

d. In 1991, it was discovered that several banks had given out $5,000,000 in fraudulent* loans.
   _R_

Explanation: To be credible the opening statement needs justification. After all, what one person calls corruption another person may call smart business practices. That justification comes from statements *a* and *d*, both of which offer evidence of illegal behavior. Sentence *b*, however, does not justify the opening statement. If anything, it suggests how bribery might be interpreted as an acceptable practice. Sentence *c* is no help either. It simply restates the original opinion.

Use the same labels to complete the rest of this exercise.

---

* fraudulent: illegal, dishonest, deceitful.

1. Katherine Dunham is an extraordinary woman.

   a. In the forties and fifties she toured the United States and Europe introducing audiences to Caribbean and African music.
      R

   b. Katherine Dunham is a unique personality.
      C

   c. Now in her eighties, Dunham runs workshops that teach disadvantaged children the discipline of dance.
      R

   d. Her husband was John Pratt, who designed the costumes worn by her troupe of dancers.
      I

2. Despite decades of intended reforms, many migrant farm workers can barely scrape out a decent living.

   a. Because they are defined as subcontractors, farm workers must pay 15.3 percent of their income in Social Security taxes.
     <u>R</u>

   b. In 1960 the television program "Harvest of Shame" provoked public outrage at the plight of migrant workers, but thirty years later a new generation of farm laborers struggles to make a living.
     <u>C</u>

   c. Federal regulations do not require that farm laborers be informed about the pesticides they use and their potential dangers.
     <u>R</u>

   d. If they are temporarily laid off, farm workers cannot collect unemployment or worker's compensation.[4]
     <u>R</u>

3. President Zachary Taylor probably died as much from the help of his doctors as he did from his disease.

   a. When Taylor came down with acute gastroenteritis, his doctors began dosing him with ipecac, calomel, opium, and quinine.
     <u>R</u>

   b. Some biographers believe Taylor died of arsenic poisoning.
     <u>I</u>

   c. Zachary Taylor might well have survived had he not been subjected to the care of his doctors.
     <u>C</u>

   d. After they gave him high doses of drugs, Zachary Taylor's doctors bled and blistered* him.
     <u>R</u>

4. Movies treat fist fights as if they were just so much horse play, but the reality is not so much fun.

---

4. Source: Jason DeParle, "New Rows to Hoe in the 'Harvest of Shame,'" *New York Times*, July 28, 1991, p. E3.

* In the nineteenth century, many physicians believed that taking blood from the body could cure disease. They also believed that applications of heat hot enough to cause blisters were beneficial.

a. On screen, actors trade numerous punches, but emergency room statistics show that most fist fights last only one punch, and that punch results in a broken hand and broken jaw.
   <u>R</u>

b. Fist fights may be fun on screen, but they are anything but fun in reality.
   <u>C</u>

c. Breaking a chair over someone's head in a movie may get a laugh, but in reality it frequently results in a concussion that can produce a coma.
   <u>R</u>

d. In 1991 the Terminator returned to the screen, this time as a hero rather than a villain.
   <u>I</u>

Exercise 4

Directions: All of the following passages express opinions. Read each one then write *J* for justified or *U* for unjustified in the accompanying blanks.

Example: *Although the shift to food domestication was traditionally viewed as progress, the current anthropological thinking is that* foraging—*the reliance on wild foods for survival—had its advantages. Judging from the few groups that still practice hunting and gathering, ways of life based on foraging are usually quite satisfactory in their ability to meet the needs of people.* Population density is generally low, and the communities of cooperating individuals are never very large. Under these circumstances, it is simple for the local group to move quickly from place to place. As a result, food shortages are rare among hunters and gatherers. Nomadic or seminomadic hunters and gatherers do not live amidst their own refuse, one contributor to many of the diseases with which more sedentary peoples must contend. This factor, plus the low population densities that are characteristic of foragers, means that the epidemics that often plague peoples who live under crowded conditions are also rare. Furthermore, Marvin Harris (1977) has pointed out that foragers have a much shorter work week than do food domesticators. For instance, the southern African !Kung foragers need to work only about three hours a day to obtain a nutritious diet, even though their desert environment is not nearly so lush as most of the areas occupied by hunting and gathering peoples before the rise of farming. (Crapo, *Cultural Anthropology*, p. 222.) <u>J</u>

Explanation: This passage opens with two statements of opinion. Notice how the author justifies those opinions by including the facts on which they are based.

Now it's your turn to decide which opinions are justified and which ones are not.

1. Transcendental meditation is a simple technique that can improve the quality of life. To practice TM, as it is commonly called, individuals just have to close their eyes and concentrate on a *mantra*, a word or sound used to focus concentration. Although meditators can let any and all thoughts enter minds, they must always come back to their point of concentration, the mantra. When that simple procedure is followed twice a day for twenty minutes, meditators report some very beneficial effects. For example, in one study, conducted by Kenneth Pelletier at the University of California, those trained in meditation indicated an increased ability to concentrate and remember. L. C. Doucette of McMaster University in Canada has shown that university students practicing TM experienced less anxiety than other subjects in the study. The *New York Times* reported that transcendental meditation was being put to use in the men's prison of São Paulo, Brazil, and prison authorities have noted a reduction in violence as well as a decreased use of drugs and alcohol among prisoners practicing meditation. ___J___

2. There appears to be growing evidence that differences in empathy and compassionate behavior in toddlers and preschool children are related to differences in parenting styles (Zahn-Waxler et al., 1979; Mussen & Eisenberg-Berg, 1977; Radke-Yarrow, Zahn-Waxler, & Chapan, 1983; Main & George, 1985). In a study of the reactions of children to other children's distress and the reactions of parents when their own children were the cause of the distress, parents of less compassionate toddlers tended to respond to the child's misbehavior in more authoritarian ways, using physical restraint, physical punishment, or unexplained commands to stop. Parents of highly compassionate children were more likely to use explanations that focused on helping the child see the connections between his unacceptable actions and the upset and distress that they caused (Zahn-Waxler et al., 1979; Radke-Yarrow, Zahn-Waxler, & Chapan, 1983). (Adapted from Seifert and Hoffnung, *Child and Adolescent Development*, p. 364.) ___J___

3. Despite attempts to improve the use of questionnaires to measure personality or performance, they do have a number of drawbacks.

Popular as they might be as tests of competence or adjustment, questionnaires are fallible.* They do not necessarily test or identify what they purport or claim they can. The questionnaire is simple to administer, hence its popularity. But it has several problems that make it a faulty instrument of measurement or diagnosis. __U__

4. For East Germans, the unification† with West Germany has enormously improved their lives. As a result of unification, travel restrictions have been lifted. East Germans can now visit relatives, some of whom they have not seen for years. There are even plans to improve the environment. Under the communist regime, whole sections of forest died because more than five million tons of sulfur dioxide were emitted‡ into the air.[5] But after the two countries were united, emissions were reduced and measures are being taken to control the discharge of chemicals into streams and rivers. __J__

A Word About Generalizations

Some opinions are **generalizations.** They are conclusions about whole groups drawn from knowledge of individual cases, examples, or studies. Here are three illustrations:

Women executives are having a hard time reaching the highest levels of management.

The only child tends to be a high achiever.

Big weddings are back in style.

In order to be taken seriously, these statements of opinion should be justified by facts. However, where such *broad* generalizations are concerned—generalizations meant to account for large numbers of people or events—the *number* of facts cited becomes significant. To win a critical reader's respect, authors must avoid **hasty generalizations** based on or justified by only one or two individual cases or examples. In short, **the broader the generalization, the more factual evidence a writer needs to supply.**

---

5. Source of statistics: William S. Ellis, "The Morning After," *National Geographic*, September 1991, p. 28.

* fallible: capable of error.

† unification: combining or bringing together into one.

‡ emitted: sent forth.

For example, the following author claims that fathers prepare excitedly for the birth of a child but do relatively little to prepare for actual fatherhood. Notice how many studies the author cites in support of his generalization.

Transition to Fatherhood

The fatherhood role begins with the woman's pregnancy and the [1] husband relating to his wife as a mother-to-be. This means sharing her excitement about the pregnancy with parents and close friends. "It was like telling people that we were getting married," said one father. "We delighted in breaking the news to people who were as excited as we were."

Opinion: *Beyond this, husbands do very little to prepare for fatherhood.* In [2] a study of 102 first-time fathers (Knox & Gilman, 1974), only one-
Study #1:   third attended parenthood classes offered by a local university, whereas one-fourth attended Lamaze classes. It would be inaccurate to assume that the fathers-to-be already knew what to expect from the fatherhood role. In fact, only 25 percent of them had discussed fatherhood with another male on several occasions, and more than 40 percent had never fed a baby or changed a baby's
Study #2:   diapers. In another study (Price-Bonahm & Skeen, 1979), 160 fathers reported that "trial and error" was their first source of help with fatherhood.

When 30 husbands whose wives were in their last month of preg- [3]
Study #3:   nancy were asked about their impending new role (Fein, 1976), most were concerned about what labor and delivery would be like and worried about how to actually take care of a baby. Others said their fathers had been emotionally distant with them when they were growing up, and they did not want to repeat this pattern when they became fathers. □ (Knox, *Choices in Relationships,* pp. 477–478.)

In this example, the author used three different studies to justify the opinion offered to his readers. You should expect this kind of justification when an author generalizes about a large group or class of people.

Although the next generalization might also express a justified opinion, critical readers would probably reserve judgment until they had a bit more information.

Members of the lower middle class show a special concern for prestige and status and tend to be *status seekers* (Mills, 1951). That is, they invest much of their disposable income in goods and services that can be used as status symbols. These include cars, homes, and certain leisure activities. (Poponoe, *Sociology*, p. 244.)

Here the author offers only one reference to support a very broad generalization. In addition, that reference, (Mills, 1951), refers to a book called *White Collar* by C. Wright Mills. The book, although highly influential, contains as much opinion as fact.

In evaluating broad generalizations, you should also be wary of those that presume to cover *all* members of a very large and varied group, for example:

Men don't like to cook.
Children are the greatest joy of a woman's life.
Old age is a time of depression and despair.

Just think of how many people you are referring to when you use words like "men," "women," "children" or "the elderly." Given the number of people these words represent, it is awfully hard to find one consistent generalization that applies to every member of the group. Thus, if authors do not supply the qualifying words like "some," "many," "most," or "in general," which make these generalizations more plausible, critical readers mentally do it for them.

Many men don't like to cook.
For many women, children are the greatest joy in life.
For some elderly people, old age is a time of depression and despair.

Exercise 5

Directions: Read each passage. Then decide if the passage offers a hasty generalization (*H*), circular reasoning (*C*), or a justified opinion (*J*).

Example: In some South American tribes, men and women speak different languages. The men cannot understand the women's language, but the women can understand the men's. On the surface, American men and women appear to speak a common language, but, in fact, we are not so different from those South American tribes. Here too the sexes speak two different languages. As the linguist Robin Lakoff has shown in a study of speech differences, women use more questions than men do. They interrupt less frequently, and are more likely to suggest than assert. They also make greater use of qualifiers like "might," "could," and "probably."
    H

Explanation: There may be distinct differences in the way men and women speak. But you should hold off judgment until you receive more evidence. One study, particularly if you don't know how many people participated, is not adequate support for such a broad generalization.

1. A costly and complicated federal program, the distribution of food stamps has been severely criticized in the past as too expensive and too inefficient. Recently, food stamp fraud has been documented in at least four different states in the United States. Given the evidence of fraud, where the individuals using food stamps were far from needy, it is a good idea to consider limiting—perhaps even abolishing—the program since food stamps are not going to the needy as they should. __H__

2. As the National Rifle Association (NRA) points out: "Persons willing to risk the penalties for criminal activity . . . don't worry about the penalty for possessing an unregistered firearm." The State of Texas, for example, prohibits the carrying of a handgun, either openly or concealed. Yet Dallas, Texas, has the eleventh highest murder rate among the U.S.'s major cities.[6] __H__

3. In presidential campaigns, the status of front runner is not always a benefit. For example, in the 1972 New Hampshire primary, Edmund Muskie was the Democratic front runner. He beat George McGovern by only one percentage point, but because he was the front runner, that narrow victory was considered a defeat. Similarly, in 1984 Walter Mondale was the Democratic front runner in New Hampshire. When he lost to Gary Hart of Colorado, his credibility as a candidate was damaged. For that matter, it was Mr. Hart's status as a front runner in the 1988 campaign that led the press to scrutinize his personal life and publish photos of him with a young model. The resulting scandal caused him to resign from the campaign. __J__

4. Recent statistics suggest that major changes have occurred in the American family over the past two or three decades. Single-parent

---

6. Cited in Allon Sack and Jack Yourman, "Gun Controls: Aimless," *Speed Reading.* Baltimore: College Skills Center, 1984, p. 163.

families increased from 11 percent to 22 percent of all families with children between 1970 and 1986. For example, almost 90 percent of single-parent families today are headed by women (U.S. Bureau of the Census, 1987a, 1987c). The profile of women as full-time homemakers has also changed. In 1960, 30 percent of married women held paying jobs; by 1987, the percentage had increased to about 56. Of wives with children under the age of 18, 64 percent were in the labor force in 1987 (U.S. Bureau of Labor Statistics, 1987b, 1987c). (Poponoe, *Sociology*, p. 354.) __J__

5. Divorce is hard on children. Although splitting up may make the parents feel better, the divorce does not necessarily have the same effect on the children. Quite the contrary, children who go through a divorce probably suffer as much as or more than the parents. It is the children who are the real victims of divorce. Parents considering divorce should keep that fact in mind. __C__

Arguing to Persuade

Usually the primary purpose or goal of textbook writing is to inform. In textbooks, authors versed in a particular subject or discipline identify the terms, facts, and opinions considered essential to an understanding of their field. While an author's personal bias or point of view plays a role in what terms or facts are selected and how they are interpreted, the writer's *primary* or central goal is not to persuade you to see things from the same perspective. In fact textbook authors frequently give equal time to opposing points of view so that readers can draw their own conclusions.

However, as you turn from your textbooks to the pages of newspapers and magazines, you will encounter writers with other primary goals or purposes. Some write to entertain; others write simply to air a personal preference. However, a good portion of the writers you encounter, particularly on the editorial pages, write in the hopes that you will share or at least seriously consider adopting their opinion. They write, in short, with the desire to **persuade.** To achieve that goal, they may well give you an **argument.** That does not mean they badger or browbeat you. It means they offer a **conclusion**—the opinion they want you to share—along with some **reasons** why you should share it. Critical readers try, first of all, to recognize those writers who wish to persuade. Then they analyze the arguments those writers provide.

Analyzing Arguments

Authors who give you arguments frequently offer a value judgment—"While zoos may be fun for people, they are not so pleasant for animals." Or they claim that some event, action, or behavior should or should not take place—"If the name of the accused rapist is published, the name of the alleged victim should be published as well." Or else they insist that some belief or attitude should or should not be shared—"Americans must stop believing that the earth can absorb repeated environmental damage and continue to sustain life."

In the following reading, the author offers a value judgment. She claims that product placement—the paid use of name brands in films—is a perfectly legitimate practice. To justify her opinion, she offers three reasons. In short she gives you an argument:

The Ethics of Product Placement

Statement of opinion

"Product placement," the paid use of name brands in film, is currently a source of controversy. In fact, the Federal Trade Commission has been asked to investigate the practice. *Yet criticism of product placement seems misguided. The practice is a legitimate and important part of making movies.*

Transitional phrase introduces first reason

First of all, *brand name products are part of American life.* Moviemakers intent on creating a realistic atmosphere are forced to use brand names. Were an actor in a scene to open a can simply labeled "tuna," the audience's attention would be distracted by the label, and the effect of the scene would be destroyed. People are used to seeing brand names like "Chicken of the Sea" and "Bumble Bee." Filmmakers who want realism in their films have to use brand names.

Transitional word introduces second reason

Secondly, *using name brands in films is just like paying famous people to wear name brands in public.* Athletes like Ivan Lendl, Magic Johnson, and Jennifer Capriati have all worn shoes or clothing identifying their sponsors' products. Yet no one complained about that practice.

Transitional word introduces third reason

Finally, *product placement is an important source of revenue for filmmakers.* The average cost of a film today is 26 million dollars, and producers cannot keep hiking up ticket prices to pay their bills. The practice of product placement, however, can help defray* some of the expense. □

---

*   defray: absorb, to meet or satisfy by payment.

To evaluate arguments like the above, first identify the opinion being put forth. Then look for the reasons used to convince. To discover the author's conclusion, ask yourself questions like these:

1. What value judgment does the author hope readers will make after reading this article?
2. What action, event, belief, attitude or behavior does the author want readers to support or oppose?

Once you can identify the conclusion the author wants you to share, use partial sentences like the following to identify the author's reasons: The author wants me to believe this because _____; or the author wants me to do this because _____.

Applied to the article on product placement, these questions would produce the following skeletal outline of the author's argument:

Opinion: "Criticism of product placement is misguided. The practice is a legitimate and important part of making movies."

Reasons: 1. Moviemakers need to use brand name products to create a realistic atmosphere.
2. There is no difference between athletes paid to sport brand names and moviemakers who use brand names in their films.
3. Product placement produces revenue needed to defray the cost of films.

In the next section, we will talk more about evaluating arguments. But first, use Exercise 6 to practice (1) identifying the author's opinion and (2) locating the reasons meant to convince.

DIGGING DEEPER

What's your opinion of product placement? Can you find any holes or flaws in the author's argument?

Exercise 6

Directions: Read each selection. Then in the accompanying blanks identify the author's opinion and reasons.

Think Twice About Using C.P.R.

Cardiopulmonary resuscitation (C.P.R.) is an important procedure *1* that has saved countless lives in the past and will continue to do so in the future. It is, however, a procedure that can be abused when it is applied indiscriminately.* If patients are elderly and already terminally ill, we should think twice about pounding their fragile bodies back into life.

In most hospitals, C.P.R. is performed routinely without regard *2* to the patient's status prior to cardiac arrest. That means an eighty-five-year-old male terminally ill from diabetes, hypertension, and liver cancer would automatically receive C.P.R., even if bones in his chest were broken as a result and his life extended for only a few more weeks. In effect, the procedure increases his suffering and further decreases the quality of his life.

Often in such cases, C.P.R. is routinely applied because the patient has not expressed his or her desire to be allowed to die. When a crisis arises, and the family feels unable to make a quick decision, the physician revives the patient, even if the application of C.P.R. causes only additional pain and suffering. Viewed from this perspective, the routine application of C.P.R. to those who are old, terminally ill, and in pain, is not necessarily a humane act. It is simply a by-product of our society's refusal to deal directly and openly with death.[7] □

Opinion: We should reconsider using C.P.R. on patients who are terminally ill, old, and in pain.

Reasons: 1. We increase their suffering and offer only a few weeks more of life.

2. We do it because no one has thought about discussing an alternative.

Explanation: Here the author offers two reasons why C.P.R. should not be routinely administered to terminally ill patients.

Now it's your turn to analyze the following arguments.

---

7. Based on an editorial by Fazlur Rahman, "Why Pound Life into the Dying," *New York Times*, February 20, 1989.

* indiscriminately: without thought.

1. Radon Scare—Where's the Proof?

Before people rush to have radon levels in their homes reduced, as *1* Federal officials advise, they might ask themselves whether such advice is premature.

E.P.A.* officials say the cost to install pipes and ventilation to *2* decontaminate a home would be $1,000 or $2,000. This could translate into billions of dollars for the millions of homes that slightly exceed the E.P.A.'s standard. Yet evidence to warrant such costs is surprisingly thin.

No relationship between illness and radon in homes has ever *3* been established in a scientific study. A presumed relationship exists only because of earlier experiences of miners, particularly uranium miners.

Radon is a breakdown product of uranium, and miners exposed *4* for years to high levels of it suffered higher rates of lung cancer than the general population. But to assume that the radon concentrations affecting miners automatically apply to homeowners disregards important differences between the two environments. □ (Excerpted from Cole, *New York Times*, October 6, 1988, p. A31.)

Opinion: People should think twice before they have the levels of radon gas in

their homes reduced.

Reasons: 1. Cost to install pipes and ventilation, according to the E.P.A.,

     1 or 2 thousand dollars

   2. No relationship between illness and radon in homes ever established.

     a. Miners exposed to high levels suffered lung cancer.

     b. But there are differences between the mines and American homes.

* Environmental Protection Agency.

2. If Felons Publish, They Should Profit

The New Jersey Assembly, by a 78–0 vote, recently approved an amendment to existing legislation that would prevent imprisoned criminals from realizing any profits whatsoever from any book or movie they have written while in prison. This measure, if enacted into law, would discourage me from using my First Amendment rights. It also would shortchange the reading public. [1]

The existing law strips criminals of profits if their work re-enacts their crime. The new, amended legislation would blanket everything written by anyone who was ever imprisoned for a crime— whether or not their crime was re-enacted in that work. [2]

Assemblymen Gary W. Stuhltrager and C. Richard Kamin have made a gross error in sponsoring the Assembly bill, which would ultimately prevent the public from reading thrilling and important informational literature. [3]

We would all remain in a vacuum about penitentiary life without books by felons that contain information about the routines that go on behind prison walls. [4]

The new legislation is all-inclusive. It covers fiction and nonfiction, and earmarks the profits for an escrow fund that reimburses the victims of the imprisoned criminal's crime. [5]

What the Assemblymen are trying to do is definitely a breach of the United States Constitution. Moreover, they're attempting to restrict the way people can earn income on the grounds that they were once in prison.   □   (Excerpted from Lavin, *New York Times*, April 14, 1988, p. 27.*) [6]

Opinion: It's not right to take profits away from felons who write about their crimes.

Reasons:

1. Public would be deprived of exciting and important information.

— Wouldn't know anything about prison life

2. A breach of constitution

3. Restricting how people in prison earn an income

---

*   In 1992 the Supreme Court decided in favor of allowing prisoners to profit from their writing.

_____

_____

_____

DIGGING DEEPER

Do you think people in jail should profit from what
they publish? Why or why not?

WRITING SUGGESTION

Write a paper in which you argue for or against using
C.P.R. to revive the terminally ill.

Diversionary Tactics

Those authors who can't make their arguments convincing
through facts and reasons may be forced to use **diversionary tactics.** They will offer reasons that are not relevant or logical. The
following pages list several of the most common diversionary
tactics.

Attacking the Person Rather than the Opinion

Authors who cannot come up with reasons to support their opinions sometimes resort to character attacks. Here is an example:

> Professor Damian argues that there is no fixed meaning in litera-
> ture. Of course such a position is appropriate for a man who has
> acknowledged that he fled the country during the Vietnam War.
> In life as in literature, then, this act has no fixed meaning. How
> very convenient for a man with such a disgraceful past.

In this example the author does not address Professor Damian's conclusion; instead, she attacks his behavior. Critical readers would not be fooled by such a tactic. They would evaluate Professor Damian's argument on its own merits.

Offering False Alternatives

Authors determined to persuade may insist that there are only two possible alternatives or answers to a problem or question when, in fact, there are several. Remember the reasoning offered in support of product placement:

> Moviemakers intent on creating a realistic atmosphere are forced to use brand names. Were an actor in a scene to open a can simply labeled tuna, the audience's attention would be distracted by the label, and the effect of the scene would be destroyed. People are used to seeing brand names like "Chicken of the Sea" and "Bumble Bee." Filmmakers who want realism in their films must use brand names.

According to the reasoning here, there are only two alternatives: Moviemakers accept money for using brand names *or* they use general names that distract the audience. What's left out here are some other alternatives: (1) Accept no money for product placement and use a variety of brand names, (2) Arrange the scene so that audiences don't see labels, or (3) Invent brand names that resemble the real ones. Faced with the above either-or thinking, critical readers would start looking for other alternatives.

Making Careless Comparisons

Comparisons used to illustrate a point are a useful tool for writers. Look how Gail Sheehy uses a comparison between humans and lobsters in order to illustrate the stages we go through in life.

> We are not unlike a particularly hardy crustacean. The lobster grows by developing and shedding a series of hard, protective shells. Each time it expands from within, the confining shell must be sloughed off. It is left exposed and vulnerable until, in time, a new covering grows to replace the old shell.
>
> With each passage from one stage of human growth to the next we, too, must shed a protective structure. We are left exposed and vulnerable. (Sheehy, *Passages*, p. 24.)

Be wary, however, of authors who use comparisons not to illustrate a point, but to prove it. Often the differences between the two things compared are more crucial than the similarities. For example, remember the author who compared paying for product placement in films with athletes who wore their sponsor's clothing.

> Using name brands in films is just like paying famous people to wear name brands in public.

While that reasoning might sound convincing at first, the differences between the two practices may, in fact, be more important than the similarities. Certainly that is what the following writer believes:

> Product placement and celebrity endorsements are not the same at all. Highly publicized celebrity contracts have made the public fully aware that athletes are paid large sums of money to sport a sponsor's clothing or footwear. In contrast, however, the average moviegoer is not so knowledgeable about the fees paid to filmmakers using brand names. Thus the effects of product placement in films work on a far more subconscious level. Members of the audience have no idea they are seeing paid advertising.

As the author of this passage points out, there are some crucial differences between athletes who wear name brand clothing and filmmakers who use name brands in their movies. Those differences considerably weaken the first author's argument for product placement.

Exercise 7

Directions: The following passages all present you with arguments. Read each one, then circle the appropriate letter to indicate the diversionary tactic used.

Example: If this gun control bill passes, law abiding citizens will suffer. Easy access to a gun gives men and women the chance to protect themselves. If that access is strewn with obstacles, people will not even try to obtain a gun. Their only choice, then, will be to submit to their status as victims.

  a. attack on the person
  ⓑ. false alternatives
  c. careless comparisons

Explanation: Here the author suggests two alternatives to the question of gun control. Either we abandon attempts to control the use of guns or we turn our lives over to criminals. These are certainly not the only alternatives. First of all, gun control does not automatically mean that "access is strewn with obstacles." In most cases it means a seven-day waiting period while a person's references and background can be checked. Secondly, it's absurd to claim that anyone without a gun automatically becomes a victim. There are certainly other ways to control crime.

1. The poet Ezra Pound has again been suggested as a candidate for a posthumous* literary award. The suggestion has caused an uproar among many members of the literary community, and there are those who insist that Pound's name be withdrawn because of his treasonous behavior during World War II, when he made broadcasts for Hitler's supporters. It is hard not to agree with this position. How can we praise the man's poetry when we despise his character?

   (a). attack on the person
   b. false alternatives
   c. careless comparisons

2. Those who object to letting police into the schools should look at our city's statistics on classroom assault. They are the highest in the country. Either we put police in the schools or we expose both teachers and students to violence.

   a. attack on the person
   (b). false alternatives
   c. careless comparisons

3. The city council has proposed an ordinance† that would make owners of pit bulls muzzle their pets while they are outdoors. This ordinance is unfair. No such ordinance exists governing other dogs in the city. If they are not forced to wear muzzles, there is no reason why pit bulls should have to.

   a. attack on the person
   b. false alternatives
   (c). careless comparisons

---

* posthumous: after death
† ordinance: regulation, rule, or statute.

4. Senator Blake has been very vocal in his attacks on defense spending. However, he has remained remarkably silent about accusations that he smoked marijuana in college. Before we listen to any more high sounding claims about waste in the military, we should demand that the senator lay these rumors to rest.

    (a). attack on the person
    b. false alternatives
    c. careless comparisons

5. "There is no other course than the one we have chosen, except the course of humiliation and darkness after which there would be no bright sign in the sky or brilliant light on earth."[8]

    a. attack on the person
    (b). false alternatives
    c. careless comparisons

Thinking About Bias

Like the rest of us, writers are influenced by the language they speak and the society in which they live. In addition, they too have been shaped or molded by their background and training. In short it is all but impossible for a writer to be completely free of personal bias.

But to assume that an author has a bias in favor of one side or another is not to claim that he or she distorts the truth. Occasionally an author may be so biased that he or she passes on false information or omits crucial details. But that degree of bias, the kind that leads to dishonesty, is rare. Most authors try to give their readers a true and honest picture of the world **as they see it.**

Critical readers, aware that bias plays a crucial role in most writing, try to discover how an author's personal stance or leaning influences a text. To that end they pay close attention to tone.

Tone and Bias

Tone in writing is like tone of voice in speaking. It is the attitude or feeling that comes through an author's words and suggests the author's relationship to both audience and subject matter. Critical

---

8. From a speech by Saddam Hussein, *USA Today*, February 22, 1991, p. 8A.

readers pay careful attention to tone because they know it can reveal an author's *degree of bias*.

For an illustration read the following excerpt:

> Latinos in this country are constantly subjected to stupid comments that insult them as a people. In every group, for example, there is always some idiot who wants the lone Latino present to explain the actions, attitudes, or beliefs of all Latinos. The racist assumption here is that we are all alike. Not quite, my friends.

The author of this excerpt may well have a point, but the tone she assumes is so furious, it suggests she may be *overly* biased in favor of her own point of view. She cannot, it appears, consider an opposing perspective.

Compare, now, the tone of the next excerpt. The author makes almost the same point. However his tone is firm without being overbearing. It suggests someone who knows what he thinks but is not unwilling to listen to another point of view.

> A common experience among Latinos is to be asked by a non-Latino colleague or boss to explain the particular actions of other Hispanics. Latinos are a large and varied group of people, with as many different personalities as there are people. They don't all know each other and should not be expected to. (Sepulveda, "As I See It," *New Haven Register*, January 23, 1992, p. 12.*)

Critical readers know that tone is a good indicator of bias. They use it to determine not just an author's personal leaning or prejudice but also to decide how objective or open-minded the author is capable of being.

Critical readers also try to determine the effect a particular tone has on their response to a reading. They don't, for example, let an author's passionate, angry tone intimidate them into accepting a position they do not really believe in. Nor do they allow an author's friendly, good-natured tone to lull them into sharing a point of view they might normally reject.

Slanted Language

While there are many elements that create tone—grammatical correctness or lack of it, long or short sentences, use of pronouns, and degree of distance from the audience—perhaps the most es-

---

* For the rest of this reading, see page 459.

sential element is *word choice*. Critical readers, therefore, are particularly alert to the presence of **slanted language**, language highly charged with positive or negative connotations. The presence or absence of slanted language does a good deal to determine tone. Consider, for example, these two descriptions of a teacher's strike:

1

Once again the community has been confronted with the sad spectacle of teachers refusing to teach. Motivated more by greed than dedication, these men and women have abandoned their responsibility to our children.

2

As in the past, teachers in this community have been forced to go out on strike. No matter how dedicated or idealistic they might be, teachers need a decent wage. They too have families to feed.

In the first example the teachers have "confronted" the community with the "sad spectacle" of a strike. "Motivated by greed," they don't care about their pupils. The language here is charged with negative connotations, resulting in a passionately angry tone. It strongly suggests the author has little sympathy with the strike.

In the second example, the teachers have been "forced to go out on strike." "Dedicated" and "idealistic," they still need a "decent wage" in order to feed their families. Here the words are positively charged. They help create a sympathetic tone that suggests the author would like his readers to support the teachers and their strike.

When they recognize slanted language, critical readers respond with several questions:

1. What does the language tell me about the author's attitude toward the person or events discussed?
2. What would happen if I reworded the author's statements?

Here's an example of how these questions can be applied:

Aging bachelors over forty tend to be *isolated, solitary* people who *avoid* romantic relationships. They are *fearful* of emotional commitments.

Here the words *aging, isolated, solitary,* and *fearful* all have negative connotations. They help create a critical tone, suggesting the author has little sympathy for bachelorhood and would like her readers to feel the same way. But how might readers respond to this next passage, in which the language has positive connotations?

> *Confirmed* bachelors who are over forty *relish* a certain amount of *solitude*. For many, romantic relationships are a pleasant but hardly essential part of life. If romance comes knocking, fine, but seeking it out is not a high priority with men in this age group.

The language used here helps establish a tone that celebrates confirmed bachelorhood and encourages readers to do the same.

Exercise 8

Directions: Read each passage, looking carefully at the italicized words. When you finish, identify the author's tone and check the box that best expresses your impression of the language used.

> Americans have always lusted for heroes. Lacking them, we have sometimes been driven to invent them. This was certainly the case with the man born Joel Hagglund and christened Joe Hill. A poet and songwriter, Hill first came to public attention when he wrote a series of songs that were adopted by the early American labor movement. His name, however, did not become *notorious* until he was arrested for armed robbery and murder. According to the legend, Hill never committed the murder; he was executed in an attempt to destroy the labor movement. Although it is true that Hill was tried and convicted on circumstantial evidence, it is equally true that his story contained numerous *distortions* and *loopholes*. At his best, he was a man unfairly tried and convicted; at his worst, he was a criminal who boldly proclaimed himself innocent. But in neither case was he a legendary hero, and the *ridiculous* tendency to eulogize him is a *misguided* attempt to create a hero where none existed.

The author's tone is

a. sympathetic.
ⓑ. critical and irritated.
c. emotionally neutral.

☐ The author's language suggests a favorable bias.
☑ The author's language suggests a negative bias.
☐ The author's language suggests a neutral or impartial attitude.

Explanation: The author's tone is critical of and angry about the tendency to make Hill a hero. Words like "notorious," "distortions," "ridiculous," and "misguided" all carry negative connotations and suggest a bias against the idea that Hill was a hero.

1. In the last year, the state legislature approved the allocation of more than fifty thousand dollars for the improvement of city jails. This decision was *ill-timed, ill-conceived,* and above all *misguided.* The men and women inside those jails are *criminals,* guilty of *vicious* crimes like robbery, rape, and murder. As free individuals, they were a *menace* to society, and they have been placed in prison in order to be punished. They should not be rewarded with fancy surroundings.

    The author's tone is

    a. supportive.
    ⓑ. furious.
    c. emotionally neutral.

    ☐ The author's language suggests a favorable bias.
    ☑ The author's language suggests a negative bias.
    ☐ The author's language suggests a neutral or impartial attitude.

2. Within less than a century, factories may be filled not with people but with *industrial robots.* At the present time, production workers make up about 15 percent of the *labor force,* but the increased use of robots in industry may eventually reduce that number to less than 5 percent. Although robots now perform the simplest tasks on the assembly line, robots in the future will be guided by sophisticated *computer programs.* Able to see and touch, they will be able to make complicated decisions and complete complex tasks. In fewer than fifty years from now, robots may be standing on assembly lines that produce more robots. This will undoubtedly be necessary if the request for *mechanical people* grows at the expected rate.

    The author's tone is

    a. highly critical.
    b. extremely enthusiastic.
    ⓒ. emotionally neutral.

388   CHAPTER 8 • CRITICAL READING

☐ The author's language suggests a favorable bias.
☐ The author's language suggests a negative bias.
☑ The author's language suggests a neutral or impartial attitude.

3. Just about every aspect of America's zoos has dramatically changed—and improved—from what viewers saw a generation ago. Gone are the sour cages full of frantic cats and the concrete tubs of thawing penguins. Instead the *terrain* is uncannily *authentic*, and animals are *free* to behave like, well, animals, not inmates. Here is a Himalayan highland full of red pandas, there a subtropical jungle where it rains indoors, eleven times a day. The effect is of an entire globe *miraculously* concentrated, the wild kingdom contained in downtown Chicago or the North Bronx. As American zoos are *renovated* and redesigned—at a cost of more than a billion dollars since 1980—hosts of once jaded visitors, some even without children, are flooding through the gates. "In the past 15 years," says Cincinnati zoo director Edward Maruska, "we've probably changed more than we've changed in the past hundred." (Gibbs, "The New Zoo: A Modern Ark," *Time*, August 21, 1989, p. 21.)

The author's tone is

a. critical.
ⓑ. enthusiastic.
c. emotionally neutral.

☑ The author's language suggests a favorable bias.
☐ The author's language suggests a negative bias.
☐ The author's language suggests a neutral or impartial attitude.

4. How can such pain and suffering also be funny? This is not a question many of Hollywood's *overpaid* stars and directors are brooding about this summer. But as real-life violence becomes more *inescapable*—the FBI says violent crime rose 22 percent in the 1980s—others have begun to wonder whether the *massive* amount of casual violence in movies and on TV really is as harmless as its creators often say it is.

Is it possible that, like *addicts*, we are getting high from the excitement of automatic weapons fire, thrill killings, timely *mutilation*, jokey avengers, and other forms of *stylish sadism*? Is it possible that the high-tech killing and routine *savagery* made entertaining in such action movies as *Total Recall*, *Lethal Weapon*, *Die Hard*,

Out for Justice, Robocop, and countless others have *numbed* us to what real violence feels like, while inspiring us to try some?

"The consensus among social scientists is that very definitely there's a causal connection between exposure to violence in the media and violent behavior," says Daniel Linz, a psychologist and professor at the University of California, Santa Barbara, who has extensively researched the subject of screen pornography and violence. (Mitchell, "Have We Become Violence Junkies?" *USA Weekend*, July 12, 1991, p. 4.)

The author's tone is

ⓐ. highly critical.
 b. mildly humorous.
 c. emotionally neutral.

- ☐ The author's language suggests a favorable bias.
- ☑ The author's language suggests a negative bias.
- ☐ The author's language suggests a neutral or impartial attitude.

Working with Words

Here are seven more prefixes and roots you should know. Use them to figure out the meaning of the italicized words. Then add them to your vocabulary notebook for regular review.

1. re	(Latin prefix)	back, again
2. com, con, col	(Latin prefix)	together, with, jointly
3. bene	(Latin adverb used as prefix)	good, well
4. mal	(Latin prefix)	bad, badly
5. sub	(Latin prefix)	under
6. string, strict	(Latin root)	draw, bind
7. ver	(Latin root)	true

1. The private eye stalked the surgeon for several months, but always seemed to be one step behind. Moving from state to state, the surgeon set up practice and vanished, leaving behind a trail of botched operations and mutilated patients. When the investigator finally caught up with him, he turned the surgeon over to the

authorities who suspended the doctor's license and *revoked* all hospital privileges.

to cancel, take away, make void
_____

2. Although Catholic services were banned in the small South American village, the people refused to abandon their religion. They met in secret, and the priest offered mass. After he gave his *benediction*, the priest and his parishioners vanished into the night.

blessing
_____

3. Raccoons can be charming pets, but they never become fully domesticated. If neglected for any length of time, they quickly *revert* to their wild ways. They have been known to attack their owners, using sharp teeth and claws to inflict serious wounds.

change back
_____

4. In his early years, there was little if any evidence that Albert Einstein was a *veritable* genius. Because he was slow to talk and even slower to read, his teachers thought him hopeless. No one who knew him as a child guessed that he would one day revolutionize the world of science.

true, actual, unquestionable
_____

5. If a tumor remains localized and does not spread, there is no danger. It is said to be benign. But if the cells in the tumor break off and spread to other parts of the body, the tumor is *malignant*. Then it must be treated immediately.

injurious
_____

6. Seventeenth-century Puritans believed that humiliation was a good way to reduce petty crime. Pickpockets, for example, were confined to the stocks and displayed to the public. The culprit's wrists and ankles were put into the holes of a wooden frame placed in the middle of the town square. And there he or she would sit in front of a large sign identifying the nature of the crime. The townspeople would then gather around to view the humiliated *malefactor*.

criminal, evildoer

7. On April 14, 1912, the British White Star ocean liner named the *Titanic* struck an iceberg and sank into the ocean's depths. Of more than 2,000 people on board only 706 were saved. Seventy-five years later, when an expedition was formed to find and explore the long *submerged* ship, some relatives of those who had been on board were appalled. They did not want old memories revived; the pain was too great.

remaining under water, hidden

8. Members of the snake family *Boa* are found all over the world. These snakes do not kill by poisoning their victims. They kill by *constriction*—by wrapping victims in their huge coils and then swallowing the body whole. A particularly large specimen of the Boa family could kill a person in this way. However, even the largest would have difficulty swallowing the body of a human being.

strangling

9. PCP is a dangerous drug with horrifying side effects. The drug can induce violent behavior in those who take it and seems to give individuals under its influence unnatural strength. It often takes two or three people to *subdue* a person who is on the drug and out of control.

control, put down, conquer

10. When they arrive from the airport, one of the first spots visitors to Pittsburgh see is the Golden Triangle Park. A scenic spot, the park marks the *confluence* of three rivers: the Allegheny, the Monongahela, and the Ohio. It is from the meeting of these three rivers that the park derives its name.

joining, coming together

Stories Behind the Words

1. *Draconian.* Draco was an Athenian law giver who lived around 620 B.C. and ruled with a stern hand. His laws were known for their strictness and cruelty. Today when we call laws, measures, or procedures *draconian*, we refer to their extreme severity.

   Sample sentence: Although there was disorder in the city, it did not merit the *draconian* measures taken by the secret police.

   Definition: extremely harsh or cruel

2. *Pandemonium.* When John Milton wrote *Paradise Lost*, he needed a name for the center of Hell, the place where all demons and devils would gather. The name he chose was pandemonium. However, today the word *pandemonium* is not associated with evil spirits. It refers instead to any place filled with noise and confusion.

   Sample sentence: When Madonna arrived at the AIDS benefit, the room was *pandemonium*.

   Definition: place of wild disorder or chaos

3. *Stoical.* In 308 B.C. the philosopher Zeno founded a school of philosophy called stoicism. One of the major principles was that wisdom should be untouched by passion. Today someone who is *stoical* does not seem to be affected by any intense emotions like joy, grief, or anger.

   Sample sentence: I don't know how he could be so *stoical* in the face of such a loss.

   Definition: indifferent to pleasure or pain

   Other forms: stoically, stoicalness

4. *Meander.* The Maiandros River is famous for the way it curves and twists its way through Asia Minor. Throughout history writers have been struck by the twisted route it follows so that the word *meander* means to follow a winding course. It also means to drift aimlessly.

Sample sentence: He *meandered* his way through the park until his dog got impatient and began pulling
against her leash.

Definition: to follow a winding course, to wander aimlessly

Other forms: meandering, meanders

5. *Augur.* In ancient Rome an augur was an official person who
could read signs and predict the future. He would then offer
his advice to the emperor. While augurs, official ones at least,
have disappeared, we still have the word *augur* which means
to predict the future.

Sample sentence: The misery of the honeymoon did not *augur*
well for the marriage.

Definition: predict from signs, foretell, be a sign or
promise of

Other forms: augury, augurs

Review Test: Chapter 8

Part A: Label each of the following passages *J* for justified opinion, *C* to indicate circular reasoning, or *H* to indicate a hasty generalization.

1. Being an only child is not a good experience. Only children are not as happy as other children. They are, for the most part, lonely. Parents thinking about having just one child should keep the child's happiness in mind and give him or her a sibling. One child simply does not make a family; children need brothers and sisters. Without siblings they can't have a normal childhood. __C__

2. Giving birth underwater is the best way to have a baby. In the United States several babies have been born underwater with no ill effects. Thus it's time for women to consider the pool as opposed to the delivery room. If given a chance, underwater birth will revolutionize maternity care. __H__

3. Dorothea Dix was an energetic New England school teacher who enormously improved the treatment of mental illness. Through her work as a teacher in a women's prison, she became acquainted with the horrible conditions prevalent in jails and asylums. Not only did she submit her findings to Congress in a report but she also carried out a ten-year-long campaign to improve the treatment of the mentally ill. Through her efforts, millions were raised and spent on improving hospital conditions. She herself established thirty-two hospitals devoted to the enlightened treatment of mental illness. __J__

4. Victims' rights groups have fought long and hard to allow victims of violent crime, or their survivors, to describe their suffering and anguish in court. During the last decade, at least thirty states have enacted laws that allow victims what is called the *right of allocution*. That means they have the right to describe in court the grief and suffering the crime has caused. However, those laws don't seem to be making much of a difference. According to two different studies—one in California, the other nationwide, the right of allocution is rarely used. The California Council on Criminal Justice found that fewer than three percent of all victims actually partici-

pate in sentencing, while the American Bar Association reported only a 10 percent figure.[9] __J__

Part B: Read the following selection. Use the blanks to outline the author's argument.

In Search of Character

Sow an act, and you reap a habit. Sow a habit, and you reap a character. Sow a character, and you reap a destiny.
—Charles Reade, 1814–1884

Character has been an important consideration in our selection of national leaders since the time of George Washington. Even our first president—by nature a retiring man—drew on the reserves of respect and trust he had stored up among the people as he campaigned in the churches of Philadelphia to sell the Constitution.

After thinking about it for several years, I see three key reasons why it is not only useful, but essential, that we examine the character of those who ask us to put our country in their hands. Chiefly, it is to protect ourselves from electing a person whose character flaws, once subjected to the pressures of leading a superpower through the nuclear age, can weaken or endanger the course of our future.

Second, we need the cold slap of insight to wake us up from the smoothly contrived images projected by highly paid professional media experts who market the candidates like perfumed soap.

Third, we can benefit personally as we peer into the mirror afforded by our leaders, whose aspirations are more highly motivated and magnified versions of what we all dream of doing. What these people are made to reveal about themselves can offer us tools to do a better job in developing ourselves.

Character is more than just a factor in our evaluation of how we are going to vote. It affects us all as an essential ingredient in how we work, play, and deal with other people. (Adapted from Sheehy, *Character: America's Search for Leadership*, pp. 11, 20, 35.)

Conclusion: It is important for us to know the character of our national leaders.

_____

_____

9. Source of statistics: Lis Wiehl, "Victim and Sentence: Resetting Justice's Scales," *New York Times*, 1989, p. 85.

Reasons:

1. We want to protect ourselves from electing a person whose character could weaken under the pressures of leadership and endanger our future.

2. We need to know the person behind the media image.

3. Our national leaders hold up a mirror for us, so that we can better understand and improve ourselves.

_____

_____

_____

_____

Part C: Read each of the following passages. Look for diversionary tactics, and circle the appropriate letter of any you find.

1. Although anti-depressants are a popular form of treatment for depression, they may actually do more harm than good. While it is easy enough to give patients pills and send them on their way, physicians should think twice before prescribing anti-depressants. Taking a pill is not the answer to depression. It's just the easiest solution for both doctors and patients. But, as with most problems, the easy solution is not necessarily the best solution.

   a. attack on the person
   b. circular reasoning
   c. false alternatives
   d. careless comparisons
   e. sound argument

2. Surprising as it may seem, there are actually people who were appalled by recent attempts to censor performances by some rap groups. Yet these same people would silence anyone who wanted to cry "fire" in a crowded theatre. In fact, they would censor that

person's freedom of speech. Unfortunately those protecting the rights of rap groups do not see the hypocrisy of their position. They can't or won't see that censorship is necessary in both cases and for exactly the same reasons.

a. attack on the person
b. circular reasoning
c. false alternatives
(d). careless comparisons
e. valid opinion

3. In far too many American cities, homelessness has become a major problem. In some cities whole families live on the streets. In a country this rich, homelessness is a national disgrace. In response to this social problem, Americans must dig more deeply into their pockets to support the work of local charities. Unless we as individuals increase our charitable donations, those already homeless will continue to suffer and their numbers will continue to grow.

a. attack on the person
b. circular reasoning
(c). false alternatives
d. careless comparisons
e. valid opinion

4. Tempting as it might be to censor musical lyrics that insult women and celebrate violence, this is not the path we should take. As we have seen in the case of *2 Live Crew*, censorship only increases public interest and ultimately profits. Sales of *2 Live Crew*'s albums doubled after their music ran into censorship problems. Then, too, there are other ways to control or monitor what our kids hear. For example, parents can demand that record companies label those records, tapes, or compact discs which feature explicitly sexual or violent lyrics. Parents can then put pressure on local music stores to refuse children or adolescents trying to buy labeled records.

a. attack on the person
b. circular reasoning
c. false alternatives
d. careless comparisons
(e). sound argument

5. In a recent column attorney John Niemand argued that it should be mandatory for lawyers to volunteer a certain portion of their time to working for the poor. Mr. Niemand claims that with 750,000 lawyers in the United States donating a few hours a week, those who cannot afford a lawyer would be guaranteed justice. He claims, too, that half the homeless in America would have remained in housing if they had had the benefit of legal services. What is interesting about this argument is that Mr. Niemand winters in Florida and spends his summers in Maine. In both places, he has a luxurious home. How easy it must be to make these kinds of proposals when one is as rich as Mr. Niemand.

ⓐ. attack on the person
b. circular reasoning
c. false alternatives
d. careless comparisons
e. sound argument

Part D: Read these two passages discussing the same event. When you finish, circle the letter that best identifies the author's bias or leaning.

1. In 1838, regular troops under General Winfield Scott rounded up the Cherokee and started them on the long trail to Indian Territory. This journey cost them one-quarter of their number, but the remainder reorganized their national government, prospered, and have retained their language and alphabet to the present day. Several hundred diehards in the Great Smokies, who resisted removal, were eventually given the Qualla reservation in North Carolina. . . .

In a sense, the removal policy was justified by the later history of the "five civilized Indian Nations"—Creek, Cherokee, Choctaw, Chickasaw, and Seminole—in Oklahoma. Removal gave them the necessary respite* to recover their morale, and until the Civil War they succeeded in keeping white men out.

Looking backward, it is now evident that, in view of the irresistible push of the westward movement, Indian removal was the lesser evil. It had to be, but the process was carried out with un-

---

* respite: interval of rest and relief.

necessary hardship to the victims. (Morrison, *The Oxford History of the American People*, pp. 450–451.)

   a. The author is sympathetic to the Indians and does not approve of the government's actions.

   ⓑ. The author is sympathetic to the Indians but wants to justify the government's actions.

   c. The author has little or no sympathy with the Indians and approves of the government's actions.

2. When the time for evacuation came in 1838, most Cherokee refused to move. President Martin Van Buren then sent federal troops to round up the Indians. About twenty thousand Cherokee were evicted, held in detention camps, and marched to Oklahoma under military escort. Nearly one-quarter died of disease and exhaustion on the infamous Trail of Tears. When it was all over, the Indians had traded about 100 million acres of land east of the Mississippi for 32 million acres west of the river plus $68 million.

A complex set of attitudes drove whites to force Indian removal. Most merely wanted Indian lands; they had little or no respect for the rights or culture of the Indians. Manifest Destiny* and westward migration justified bulldozing Indians aside. Others were aware of the injustice, but believed the Indians must inevitably give way to white settlement. Some, like John Quincy Adams, believed the only way to preserve Indian civilization was to remove the tribes and establish a buffer zone between Indians and whites. Others, including Thomas Jefferson, doubted that white civilization and Indian "savagery" could coexist. Supported by missionaries and educators, they hoped to "civilize" the Indians and assimilate them slowly into American culture. Whatever the source of white behavior, the outcome was the same: the devastation of Native American people and their culture. (Norton et al. *A People and a Nation*, pp. 290–291.)

   ⓐ. The author is sympathetic to the Indians and does not approve of the government's actions.

   b. The author is sympathetic to the Indians but wants to justify the government's actions.

   c. The author has little or no sympathy with the Indians and approves of the government's actions.

---

* Manifest Destiny: the 19th century doctrine or belief that the U.S. had the right and duty to expand throughout North America.

DIGGING DEEPER

What is your opinion of Manifest Destiny? Do you think we had a *right* and a *duty* to make North America our own?

WRITING SUGGESTION

In the last two presidential campaigns, much attention was paid to the private lives of candidates. Write a paper in which you argue that voters do *or* do not need to know about the private lives of presidential candidates.

Vocabulary Review

Part E: Here is a list of words drawn from the chapter. Some actually appear in the chapter. Some have been derived from the prefixes and suffixes introduced on page 390. Your job is to match words and blanks.

In some cases, you may have to change the endings of words to make them fit the context. If you need to, consult your dictionary to decide which ending to use. *Note:* You may use some words more than once and others not at all.

stringent	pandemonium	subdue	reunification
equitable	benevolence	fraudulent	ordinance
draconian	malevolent	malicious	stoical
annals	meander	augur	
subjugated	defray	vigilante	

1. When the Spanish explorer Hernando Cortez first set sail, he was certainly not motivated by <u>benevolence</u>. Under the leadership of Diego Valáquez, he had gone to the island of Hispaniola to put down a revolt. The Indians on the island had been driven to rebellion by the __stringent__ and __draconian__ measures of their Spanish rulers.

But after the rebellion was __subdued__, tales of the gold and precious stones on the mainland led Cortez to the Kingdom of Montezuma. Believing Cortez to be a god, Montezuma's ambassadors plied him with gifts of gold, silver, and jewels. But the gifts did no good. Cortez continued his conquest until the country was in __pandemonium__, Montezuma was dead, and his people were in chains.

2. Initially the __reunification__ of the two Germanies was cause for joy in both Europe and the United States, and the signs __augured__ well for a bright future. However, in the past year some of that initial optimism has begun to fade. In parts of what was once East Germany, __vigilante__ groups have been terrorizing foreigners and chanting an old slogan reminiscent of the years when Adolf Hitler was in power: "Germany for the Germans." And their __malicious__ behavior has not been confined to slogans; groups of right-wing skinheads have attacked and beaten numerous men and women who were clearly foreigners. During the communists' reign in East Germany, it was claimed that bigotry and racism had been defeated by the power of socialist brotherhood. Unfortunately the resurgence of such right-wing viciousness illustrates just how __fraudulent__ that claim was.

3. The city council unanimously approved a new __ordinance__ that levied a fine of fifty dollars on anyone owning a dog without a license. Although the initial reaction of dog owners was __stoical__, they were outraged when the fine was doubled. From their perspective, the council was fin-

ing them in order to _defray_____ some of the city's debts and there had to be a more _equitable_____ solution, one that might pick the pockets of cat owners as well. The issue was debated at the first council meeting, and as one might expect, the meeting was complete _pandemonium_____.

4. Although physically the Russian leader, Joseph Stalin, looked the part of someone's _benevolent_____ old uncle, he was in reality a merciless and _malevolent_____ dictator. Responsible for the slaughter of thousands, Stalin ruthlessly _subjugated_____ his own people, murdering anyone suspected of disloyalty. Under the leadership of Lavrenti Beria, Stalin's secret police were everywhere looking for evidence of dissent or protest. When they found it, punishment was swift and immediate. In the _annals_____ of history, only Adolph Hitler can rival Joseph Stalin's evil influence.

Additional Readings

Increasing Reading Rate

Because they have so much to read, many college students want to work on increasing their reading rate. They hope that by reading at high rates of speed they can complete their assignments in a shorter period of time. In response to those students, the following pages offer instruction and practice for increasing reading rate. However, before introducing either, a word of caution is in order. "Speed reading," as many students like to call it, has a place in your repertoire of reading strategies. But it needs to be used selectively. If, for example, you want to read at high rates of speed in order to be generally informed about current events, go ahead and read as fast as you can. Reading at high rates of speed is also extremely useful for pre-reading your textbooks. Without investing a great deal of time, you'll be able to decide which sections need a close and careful reading and which, if any, do not.

However, keep in mind that high reading rates do not usually produce a high level of comprehension.[1] At six or seven hundred words per minute, you can probably discover the author's controlling idea. You might even be able to recognize some supporting details. It's doubtful, however, that you could paraphrase all of the key points, draw the appropriate inferences, or evaluate the author's arguments. At accelerated speeds, you just can't do the kind of reading required of college students. When you need to understand how the author marshals support for the controlling

---

1. Carver, Ronald P. "How good are some of the world's best readers?" *Reading Research Quarterly*, Summer 1985, 20, p. 389–419.

idea, uses language to persuade, or implies without stating, it's time to switch gears and lower your reading rate.

Reading Rates[2] and Purposes

Rate	Purpose
Slow and careful: 150–250	• to reread passages that confused you initially • to understand dense and difficult texts like chemistry and philosophy • to read poetry
Average: 250–350	• to read material that is not completely unfamiliar in content or style, like psychology or sociology
Rapid: 350–450	• to understand material that is fairly familiar in both content and style, like child development or health
Very rapid: 450–600	• to read magazines or newspapers strictly for personal interest or pleasure
Skimming: 600–1,000	• to discover the general point of a chapter or article
Scanning: 1,000–1,500	• to glance down an article and locate specific pieces of information

Pointers for Improving Reading Rate

1. *Tell yourself you "can" read faster.*

   Many students read slowly because they don't trust their own intelligence. They convince themselves they have to read every word twice in order to understand the material. To fight that tendency, *define your purpose in reading*—"I just want to get a general idea of what the author wants to say; I don't have to understand every detail." Then force yourself to go full speed ahead, knowing that your purpose does not require you to read every word.

2. *Use your finger or a pen as a pacer.*

   When readers **regress,** they move their eyes backward and reread the same words. Sometimes regressions are absolutely

---

2. Rates cited are adapted from Beers, Penny G. "Accelerated Reading for High School Students." *Journal of Reading*, Vol. 29, January 1986, p. 313.

necessary in order for readers to create the necessary links between sentences. But sometimes regressions are nothing more than a bad habit, grounded in a lack of confidence.

To avoid regressions, imagine that your finger or a pen is a battery-fueled pointer, forcing your eyes across the page. As you read, move that pointer back and forth from left to right in a zig-zag movement just underneath the lines of print. If you start to slow down, force yourself to keep the pointer moving at a steady pace from left to right and down the page.[3]

3. *Improve your vocabulary.*

The more "automatically" you can respond to words, the faster you will be able to read. Responding automatically means that you can look at a word and, without consciously searching, retrieve the appropriate meaning from memory. If you want to increase your reading rate, review new words in different contexts until you can recall the appropriate meaning in a split second.

4. *Read regularly.*

The more familiar you are with different sentence patterns, styles of writing, and methods of organization, the easier it will be to anticipate the author's words. As you read, you'll discover that your eyes automatically skip to the next word or phrase essential to the author's meaning. Guided by your knowledge of typical language patterns, you will be able to stop reading every word. However, that change in your reading habits can happen only if you read often enough to *become familiar with words in print.*

Repeated readings of the same material will help familiarize you with the various forms written language can take. Because you know the material, you'll feel freer to let yourself go and practice reading for speed.

5. *Use the author's organization to focus your attention.*

Everything you have learned about patterns of organization comes in handy when you are trying to read at high rates of speed. Say, for example, that the author's text links cause to effect. Once you recognize this pattern, you can concentrate on locating the cause and the effect. Then you can skim everything else at high rates of speed.

---

3. Some people who write about reading rate do not support this strategy while others do. However, in my experience it works. L.F.

Putting the Pointers into Practice

The following pages contain ten readings you can use to practice what you have learned about increasing your reading rate. Start by studying the definitions that open each reading. Remember, you don't want to waste time laboring over word meaning while you are trying to read at high rates of speed.

Next preview the first set of questions—*Questions for Accelerated Reading*. These are the questions you should be able to answer even if you have been reading at six, seven, or even eight hundred words per minute. (The second set—*Questions for Understanding and Review*—requires a slower, more careful reading). Previewing the first set of questions will help you define your purpose while reading. Knowing precisely what questions you want to answer, you will be less tempted to slow down and try to read every word.

After spending a few minutes previewing the vocabulary and questions, jot down the time and start reading, pushing your eyes as fast as you can back and forth down the page. Although the words should not become a blur, *you should feel somewhat uncomfortable while you are reading.* You should feel as if you are making only partial sense out of the words before you force your eyes to move on.

As soon as you finish, jot down the time. Then use this formula to determine and record your reading rate.

number of words ÷ by number of minutes = number of words per minute

$$\frac{800 \text{ words}}{2.5 \text{ minutes}} = 320 \text{ wpm}$$

Next answer the *Questions for Accelerated Reading* and write down your score (Answer key appears on page 481). If your score is 80 or above, try to complete the next reading at an even higher rate of speed.

If your score is below 80, do not try to read the next article at a higher rate of speed. In fact, you might try to slow yourself down a bit. Don't be impatient. If you practice with confidence and consistency, your reading rate will increase.

Questions for Understanding and Review

The second set of questions is designed to test your understanding of the reading *and* review the skills introduced in this book. Answer them only after you have reread the article at a normal or comfortable rate of speed.

When you correct your answers to these questions, record those you got wrong in the accompanying boxes. After you have completed at least three readings, check to see if you have consistently missed the same type of question, say, those concerning supporting details or inferences. If this is true, ask your instructor for some review work in this particular area.

Reading 1

Convenience Friends, and Historical Friends, Etc.

Vocabulary to Learn:
☐ dormant: temporarily inactive.
☐ disparities: differences.

Friends broaden our horizons. They serve as new models with *1* whom we can identify. They allow us to be ourself—and accept us that way. They enhance our self-esteem because they think we're okay, because we matter to them. And because they matter to us—for various reasons, at various levels of intensity—they enrich the quality of our emotional life.

Even though, with most of our friends, we form imperfect con- *2* nections. Even though most of our friends are "friends in spots."

In my discussions with several people about the people we call *3* our friends, we established the following categories of friendship:

1. Convenience friends. These are the neighbor or office mate or *4* member of our car pool whose lives routinely intersect with ours. These are the people with whom we exchange small favors. They lend us their cups and silverware for a party. They drive our children to soccer when we are sick. They keep our cat for a week when we go on vacation. And, when we need a lift, they give us a ride to the garage to pick up the Honda. As we do for them.

But we don't, with convenience friends, ever come too close *5* or tell too much: We maintain our public face and emotional distance. "Which means," says Elaine, "that I'll talk about being overweight but not about being depressed. Which means I'll admit being mad but not blind with rage. And which means I might say that we're pinched this month but never that I'm worried sick over money."

But which doesn't mean that there isn't sufficient value to *6* be found in these friendships of mutual aid, in convenience friends.

2. Special-interest friends. These friendships depend on the shar- ₇ ing of some activity or concern. These are sports friends, work friends, yoga friends, nuclear-freeze friends. We meet to participate jointly in knocking a ball across a net, or saving the world.

    "I'd say that what we're doing together is *doing* together, not ₈ being together," Suzanne says of her Tuesday-doubles friends. "It's mainly a tennis relationship but we play together well." And as with convenience friends, we can, with special-interest friends, be regularly involved without being intimate.

3. Historical friends. With luck we also have a friend who knew ₉ us, as Grace's friend Bunny did, way back when . . . when her family lived in that three-room flat in Brooklyn, when her father was out of work for seven months, when her brother Allie got in that fight where they had to call the police, when her sister married the endodontist from Yonkers, and when, the morning after she lost her virginity, Bunny was the person she ran to tell.

    The years have gone by, they have gone separate ways, they ₁₀ have little in common now, but they still are an intimate part of each other's past. And so, whenever Grace goes to Detroit, she always goes to visit this friend of her girlhood. Who knows how she looked before her teeth were straightened. Who knows how she talked before her voice got un-Brooklyned. Who knows what she ate before she learned about artichokes. Who knew her when.

4. Crossroads friends. Like historical friends, our crossroads ₁₁ friends are important for what was—for the friendship we shared at a crucial, now past, time of life: a time, perhaps, when we roomed in college together; or served a stint in the U.S. Air Force together; or worked as eager young singles in Manhattan together; or went through pregnancy, birth, and those first difficult years of motherhood together.

    With historical friends and crossroads friends we forge links ₁₂ strong enough to endure with not much more contact than once-a-year letters at Christmas, maintaining a special intimacy—dormant but always ready to be revived—on those rare but tender occasions when we meet.

5. Cross-generational friends. Another tender intimacy—tender ₁₃ but unequal—exists in the friendships that form across generations, the friendships that one woman calls her daughter-mother and her mother-daughter relationships. Across the generations the younger enlivens the older, the older instructs the

younger. Each role, as mentor or quester, as adult or child, offers gratifications of its own. And because we are unconnected by blood, our words of advice are accepted as wise, not intrusive, our childish lapses don't summon up warnings and groans. Without the risks, and without the ferocious investment, which are always a part of a real parent-child connection, we enjoy the rich disparities to be found among our crossgenerational friends.

6. Close friends. Emotionally and physically (by seeing each 14 other, by mail, by talks on the phone) we maintain some ongoing friendships of deep intimacy. And although we may not expose as much—or the same kinds of things—to each of our closest friends, close friendships involve revealing aspects of our private self—of our private feelings and thoughts, of our private wishes and fears and fantasies and dreams.

We reveal ourself not only by telling but also by wordlessly 15 showing what we are, by showing the unattractive—as well as the nice. And intimacy means trusting that our friends— although they don't, and should not, think we're perfect—will see our virtues as foreground, our vices as blur. "To be her friend," said a friend of the late political-activist and writer Jenny Moore, "was to be for a little while as good as you wish you were." And sometimes, with a little help—including some helpful don't-do-thats—from our friends, we can get there, and stay there. □ (Viorst, *Necessary Losses*, pp. 197–199.)

908 words

Questions for Accelerated Reading

Based on your reading, decide if the following statements are true (T) or false (F) and circle the correct answer.

1. Convenience friends are a waste of time; they have little or nothing to offer.   **T**   **(F)**

2. With special-interest friends, we can unburden our souls. **T**   **(F)**

3. It's impossible to be friends with those who are two generations older than we are.   **T**   **(F)**

4. With close friends we are afraid of revealing the unattractive side of ourselves for fear of losing them.   **T**   **(F)**

5. Crossroads friends do not require a great deal of contact. **(T)**   **F**

Choose the correct answer for each of the following questions.

6. Crossroads friends are important because

    a. they were present during a crisis.
    b. they helped us when we were depressed.
    ⓒ. they shared a crucial but now past time in our lives.

7. A close friend

    a. sees you as perfect.
    ⓑ. accepts your flaws.
    c. tells you when you make a mistake.

8. With convenience friends we

    ⓐ. exchange small favors.
    b. gossip.
    c. have dinner parties.

9. Special-interest friends

    a. like to laugh a lot.
    ⓑ. share some activity or concern.
    c. pay special attention to birthdays.

10. Cross-generational friends have an intimacy that is

    a. tender and equal.
    ⓑ. tender but unequal.
    c. filled with violent emotion.

Give yourself ten points for each correct answer.

Score = _____

Questions for Understanding and Review

Unless the question directs you to do otherwise, circle the correct answer. (Use the boxes to record incorrect answers.)

Discovering the Controlling Idea

☐ **1.** Which of the following statements best paraphrases the controlling idea?

    a. Close friendships can enormously enrich a person's life.

(b). There are many different kinds of friendship, each with its own rewards.

☐ **2.** The controlling idea was

    a. summed up in a thesis statement.
    (b). had to be inferred.

Looking for Support

☐ **3.** Which of the following does *not* support the controlling idea?

    (a). Bonding among men is different from bonding among women.
    b. With most of our friends we form imperfect connections.
    c. With some friends we simply share activities.
    d. Historical friends are important because they provide us with a connection to the past.

☐ **4.** To make her point, the author relies heavily on

    a. reasons.
    b. studies.
    (c). examples.
    (d). definitions.
    e. quotations.

☐ **5.** For each kind of friendship, the author begins with

    a. an example.
    (b). a definition.
    c. a reason.

☐ **6.** Identify the relationship between paragraphs 4 and 5.

    (a). Both are major supporting paragraphs.
    b. Both are minor supporting paragraphs.
    c. 4 is a major supporting paragraph; 5 is a minor supporting paragraph.

Analyzing Paragraphs

☐ **7.** *Identify each of the following sentences as a main idea statement (MI), major supporting sentence (M), or minor supporting sentence (m).*

Convenience friends. These are the neighbor or office mate or member of our car pool whose lives routinely intersect with ours. ___MI___ These are the people with whom we exchange small favors. ____MI____ They lend us their cups and silverware for a party. ____M____ They drive our children to soccer when we are sick. ____M____ They keep our cat for a week when we go on vacation. ____M____ And, when we need a lift, they give us a ride to the garage to pick up the Honda. ____M____ As we do for them. ____m____

☐ **8.** Which statement best sums up the main idea of paragraph 10?

    a. With historical friends, the years go by and we no longer have anything in common. This is the time to let go.

    (b). Historical friends may have little in common as times goes by, but they can still give one another a sense of connection to the past.

Organizational Patterns

☐ **9.** What organizational pattern underlies this reading?

    a. comparison and contrast

    (b). classification

    c. cause and effect

    d. sequence of dates and events

Transitions

☐ **10.** What transitional words appear in paragraphs 10 and 13?

But, And, And so

Inferences

☐ **11.** In paragraph 13, the author expects you to draw what inference from the following sentence: "And because we are unconnected by blood, our words of advice are accepted as wise, not intrusive, our childish lapses don't summon up warnings and groans"?

The opposite might occur when two people are members of the

same family.

☐ **12.** The author expects you to infer the difference between "doing together not being together." That inference can be defined as

    (a). sharing an activity without being particularly close or intimate.

b. sharing an activity without particularly liking one another.

c. sharing an activity without ever being introduced to the other person involved.

☐ **13.** Does the author imply that these are the only categories of friendship possible? Yes or (No.)

Explain your answer. <u>She makes it clear that these categories</u>

<u>are based on discussions with friends.</u>

☐ **14.** Most of the author's conclusions apply to

a. men and women equally.

(b). women.

Explain your answer. <u>Although she tries to give examples that</u>

<u>would apply to men, she uses only women's names.</u>

☐ **15.** The author says of Jenny Moore that "to be her friend was to be for a little while as good as you wish you were." This woman probably

(a). brought out the best in her friends.

b. encouraged her friends to feel good about themselves.

c. made her friends feel attractive and popular.

Distinguishing Between Fact and Opinion

☐ **16.** This reading

a. balances fact and opinion.

(b). relies primarily on opinions.

c. relies primarily on facts.

Purpose

☐ **17.** The author wants to

(a). inform you of her personal views about friendship.

b. persuade you to share her personal views about friendship.

Tone

☐ **18.** The author's tone is

a. distant and formal.

(b). friendly and informal.

c. emotionally neutral.

☐ **19.** Do you think the author reveals any personal bias for or against any one type of friendship? Yes or (No.)

Analyzing Language

☐ **20.** When the author says "we forge links" with historical friends, she suggests

    a. a prison.
    (b). a chain.
    c. a chain letter.

Do you think that the word "forge" in this context has positive or negative connotations? Explain your answer.

Positive, the word suggests strong connections that will not break.

WRITING SUGGESTION

Write a paper in which you describe the kinds of friendship most essential in your life. Use the author's categories if you wish or create new ones based on your own experience.

Reading 2

'Reel' Vs. Real Violence

Vocabulary to Learn:

☐ mayhem: violent disorder.
☐ cautionary: warning.
☐ nefarious: evil.
☐ dementia: deterioration of intellectual abilities.
☐ spawn: give birth to, produce.
☐ vicarious: experienced or enjoyed from afar.
☐ pragmatic: practical.
☐ gratuitously: unnecessarily, without reason.

One day I switched on the evening news just in time to see a Pennsylvania politician waving around a .357 magnum, warning reporters to back off so they wouldn't get hurt, then sticking the gun in his mouth and . . .

Mercifully, the station I was watching didn't show him pulling 2 the trigger, but I learned later that another Pittsburgh station showed the whole suicide unedited. What I saw was enough to make me ill. My stomach was in a knot, and I couldn't get the incident out of my mind. I still can't, even though three years have gone by.

I have a special reason for wondering and worrying about blood 3 and violence on TV and movie screens. I write, produce and direct horror movies. I coauthored "Night of the Living Dead," the so-called "granddaddy of the splatter flicks." And since then I've made a string of movies depicting murder and mayhem.

I can watch these kinds of movies when they've been made by 4 other people, and I can even help create the bloody effects in my own movies without getting a knot in my stomach. Yet I still retain my capacity to be shocked, horrified and saddened when something like this happens in real life.

So there must be a difference between real violence and "reel" 5 violence. And if I didn't feel that this is true, I'd stop making the kinds of movies that I make. What are those differences?

My movies are scary and unsettling, but they are also cautionary 6 tales. They might show witches at work, doing horrible things or carrying out nefarious schemes, but in doing so they convey a warning against superstition and the dementia it can spawn. They might show people under extreme duress, set upon by human or inhuman creatures, but in doing so they teach people how duress can be handled and blind, ignorant fear can be confronted and conquered. My purpose hasn't been to glorify or encourage murder and mayhem, but to give horror fans the vicarious chills and thrills that they crave.

The most powerful and, consequently financially successful hor- 7 ror movies—"Night of the Living Dead," "The Texas Chainsaw Massacre," "Halloween" and "Friday the 13th"—feature a small cast in a confined situation that is made terrifying by the presence of a monster/madman/murderer. Usually the victims are young, beautiful women. Often the murders are filmed from the point of view of the murderer. For all these reasons, we filmmakers have been accused of hating women and portraying them as objects to be punished for being sexually desirable. Horror fans have been accused of identifying with the psychopathic killers portrayed in these movies and deriving vicarious enjoyment from watching the killers act out the fans' dark fantasies.

But there are two simple, pragmatic reasons why the victims 8 are often filmed from the point of view of the killer. First, it's an effective technique for not revealing who the killer is, thus preserving an aura of suspense. Second, it affords dramatically explicit angles for showing the victim's terror—and the horror of what the killer is doing.

These films *are* horrifying because they reflect—but do not create—a frightful trend in our society. Murders, assaults and rapes are being committed with more frequency and with increasing brutality. Serial killers and mass murderers are constantly making headlines. Most of these killers are men, often sexually warped men, and they most often kill women. So we filmmakers have stuck to the facts in our portrayal of them. That's why our movies are so scary. Too many of our fellow citizens are turning into monsters, and contemporary horror movies have seized upon this fear and personified it. So now we have Jason, Michael and Freddy instead of Dracula and Frankenstein. Our old-time movie monsters used to be creatures of fantasy. But today, unfortunately, they are extensions of reality. 9

Recently, at a horror convention in Albany, I was autographing videocassettes of a show I had hosted, entitled "Witches, Vampires & Zombies," and a young man asked me if the tape showed actual human sacrifices. He was disappointed when I informed him that the ceremonies on the tape were fictional depictions. He was looking for "snuff movies"—the kind that actually show people dying. 10

Unfortunately, tapes showing real death are widely available nowadays. A video of the Pennsylvania politician blowing his brains out went on sale just a few weeks after the incident was broadcast. But I don't think that the people who are morbidly fixated on this sort of thing are the same people who are in love with the horror-movie genre. 11

I'm afraid that the young man I met in Albany has a serious personality disorder. And I don't think he's really a horror fan. He didn't buy my tape, but he would have bought it if the human sacrifices had been real. "Reel" violence didn't interest him. He didn't care about the niceties of theme, plot or character development. He just wanted to see people die. 12

I haven't seen any snuff movies for sale at the horror conventions I've attended. True horror fans aren't interested. They don't go to the movies just to see artificial blood and gore, either. The films that gratuitously deliver those kinds of effects usually are box-office flops. The hit horror films have a lot more to offer. While scaring us and entertaining us, they teach us how to deal with our deepest fears, dreads and anxieties. 13

But modern horror movies aren't to blame for these fears, dreads and anxieties. They didn't create our real-life Jasons, Michaels and Freddys any more than the gangster movies of the 1920s and 1930s created Al Capone and Dutch Schultz. If the movies reflect, with disturbing accuracy, the psychic terrain of the world we live in, 14 then it's up to us to change that world and make it a safer place. (Russo, " 'Reel' vs. Real Violence," *Newsweek*, February 19, 1990, p. 10.)

979 words

Questions for Accelerated Reading

Based on your reading, decide if the following statements are true (T) or false (F) and circle the correct answer.

1. The author believes that movie violence contributes to real violence.   **T**   **(F)**

2. The author believes there are real differences between screen violence and real violence.   **(T)**   **F**

3. According to the author, violent movies reflect real violence.   **(T)**   **F**

4. The author feels ill when he sees real violence on television.   **(T)**   **F**

5. The author believes that horror fans are morbidly fixated on death.   **T**   **(F)**

Choose the correct answer for each of the following questions.

6. Which of these horror movies is *not* mentioned in the article?

   a. *Halloween*
   b. *Friday the 13th*
   (c). *Child's Play*

7. The author co-authored which horror movie?

   a. *Halloween*
   (b). *Night of the Living Dead*
   c. *Friday the 13th*

8. Makers of horror films have been accused of hating

   a. people.
   (b). women.
   c. homosexuals.

9. According to the author, "true" horror films

   a. emphasize blood and gore.
   (b). explore our deepest fears and anxieties.
   c. feature witchcraft.

10. According to the author, if we are frightened by the level of violence in our society, we should

    a. stop going to horror movies.
    (b). change the world and make it a safer place.
    c. censor special effects in horror films.

Give yourself ten points for each correct answer.

Score = _____

Questions for Understanding and Review

Unless the question directs you to do otherwise, circle the correct answer. (Use the boxes to record incorrect answers.)

Discovering the Controlling Idea

□ 1. Which of the following statements paraphrases the author's controlling idea?

    (a). There are real differences between violence in reality and violence on the screen. If there weren't, I would not continue to create horror films.
    b. There are practical reasons why horror films are often told from the killer's point of view.

□ 2. The controlling idea

    (a). appears in a thesis statement.
    b. has to be inferred.

Looking for Support

□ 3. Which of the following statements does the author make in support of his controlling idea?

    a. *Night of the Living Dead* is still shown regularly on Halloween night.
    (b). My movies are scary and unsettling but they are also cautionary tales.
    c. Research has not revealed a connection between violent behavior on film and violent behavior in reality.

□ 4. Identify the relationship between paragraphs 7 and 8.

(a). Both are major supporting paragraphs.

   b. 7 is a minor supporting paragraph while 8 is a major supporting paragraph.

   c. 7 is a major supporting paragraph while 8 is a minor supporting paragraph.

☐ **5.** The author says "there must be a difference between real violence and 'reel' violence." What specific statements does he make in support of this general claim?

In paragraphs 4 and 5, the author says that he, a creator of horror films,

still gets shocked and horrified by real life violence; therefore, there must

be a difference between violence on film and violence in reality.

In answer to the question, "what are those differences?" he points out

that his movies also have a moral or a warning.

_____

_____

_____

Reread the paragraphs listed below. Then identify each of the following statements as major (M) or minor (m) supporting details.

Analyzing Paragraphs

☐ **6.** *Paragraph 6:*

   a. My movies are scary and unsettling, but they are also cautionary tales. __M__

   b. They convey a warning against superstition and the dementia it can spawn. __m__

☐ **7.** *Paragraph 9:*

   a. Murders, assaults and rapes are being committed with more frequency and increasing brutality. __m__

   b. These films *are* horrifying because they reflect a frightful trend in our society. __M__

Organizational Patterns

☐ **8.** The title would lead you to expect what organizational pattern?

    a. cause and effect
    ⓑ. comparison and contrast
    c. sequence of events
    d. classification

Transitions

☐ **9.** Underline the transitions in the following paragraph.

<u>But</u> there are two simple, pragmatic reasons why the victims are often filmed from the point of view of the killer. <u>First</u>, it's an effective technique for not revealing who the killer is, thus preserving the aura of suspense. <u>Second</u>, it affords dramatically explicit angles for showing the victim's terror—and the horror of what the killer is doing.

Inference

☐ **10.** The author describes in detail his reaction to a news story about a man who committed suicide in front of reporters. From this description he wants you to infer that he is a

    a. person versed in current events.
    ⓑ. sensitive and caring human being.
    c. director who uses real life events in his films.

☐ **11.** Reread paragraphs 7 and 8. Then choose the inference the author expects you to draw.

    ⓐ. The makers of horror films do not hate women. Such accusations are unjust.
    b. It is the fans of horror films who hate women, not the creators.

Distinguishing Between Fact and Opinion

Label the following statements fact (F), opinion (O), or both (B).

☐ **12.** True horror fans don't go to the movies just to see blood and gore. __0__

☐ **13.** The hit horror films have a lot more to offer than blood and gore. __0__

Purpose

☐ **14.** The author's primary purpose is to

a. inform.

ⓑ. persuade.

c. entertain.

d. share a personal experience.

Tone

☐ **15.** The author's tone is

a. angry and outraged.

ⓑ. serious and concerned.

c. emotionally neutral.

Bias

☐ **16.** John Russo's background suggests he would

ⓐ. lean toward supporting the portrayal of violence in films.

b. be inclined to oppose the use of violence in films.

c. be as impartial as possible.

Evaluating opinions

☐ **17.** The author claims that horror films reflect—but do not create—a frightful trend in our society. What justification does he offer for that claim?

Violent crimes are increasing, so "we filmmakers have stuck to

the facts." We are no more responsible than creators of gangster films

of the 1920s and 1930s were for Al Capone and Dutch Schultz.

☐ **18.** Based on what you learned about evaluating opinion, would you say the author's opinion is justified or unjustified? Explain your answer.

Unjustified. The author does not really argue this point. He simply asserts it.

☐ **19.** The author generalizes about **true** horror fans. Which statement best paraphrases his generalization?

ⓐ. True horror fans have taste. They are not interested in blood and gore. They want films that explore human fears and desires.

b. True horror fans are fixated on death. Thus horror films help them face their fear of dying.

The author does or (does not) provide a basis for his generalization?

Forming Your Own Opinion

☐ **20.** Do you agree or disagree that horror films "reflect—but do not create—" violence in reality? What is your justification for that opinion?

_____

_____

Reading 3:

Raised on Rock-and-Roll

Vocabulary to Learn:

☐ devotee: follower, someone deeply attached or devoted.
☐ decrepit: old, broken down.
☐ decipher: figure out.
☐ poet laureate: a poet considered to be the best.
☐ thrash: to move about violently.

I was born in Philadelphia, a city where if you can't dance you might as well stay home, and I was raised on rock-and-roll. My earliest television memory is of *American Bandstand,* and the central question of my childhood was: Can you dance to it?

When I was fifteen and a wild devotee of Mitch Ryder and the Detroit Wheels, it sometimes crossed my mind that when I was thirty-four years old, decrepit, wrinkled as a prune and near death, I would have moved on to some nameless kind of dreadful show music, something akin to Muzak. I did not think about the fact that my parents were still listening to the music that had been popular when they were kids; I only thought that they played "Pennsylvania 6–5000" to torment me and keep my friends away from the house.

But I know now that I'm never going to stop loving rock-and-roll, all kinds of rock-and-roll: the Beatles, the Rolling Stones, Hall and Oates, Talking Heads, the Doors, the Supremes, Tina Turner, Elvis Costello, Elvis Presley. I even like really bad rock-and-roll, although I guess that's where my age shows; I don't have the tolerance for Bon Jovi that I once had for the Raspberries.

We have friends who, when their son was a baby, used to put a record on and say, "Drop your butt, Phillip." And Phillip did. That's what I love: drop-your-butt music. It's one of the few things left in my life that makes me feel good without even thinking about it. I can walk into any bookstore and find dozens of books about motherhood and love and human relations and so many other things that we once did through a combination of intuition and emotion. I even heard recently that some school is giving a course on kissing, which makes me wonder if I'm missing something. But rock-and-roll flows through my veins, not my brain. There's nothing else that feels the same to me as, say, the faint sound of the opening dum-doo-doo-doo-doo-doo of "My Girl" coming from a radio on a summer day. I feel the way I felt when I first heard it. I feel good, as James Brown says.

There are lots of people who don't feel this way about rock-and-roll. Some of them don't understand it, like the Senate wives who said that records should have rating stickers on them so that you would know whether the lyrics were dirty. The kids who hang out at Mr. Big's sub shop in my neighborhood thought this would make record shopping a lot easier, because you could choose albums by how bad the rating was. Most of the people who love rock-and-roll just thought the labeling idea was dumb. Lyrics, after all, are not the point of rock-and-roll, despite how beautifully people like Bruce Springsteen and Joni Mitchell write. Lyrics are the point only in the case of "Louis, Louis"; the words have never been deciphered, but it is widely understood that they are about sex. That's understandable, because rock-and-roll is a lot like sex: If you talk seriously about it, it takes a lot of the feeling away—and feeling is the point.

Some people over-analyze rock-and-roll, just as they over-analyze everything else. They say things like "Bruce Springsteen is the poet laureate of the American dream gone sour," when all I need to know about Bruce Springsteen is that the saxophone bridge on "Jungleland" makes the back of my neck feel exactly the same way I felt the first time a boy kissed me, only over and over and over again. People write about Prince's "Psychedelic masturbatory fantasies," but when I think about Prince, I don't really think, I just feel—feel the moment when driving to the beach, I first heard "Kiss" on the radio and started bobbing up and down in my seat like a seventeen-year-old on a day trip.

I've got precious few things in my life anymore that just make me feel, that make me jump up and dance, that make me forget the schedule and the job and the mortgage payments and just let me thrash around inside my skin. I've got precious few things I haven't studied and considered and reconsidered and studied some more. I don't know a chord change from a snare drum, but I know what I like, and I like feeling this way sometimes. I love rock-and-roll because in a time of talk, talk, talk, it's about action.

Here's a test: Get hold of a two-year-old, a person who has never ⁸ read a single word about how heavy-metal musicians should be put in jail or about Tina Turner's "throaty alto range." Put "I Heard It Through the Grapevine" on the stereo. Stand the two-year-old in front of the stereo. The two-year-old will begin to dance. The two-year-old will drop his butt. Enough said. (Excerpted from Quindlen, *Living Out Loud*, pp. 267–274.)

811 words

Questions for Accelerated Reading

Based on your reading, decide if the following statements are true (T) or false (F) and circle the correct answer.

1. The author feels that getting older made her fall out of love with rock-and-roll.   **T**   **(F)**

2. The author believes that everybody loves rock-and-roll. **T**   **(F)**

3. The author is an accomplished musician.   **T**   **(F)**

4. For the author, rock-and-roll is about action not thought. **(T)**   **F**

5. According to the author, in Philadelphia if you can't dance you might as well stay home.   **(T)**   **F**

Choose the correct answer for each of the following questions.

6. This article is about

   a. American Bandstand.
   (b). loving rock-and-roll.
   c. musical taste in different generations.

7. The author believes rock-and-roll should be

   a. the subject of scholarly study.
   (b). experienced rather than analyzed.

8. The author was born in

a. Boston.
ⓑ. Philadelphia.
c. New York.

9. According to the author, the central question of her childhood was

a. Where's the party?
ⓑ. Can you dance to it?
c. Who will dance with me?

10. The author tests for rock-and-roll by playing

a. "Dancing in the Streets."
b. "Proud Mary."
ⓒ. "I Heard it Through the Grapevine."

Give yourself ten points for each correct answer.

Score = _____

Questions for Understanding and Review

Unless the question directs you to do otherwise, circle the correct answer. (Use the boxes to record incorrect answers.)

Discovering the Controlling Idea

☐ 1. Which of the following statements expresses the controlling idea?

a. Parents and kids will never like the same music at the same time. It is genetically impossible for them to share musical tastes.
b. Putting stickers on rock-and-roll music is a waste of time because it only encourages kids to buy albums with stickers.
ⓒ. Because of the way it makes the author feel, rock-and-roll will always be part of her life.

☐ 2. The controlling idea

a. is expressed in a thesis statement.
ⓑ. had to be inferred.

Looking for Support

Put an I next to those statements that help introduce the controlling idea and an S next to those statements that support the controlling idea.

☐ **3.** I thought they [her parents] played "Pennsylvania 6–5000" to torment me and keep my friends away from the house. __I__

☐ **4.** I've got precious few things in my life that just make me feel, that make me jump and dance. __S__

☐ **5.** Some people over-analyze rock-and-roll just as they over-analyze everything else. __S__

☐ **6.** I was born in Philadelphia where if you can't dance you might as well stay home. __I__

☐ **7.** What is the relationship between paragraphs 4 and 5?

ⓐ. Both are major supporting paragraphs.
b. 4 is a major supporting paragraph; 5 is a minor supporting paragraph.
c. Both are minor supporting paragraphs.

Analyzing Paragraphs

☐ **8.** Which statement best paraphrases the main idea of paragraph 7?

a. I love rock-and-roll because it makes me want to dance.
ⓑ. I love rock-and-roll because it's one of the few things that allows me to feel instead of think.

Transitions

☐ **9.** In paragraph 2, the author says that when she was younger, she thought she would hate rock-and-roll as she got older. Then she reverses that train of thought. What transition introduces the reversal?

But _____

_____

Inferences

☐ **10.** Reread the last paragraph. Then identify the inference you are expected to supply.

a. Two-year-olds have natural rhythm; they are not afraid to dance in public.
ⓑ. The love of rock-and-roll can't be taught or explained. It's an instinct.

11. Reread paragraph 2. Then identify the inference the author expects you to supply.

(a). I should have known that I'd never stop loving rock-and-roll. After all, my parents still loved the music of their youth.

b. My parents played "Pennsylvania 6–5000" because it reminded them of how they first met and fell in love. It made them feel young again.

12. In paragraph 4 the author says, "I even heard recently that some school is giving a course on kissing, which makes me wonder if I'm missing something." The inference here is:

a. She would have liked to take such a course when she was in high school.

(b). It seems odd to take a course in kissing, which should come naturally.

Distinguishing Between Fact and Opinion

Label the following statements fact (F), opinion (O), or both (B).

13. Lyrics are not the point of rock-and-roll. __O__

14. Bruce Springsteen and Joni Mitchell write many of their own lyrics; that's what makes their songs so special. __O__

Purpose

15. The author's primary goal is to

a. inform her readers.

b. persuade them to share her opinion.

(c). share a personal feeling.

Tone

16. The author's tone is

(a). good natured and humorous.

b. annoyed and sarcastic.

c. emotionally neutral.

Evaluating Opinions

17. The author says that "Most of the people who love rock-and-roll just thought the labeling idea was dumb." This is an example of a

a. hasty generalization.

(b). unsupported generalization.

c. supported generalization.

Analysis of Language

☐ **18.** The author refers to the women who proposed labeling records as "Senate wives." What kind of connotation do you think this phrase has?

a. positive

(b). negative

c. neutral

Explain your answer. <u>Suggests they have no authority or importance</u>

<u>on their own</u>

☐ **19.** The author says that "some people over-analyze rock-and-roll, just as they over-analyze everything else." What connotation does the word *over-analyze* carry for you?

a. positive.

(b). negative

c. neutral

Explain your answer. <u>Usually the word "over-analyze" suggests</u>

<u>unnecessary or extensive analysis.</u>

☐ **20.** The author says that rock-and-roll makes her "thrash around inside my skin." The word *thrash* suggests

a. that her movements are painful.

(b). that the feeling is intense.

c. that her movements are awkward and clumsy.

Reading 4

Some Reasons for Wilding

Vocabulary to Learn:
☐ heinous: horrible.
☐ lurid: gruesome, sensational.
☐ remorseless: without pity or compassion.
☐ methodically: systematically, carefully.
☐ litany: list.
☐ advocate: support, propose.
☐ reticence: holding back, restraint

"Wilding." It's a new word in the vocabulary of teenage violence. The crime that made it the stuff of headlines is so heinous, the details so lurid as to make them almost beyond the understanding of any sane human being.

When it was over, a 28-year-old woman, an investment banker out for a jog, was left brutally beaten, knifed and raped by teenagers. She was found near an isolated road in New York's Central Park, covered with mud, almost dead from brain damage, loss of blood and exposure. "It was fun," one of her suspected teenage attackers, between 14 and 17 years old, told the Manhattan district attorney's office. In the lockup, they were nonchalant, whistling at a policewoman and singing a high-on-the-charts rap song about casual sex: "Wild Thing."

Maybe it's the savagery, the remorseless brutality that brought the national attention to this crime. We all heard about this one, either directly or from a friend or family member who would end the story with an "I can't believe it."

Believe it. Because it's happening elsewhere too.

In 1987, in Brooklyn, N.Y., three teenagers methodically set fire to a homeless couple. When at first rubbing alcohol wouldn't ignite the couple, they went to a local service station for gasoline. It worked.

In 1988, in rural Missouri, three teenagers killed a friend— partly out of curiosity! They just wanted to know what it would feel like to kill someone. One of the teenagers claimed the fascination with death began with heavy-metal music. When the victim asked, "Why?" over and over as his friends brutally attacked with baseball bats, the answer was, "Because it's fun."

In 1988 a record 406 people died in the county of Los Angeles alone in teen-gang-related attacks. One victim who survived was a pregnant woman who was shot, allegedly by a 16-year-old as a gang initiation rite.

This is truly a "generation at risk." Indeed, the statistics reflect its pain and confusion:

☐ The three leading causes of death among adolescents are drug- and alcohol-related accidents, suicide and homicide.

☐ Every year 1 million teenagers run away from home.

☐ Every year 1 million teenagers get pregnant.

☐ Every year over half a million—600,000 teenagers—attempt suicide; 5,000 succeed.

☐ Alcohol and drug abuse are so prevalent among the young that a *Weekly Reader* survey recently reported that 10-year-olds often feel pressure to try alcohol and crack.

☐ According to the Department of Education, 81 percent of the victims of violent crime are preteens and teenagers, 19 or younger. For the first time, teenagers have topped adults in the percentages of serious crimes committed per capita.

There are many complex reasons for this sad litany. Divorce and working parents strain the family's ability to cope. Latchkey kids are the rule more than the exception. Our schools and neighborhoods have become open-air drug markets. But it is not enough to excuse these children as products of a bad environment. *10*

As a society, we must take full responsibility. Our music, movies and television are filled with images of sexual violence and killing. The message to our kids is: it's OK to enjoy brutality and suffering: "It's fun." *11*

The American Academy of Pediatrics released a national policy statement on the impact of rock lyrics and music videos on adolescents last November. In it, they noted that some lyrics communicate potentially harmful health messages in a culture beset with drug abuse, teenage pregnancy, AIDS and other sexually transmitted diseases. *12*

The No. 2 album in the country this week is "GN'R Lies" from the very popular group, Guns N' Roses. This band is a favorite of sixth through 12th graders. It contains the following lyrics: "I used to love her but I had to kill her, I had to put her six feet under, and I can still hear her complain." *13*

Teen "slasher" films, featuring scenes of graphic, sadistic violence against women are so popular that characters like Jason from "Friday the 13th" and Freddie from "Nightmare on Elm Street" are considered cult heroes, and now there are spinoff television shows. *14*

As parents, it is our responsibility to teach our children to make wise decisions. This responsibility is not only to feed and clothe their bodies, but also to feed and nurture their spirits, their minds, their values. The moral crisis facing our nation's youth requires that we *all* share the responsibility, parents and the entertainment industry. *15*

Too often, those who produce this violence evade any discussion of their own responsibility by pretending the entire debate begins and ends with the First Amendment. We are strong advocates of its protections of free speech and free expression. We do not and have not advocated or supported restrictions on these rights; we have never proposed government action. What we are advocating, and what we have worked hard to encourage, is responsibility. *16*

For example, producers and songwriters don't consider putting out songs, movies or videos that would portray racism in a positive way. They could. The First Amendment provides that freedom. But they don't. In part, perhaps it's because they think those products wouldn't sell. But in part, they recognize it would be irresponsible. *17*

Why is there no similar reticence when the issue is glorifying violence, generally against women?

Responsibility should be brought to a marketplace so saturated *18* with violence that it legitimizes it for our children. It's time to stop the spilling of blood both as "entertainment" and in real life. (Excerpted from Baker and Gore, *Newsweek,* May 29, 1989, pp. 6–7.)

903 words

Questions for Accelerated Reading

Based on your reading decide if the following statements are true (T) or false (F) and circle the correct answer.

1. The authors believe that violence in movies, music, and television encourages violence among teenagers. **(T)** **F**

2. The authors do not believe that musical lyrics can be harmful but images can. **T** **(F)**

3. The authors advocate censorship of violence in movies, music, and television. **T** **(F)**

4. The authors think the current generation of teenagers is at risk. **(T)** **F**

5. The authors believe record producers must take more responsibility for their product. **(T)** **F**

6. The American Academy of Pediatrics released a policy statement saying that rock-and-roll lyrics were harmless. **T** **(F)**

Choose the correct answer for each of the following questions.

7. The rock-and-roll group mentioned in the article is

   a. Bon Jovi.
   (b). Guns N' Roses.
   c. The Grateful Dead.

8. The First Amendment provides for

   (a). freedom of speech.
   b. the right to assemble.
   c. the right to bear arms.

9. The authors believe that violent crimes involving teenagers

   a. receive too much publicity.

(b). are happening all over the country.
c. are happening primarily in New York.

10. The authors believe that movies, music, and television send the following message to kids:

a. Money is the key to happiness.
b. Drugs are fun and drinking is glamorous.
(c). It's OK to enjoy brutality and suffering.

Give yourself ten points for each correct answer.

Score = _____

Questions for Understanding and Review

Unless the question directs you to do otherwise, circle the correct answer. (Use the boxes to record incorrect answers.)

Discovering the Controlling Idea

☐ **1.** Which of the following statements paraphrases the controlling idea?

a. Today more and more teenagers are the victims or the perpetrators of crimes. Some of those crimes are so appalling and gruesome they are almost beyond human comprehension.
(b). As adults we have to take more responsibility for the messages our children receive from music, movies, and television. Our children learn repeatedly that violence and cruelty are without any serious consequences.

☐ **2.** The controlling idea

(a). was expressed in a thesis statement.
b. had to be inferred.

Looking for Support

☐ **3.** Paragraphs 5, 6, and 7 do not explicitly state a main idea. But taken together they combine to suggest that

(a). what happened to the Central Park jogger was not an isolated incident but an example of a national problem.
b. teenagers today are more likely to commit violent crimes than they were twenty years ago.

4. Which of the following statements are used to support the author's controlling idea?

    a. Divorce and working parents strain the family's ability to cope.

    ⓑ. The American Academy of Pediatrics noted that some lyrics communicated potentially harmful health messages.

    ⓒ. Characters like Jason from *Friday the 13th* and Freddie from *Nightmare on Elm Street* are considered cult heroes.

5. The authors say that our music, movies, and television are filled with images of sexual violence and killing. What specific support do they offer for this claim?

(1) lyrics from a "Guns N' Roses" album   (2) examples of slasher films like

"Friday the 13th" and their television spinoffs   (3) policy statement by

American Academy of Pediatrics noting "harmful" lyrics

6. What is the relationship between paragraphs 12 and 13?

    a. Both are major supporting paragraphs.

    ⓑ. 12 is a major supporting paragraph, while 13 is a minor supporting paragraph.

    c. 12 is a minor supporting paragraph; 13 is a major supporting paragraph.

7. What is the relationship between paragraphs 16 and 17?

    a. Both are major supporting paragraphs.

    b. Both are minor supporting paragraphs.

    ⓒ. 16 is a major supporting paragraph, while 17 is a minor supporting paragraph.

Analyzing Paragraphs

8. What is the purpose of paragraph 1?

    a. introduces the thesis statement

    ⓑ. provides an introduction for the thesis statement, which follows in another paragraph

    c. both

9. In paragraph 10 the last sentence is

    a. a major supporting sentence.

b. a minor supporting sentence.

ⓒ. a transitional sentence.

Organizational Patterns

☐ **10.** The pattern of organization underlying the entire article is

a. comparison and contrast.

ⓑ. cause and effect.

c. classification.

Inferences

☐ **11.** The authors do not use a transition between paragraphs 12 and 13. What kind of transition are you expected to infer?

a. one that signals reversal

ⓑ. one that signals illustration

c. one that signals addition

☐ **12.** Why do the authors mention that teenagers suspected of an attack were singing "Wild Thing" when they were locked up? What inference do they want their readers to draw?

a. They were scared and trying to act tough.

ⓑ. They just didn't care about being accused of the crime.

☐ **13.** How does that inference help support the author's thesis statement?

It reinforces the notion that today's kids do not seem to take brutality and

suffering seriously.

Distinguishing Between Fact and Opinion

Label the following statements fact (F), opinion (O), or both (B).

☐ **14.** Our music, movies, and television are filled with images of sexual violence and killing. __O__

☐ **15.** The American Academy of Pediatrics released a national policy statement on the impact of rock lyrics and music videos on adolescents. __F__

Choose the correct answer for each of the following questions.

Purpose

☐ **16.** The authors' objective is to

    a. inform.
    ⓑ. persuade.
    c. express a personal opinion.

Tone

☐ **17.** The authors' tone is

    ⓐ. sad and deeply concerned.
    b. outraged and furious.
    c. emotionally neutral.

Evaluating Opinions

☐ **18.** What generalization do the authors make about the content of movies, music, and television?

All three—movies, music, and television—are filled with sexual violence

and killing.

☐ **19.** What essential modifier do they leave out of their generalization that appears in the statement by the Academy of Pediatrics?

some

Forming Your Own Opinion

☐ **20.** Do you agree or disagree with the authors' claim that "music, movies, and television are filled with images of sexual violence and killing"? How would you justify your opinion?

Reading 5

Disability

Vocabulary to Learn:
- ☐ representations: images.
- ☐ distinctive: noticeable, characteristic.
- ☐ capitulation: giving in.
- ☐ premise: basis.
- ☐ embodiment: a representation in physical form, a concrete example.
- ☐ effaced: erased.
- ☐ feasible: possible.
- ☐ degradation: humiliation.
- ☐ imperils: endangers.
- ☐ integration: coming together.

For months now I've been consciously searching for representations of myself in the media, especially television. I know I'd recognize this self because of certain distinctive, though not unique, features: I am a forty-three-year-old woman crippled by multiple sclerosis; although I can still totter short distances with the aid of a brace and a cane, more and more of the time I ride in a wheelchair. Because of these appliances and my peculiar gait, I'm easy to spot even in a crowd. So when I tell you I haven't noticed any woman like me on television, you can believe me.

Actually, last summer I did see a woman with multiple sclerosis [2] portrayed on one of those medical dramas that offer an illness-of-the-week like the daily special at your local diner. In fact, that was the whole point of the show: that this poor young woman had MS. She was terribly upset (understandably, I assure you) by the diagnosis, and her response was to plan a trip to Kenya while she was still physically capable of making it, against the advice of the young, fit, handsome doctor who had fallen in love with her. And she almost did make it. At least, she got as far as a taxi to the airport, hotly pursued by the doctor. But at the last she succumbed to his blandishments and fled the taxi into his manly protective embrace. No escape to Kenya for this cripple.

Capitulation into the arms of a man who uses his medical powers [3] to strip one of even the urge toward independence is hardly the sort of representation I had in mind. But even if the situation had been sensitively handled, according the woman her right to her own adventures, it wouldn't have been what I'm looking for. Such a television show, as well as films like *Duet for One* and *Children of a Lesser God*, in taking disability as its major premise, excludes the complexities that round out a character and make her whole. It's not about a woman who happens to be physically disabled; it's about physical disability as the determining factor of a woman's existence.

Take it from me, physical disability looms pretty large in one's [4] life. But it doesn't devour one wholly. I'm not, for instance, Ms. MS, a walking, talking embodiment of a chronic incurable degenerative disease. In most ways I'm just like every other woman of my age, nationality, and socioeconomic background. I menstruate, so I have to buy tampons. I worry about smoker's breath, so I buy mouthwash. I smear my wrinkling skin with lotions. I put bleach in the washer so my family's undies won't be dingy. I drive a car, talk on the telephone, get runs in my pantyhose, eat pizza. In most ways, that is, I'm the advertisers' dream: Ms. Great American Consumer. And yet the advertisers, who determine nowadays who will get represented publicly and who will not, deny the existence of me and my kind absolutely.

I once asked a local advertiser why he didn't include disabled [5] people in his spots. His response seemed direct enough: "We don't want to give people the idea that our product is just for the handicapped." But tell me truly now: If you saw me pouring out puppy biscuits, would you think these kibbles were only for the puppies of cripples? If you saw my blind niece ordering a Coke, would you switch to Pepsi lest you be struck sightless? No, I think the advertiser's excuse masked a deeper and more anxious rationale:

To depict disabled people in the ordinary activities of daily life is to admit that there is something ordinary about disability itself, that it may enter anybody's life. If it is effaced completely, or at least isolated as a separate "problem," so that it remains at a safe distance from other human issues, then the viewer won't feel threatened by her or his own physical vulnerability.

This kind of effacement or isolation has painful, even dangerous 6 consequences, however. For the disabled person, these include self-degradation and a subtle kind of self-alienation not unlike that experienced by other minorities. Socialized human beings love to conform, to study others and then to mold themselves to the contours of those who images, for good reasons or bad, they come to love. Imagine a life in which feasible others—others you can hope to be like—don't exist. At the least you might conclude that there is something queer about you, something ugly or foolish or shameful. In the extreme, you might feel as though you don't exist, in any meaningful social sense, at all. Everyone else is "there," sucking breath mints and splashing on cologne and swigging wine coolers. You're "not there." And if not there, nowhere.

But this denial of disability imperils even you who are able- 7 bodied, and not just by shrinking your insight into the physically and emotionally complex world you live in. Some disabled people call you TAPs, or Temporarily Abled Persons. The fact is that ours is the only minority you can join involuntarily, without warning, at any time. And if you live long enough, as you're increasingly likely to do, you may well join it. The transition will probably be difficult from a physical point of view no matter what. But it will be a good bit easier psychologically if you are accustomed to seeing disability as a normal characteristic, one that complicates but does not ruin human existence. Achieving this integration, for disabled and able-bodied people alike, requires that we insert disability daily into our field of vision: quietly, naturally, in the small and common scenes of our ordinary lives. (Mairs, *Carnal Acts*, pp. 30–35.)

944 words

Questions for Accelerated Reading

Based on your reading, decide if the following statements are true (T) or false (F) and circle the correct answer.

1. The author complains about seeing too many commercials that focus on housewives.   **T**   **(F)**

2. The author is in her sixties.   **T**   **(F)**

3. The author has multiple sclerosis. (T) F

4. The author thinks there should be more disabled people represented on television. (T) F

5. The author believes that many advertisers simply deny the existence of people like her. (T) F

Choose the correct answer for each of the following questions.

6. The author believes that having a physical disability

   (a). profoundly affects but does not destroy a person's life.
   b. ruins a person's life forever.
   c. doesn't make much of a difference.

7. Which of the following movies does the author mention?

   a. *Playing for Time*
   (b). *Children of a Lesser God*
   (c). *Duet for One*

8. The author claims that she

   (a). is always looking for representations of people like herself.
   b. doesn't care if she sees herself represented in the media.
   c. never watches television or goes to movies.

9. The author believes that

   (a). she is, in most ways, just like any other woman her age.
   b. she has little in common with other women.
   c. she has been ostracized by other women her age.

10. The author refers to herself as

    a. the woman who will stop at nothing.
    (b). Ms. Great American Consumer.
    c. Towanda, the Amazon.

Give yourself ten points for each correct answer.

Score = _____

Questions for Understanding and Review

Unless the question directs you to do otherwise, circle the correct answer. (Use the boxes to record incorrect answers.)

Discovering the Controlling Idea

□ **1.** Which of the following statements best paraphrases the controlling idea?

    a. Television does not realistically reflect the lives of disabled people. Too often the disability is made the focus of their lives.

    ⓑ. Television tends to deny the existence of the disabled. That denial has dangerous consequences for everyone, even those who are not disabled.

□ **2.** The controlling idea was

    a. summed up in a thesis statement.

    ⓑ. had to be inferred.

Looking for Support

□ **3.** To make her point the author relies heavily on

    a. statistics.

    b. quotations.

    ⓒ. personal experience.

    d. definitions.

□ **4.** Identify the relationship between paragraphs 5 and 6.

    ⓐ. Both are major supporting paragraphs.

    b. Both are minor supporting paragraphs.

    c. 5 is a major supporting paragraph; 6 is a minor supporting paragraph.

□ **5.** The author mentions the television drama *Duet for One* to illustrate that

    a. television ignores those with a disability.

    ⓑ. television does not realistically represent the complex lives of people with a disability.

Analyzing Paragraphs

□ **6.** Which statement best paraphrases the main idea of paragraph 4?

    a. Having a physical disability has a dramatic effect on a person's life, an effect that is impossible to ignore.

    ⓑ. People with a disability do not make that disability the focus of their life. For them, life goes on as it does for everyone else.

Organizational Patterns

□ **7.** What organizational pattern underlies paragraph 6?

a. comparison and contrast
b. classification
c. cause and effect
d. sequence of dates and events

Transitions

☐ **8.** In order, list the transitions used in paragraph 7.

But, And, But

Inferences

☐ **9.** The word *rationale* appears in paragraph 5. Although it was not initially defined for you, you can probably infer a meaning from context: "I think the advertiser's excuse masked a deeper and more anxious rationale." What definition were you able to infer?

reason

☐ **10.** Within paragraph 7, the author does not explicitly state how disability can be inserted "in the small and common scenes of our ordinary lives." But given the rest of the reading, what is your inference? What do you think she would like to see happen?

She would like to see more disabled people in the media, particularly

on television.

☐ **11.** The author discusses a movie of the week in which a young woman discovered she had multiple sclerosis. You can infer from her description that she

a. enjoyed the program.
b. did not enjoy it.

Explain what statements in the reading led to your conclusion.

(1) Capitulation into the arms of a man who uses his medical powers to

strip one of even the urge toward independence is hardly the sort of

representation . . . (2) But even if the situation had been sensitively

handled. . . .

Distinguishing Between Fact and Opinion

☐ **12.** This reading

    a. balances fact and opinion.
    (b). relies primarily on opinions.
    c. relies primarily on facts.

Analyzing Arguments

☐ **13.** What conclusion does the author hope you will share as a result of reading this article?

Disabled people need to be represented in the media so that we accept

disability as something that complicates but does not ruin life.

☐ **14.** What reasons does she offer as part of her argument?

(1) If we isolate or ignore the disabled, we make them feel ugly and shameful.

(2) We make it harder on those who could become disabled in the future.

☐ **15.** In paragraph 6, the author offers what generalizations about the nature of human beings?

Socialized human beings enjoy conforming to the images of those

they love.

Identifying Tone

☐ **16.** The author's tone is

    (a). informal but still serious.
    b. humorous yet angry.
    c. casual and relaxed.

Analyzing Language

☐ **17.** In the last two paragraphs, the author repeatedly addresses the audience with the pronoun "you." Why do you think she does this?

To emphasize that her audience, disabled or not, must take this issue

personally.

□ **18.** In paragraph 1, the author describes her "unique features." Then in paragraph 4, she focuses on her similarities to other women. What is the purpose of those descriptions?

Paragraph 1 focuses on the difficulties the disease creates. Paragraph 4

emphasizes that, nevertheless, the author is much like anyone else.

□ **19.** In paragraph 1, the author says she "can still 'totter' short distances with the help of a cane and a brace." Why do you think she chose this verb?

To suggest the difficulties the disease imposes on her life.

Forming Your Own Opinion

□ **20.** The author says that the failure to depict disabled people on television has "painful, even dangerous consequences." According to her, what are those consequences?

People feel queer and ashamed. They have the feeling that socially, at least,

they do not exist.

Explain why you agree or disagree with her opinion.

DIGGING DEEPER

This essay was written in 1987. Do you see any evidence that things are changing? Explain your answer.

Reading 6:

Red, White, Blue and Yellow

Vocabulary to Learn:

- □ signified: identified, defined, represented.
- □ coalition: group working together.
- □ apolitical: lacking an interest in politics.
- □ collective: assembled, combined.
- □ disheartening: depressing.

Of the two signs Americans are using to show one another their *1* relation to the gulf war—the yellow ribbon and the Star-Spangled Banner—I confess that I'm cheered more by the former than the latter. The yellow ribbons make me love and respect my fellow citizens; the flags make me fear them.

From Day 1 through Day 12 or so, we saw mainly yellow rib- *2* bons—tied to mailboxes, trees, lamp posts, hats and lapels—but no flags or, at least in my area of New Jersey, no more than usual. There was Old Glory waving alongside the red Marine Corps and black "Remember the M.I.A.'s" banners at the Gulf station on Route 1, which is run by a Vietnam vet who seems to hire only Vietnam vets; and the huge flag at the self-storage outfit in South Brunswick, which is mainly an attention-getting device for a business one would otherwise pass without noticing.

The ribbons were the new thing. And early on in the gulf crisis, *3* I decided I liked them, even though they kept alive for another season the terrible country-western love song that first brought them into public life, back when the Ayatollah Ruhollah Khomeini was Satan and Jimmy Carter was President, and instead of soldiers in the gulf we had hostages.

Today, as then, yellow ribbons have signified our desire to bring *4* home Americans who were being held against their wills in foreign lands (which, since Vietnam, is how I have regarded enlisted men and women anyhow). We would keep dinner in the stove, sheets on their beds, until our kids were brought home again. The yellow ribbons expressed loyalty to our military on an individual basis, one young man or woman at a time, and not loyalty to the whole, the coalition forces, as the Pentagon calls this armada. And certainly not loyalty to something as abstract and out of our control as Republican foreign policy in the gulf.

But then, somewhere around Day 12, I started seeing Star- *5* Spangled Banners all over town. Suddenly, every merchant on Nassau Street in Princeton had a flag out front, and even my generally apolitical neighbors, mostly academics and scientists, had flags fluttering above their two-car garage doors. It was Veterans

Day, July Fourth and Presidents Day all rolled into one. Now, on Day 40, with the ground war proceeding, we can expect to see even more flags.

This has made me nervous. Flags signify a wholly different rela- 6 tion to the war than the yellow ribbons do. This is Us vs. Them. The flags express a Super Bowl mentality—identification with a team (in our case, the visiting team) instead of with the individual players. From hoping that the Republicans or God or Jimmy Carter or Jesse Jackson—anyone—would soon bring our sons and daughters home alive, we'd gone to declaring our collective desire to kick collective butt.

The saddest, most disheartening symbolism I've seen lately is 7 the joining of the two emblems—the mailbox with both flag and big yellow bow attached, the pole with Old Glory above and ribbons swirling below, the tiny paper flag against a swatch of yellow acetate pinned to a lapel.

What's being symbolized here is a profound conflict between 8 two irreconcilable, painfully opposed desires—to protect our children and to destroy the Iraqi military. For us to affirm that contradiction openly, publicly, as if it did not exist, we must go into deep denial. And when that happens, the symbol no longer stands for reality; it has replaced it. (Banks, "Red, White, Blue, and Yellow." *New York Times*, February 26, 1991, p. A23.)

588 words

Questions for Accelerated Reading

Based on your reading, decide if the following statements are true (T) or false (F) and circle the correct answer.

1. The author liked the combination of yellow ribbons and American flags that was common during the 1991 Gulf War.   **T**   **(F)**

2. According to the author, the ribbons and flags meant much the same thing.   **T**   **(F)**

3. The author apparently resented those people who did not display American flags during the Gulf War.   **T**   **(F)**

4. The author definitely supported the Gulf War.   **T**   **(F)**

Choose the correct answer to each of the following questions.

5. The author refers to the flag as

   a. Old Glory.

    (b). The Star-Spangled Banner and Old Glory.

    c. The Stars and Stripes.

6. The author lives in

    a. Philadelphia.

    (b). New Jersey.

    c. New York.

7. The custom of displaying yellow ribbons started with

    a. a movie.

    (b). a song.

    c. a ribbon salesperson.

8. According to the author, yellow ribbons represent

    a. Americans' love of their country.

    (b). the desire to bring home Americans held against their will in other countries.

    c. the hope of winning a war.

9. When the flags began to appear the author felt

    a. patriotic.

    b. angry.

    (c). nervous.

10. The author says that the flags he saw everywhere symbolized

    a. love of country.

    b. anxiety about the soldiers.

    (c). feelings of Us vs. Them.

Give yourself ten points for each correct answer.

Score = _____

Questions for Understanding and Review

Unless the question directs you to do otherwise, circle the correct answer. (Use the boxes to record incorrect answers.)

Discovering the Controlling Idea

☐ 1. Which of the following statements best paraphrases the controlling idea?

a. The flags and ribbons that appeared during the Gulf War made me feel out of touch with my fellow Americans.

(b). The yellow ribbons that blossomed during the Gulf War made me proud to be American but the flags made me afraid.

☐ **2.** The thesis statement appears in

(a). paragraph 1.
b. paragraph 2.
c. paragraph 3.

Looking for Support

☐ **3.** Describe the author's feelings about the yellow ribbons that appeared.

He liked them because they represented the desire to bring home Americans

held against their will. They expressed loyalty to the military on an individual

basis.

☐ **4.** Describe how he felt about the flags.

He thought the flags expressed a feeling of "Us vs. Them." They symbolized

a collective desire to get even.

Analyzing Paragraphs

☐ **5.** Which statement best paraphrases the main idea of paragraph 8?

a. The display of both symbols together suggests that people do not really understand what each one means.

(b). In displaying the two symbols together, people refuse to recognize that the symbols contradict one another.

☐ **6.** What is the relationship between paragraphs 7 and 8?

(a). Both are major supporting paragraphs.
b. Both are minor supporting paragraphs.
c. 7 is a major supporting paragraph; 8 is a minor supporting paragraph.

Transitions

☐ **7.** In what paragraph does the author make the transition from de-

scribing the meaning of yellow ribbons to describing the meaning
of flags?

   a. paragraph 3
   b. paragraph 4
   ⓒ. paragraph 5

☐ **8.** Write down the transitional word the author uses to introduce
that change in meaning.

But
_____

☐ **9.** In the first four paragraphs, the author uses the following transitions: "From Day 1 through Day 12," "And early on," "Today as
then." How do these transitions help the reader?

They help the reader follow a sequence in time.
_____

Organizational Patterns

☐ **10.** What pattern of organization can you identify in paragraph 6?

   a. sequence of dates and events
   b. comparison and contrast
   ⓒ. cause and effect

☐ **11.** What pattern organizes the reading as a whole?

   a. sequence of dates and events
   b. classification
   ⓒ. comparison and contrast

Inferences

☐ **12.** On the basis of this article, you could logically infer that

   a. the author supported the Gulf War.
   ⓑ. the author did not support the war.
   c. the author is against all wars.

☐ **13.** What statements in the article led you to your inference?

Paragraph 4: The statement ending "(which since Vietnam is how I have

regarded enlisted men and women anyhow)." The statement ending "and

out of our control as Republican foreign policy in the Gulf."
_____

☐ **14.** From the article you could logically infer that the author is

    a. generally against displaying the flag.
    b. against displaying the flag during wartime.
    ⓒ. against using the flag to show support for America's soldiers in combat.

Distinguishing Between Fact and Opinion

Label the following statements fact (F), opinion (O), or both (B).

☐ **15.** Flags signify a wholly different relation to the war than do yellow ribbons. __O__

☐ **16.** The flags displayed during the Gulf War showed a Super Bowl mentality. __O__

Purpose

☐ **17.** The author's purpose was

    a. to inform.
    b. to persuade.
    ⓒ. to express a personal opinion.

Bias

☐ **18.** Does the author suggest anywhere that displaying flags during the Gulf War might mean something else besides a "Us versus Them" mentality? Yes or No.

Analyzing Language

☐ **19.** The author says in paragraph 6 that the American public had gone from hoping that individual sons and daughters would survive to "our collective desire to kick collective butt." Why does he use such informal, even crude language? What does he imply?

A more aggressive and unthinking attitude had asserted itself.

Forming Your Own Opinion

☐ **20.** Do you agree or disagree that the flags and yellow ribbons displayed during the Gulf War represented opposite desires as the author claims? How would you justify your opinion?

_____

_____

_____

_____

Reading 7:

The Wild Boy of Aveyron

Vocabulary to Learn:

- ☐ inculcate: teach.
- ☐ obstinate: stubborn.
- ☐ congenital: inborn.
- ☐ proximity: nearness.

In 1800, long before the development of psychotherapy, Jean-Marc *1* Itard attempted to inculcate normal human abilities in a "wild boy" who had been captured by peasants in the forests of Aveyron, France. The boy, who appeared to be between 10 and 12 years old, had been exhibited in a cage for about a year by his captors when Itard rescued him. By examining scars on the boy's body, as well as the observation of his personal habits, Itard concluded that he had been abandoned at the age of two or three.

At first Victor (as Itard named the boy) seemed more animal *2* than human. He was oblivious to other human beings, could not talk, and howled and ate off the ground on all fours like an animal. He evidenced unusual sensory reactions; for example, he did not react if a pistol was fired next to his ear, but he could hear the crack of a nut or the crackling of underbrush at a great distance. No adverse reaction seemed to result from his going unclothed even in freezing weather. In fact, Victor had velvety skin, despite his years of exposure.

Victor exhibited animal-like behavior in many ways. He had an *3* obstinate habit of smelling any object that was given to him—even objects we consider void of smell. He knew nothing of love and perceived other human beings only as obstacles—in other words, like the wild animals he had known in the forest. He was typically indifferent and uncomplaining but, very occasionally, he showed a kind of frantic rage and became dangerous to those around him. If he had any sense of self-identity, it was apparently more that of an animal than a human.

Philippe Pinel, Itard's teacher, diagnosed Victor's condition as ₄ congenital idiocy—concluding that the boy was incapable of profiting from training. But Itard, although only 25 years old and inexperienced in comparison with Pinel, disagreed; in his view, Victor's savage behavior was the result of early and lengthy isolation from other humans. He believed that human contact and intensive training would enable the boy to become a normal person, and, ignoring Pinel's advice, he began his attempt to civilize "the wild boy of Aveyron."

No procedures had yet been formulated that Itard could use in ₅ treating Victor; thus he developed a program based on principles that included the following: (a) without contact with its own kind, a human infant—unlike a lower animal—cannot develop normally; (b) the instinct to imitate is the learning force by which our senses are educated, and this instinct is strongest in early childhood and decreases with age; and (c) in all human beings, from the most isolated savage to the most educated individual, a constant relationship exists between needs and ideas—the greater the needs, the greater the development of mental capacities to meet them.

In attempting to train Victor, Itard developed methods that have ₆ had considerable impact on the subsequent treatment of children with serious learning disabilities. Instructional materials were provided to broaden Victor's discrimination skills in touch, smell, and other sensory modalities, appropriate to his environment; language training was begun through the association of words with the objects Victor wanted; and modeling and imitation were used to reinforce Victor's learning of desired social behaviors.

Initial results were indeed promising. Victor learned to speak a ₇ number of words and could write in chalk to express his wants. He also developed affectionate feelings toward his governess.

In June 1801, Itard reported to the Academy of Science in Paris ₈ on the rapid progress in the first nine months of training. But in November 1806, he could only report that despite significant advances in several areas, Victor had not been made "normal" in the sense of becoming a self-directing and socially adjusted person. Being brought into the proximity of girls, for example, only upset the boy, leaving him restless and depressed, and Itard had to abandon his hope for a normal sexual response as a means of fostering Victor's motivation and socialization.

After devoting five and a half years to the task, Itard gave up ₉ the attempt to train "the wild boy of Aveyron." As for Victor, he lived to be 40, but never progressed appreciably beyond the achievements of that first year.

The story of Victor is of absorbing interest to both laymen and ₁₀ scientists. A motion picture that portrays Itard's work with Victor—*The Wild Child*—was produced by François Truffaut. In scientific circles, the lack of conclusive answers will keep psychologists and others puzzling over the question of whether Victor was a congenital mental retardate, a brain-damaged child, a psychotic, or simply a child who had been so deprived of human contact during early critical periods of development that the damage he had sustained could never be completely remedied. (Carson, Butcher, and Coleman, *Abnormal Psychology and Modern Life*, p. 482.)

797 words

Questions for Accelerated Reading

Based on your reading, decide if the following statements are true (T) or false (F), and circle the correct answer.

1. Jean Marc Itard transformed the wild boy of Aveyron into a happy and normal human being.   **T**   **(F)**

2. The boy never developed any affection for other human beings. **T**   **(F)**

3. In training the boy, Itard used well-established procedures. **T**   **(F)**

4. Itard never gave up on the boy.   **T**   **(F)**

5. In the beginning the boy made real progress.   **(T)**   **F**

Choose the correct answer for each of the following questions.

6. Itard's belief in the boy was not shared by

   (a). Pinel.
   b. Charcot.
   c. Freud.

7. When Itard found him, the boy appeared to be

   a. 8 years old.
   b. between 8 and 9 years old.
   (c). between 10 and 12 years old.

8. By the time he was an adult, Victor

   a. could speak a foreign language.

(b). had not gone beyond the achievements of the first year.
   c. had become wilder than he was as a child.

9. Victor lived to be

   a. 60
   (b). 40.
   c. 30.

10. The motion picture based on Victor's life was called

   a. *Wild in the Jungle.*
   (b). *The Wild Child.*
   c. *Jungle Child.*

Give yourself ten points for each correct answer.

Score = _____

Questions for Understanding and Review

Unless the question directs you to do otherwise, circle the correct answer.

Discovering the Controlling Idea

☐ 1. Which of the following statements best paraphrases the author's controlling idea?

   (a). Almost two centuries ago, Jean-Marc Itard tried to teach the "wild boy" of Aveyron how to behave like a normal little boy of his age. However, despite some initial success, the attempt was a failure.
   b. In an attempt to train the "wild boy" of Aveyron, Jean-Marc Itard developed new methods for teaching children with learning disabilities, methods still widely used today.

☐ 2. The controlling idea

   a. was summed up in a thesis statement.
   (b). had to be inferred.

Looking for Support

☐ 3. Which of the following statements does the author use to support the controlling idea?

a. *The Wild Child*, a motion picture that portrays Itard's work with Victor, was a very successful French film.
(b). At first Victor seemed more animal than human.
(c). Victor learned to speak a number of words, and could express his wants by writing in chalk.
(d). In November of 1806, Itard had to report to the Academy of Science in Paris that Victor had not become socially adjusted.

☐ **4.** Paragraph 3 is a

a. major supporting paragraph.
(b). minor supporting paragraph.

☐ **5.** What support does the author offer for the claim that Victor initially behaved more like an animal than a human being?

He was oblivious to others, could not talk, howled, ate off the ground, showed

unusual sensory reactions, smelled everything, treated humans as obstacles.

Analyzing Paragraphs

☐ **6.** Which statement best paraphrases the main idea of paragraph 3?

a. Victor's furious rage made him dangerous to those around him.
(b). In many ways, Victor's behavior resembled an animal's.

Label the sentences in the following paragraph M.I. *for main idea statement,* M *for major supporting sentence and* m *for minor supporting sentence:*

☐ **7.** Initial results were indeed promising. ____M.I.____ Victor learned to speak a number of words and could write in chalk to express his wants. ____M____ He also developed affectionate feelings toward his governess. ____M____

Transitions

☐ **8.** Reread the first two sentences of paragraph 2. What transitional word or phrase could you use to link those two sentences?

a. on the other hand
(b). for example
c. however

Inferences

☐ **9.** The reading does not explicitly say *why* Itard gave up on trying to train Victor. What inference can you logically draw given what you know from the article?

He got discouraged because Victor stopped making progress.

☐ **10.** Based on the article, you could logically infer

    a. that Pinel was right about the boy being unable to profit from training.
    b. that Itard was correct in assuming that the boy could, with training, learn to behave like a normal person.
    ⓒ. that it is not clear who was right.

Distinguishing Between Fact and Opinion

Label the following statements fact (F), opinion (O), or both (B).

☐ **11.** In 1800 Jean-Marc Itard tried to train and teach a "wild boy" who had been captured by peasants in the forest of Aveyron. _F_

☐ **12.** In June 1801, Itard reported to the Academy of Science in Paris on Victor's rapid progress in the first nine months of training. _F_

☐ **13.** Victor's savage behavior was the result of early and lengthy isolation from other human beings. _O_

Purpose

☐ **14.** The author's goal in this reading is to

    a. entertain.
    b. persuade.
    ⓒ. inform.

Tone

☐ **15.** The author's tone is

    a. serious but still amused.
    b. angry and upset.
    ⓒ. emotionally neutral.

Bias

☐ **16.** The author appears to be

a. critical of such experiments.
b. supportive of what Itard tried to accomplish.
ⓒ. unbiased in either direction.

Evaluating Opinions

☐ **17.** What generalization does the author make about the effects Itard's methods had upon future generations?

That his methods had an important effect on the education of children

with learning disabilities.

☐ **18.** Does the author offer specific support for that generalization? Yes or ⓃⓄ If your answer is *yes*, describe the support. If your answer is *no*, explain why the author might have chosen not to support the generalization.

The author might have assumed that readers already know how children

with disabilities are trained, and therefore would immediately recognize

how Itard's methods resemble those currently used to teach children

with disabilities.

Analyzing Language

☐ **19.** The language of this essay is

a. more connotative than denotative.
ⓑ. more denotative than connotative.

Forming Your Own Opinion

☐ **20.** What do you think about Itard's work with Victor? Do you think that, in the long run, it benefitted or hurt the boy?

DIGGING DEEPER

Do you think Itard should or should not have given up on Victor? Why or why not?

Reading 8:

As I See It

Vocabulary to Learn:

- □ stereotype: an oversimplified and often negative opinion or belief about some group or event.
- □ divisive: creating difference or disagreement.
- □ caricature: an exaggerated or distorted picture created for comic effect.
- □ genealogy: origin.
- □ tapestry: weaving.
- □ disparate: different.
- □ misconception: mistaken idea or notion.

Ignorance, intolerance and insecurity about particular groups of people breed stereotypes. They are used to disregard, or worse to subordinate, the people who are the victims of stereotypes. 1

But if racial and ethnic stereotypes weren't so divisive and destructive, they would be funny. By ascribing absurd and mythical characteristics to whole groups of people, stereotypes create caricatures. Here are only only a few of my favorite ones about Latinos. 2

"All Latinos carry knives." A roll of Wintergreen Life Savers is usually the most dangerous thing Latinos carry. (By the way, I am afraid of knives.) 3

"Most Latinos can't speak English." Most Latinos in the United States do speak English. And those who don't can be found in crowded English-language classes. In fact, most Latinos speak both English and Spanish. Not bad, given the increasing need for foreign language skills in our globalized economy. 4

"Most Latinos in the United States are not American citizens." The vast majority of Hispanics living in the United States are American citizens by birth or naturalization. Puerto Ricans are a case in point. If I had a nickel for every time I had to explain that Puerto Ricans born on the island are automatically Americans, 5

and have been so since 1917, I'd be able to lend money to "the Donald."

"All Latinos are related." Not quite. While it might appear that there is an overabundance of Latinos who answer to Rodriguez or Rivera or Ortiz, trust me, they are not all related, any more than all people named Jones or Smith are related. 6

"All Latinos know each other." A common experience among Latinos is be asked by a non-Latino colleague or boss to explain the particular actions of other Hispanics. Latinos are a large and varied group of people, with as many different personalities as there are people. They don't all know each other and should not be expected to. 7

"Latinos are all poor and lazy." While the percentage of Latinos nationwide who live in poverty remains high, the latest census revealed an impressive improvement in their socio-economic situation. The total income of Latinos grew from $71.1 billion in 1980 to $188.3 billion in 1990. Analysts project Hispanic income to grow to nearly $330 billion by the year 2000. 8

Additionally, the number of Hispanic-owned businesses jumped from 219,355 in 1977 to 422,373 in 1987. The total revenue of these businesses more than doubled during the same period, going from $10.4 billion to $24.7 billion, and it is projected to increase to nearly $58 billion in eight years. 9

If "lazy Latinos" can generate this kind of skyrocketing statistics, I wonder what would happen if they decide to really get to work. Japan, watch out! 10

"Funny, you don't look Hispanic." Again, if only I had a nickel . . . Come on folks, what's a Latino supposed to look like anyway? Like Baskin Robbins, we come in a wide and wonderful selection of colors, races, shapes and sizes, courtesy of an African, Indian and European genealogy. 11

"All Latinos are the same." Wrong. Although Spanish is the common denominator among Latinos, this community must also be viewed as a tapestry of disparate nationalities, with significant linguistic, historical and cultural differences. This is because Latinos have come to the United States from such a variety of places as Puerto Rico, Cuba, Mexico, Dominican Republic and Central and South America. 12

What's a non-Latino to do given this diversity among Latinos? Be sensitive to, and respectful of, the differences. Don't try to lump people together just because they speak Spanish. 13

Latinos are the fastest growing population in the United States. Over the next few years we will be seeing more and more Hispanics in the workplace, in schools, in stores, on the street, on television and even in public office. 14

How well Latinos are accepted into America's mainstream will 15 depend on whether we can put an end to the misconceptions and stereotypes that have for too long hindered their progress and made them seem to be much less than they really are. (Sepulveda, "As I See It," *New Haven Register*, January 23, 1992, p. 12.)

667 words

Questions for Accelerated Reading

Based on your reading, decide if the following statements are true (T) or false (F), and circle the correct answer.

1. The author does not believe that stereotyping people has any harmful results.   **T**   **(F)**

2. He believes that most Latinos carry knives.   **T**   **(F)**

3. The author himself is Hispanic.   **(T)**   **F**

4. The author suggests that non-Latinos should be more sensitive to and respectful of differences among Latinos.   **(T)**   **F**

5. According to the author, the number of Hispanic-owned businesses is decreasing.   **T**   **(F)**

Choose the correct answer for each of the following questions.

6. The author says that the vast majority of Hispanics living in the United States are

   a. not citizens.
   b. American citizens by birth.
   (c). American citizens by birth or naturalization.

7. According to the author, the Latino population is

   (a). growing.
   b. declining.
   c. staying the same.

8. The author says that most Latinos

   a. speak only Spanish.
   (b). speak English and Spanish.
   c. speak English without an accent.

9. The author makes it clear that Latinos

   a. have a close-knit family group.

    ⓑ. are as varied and different as any other group of people.

    c. all have similar tastes and attitudes.

10. The author suggests that

    a. Latinos need better representation on television.

    ⓑ. Latinos have been the target of stereotypes.

    c. he is personally resentful of his treatment in this country.

Give yourself ten points for each correct answer.

Score = _____

Questions for Understanding and Review

Unless the question directs you to do otherwise, circle the correct answer.

Discovering the Controlling Idea

☐ **1.** Which of the following statements best paraphrases the controlling idea?

    a. Stereotypes are the product of insecurity and ignorance.

    ⓑ. As a Latino, the author has had first-hand experience with being stereotyped.

☐ **2.** The controlling idea

    a. was expressed in a thesis statement.

    ⓑ. had to be inferred.

Looking for Support

☐ **3.** The author develops the controlling idea by means of

    a. examples.

    b. personal experiences.

    c. statistics.

    ⓑ. all of the above.

☐ **4.** What is the relationship between paragraphs 8 and 9?

    a. Paragraph 8 is a minor supporting paragraph, while 9 is a major supporting paragraph.

    ⓑ. Paragraph 8 is a major supporting paragraph, while 9 is a minor supporting paragraph.

    c. Both are major supporting paragraphs.

☐ **5.** What is the relationship between paragraphs 9 and 10?

    a. Both are major supporting paragraphs.

    ⓑ. Both are minor supporting paragraphs.

    c. Paragraph 9 is a major supporting paragraph, while 10 is a minor supporting paragraph.

☐ **6.** The author opens paragraphs 3–12 with what he believes are common stereotypes about Latinos. What is the purpose of the stereotypes?

To demonstrate how foolish or inaccurate such stereotypes are.

Analyzing Paragraphs

☐ **7.** In paragraph 4, the last sentence is a

    a. major supporting sentence.

    ⓑ. minor supporting sentence.

☐ **8.** Which of the following statements paraphrases the main idea of paragraph 8?

    a. There is still a high percentage of Latinos who live in poverty.

    ⓑ. Census figures show an impressive gain in the living standard and earning power of Latinos.

☐ **9.** How does the author answer the question he poses in paragraph 13?

Non-Latinos should be sensitive to and respect differences among Latinos.

Organizational Patterns

☐ **10.** The organizational pattern underlying paragraph 1 is cause and effect. What cause and effect relationship does the author describe?

Ignorance, insecurity, and intolerance cause or breed stereotypes.

Transitions

☐ **11.** Identify the transitional sentence that appears somewhere in the first three paragraphs.

Here are only a few of my favorite ones about Latinos.

Inferences

☐ **12.** In paragraph 5, the author says "If I had a nickel for every time I had to explain that Puerto Ricans born on the island are automatically Americans and have been since 1917, I'd be able to lend money to 'the Donald'." What inference can you draw from that statement?

He has had to explain this fact very frequently.

☐ **13.** What does the author imply when he says "trust me, they are not all related, any more than all people named Jones or Smith are related"?

No one would be silly enough to think all people named Jones are

related.

Distinguishing Between Fact and Opinion

Label the following statements fact (F), opinion (O), or both (B).

☐ **14.** The number of Hispanic-owned businesses jumped from 219,355 in 1977 to 422,373 in 1987. __F__

☐ **15.** If racial and ethnic stereotypes weren't so divisive and destructive, they would be funny. __O__

Purpose

☐ **16.** The author's objective is to

    a. inform.
    ⓑ. persuade.
    c. entertain.

Tone

☐ **17.** The author's tone is

    a. passionate and angry.
    ⓑ. good-natured but quite serious.
    c. emotionally neutral.

Analyzing Language

☐ **18.** Identify some of the language that helped create that tone.

(1) "A roll of Wintergreen lifesavers is usually the most dangerous thing

Latinos carry. (By the way, I am afraid of knives)" (2) "If I had a nickel. . . ."

(3) "Not quite." (4) "Japan watch out!" (5) "Come on folks. . . ."

Evaluating Opinions

☐ **19.** The author generalizes that the Latino population has shown "an impressive improvement in their socio-economic situation." Would you say that opinion is

(a). justified.
b. unjustified.

Explain why you chose *a* or *b*.

The author offers several different statistics in support of his claim.

Forming Your Own Opinion

☐ **20.** Do you think the author overstates his case? Or, do you think many non-Latinos are prone to stereotype the Latino population of this country? How do you justify your opinion?

DIGGING DEEPER

What are some other groups that have been hurt by stereotyping? Have you personally ever tended to stereotype other people different from yourself?

Write a paper in which you explain how parents or teachers might help children avoid the trap of stereotyping others.

Reading 9:

It's Not My Fault

Vocabulary to Learn:

☐ compulsive: irresistible, uncontrollable.
☐ rationalize: to explain one's behavior with reasons that seem appropriate but that really help disguise the actual motives for the behavior.
☐ transgressions: mistakes, crimes, errors.
☐ attribute: to regard as the cause.
☐ organic: derived from the body, physical rather than psychological.

In California, a woman was accused of murdering her infant son. 1
She killed him, the defense claimed, while suffering from postpartum depression. In San Antonio, Texas, a man confessed to raping a woman three times. But the jury agreed that *he* was the victim— of a high testosterone level. Michael Deaver* excused his perjury by saying he was "forgetful" due to his drinking problem. We are in the midst of an excuse epidemic in America.

William Wilbanks, professor of criminal justice at Florida Inter- 2
national University in North Miami, thinks these excuses are all variations on the same theme: "I can't help myself." Wilbanks calls this phrase the "new obscenity," because, he says, "it is offensive to the core concept of humanity": that human beings have free will and are capable of self-discipline and responsibility.

Across the country, clinicians are treating the "sexually compul- 3
sive" man who can't control his sexual desires, the "love-addicted" woman who can't break out of bad relationships, and millions of people addicted to drugs or alcohol—or who are allegedly addicted to those who are.

"There is a growing tendency in the scientific community to 4

---

* Michael Deaver served under President Ronald Reagan.

view human beings as objects who are acted upon by internal and external forces over which they have no control," says Wilbanks. "We mistakenly infer that people *cannot* exercise self-control." We overlook the millions of men with high testosterone levels who do not rape, the depressed women who do not murder their children, and the great majority of addicts who decide to quit and do.

"The new obscenity of 'you can't help yourself' only convinces 5 the person that her problem is hopeless and she might as well give up," says Wilbanks."It thereby produces the very kind of problem behavior it attempts to explain. The problem with the medical model of misbehavior is that it completely ignores the idea of moral choice and resistance to temptation."

At the University of Kansas, C. R. Snyder, Ph.D., and Raymond 6 L. Higgins, Ph.D., are also interested in the growing number of categories the public accepts as legitimate excuses for irresponsible, self-defeating, or criminal behavior. While Wilbanks is concerned about the effect of excuses on the legal system and society at large, Snyder is concerned about the effects of excuses on individual health and well-being.

Snyder has been studying the psychology of excuses for years. 7 "Excuses—such as, 'It's not my fault,' 'The dog ate it,' 'I didn't *mean* to break her jaw'—soften the link between you and an unfortunate or negative action," says Snyder. "Of course, without excuses, we would be exposed and vulnerable. They protect our self-esteem. But sometimes, people also use excuses to rationalize the destructive things they do."

Excuses become self-defeating, says Snyder, when their costs 8 outweigh their benefits. "A woman who blames unacceptable behavior on her depression or an 'addiction,'" he says, "finds that her future transgressions are automatically attributed to her problem—thus, her excuse becomes what's known as a self-handicapping strategy. It excuses her behavior in the short run, but in the long run it undermines her self-esteem and sense of personal control."

As a psychotherapist as well as a researcher, Snyder is particu- 9 larly concerned about people who move from making the excuse to being the excuse. "With some people, the excuse becomes part of their identities," says Snyder. "I couldn't help myself; I *am* an addict/rapist/abuser; I *am* depressed/shy/angry."

Snyder observes that it is particularly difficult to treat those 10 with built-in excuses. Once people define themselves as helpless slaves to a problem, they hand over control of the problem to others. Or they find an explanation for the problem that is out of their hands: "I can't help the way I am; my mother made me this way"—an ever-popular choice for blame. (As a client of one of Snyder's colleagues told him: "It's like this: if it's not my fault,

it's her fault, and if it's not her fault, it's still not my fault.")
For people whose excuses have become a problem, says Snyder,
successful therapy depends on breaking down their self-deceptive,
self-protective excuses and making them face the link between
themselves and their actions.

Both Wilbanks and Snyder recognize that a humane legal sys- 11
tem will consider some conditions—such as defending oneself or
one's family, or having an organic brain disorder—to be legitimate
excuses for a defendant's behavior. But they oppose the growing
tendency in psychology and law to excuse behavior we don't like:
to confuse moral judgments with scientific ones, and to confuse
learned habits with organic deficiencies.

Furthermore, Wilbanks believes that for society's sake, as well 12
as for the thousands of people who are being taught to think of
themselves as helpless victims of life or biology, it is time to restore confidence in self-control and self-determination. "People
can learn to respond to temptations by asking themselves, 'Does
this behavior fit my self-image?'" says Wilbanks, "rather than,
'Can I get away with it?'" (Tarvis, *Vogue*, January, 1989, p. 116.)

824 words

Questions for Accelerated Reading

*Based on your reading, decide if the following statements are true (T)
or false (F), and circle the correct answer.*

1. According to the article, there is a tendency in the scientific community to view human beings as objects acted upon by forces they
cannot control. (T) F

2. William Wilbanks called the tendency to say "I can't help myself"
the new obscenity. (T) F

3. According to C. R. Snyder, excuses become self-defeating when
their costs outweigh their benefits. (T) F

4. People with built-in excuses for their behavior are easy to treat.
T (F)

5. Our legal system should not accept any excuse for criminal
behavior. T (F)

Choose the correct answer for each of the following questions.

6. Which of the following excuses is *not* mentioned in the article?

a. forgetfulness due to drinking

b. rape because of a high testosterone level

ⓒ. murder because of a junk food addiction

7. Excuses such as "I didn't mean to do it" and "It's not my fault"

   a. are diminishing in popularity.
   b. make people feel exposed and vulnerable.
   ⓒ. soften the link between the person and the action.

8. Once people define themselves as helpless slaves to a problem, they

   a. are likely to be taken advantage of.
   b. are likely to feel a lot better.
   ⓒ. hand control of the problem over to others.

9. People should respond to temptation by saying:

   a. Get thee behind me Satan!
   b. I can't help myself.
   ⓒ. Does this behavior fit my self-image?

10. The researchers cited in this article generally agree that

    a. it's time to get tough on crime.
    b. excuses can help improve our self-esteem.
    ⓒ. there needs to be more emphasis on self-control and self-discipline.

Give yourself ten points for each correct answer.

Score = _____

Questions for Understanding and Review

Unless the question directs you to do otherwise, circle the correct answer.

Discovering the Controlling Idea

☐ 1. Which of the following statements best paraphrases the controlling idea?

   a. More and more criminals are going free because juries accept the idea that some people cannot help themselves.
   ⓑ. In America today, there is a dangerous tendency for people to make and accept the excuse: "I can't help myself."

c. An increasing number of people are excusing bad behavior by claiming they have a drinking problem.

☐ **2.** The controlling idea

a. was summed up in a thesis statement.
ⓑ. had to be inferred.

☐ **3.** How does the author introduce the thesis statement?

Through examples of people making excuses.

Looking for Support

☐ **4.** Which of the following statements does *not* support the controlling idea?

a. C. R. Snyder is concerned about the effects of excuses on an individual's health and well-being.
ⓑ. In England there is a much greater acceptance of the idea that post-partum depression can excuse some crimes committed by women.
c. William Wilbanks thinks the trend toward making excuses can undermine the development of self-discipline and personal responsibility.

☐ **5.** According to the article, what are some of the things that can happen if people assume they cannot help themselves?

(1) They hand over control of the problem to others

(2) They undermine their own self-esteem.

Analyzing Paragraphs

☐ **6.** Which statement best paraphrases the main idea of paragraph 10?

a. Too many people want to blame their mothers for everything that goes wrong.
ⓑ. People who have built-in excuses for their behavior do not respond well to therapy.

☐ **7.** *Label the sentences in the following paragraph* M.I. *for main idea statement,* M *for major supporting sentence, and* m *for minor supporting sentence.*

Excuses become self-defeating, says Snyder, when their costs outweigh their benefits. ____M.I.____ "A woman who blames unacceptable behavior on her depression or addiction," he says, "finds that her future transgressions are automatically attributed to her problem—thus her excuse becomes what's known as a self-handicapping strategy. ___M___ It excuses her behavior in the short run, but in the long run it undermines her self-esteem and sense of personal control." ___m___

Organizational Patterns

☐ **8.** What pattern of organization do you recognize in paragraph 5?

    a. comparison and contrast
    ⓑ. cause and effect
    c. sequence of steps

☐ **9.** What verb in that paragraph is a clue to the method of organization?

produces

Transitions

☐ **10.** What transitions appear in paragraph 7?

of course, but

☐ **11.** What transitions appear in paragraphs 11 and 12?

but, furthermore

Inferences

☐ **12.** What inference could you logically draw on the basis of this article?

    a. None of the people mentioned would accept mental retardation as an excuse for criminal behavior of any kind.
    ⓑ. Wilbanks and Snyder would probably accept mental retardation as a legitimate excuse for some kinds of criminal behavior.

What statements in the article led you to choose this inference?

"Both Wilbanks and Snyder recognize that a humane legal system

will consider some conditions. . . ."

Distinguishing Between Fact and Opinion

Label the following statements fact (F), opinion (O), or both (B).

☐ **13.** Excuses help undermine a person's belief in free will and personal responsibility. __O__

☐ **14.** America is in the midst of an excuse epidemic. __O__

Purpose

☐ **15.** The author's primary goal is

(a). to inform.
b. to persuade.

Tone

☐ **16.** The author's tone is

a. annoyed and disgusted.
b. cool and humorous.
(c). emotionally neutral.

Bias

☐ **17.** The author is

a. biased against the idea that excuses can be dangerous.
b. biased in favor of the idea.
(c). relatively neutral or impartial.

Evaluating Opinions

☐ **18.** According to the article, America is in the midst of an excuse epidemic. What specific examples support this generalization?

The three examples in the opening paragraph
_____

_____

☐ **19.** This is an example of

a. a supported generalization.
b. an unsupported generalization.
(c). a hasty generalization.

Analyzing Language

☐ **20.** In the article, William Wilbanks calls the growing tendency to make and accept excuses the "new obscenity." The word *obscenity* is usually used to describe pornography or foul language. Why do you think Wilbanks chose this particular word?

He wants to emphasize how repulsive he finds this tendency.

Reading 10:

The Milgram Experiment

Vocabulary to Learn:
- ☐ atrocities: horrible crimes.
- ☐ ingenious: clever, imaginative.

After World War II the Nuremberg war trials were conducted in order to try Nazi war criminals for the atrocities they had committed. In many instances the defense offered by those on trial was that they had "only followed orders." During the Vietnam War American soldiers accused of committing atrocities in Vietnam gave basically the same explanation for their actions.

Most of us reject justifications based on "obedience to authority" as mere rationalizations, secure in our convictions that we, if placed in the same situation, would behave differently. However, the results of a series of ingenious and controversial investigations performed in the 1960s by psychologist Stanley Milgram suggest that perhaps we should not be so sure of ourselves.

Milgram wanted to determine the extent to which people would obey an experimenter's commands to administer painful electric shocks to another person. Pretend for a moment that you are a subject in one of his studies. Here is what would happen. On arriving at a university laboratory in response to a classified ad offering volunteers $4 for one hour's participation in an experiment on memory, you meet another subject, a pleasant, middle-aged man with whom you chat while awaiting the arrival of the experimenter. When the experimenter arrives, dressed in a laboratory coat, he pays you and then informs you and the other person that one of you will be the subject in the experiment and that the other will serve as his assistant. You are chosen by lot to be the assistant, but in reality you are the subject.

The experimenter explains that the study is concerned with the effects of punishment on learning. Accompanied by you, the "subject" is conducted into a room and strapped into a chair, and a large electrode is attached to his wrist. He is told that he is to learn a list of word pairs and that whenever he makes an error he will receive electric shocks of increasing intensity. On hearing this, the "subject" responds, "When I was at the West Haven V. A. Hospital a few years ago, they detected a slight heart condition.

Nothing serious, but are these shocks dangerous?" The experimenter replies in an unconcerned manner that although the shocks may be painful, they will cause no permanent tissue damage.

You and the experimenter then proceed to an adjoining room 5 connected by an intercom so that the "subject's" responses can be heard. You are seated in front of an apparatus with 30 toggle switches ranging from 15 volts to 450 volts. Your task is to administer the learning task to the "subject." Whenever he gives an incorrect answer, you must give him an electric shock, starting at the lowest level (15 volts) and increasing the level by 15 volts each time. You are given a sample shock of 45 volts and find it moderately painful.

What you are unaware of at this point is that you are in a care- 6 fully contrived situation. The learner is actually an actor who receives no shock at all, and the responses you hear over the intercom are tape-recorded so that they will be exactly the same for each "assistant." The experimenter's actions are also carefully programmed.

As the experiment proceeds, the learner makes error after error. 7 You increase the shock level steadily until he is clearly experiencing pain. The tape-recorded responses are programmed to correspond to the shock intensities as follows:

75 volts	Ugh!
90 volts	Ugh!
105 volts	Ugh! (louder)
120 volts	Ugh! Hey, this really hurts.
135 volts	Ugh!!
150 volts	Ugh!!! Experimenter! That's all. Get me out of here. I told you I had heart trouble. My heart's starting to bother me now. Get me out of here. I told you I had heart trouble. My heart's starting to bother me. I refuse to go on. Let me out.
165 volts	Ugh! Let me out. (shouting)
180 volts	Ugh! I can't stand the pain. Let me out of here! (shouting)
195 volts	Ugh! Let me out of here. Let me out of here. My heart's bothering me. Let me out of here! You have no right to keep me here! Let me out! Let me out of here! My heart's bothering me. Let me out! Let me out!
210 volts	Ugh!! Experimenter! Get me out of here. I've had enough. I won't be in the experiment any more.
225 volts	Ugh!
240 volts	Ugh!
255 volts	Ugh! Get me out of here.

270 volts	(*Agonized scream*). Let me out of here. Let me out of here. Let me out of here. Let me out. Do you hear! Let me out of here.
285 volts	(*Agonized scream.*)
300 volts	(*Agonized scream*). I absolutely refuse to answer any more. Get me out of here. You can't hold me here. Get me out. Get me out of here.
315 volts	(*Intensely agonized scream*). *I told you I refuse to answer.* I'm no longer part of this experiment.
330 volts	(*Intense and prolonged agonized scream*). Let me out of here. Let me out of here. My heart's bothering me. Let me out, I tell you. (*Hysterically*) Let me out of here. Let me out of here. You have no right to hold me here. Let me out! Let me out! Let me out of here! Let me out! Let me out!
345 volts	(*At 345 volts and thereafter, there was only silence*)

But supposing you express unwillingness at some point to continue shocking the learner? In that event the experimenter, sitting at a nearby desk, would respond in one of the following ways: 8

"Please continue" or "Please go on."
"The experiment requires that you continue."
"It is absolutely essential that you continue."
"You have no other choice. You must go on."

Having now experienced the Milgram situation at least in your imagination, how long do you think you would continue to administer shocks? Most of our students maintained that they would not go beyond 105 volts before refusing to continue the experiment. A panel of psychiatrists predicted before the experiment that perhaps only 1 percent of the subjects would proceed to the 450-volt level. 9

In fact, however, the "shock" produced by the results of this study was much more startling than the simulated shocks in the experiment. Forty men ranging in age from 20 to 50 and representing a cross section of the population, participated in the investigation. Nearly two-thirds of them administered the 450-volt maximum shock, and the average maximum shock they administered was 368 volts. 10

Virtually all the people who administered high levels of shock exhibited extreme discomfort, anxiety, and distress. Most verbally refused to continue on one or more occasions. But continue they did when ordered to do so by the experimenter, who assured them that what happened in the experiment was his responsibility. 11

By contriving a situation with many real-life elements, Milgram [12] succeeded in demonstrating that a high percentage of "normal" people will obey an authority figure even when the destructive effects of their obedience are obvious. (Smith, Sarason, Sarason, *Psychology: The Frontiers of Behavior.*)

1165 words

Questions for Accelerated Reading

Based on your reading, decide if the following statements are true (T) or false (F), and circle the correct answer.

1. The Milgram experiment suggests that Americans will generally refuse to take orders, particularly if those orders go against their moral code.   T   (F)

2. Milgram wanted to determine the most effective methods for helping people learn.   T   (F)

3. The subjects of this experiment were always aware that they were not really inflicting pain.   T   (F)

4. The "learners" in the experiment really received electrical shocks.   T   (F)

5. Most of those who administered high levels of shock, expressed discomfort at doing so.   (T)   F

Choose the correct answer to each of the following questions.

6. Most of the people administering shocks

   a. cried and refused to continue.
   (b). verbally refused but continued when ordered to do so.

7. The subjects were told that the experiment was concerned with

   (a). the effects of punishment on learning.
   b. the ease with which people learn unfamiliar information.
   c. people's different abilities to bear pain.

8. The head of the experiment was dressed

   (a). in a white coat.
   b. in street clothes.
   c. all in black.

9. After World War II, the Nuremberg war trials were conducted to try Nazi war criminals. In many instances, the defense argued that those on trial

    a. feared for their own lives.
    ⓑ. were only following orders.
    c. were unaware of what they were doing.

10. According to the authors, Milgram's experiment succeeded in demonstrating that

    a. people are naturally cruel to one another.
    ⓑ. many people are inclined to obey authority even when their obedience is destructive to others.
    c. people are easily fooled.

Give yourself ten points for each correct answer.

Score = _____

Questions for Understanding and Review

Unless the question directs you to do otherwise, circle the correct answer.

Discovering the Controlling Idea

☐ 1. Which of the following statements paraphrases the controlling idea?

    a. The Milgram experiment proved that most people enjoy inflicting pain and suffering on others.
    ⓑ. The Milgram experiment suggests that Americans might be more obedient to authority that we like to think.

Looking for Support

Label the following statements as introduction (I) or supporting detail (S).

☐ 2. After World War II, the Nuremberg war trials were conducted in order to try Nazi war criminals for atrocities they had committed. __I__

☐ 3. Milgram wanted to determine the extent to which people would obey an experimenter's commands to administer painful shocks to another person. __S__

☐ **4.** Nearly two-thirds of the subjects administered the 450-volt maximum shock. __S__

☐ **5.** During the Vietnam War American soldiers accused of committing atrocities in Vietnam said that they "only followed orders." __I__

☐ **6.** What is the relationship between paragraphs 9 and 10?

(a). Both are major supporting paragraphs.
  b. Both are minor supporting paragraphs.
  c. 9 is a major supporting paragraph; 10 is a minor supporting paragraph.

Analyzing Paragraphs

☐ **7.** In paragraph 1 the authors describe two different wars and two different cases in which soldiers accused of atrocities defended themselves by saying they were only taking orders. Since the article is not about wartime atrocities, why do the authors open this way?

To illustrate the kind of behavior most people believe they would never

commit.

☐ **8.** What is the main idea of paragraph 11?

No matter how miserable the subjects were, they did what they were told.

☐ **9.** Is the main idea of paragraph 11 stated or implied?

implied

Organizational Patterns

☐ **10.** What pattern of organization appears in paragraphs 3 through 8?

  a. comparison and contrast
  b. classification
(c). sequence of steps

Transitions

☐ **11.** What transitional word introduces the thesis statement?

however

☐ **12.** List in order the transitions that appear in paragraphs 10 and 11.

in fact, however, but

Inferences

☐ **13.** Why do you think the man leading the experiment wore a white coat?

To give him the authority of a scientist or doctor.

☐ **14.** The subjects who did not want to continue did so when the experimenter "ordered" them to continue, and assured them that everything that was happening was "his responsibility." Why do you think they continued when they obviously felt so miserable?

    a. They were afraid of being eliminated from the experiment.
    b. They actually liked hurting other people and were only pretending to be upset.
    ⓒ. Because someone else was in charge, they no longer felt responsible for their own actions.

Purpose

☐ **15.** The authors' primary goal is to

    a. inform.
    ⓑ. persuade.

Tone

☐ **16.** The authors' tone is

    a. distant and scientific.
    ⓑ. informal and friendly.
    c. emotionally neutral.

Bias

☐ **17.** The authors

    ⓐ. lean toward accepting Milgram's conclusions.
    b. seem opposed to his conclusions.
    c. are impartial or neutral.

□ **18.** What statement or statements in the reading would you use to support your answer to the previous question?

Paragraph 2: "The results of a series of ingenious. . . ."

Paragraph 12: "By contriving a situation with many real life elements,

Milgrim succeeded in demonstrating. . . ."

_____

Analyzing Language

□ **19.** On pages 474–475 the authors describe the responses of those subjects supposedly being shocked. They begin by saying the subjects "shouted." Then they "screamed." Then they gave "agonized" screams and finally they gave out "intensely agonized screams." What do the authors want to indicate with the changes in verbs?

The increasing pain and suffering of the supposed victims and the willingness

of the subjects to continue administering the shocks.

_____

Forming Your Own Opinion

□ **20.** What do you think about Milgram's experiment? Do you think it proved that "a high percentage of normal people" will obey an authority figure even when it means they will hurt others? Why or why not?

_____

_____

_____

_____

Answer Key

Questions for Accelerated Reading

Reading 1
Convenience Friends and Historical Friends, Etc. (pp. 409–411)

1. F	5. T	8. a
2. F	6. c	9. b
3. F	7. b	10. b
4. F		

Reading 2
"Reel" vs. Real Violence (pp. 416–419)

1. F	5. F	8. b
2. T	6. c	9. b
3. T	7. b	10. b
4. T		

Reading 3
Raised on Rock-and-Roll (pp. 424–426)

1. F	5. T	8. b
2. F	6. b	9. b
3. F	7. b	10. c
4. T		

Reading 4
Some Reasons for Wilding (pp. 430–433)

1. T	5. T	8. a
2. F	6. F	9. b
3. F	7. b	10. c
4. T		

Reading 5
Disability (pp. 438–440)

1. F	5. T	8. a
2. F	6. a	9. a
3. T	7. b,c	10. b
4. T		

Reading 6
Red, White, Blue, and Yellow (pp. 446–447)

1. F	5. b	8. b
2. F	6. b	9. c
3. F	7. b	10. c
4. F		

Reading 7
The Wild Boy of Aveyron (pp. 452–454)

1. F	5. T	8. b
2. F	6. a	9. b
3. F	7. c	10. b
4. F		

Reading 8
As I See It (pp. 459–461)

1. F	5. F	8. b
2. F	6. c	9. b
3. T	7. a	10. b
4. T		

Reading 9
It's Not My Fault (pp. 466–468)

1. T	5. F	8. c
2. T	6. c	9. c
3. T	7. c	10. c
4. F		

Reading 10
The Milgram Experiment (pp. 473–476)

1. F	5. T	8. a
2. F	6. b	9. b
3. F	7. a	10. b
4. F		

Index

Memory
  long-term, 195
  visual image and, 57
Modifiers, 78–81
  in identifying topic, 106–
    108
  inferring, 108
Multiparagraph selections,
    215–264
  identifying topic in, 216
  locating controlling idea
    and thesis statement in,
    216–219, 226–231
  marking for note-taking,
    235–239
  mixed patterns of develop-
    ment in, 265, 329–340
  note-taking for, 235–257,
    295
  organized by cause and ef-
    fect, 265, 304–310
  organized by classification,
    265, 314–323
  organized by comparing
    and contrasting, 265,
    293–299
  organized by dates and
    events, 265, 271–278
  organized by sequence of
    steps, 265, 283–288
  relating supporting para-
    graphs to controlling
    idea in, 216, 218–225
  review test for note-taking
    on, 259–264
  transitions in, 231–235

Notebook, vocabulary, 57–58
Note-taking, 185–204, 266n
  condensing and abbreviat-
    ing in, 187–188, 235, 239
  four pointers for, 196
  informal outlining (inden-
    tion) in, 187, 239–240
  for longer (multipara-

graph) selections, 235–
    257, 295
  marginal annotation, 7–8,
    235
  marking text for, 235–239,
    247
  paraphrasing in, 187, 195–
    201, 235, 239, 247
  patterns of development
    and, 265–352
  recording essential ele-
    ments in, 185–204
  review tests for, 205–213,
    259–264
  selectivity in, 239
  for summaries, 246–253,
    295
  symbols for, 237

Opinions
  arguments for, 374–384
  attack on person rather
    than, 380–381
  author's language and,
    355–356, 357, 384–387
  bias and, 356, 363–364,
    374, 384–394
  circular reasoning and,
    363–364
  conflicting, comparison of,
    355
  developing one's own, 363
  evaluating, 362–374, 381
  facts vs., 353–361
  generalizations, 370–374
  identifying, 357
  justifying, 354, 362–370,
    371, 375
  valid, 354
Organization. See Patterns of
    development
Outline
  chapter, in pre-reading, 3
  informal, in note-taking,
    187, 239–240, 295

Acknowledgments

John H. Aldrich, et al.: Adapted from John H. Aldrich et al., "Broadcast and Print Media," from AMERICAN GOVERNMENT: PEOPLE, INSTITUTIONS AND POLICIES, Houghton Mifflin Company © 1986. Reprinted by permission of Houghton Mifflin Company.

Billy Allstetter: Adapted from Billy Allstetter, *American Health*, November 1991, p. 27. Reprinted by permission.

American Heritage Dictionary: Copyright © 1985 by Houghton Mifflin Company. Reprinted by permission from the AMERICAN HERITAGE DICTIONARY, SECOND COLLEGE EDITION.

S. Baker and T. Gore: From Susan Baker and Tipper Gore, "Some Reasons for Wilding," *Newsweek*, My Turn, May 29, 1989, pp. 6–7. Reprinted with permission of the authors.

Russell Banks: Russell Banks, "Red, White, Blue and Yellow," *New York Times*, February 26, 1991, p. A23. Copyright © 1991 by The New York Times Company. Reprinted by permission.

Penny G. Beers: Adapted from Penny G. Beers, "Accelerated Reading for High School Students." *Journal of Reading*, Vol. 29, January 1986, p. 313. Used by permission.

Vincent Bozzi: Vincent Bozzi, "A Healthy Dose of Religion," from *Psychology Today*, November 1988, p. 13. Reprinted by permission from Psychology Today Magazine. Copyright © 1988 (Sussex Publishers, Inc.).

R. Carson, et al.: Excerpts from ABNORMAL PSYCHOLOGY AND MODERN LIFE, 8/e by Robert C. Carson et al. Copyright © 1988, 1984 by Scott, Foresman and Company. Reprinted by permission of HarperCollins Publishers.

Robert Cialdini: From INFLUENCE: SCIENCE AND PRACTICE by Robert B. Cialdini. Copyright © 1985 by Scott, Foresman and Company. Reprinted by permission of HarperCollins Publishers

Leonard A. Cole: Leonard A. Cole, "Radon Scare—Where's the Proof?" *New York Times*, October 6, 1988, p. A31. Copyright © 1988 by The New York Times Company. Reprinted by permission.

Dennis Coon: Dennis Coon, INTRODUCTION TO PSYCHOLOGY, West Publishing Company, 1989. Used by permission of the publisher.

Robert A. Divine: From AMERICA: PAST AND PRESENT. Volume I by Robert A. Divine, et al.

Copyright © 1986, 1984 by Scott, Foresman and Company. Reprinted by permission of HarperCollins Publishers.

Jerrold Greenberg, et al.: From Jerrold S. Greenberg, Clint E. Bruess, Kathleen D. Mullen, and Doris W. Sands, SEXUALITY: INSIGHTS AND ISSUES, 2nd ed. Copyright © 1989, Wm. C. Brown Communications, Inc., Dubuque, Iowa. All Rights Reserved. Reprinted by permission.

Fred R. Harris: Excerpts from AMERICA'S DEMOCRACY: THE IDEAL AND THE REALITY, 3/e by Fred R. Harris. Copyright © 1986, 1983 by Fred R. Harris. Reprinted by permission of HarperCollins Publishers.

International Ice Cream Association: From "Ice Cream: Past and Present," The International Ice Cream Association, October 1990. Reprinted with permission.

W. Kephart, D. Jedlicka: Excerpt from THE FAMILY, SOCIETY AND THE INDIVIDUAL, 7/e, by William M. Kephart and Davor Jedlicka. Copyright © 1991 by HarperCollins Publishers, Inc. Reprinted by permission of the publisher.

David Knox: David Knox, CHOICES IN RELATIONSHIPS. Copyright © West Publishing Company, 1985. Reprinted by permission.

Michael Lavin: Michael Lavin, "If Felons Publish, They Should Profit." *New York Times*, April 14, 1988, p. 27. Copyright © 1988 by The New York Times Company. Reprinted by permission.

Nancy Mairs: Essay from CARNAL ACTS by Nancy Mairs. Copyright © 1990 by Nancy Mairs. Reprinted by permission of the publisher.

Sean Michell: Sean Michell, "Have We Become Violence Junkies," *USA Weekend*, July 12, 1991, p. 4. Reprinted by permission of the author.

Frances Munnings: From Frances Munnings, *American Health*, November 1991, p. 93. Reprinted by permission.

Mary Beth Norton, et al.: Excerpts from Mary Beth Norton, et al. A PEOPLE AND A NATION: A HISTORY OF THE UNITED STATES, 2/e, Vol. I, Houghton Mifflin Company © 1986 and A PEOPLE AND A NATION: A HISTORY OF THE UNITED STATES, 3/e, Vol. I. Houghton Mifflin Company, © 1990. Reprinted by permission of Houghton Mifflin Company.

David Popenoe: David Popenoe, SOCIOLOGY. Prentice Hall, 1989, p. 13, 218–19, 244–45, 354,

436–437. Reprinted by permission of Prentice Hall, Englewood Cliffs, N.J.

W. Pride, et al.: Excerpts from William Pride, Robert Hughes, and Jack Kapor, BUSINESS, Houghton Mifflin Company © 1991. Reprinted by permission.

Psychology Today Staff: "People Who Need People" excerpt from *Psychology Today*, November 1988, p. 8. Reprinted by permission from Psychology Today Magazine. Copyright © 1988 (Sussex Publishers, Inc.).

Anna Quindlen: From LIVING OUT LOUD by Anna Quindlen. Copyright © 1987 by Anna Quindlen. Reprinted by permission of Random House, Inc.

John Russo: " 'Reel' vs. Real Violence," *Newsweek*, February 19, 1990, p. 10. Reprinted by permission of the author.

John U. Sepulveda: John U. Sepulveda, "As I See It," *New Haven Register*, January 23, 1992, p. 12. Reprinted by permission of the author.

R. E. Smith, et al.: Excerpt from PSYCHOLOGY: THE FRONTIERS OF BEHAVIOR by Ronald E. Smith et al. Copyright © 1982 by Ronald E. Smith, Irving G. Sarason. Reprinted by permission of HarperCollins Publishers. Excerpt from OBEDIENCE TO AUTHORITY by Stanley Milgram. Copyright © 1974 by Stanley Milgram. Reprinted by permission of HarperCollins Publishers.

Deborah Tannen: From YOU JUST DON'T UNDERSTAND by Deborah Tannen, Ph. D. Copyright 1990 by Deborah Tannen, Ph. D. Reprinted by permission of William Morrow & Company, Inc.

Carol Tavris: "It's Not My Fault" Copyright © 1989 by Carol Tavris, Ph. D. Originally appeared in *Vogue*.

Jonathan and Amos Turk: Excerpt from PHYSICAL SCIENCE, Third Edition by Jonathan and Amos Turk, copyright © 1987 by Saunders College Publishing, reprinted by permission of the publisher.

Judith Viorst: Judith Viorst, "Convenience Friends and Historical Friends, Etc." from NECESSARY LOSSES, pp. 197–199. Copyright © by Judith Viorst. Reprinted by permission of Simon & Schuster, Inc.

Robert A. Wallace: Excerpts from BIOLOGY: THE WORLD OF LIFE, 4/e by Robert A. Wallace. Copyright © 1987, 1981 by Scott, Foresman and Company. Reprinted by permission of HarperCollins Publishers.